MYTHOPOETIC
PERSPECTIVES
OF MEN'S HEALING WORK

Stephen

Blessings on your
work, your passion
& your Mission.

Ed Barton 2/18/01

MYTHOPOETIC PERSPECTIVES OF MEN'S HEALING WORK

An Anthology for Therapists and Others

Edited by
Edward Read Barton

BERGIN & GARVEY
Westport, Connecticut • London

Library of Congress Cataloging-in-Publication Data

Mythopoetic perspectives of men's healing work : an anthology for therapists and others / edited by Edward Read Barton.
     p. cm.
   Includes bibliographical references and index.
   ISBN 0–89789–646–7 (alk. paper)
   1. Men's movement—United States. 2. Men—United States—Psychology. 3. Men—Mental health—United States. 4. Men—United States—Attitudes. 5. Masculinity—United States. 6. Self-help groups—United States. I. Barton, Edward Read.
HQ1090.3.M97 2000
305.32'0973—dc21   99–054739

British Library Cataloguing in Publication Data is available.

Library of Congress Catalog Card Number: 99–054739
ISBN: 0–89789–646–7

First published in 2000

Bergin & Garvey, 88 Post Road West, Westport, CT 06881
An imprint of Greenwood Publishing Group, Inc.
www.greenwood.com

Printed in the United States of America

The paper used in this book complies with the Permanent Paper Standard issued by the National Information Standards Organization (Z39.48–1984).

10 9 8 7 6 5 4 3 2 1

COPYRIGHT ACKNOWLEDGMENTS

The author and publisher gratefully acknowledge permission for use of the following material:

Excerpts from *Iron John: A Book About Men* by Robert Bly reprinted by permission of Perseus Books Publishers, a member of Perseus Books, L.L.C. Copyright © 1990 by Robert Bly. Also used by permission of Element Books Ltd. of Shaftesbury, Dorset.

To the men who have been in my mythopoetic men's peer mutual support groups, my fellow NEW Warrior Brothers, and the men who will be in my future men's peer mutual support groups, who are my family of choice, my community.

Contents

Preface

But I was from the all American family
Therefore I am from a dysfunctional family
Which means I was expected to meet their needs

But I had the all American job
Therefore I had to perform and produce
Regardless of what it cost me emotionally

But I was the all American macho man
Therefore I was expected to hide my pain and tender emotions
And only show my anger

This poem which I wrote may partially explain why a family science scholar is interested in mythopoetic men's healing work. For a partial answer to the question of why a family studies scholar has such an interest, it is necessary to provide a map of my social location. I am white, Protestant, Anglo-Saxon, divorced, and well into middle age.

I faced a number of midlife crises in the late 1980s including loss of much of the family farm, loss of profession, and loss of license. Then my wife's moving out propelled me to take a look at myself and my life. I called my minister and said I needed some help. He referred me to Bill Courter for therapy. Bill was just starting to become active in the mythopoetic branch of the contemporary men's movement, and I followed.

In the early 1990s there was a fair amount of publicity about the mythopoetic branch of the contemporary men's movement. It was portrayed in the popular media as mainly men going out into the woods for male bonding and men hugging trees. Much of the media portrayal, which was unfavorable, if not outright hostile, completely misunderstood the healing aspects of men seeking emotional healing work in mythopoetic gatherings.

My participation in mythopoetic men's mutual support groups (MMSG), mythopoetic men's events, and men's group therapy helped me along my path of recovery. In fact, for two and a half years after my wife moved out, I did one hour of individual therapy, two hours of men's group therapy, and two hours of men's mutual support group per week plus numerous mythopoetic men's weekend events.

Since the early 1990s there has been considerable writing, theory building, and research about the mythopoetic branch. As there has been more and more research and more and more men involved in it, it became apparent that there was more to mythopoetic activities than "men hugging trees."

This book is a collection of chapters that examine mythopoetic groups, activities, and men's peer mutual support groups, along with early research, theory building, and more current research, particularly on the ManKind Project (MKP), formerly known as the New Warrior Network (NWN) and its entry point, the New Warrior Training Adventure (NWTA), which today is international in scope and a main component of the mythopoetic branch of the contemporary men's movement.

From a historical perspective, the name "NEW Warrior" was chosen. The word *new* was selected to represent a different model of warrior than the currently popular domineering warrior; however, due to the continuing negative baggage associated with the word *warrior*, the name change to MKP has been approved by the network.

Another aspect of the NWTA and the MKP is developing a personal mission statement, defined as a life's work toward which a man focuses his energy. His mission is to be large enough so that he will not complete it during his lifetime. My MKP mission is that I create world peace by healing and emotionally empowering men. This book is part of my mission, it shares ways in which men are being healed and empowered through mythopoetic perspective activities. This book demonstrates ways in which old stories and poetry are being reinterpreted for today's men and today's healing professionals.

The final part of the book is an international dialogue of feminist looking at mythopoetics. It started with Holly Sweet's paper presented at NOMAS' Men's Studies Task Force at Men & Masculinity (M&M) in Portland. The second member of this group is Jorgen Lorentzen of Norway. I met Jorgen at NOMAS Men's Studies Task Force in Chicago in 1992 and San Francisco in 1993 and then we participated in an eight-day mythopoetic men's conference in Mendecino, California, with Robert Bly, John Lee, Robert Moore, Shephard Bliss, Martin Prechtel, and others. Jorgen's contribution is his review of Kimmel's "Politics of Manhood" in *Men and Masculinities*, Vol. 1, No. 1, pp. 112–115. John Rowan from England then joins the debate. John is on the editorial collective for *Achilles Heel*. I met John in Vienna, and we motored south to Hungary and participated in the First European Men's Gathering. Then Amanda Goldrick-Jones from the University of Winnipeg joins the debate and shares her experiences. I met Amanda when she came to Michigan State University to do research in the library's Special Collections Division in the Changing Men Collections about the early days of the profeminist branch of the CMM. Each has valuable insights that they share about the tensions between the profeminist and mythopoetic branches of the contemporary men's movement.

In my travels as an officer of the Jaycees (now Junior Chamber of Commerce) and Junior Chamber International, I came across this plaque, which now hangs in my office and reads as follows:

> I do not choose to be a common man
> It is my right to be uncommon if I can . . .
> It is my heritage to stand erect, proud, and unafraid:
> To think and act for myself;
> Enjoy the benefits of my creation;
> And to face the world boldly and say, "This I have done"!

I see men who participate in mythopoetic men's work as uncommon men. In many respects they are like the uncommon men who realize that help is necessary, that they cannot control everything in their lives. These are similar to the uncommon men who go to therapy and the uncommon men who participate in twelve-step programs. MPMW is and can be an adjunct to therapy. For the readers involved in the health, mental health, and healing professions, men involved in men's work, and men in general, as well as their partners, I invite you on a journey whose destination is a better understanding of mythopoetic men's healing work.

Acknowledgments

On Saturday evening of the American Men's Studies Conference in Washington, D.C., James Doyle, Douglas Hindman, and I were sitting around the table at a Potomac River bank restaurant. I mentioned to Jim that based on my archiving theses and dissertations for the Changing Men Collections (CMC) in the Special Collections Division of the Michigan State University Libraries that I knew of several potential journal articles about mythopoetic men's work for the *Journal of Men's Studies* (JMS). Jim indicated that if I gave him their names and addresses, he would contact them. The next morning I woke up thinking that I had already talked to most of those scholars, so I offered to be guest editor of a mythopoetic perspective thematic issue of the JMS.

Thanks to Jim Doyle for agreeing to allow me to be guest editor and providing me guidance as the thematic issue progressed. I also thank Jim Doyle for releasing me from the thematic issue when it outgrew JMS. That release allowed this book to go forward.

Thanks to all the reviewers who took time to review the drafts of the chapters in this book: Martin Acker, Marvin Allen, Robert Bly, Norma Bobbitt, Robert Boger, Bryan Bolwahn, Stephen B. Boyd, Marsha Carolan, Douglas Campbell, Stanley Cunningham, Bruce R. Curtis, Thomas Dean, David Dollahite, William Doty, Richard F. Doyle, Philip Dunn, Sam Femiamo, Roy Fish, Wesley Goodenough, Robert Griffore, Christopher Harding, Douglas Hindman, David Imig, Ralph Johnson, Kevin Kelly, Gary Kiveles, David Kruger, Nedra R. Lander, Robert Lee, Jordon Levin, Ross T. Lucas, Eric Mankowski, Kenneth Maton, G. Stanley Meloy, Mark W. Muesse, Danielle Nahon, Linda Nelson, Barbara H. Settles, Thomas Williamson, and Jeffrey Zeth, CSW.

Out of this group I particularly thank Douglas Hindman, now retired professor of psychology at Eastern Kentucky University (and whose NWTA adventure I had the honor to staff), Ralph Johnson, professor of philosophy at the University of Windsor, coeditor of the *Journal of Informal Logic* and immediate past chairman of the Windsor/Detroit ManKind Project Center Board; Robert Lee, associate professor of marriage and family therapy, Department of Family and Child Ecology, MSU, and advisory editor of the *Journal of Marriage and Family Therapy*, for reading and rereading various drafts of therapeutic articles; and Eric Mankowski, now at Portland State University, whose support, encouragement, and efforts at providing extra reviews and extra coauthoring of chapters I appreciate tremendously.

Thanks to Jane Garry, my editor at Greenwood, for seeing the value of these manuscripts when they were submitted as part of the book proposal. Jane's comment to me was that she had heard about "men hugging trees" in the early 1990s and it had sounded odd to her. That common reaction is another reason that the publication of these materials is so important. So, again Jane, thanks.

PART I
MYTHOPOETIC MEN'S WORK AND THEORY BUILDING

Chapter 1

Parallels Between Mythopoetic Men's Work/Men's Peer Mutual Support Groups and Selected Feminist Theories

Edward Read Barton

Bliss (1986) first applied the term *mythopoetic* to the spiritually oriented branch of the burgeoning contemporary men's movement. The word comes from *mytho-poesis*, which refers to remythologizing. Thus, the use of the mythopoetic approach "means revisioning masculinity for our time" (Bliss, 1995, p. 293). The term did not come to popular awareness until Bly's *Iron John* was published in 1990 and topped the *New York Times* best-seller list for many months, though the precursor to that was Keith Thompson's 1982 interview of Bly, "What Do Men Really Want?"

Mythopoetic men's work (MPMW) uses myths and poetry as vehicles for accessing inner emotions, inner realities, and feelings. The accessing of these feelings is part of the remythologizing of the man and his masculinity for this time. These feelings are often deeply buried in men, who have been socialized by North American culture and society to ignore or deny most feelings except anger. By using the tools of myth, poetry, and experiential processes, men can access these feelings and emotions to re-vision a form of masculinity that is healthy for himself, his family or household, his relationships, his community, and his planet.

MPMW extensively borrows from Jungian psychology (Schwalbe 1996) and humanistic psychology. Hollis (1994), for example, lists and discusses the eight secrets men carry within themselves:

1. Men's lives are as much governed by restrictive role expectations as are the lives of women.

2. Men's lives are essentially governed by fear.

3. The power of the feminine is immense in the psychic economy of men.

4. Men collude in a conspiracy of silence whose aim is to suppress their emotional truth.

5. Because men must leave Mother, and transcend the mother complex, wounding is necessary.

6. Men's lives are violent because their souls have been violated.

7. Every man carries a deep longing for his fathers and for his tribal fathers.

8. If men are to heal, they must activate within what they did not receive from without (p. 11).

This language borrowed from Jung differs from that of a decade ago when the dominant theory was of sex roles and the concept of role strain was evolving. "The cause of much of this strain [conflict caused by contradictory role expectations] can be found in the pressure social institutions exert on men's lives. Individual men feel powerless to make any changes in the face of a socialization process which militates against change and, although men seem to choose male groupings for support, these groups provide little emotional nurturance because of men's inability to be vulnerable and expressive" (Femiamo, 1986, p. 77).

TYPICAL MYTHOPOETIC ACTIVITIES

As a kind of a map, Harding (1992) provides a collage of the typical activities of men in the mythopoetic branch. "Some retreats have a pronounced neoprimitive quality. Widespread borrowing from Native American traditions includes exploration of such forms as the medicine wheel, the sweat lodge (or sweat cave), talking staff/stick council, and the giveaway ceremony" (p. xv). A number of experiential events fall under the umbrella of MPMW—for example: vision quests (Jastrab, 1995) "Wild Men" weekends (Lee, 1991), New Warrior Training Adventure (Kauth, 1992), Inner King Training (Daly, personal communication), Warrior Monk (Kauth, 1997), Gathering of Men (Barton, 1993), Metamorphosis (Planning Cooperative of the West Michigan Men's Center, personal communication), Woodland Passage (Detroit Wisdom Council, personal communication), spiritual retreats (Spiritual Warrior, personal communication); Spirit Journeys (personal communication), men's weekends (Wissocki & Andronico, 1996) plus many others.[1]

Other than sharing myths and reading poems, numerous experiential processes and activities are used to create a mythopoetic "men's work" event: sharing circles, truth-telling circles, psychodrama, mission work (developing a personal life mission) (Kauth, 1991), guided imagery, breath work and rebirthing (Grof, 1992), massage, drumming, chanting, singing, trust falls, father quests, shadow work (Shadow Work Seminars, 1998), and many others. (More elaborate discussion of events can be found in Kauth 1991; Jesser, 1996; and Wilson and Mankowski, this volume.) With such a variety of activities, there is an equally diverse type of groups that meet. Among them are "small weekly or biweekly support group meetings (5–10 men); citywide, drop-in monthly council meetings featuring drumming, rituals, and presentations (30–300 men); weekend or week long rustic retreats (20–150 men); one- or two-day lectures (100–1500 men)" (Harding, 1992, p. xv). The lecture-workshop is often less experiential. Robert Bly and John Lee use the lecture format, though not exclusively, as does the Chicago Men's Gathering, which also incorporates a number of workshops (Robinson, 1995).

MEN'S PEER MUTUAL SUPPORT GROUPS

Men's peer mutual support groups (MPMSG) take various forms. One has a fixed membership of usually five to ten men and does not accept new members until one of the members ends his participation. Then the membership is opened briefly to replace the former member, and membership is again closed. In contrast to this closed MPMSG, an open MMSG or drop-in MPMSG meets weekly or bi-weekly and is open to any man who wants to attend and participate. The group typically has a formal topic for discussion for each meeting. The main difference between an open and a closed MPMSG is the level of intimacy that is possible. The closed group tends to promote a more intimate atmosphere because of the fixed, small number of men who attend each meeting and their commitment to attend consistently. This intimacy lends itself to a higher level of safety, which tends to promote deep, intimate sharing among the members. (For an example of a closed MPMSG, see Chapters 12 and 13, this volume).

A typical MPMSG usually begins with a check-in: each man makes a brief statement about his week, what is happening in his life, and what feelings he is feeling right then. With this sharing, "The isolation of being male has now been broken and the men are connected to the group, to each other, and themselves. The group serves as a safe "container" for the feelings to be expressed. The container holds, nourishes and protects the men in the group and enables them to focus on the difficult and courageous struggle that is deep inner work" (Winter, 1992). Through this connection to one another and the group, the men realize that they are not alone, unique, or abnormal in their problems and concerns. Through their interaction with one another, they learn more about themselves. They try out new behaviors and ways of interacting and observe how problems can be resolved to mutual satisfaction and that they will not die or be abandoned by others if they are attacked (Winter, 1992).

There are a few guidelines for this interaction. First, the sharing is confidential. A man can talk to others outside the group about what he shared within the group, but not what other men shared within the MPMSG. Second, men talk about their feelings, not about what they do or how they perform as men in their jobs. Third, the events and meetings are drug free and alcohol free, and often smoking is not an option. The reason is that men often are numbed out on drugs, including alcohol, and are not able to connect with their feelings. To heal, they must be able to reach, feel, and experience their feelings, with the fear being faced and "walked" through or worked through with the support of the other men in the group.

The term *men's work* used to describe the activities of mythopoetic men and MPMG. The concept is that men are working on healing themselves, their families, their relationships, their community, and their planet, but primarily each one is working on healing himself, his spirit, his spirituality. The belief is that a man cannot heal anyone else or anything else if he is not in the process of healing himself.

Baldauf (1995) says that *men's work* is the preferable term used to describe the path men are "attempting to follow to redefine and revitalize their lives":

Men's Work is the process by which men turn inward into their hearts, souls, and minds, both by themselves and in the company of other men, in order to better understand [and access] their feelings, who they are as men, and how they relate to others in their lives. Men's Work is about creating meaning. Men's Work is heart work. Men's Work is about men healing, about self-definition, about creating healthy relationships, and about being generative [by giving back] and serving other men and the larger community. (p. 2)

Men's work, he says, signifies that there is no singular unifying theme, political or otherwise, that men are rallying around and following. Rather, there are at least eight areas in which men are working that have different, sometimes overlapping, purposes or agendas: internal movement, increased consciousness, recognition of a process orientation, the importance of initiation, the healing of the "father wound," creating relationships and friendships with men, the healing of other masculine wounds, and becoming generative, building positive connections and communities through service. (Horne, Jolliff, & Roth, 1996, map this terrain slightly differently by referring to developmental influences on men: nurturing, role modeling, initiation, mentoring, and eldering.)

Baldauf then elaborates seven processes for men's work: coming out of hiding, confronting male fears, the accepting and giving of nurturance from and to other men, separating from the world of the feminine, entering into the deep masculine, the challenging of cultural male myths, and giving back.

Regarding separating from the world of the feminine, Baldauf has this to say:

A man must be willing to break from the world of the feminine, the W-O-R-L-D OF W-O-M-E-N as Sam Keen describes it. Separating from the strong feminine pull which has engulfed him, beginning with his mother, and continued on in his relationships, is a particularly difficult task and it cannot be done alone. It requires the assistance of other men. Establishing a strong, secure male identity, is a particularly important and arduous but necessary process. This separation is especially important, ironically enough, if he is ever to have a healthy, nondependent relationship with a woman [or a partner]. If a man cannot learn to value his own maleness and deeper masculine self plus integrate his own "feminine side," he will forever be looking to women to care for him and depend on [women] emotionally. As John Lee states in, *At My Father's Wedding*, A man must be able to take his feelings to another man and have them accepted and honored if he is to have a healthy emotional relationship with a woman. The process of taking your emotions to another man and having them accepted is very healing. Men who have participated in men's groups and men's work would validate this point. (p. 4)

Baldauf well summarizes the experiences of many men actively involved in MPMW. However, he does fail to mention gay groups, black men's groups, other men's groups based on race or ethnicity, and profeminist men's activities. A second criticism is his implicit, if not explicit, assumption or position that the only possible intimate relationship for a man is with a woman. Baldauf's list specifically excludes gay men or shows a lack of sensitivity to gay men's issues and men's work for gay men.

One other consideration necessary for this stew is that there is not a single definition of masculinity in this culture; rather, there are many masculinities, and they change over time (Hansen, 1991, 1992). In this culture men are deemed to enjoy social power and forms of privilege. "But the way we have set up that world of power causes immense pain, isolation, and alienation not only for women but also for men. . . . This is men's contradictory experience of power" (Kaufman, 1994, p. 142).

Much of men's pain is that they are to live the culturally ideal definition of masculinity—hegemonic masculinity (Connell, 1987). Yet none of the groups doing men's work consists of or is represented by a single hegemonic definition of masculinity, except, perhaps, for the Promise Keepers, a Christian evangelical men's movement. Each of them is represented by various masculinities. As an example, Franklin (1992), in studying black male friendships, found that working-class black men using language like "yo-bro" had a very different meaning of male friendship—much closer, more meaningful, and less homophobic—than did upwardly mobile black males, who had begun to "display societal definitions of masculinity . . . began to change. . . . [Different traits began to be adopted] such as aggression, competitiveness, stoicism, rational thinking, and independence" (pp. 209–210).

Clearly there is more than one definition of masculinity in the black community. A third example would be the definition of masculinities in the black gay community, which is unlikely to be any more hegemonic than in the straight community that Franklin studied (Clatterbaugh, 1997). Each of these groups may relate to and need a different re-visioning of their masculinities for their time for their group.

THE WOMEN'S MOVEMENT AND THE MYTHOPOETIC BRANCH

Would there be MPMW if there were not a women's movement? In asking the question, there is an awareness that the women's movement is as diverse as the men in the various branches of the contemporary men's movement. There are cultural feminists, Christian feminists, conservative feminists, ecofeminists, liberal feminists, multicultural feminists, radical feminists, and separatist feminists, to name just a few strands of feminism.

The time line is clear. Profeminist men became involved and organized to support the women in the women's movement. The men's rights branch arose, at least in part, as a reaction to the women's movement (Clatterbaugh, 1990, 1997). MPMW also seems to have evolved as a response, not as a backlash, to the women's movement. Maybe there is not a 100 percent cause-and-effect relationship, but some correlation seems clear, even if a major piece of the father wound is because of the absent father caused by the Industrial Revolution (Bly, 1990; Goodsell, 1927).[2] Maybe men were ready for MPMW (Sheehy, 1995) and the women's movement provided the catalyst.

To answer the question of whether there are any parallels between MPMW and feminist theory, two theories will be discussed: standpoint theory and the "personal is political" theory. The conclusion is yes—there are commonalities, which should warrant more support for MPMW from feminists in the women's movement and profeminist men.

Standpoint Theory

One of the developers of standpoint theory was Nancy C. M. Hartsock (1983), who paraphrases Marxian metatheory by saying that women have a particularly unique and privileged vantage point by which to understand the way patriarchy affects women. Hartsock identified two key components of feminist standpoint: oppression of women and the unique perspective that women have to add to the discourse because of that uniquely oppressed position.

Sandra Harding (1991) subsequently expanded on standpoint theory—she calls it standpoint epistemology—as containing the following components:

1. Women's different lives have been erroneously devalued and neglected as starting points for scientific research and as the generators of evidence for or against knowledge claims.

2. Women are valuable "strangers" to the social order.

3. Women's oppression gives them fewer interests in ignorance.

4. Women's perspective is from the other side of the "battle of the sexes" that women and men engage in daily.

5. Women's perspective is from everyday life.

6. Women's perspective comes from mediating ideological dualism: natures v. culture.

7. Women, especially researchers, are "outsiders within."

Coltrane (1994), using a microstructural approach, uses men's standpoints— that is, personal experiences—to study men, although Harding says that *standpoint* means more than just personal experiences. Coltrane integrates men's standpoints into gender studies in three ways: by focusing on men's emotions, studying men in groups, and placing men's experiences in a structural context.

These consequences for knowledge from personal lived experiences are the main features of standpoint theory. This means that women have a unique way of knowing about their lives as women. Many aspects of those daily lives are routine, ordinary, and repetitive—what women refer to as the ordinariness of their daily lives.

Men also have ordinary aspects of their lives—both routine jobs (e.g., car maintenance, house maintenance, routine jobs) and routine aspects of their daily lives (e.g., morning routine, exercise routine). Sometimes, too, relationships are routine and interactions superficial, which can lead to a life of emotionless "quiet desperation." (Some of these routine aspects of men's daily lived experiences may not be as constant as daily child care, though that is changing as more and more men become full-time fathers by selecting employment that can be done in the home, is less demanding, or offers more freedom to do more parenting time.)

As opposed to the ordinariness of aspects of men's daily lives, Coltrane (1992) looked at men's ritualized displays of manliness: boastful demonstrations of strength, aggressiveness, and sexual potency. Yet there is little boastful demonstrating of strength, aggressiveness, or sexual potency in the types of routine, ordinary, even boring aspects of men's daily lived experiences. Indeed, these experiences show that there is little, if any, display of men's emotions. Coltrane suggests that showing emotions is important.

To work beyond the life of quiet desperation and learn to show and share emotions, I have participated in two open MMSG and one closed MMSG since the fall of 1989. These groups provide a forum for learning new insights into lived experiences, learning to feel feelings, and learning to share those feelings in an emotionally vulnerable way. Mythopoetic MPMSG are conducive to and supportive of a more healthful life, which is traditionally prohibited or marginalized by hegemonic forms of masculinity. From a structural context (which is Coltrane's third point), we can see the concept of sharing ordinary lived experiences, which is a new form or new role for men, men's ways of knowing, men's ways of being, men's standpoint. The poems that we write and share in the group represent each man's lived experience, or standpoint, in an emotionally vulnerable way, which is conducive to and supportive of a more healthful life.

Christian (1990) writes that it is now accepted that "literature [myths, stories, poems] is political" (p. 338). Men in the MPMSG and other men's gatherings often write poems that for the first time express their pain, their dull lives. Christian notes that these shared poems, stories, and emotions—these concepts so potentially destructive to the femininity, and even masculinity, of the dominant culture—are and must be written and spoken by men in MPMSG for their own health, mental health, sanity. He says, "I can only speak for myself. But what I write and how I write is done in order to save my own life. And I mean that literally. For me literature is a way of knowing that I am not hallucinating, that whatever I feel/know IS. It is an affirmation that sensuality is intelligence, that sensual language is language that makes sense" (p. 343).

Clearly there is a benefit to men from the support of men in a MPMSG. There is a difference between MPMSG and women's consciousness raising groups. Alarcon (1990) speaks to this difference:

Through "consciousness-raising" (from a women's point of view), women are led to know the world in a different way. Women's experience of politics, of life as sex objects, gives rise to its own method of appropriating that reality: feminist method. It challenges the objectivity of the "empirical gaze" and rejects the distinction between knowing subject and knowing object. By having women be the subject of knowledge, the so-called objectivity of men is brought into question.

Often, this leads to privileging women's way of knowing in opposition to men's way of knowing, thus sustaining the very binary opposition that feminism would like to change or transform. (p. 361)

Thus, the main difference is the emphasis of some feminists on the political (i.e., political in the traditional sense). However if Christian's statement that "literature is political," the poems and stories that men write and share in MPMW are also political statements. For example, one man spoke about his anger during a New Warrior weekend: "My father died when I was twelve. I had all the anger toward him for leaving me [but] I didn't think it was okay for me to have that. . . . [Now] I see the world in a different way. I used to want to be like Rambo. He's strong; he can kill. I learned that [mythopoetic men's work] is what should be the model for kids" (Becker, 1993, p. 419). This man was allowed to feel his pain, express his anger without hurting himself or anyone else and transform himself.

The poems that MPM write and the stories they share clearly are often about their pain as men. They often write about and share their emptiness and the routine of their daily lives. These are about men's way of knowing about these aspects of their routine, ordinary, often painful, often grief-filled daily lives. That is a man's way of knowing, a men's standpoint, an authentic man's way of knowing. This man's way of knowing is all masculine—but a new form of masculinity, re-visioned for this time, not the John Wayne stereotype of silent, strong hypermasculinity. By putting voice to that pain and anger, the voice has a political connotation because literature is political.

Alarcon (1990) sees a continuing separation between men and women by the perpetuation of the dichotomy between them. It could be seen as the perpetuation of the women's way of knowing which seems necessary until there is radical change in the dominant culture through the acceptance of women's ways of knowing.

The question here is whether there must be a women's way of knowing and a men's way of knowing. In fact, feminists have provided a new conceptual lens or framework through which, or by which, other ways of knowing have been demonstrated, can be acknowledged, and hopefully can be validated by society. The poems and stories mythopoetic men write are examples. To the extent that men adopt these similar sensitivities, insights, and intuitions and can develop healthy ways to live and express feelings, is the continuing of the binary opposition necessary? A friend said that what he thought was necessary was a "stand center" theory (Huff, personal communication, 1994), a concept echoed by Walker (1990), who talks about being "committed to survival and wholeness of entire people, MALE AND FEMALE. Not a separatist, except periodically, for health" (p. 370).

Periodically there seems to be a need for women to be with women and for men to be with men in mythopoetic groups. Part of the reason is the good that comes from men gathering in groups to support one another and help heal the pain in their lives in ways other than through demonstrating release of anger in an unhealthy way, the damage from being raised in dysfunctional families, and losses in their lives.

Walker (1990) used poetry to express and theorize about her womaness, her black femaleness—what she calls her "Womanist." She conveys her loves, the unconventional and the conventional, as follows:

A woman who loves other women, sexually and/or nonsexually. Appreciates and prefers women's culture, women's emotional flexibility (values tears as a natural counter balance of laughter), and women's strength. Sometimes loves individual men, sexually and/or nonsexually. Committed to survival and wholeness of entire people, MALE AND FE-MALE. Not a separatist, except periodically, for health. Traditionally universalist, as in: "Mama, why are we brown, pink, and yellow?" Ans.: "Well, you know the colored race is just like a flower garden, with every color flower represented." Traditionally capable, as in: "Mama, I'm walking to Canada and I'm taking you and a bunch of other slaves with me." Reply: "It wouldn't be the first time."
Loves Music. Loves dance. Loves the moon. LOVES the Spirit. Loves love and food and roundness. Loves struggle. LOVES the Folk. Loves herself. REGARDLESS. (p. 370)

As I read this definition, I was reminded of Kipnis's (1990) "New Male Manifesto," especially items IX and X:

IX. Men and women can be equal partners. As men learn to treat women more fairly they also want women to work toward a vision of partnership that does not require men to be less than who they authentically are.
X. Sometimes we have the right to be wrong, irresponsible, unpredictable, silly, in-consistent, afraid, indecisive, experimental, insecure, visionary, lustful, lazy, fat, bald, old, playful, fierce, irreverent, magical, wild, impractical, unconventional, and other things we're not supposed to be in a culture that circumscribes our lives by rigid rules.

Let us compare these two ways of knowing. Walker talks about "wholeness of entire people, MALE and FEMALE." Kipnis talks about men and women as equal partners. These are very similar concepts, not vastly different or divergent, as often thought. Walker talks about the loves of life—that part of life that is worthwhile but not necessarily within the definition of love and beauty in the dominant culture, especially those who are black. Kipnis wants men to celebrate all the aspects of masculinity that are decried and discounted by the rigid definition of masculinity of the dominant culture. He wants women to share in this celebration.

Standpoint theory and much of feminist theory is about the woman's way of knowing. Much has been contributed through new understanding to this society stemmed by the work of feminists and feminist theory, resulting in cultural shifts that have stemmed from the second great wave of feminism.

Starting with women's consciousness-raising groups in the 1960s and the establishment of profeminist men's groups at that time made up largely of husbands and significant others of the women who were active in these groups, there was a shift of consciousness on the part of women and men. Part of that shift was women speaking in their own voice about their own experiences, about the ordinariness of their daily lives. This was a cultural shift that has also influenced some men. These mythopoetic men are influenced by the ordinariness of their daily lives and how that affects their relationships with themselves, women, and other men.

I believe there is a much closer connection of standpoint theory, profeminist men, and men doing MPMW than is usually understood. As women have found their more authentic voice through consciousness-raising groups and theories like standpoint, this framework for organizing their voices has also been happening among men, particularly those mythopoetic men who are looking for their authentic voice. An example is "The New Male Manifesto," a new voice. This is a political voice in Christian's (1990) context because it is literature or poetry that is political. And it is a masculine voice speaking from the masculine experience of consciousness, pain, vulnerability, and healing. The change in consciousness resulting from the second great wave of feminism along with various types of spiritualism, seems to mean almost as if there were a permission given to seek and find this new voice for men who want to do things other than dominate in the ways that seem to be ascribed by the dominant culture. Mythopoetic men and profeminist men are challenging the unhealthy and harmful aspects of patriarchy. It is as if the consciousness raising, the cultural changes, the cultural shifts, and the challenges to patriarchy have loosened the energy. Now standpoint theory in the form of women's ways of knowing and men's ways of authentic knowing is challenging the dominant culture. Now we have poetry and stories as theory, as discourse, as praxis, for women's ways of knowing and for men's ways of knowing, women's standpoint and men's standpoint.

The mythopoetic MPMSG is one of the main areas where this men's ways of knowing—a men's standpoint, a challenge to the dominant culture, and thereby political and changing social structure—is happening on a regular, often weekly, basis. Accordingly, there are parallels between mythopoetic men's work and standpoint theory. "The men who attend such meetings typically see them-selves as being liberated from patriarchal roles and expectations, freed to be more honestly related to women and other men" (Becker, 1993, p. 418; see also Chapter 13, this volume).

Is the Personal Political?

One of the most often heard statements of feminist practice or feminist theory is that "the personal is political" (Millett, 1970). To an outsider this seemed to be the "political agenda" of the women's movement—that everything is political, that all feminist activity is politically driven no matter what the possible negative costs are to other women, men, children, or society. From the position of this outsider wear-ing a psychological lens, the image of excessive politicalization of the women's movement has been propagated and perpetuated by the media and probably by those opposed to the movement, feminism, or women's liberation. Is this true? Is the personal political? Is all consciousness raising political? Are there any excep-tions to the statement that "the personal is political"?

First some definitions are necessary. *Webster's New Collegiate Dictionary* (1993) defines *consciousness* as "1a: the quality or state of being aware espe-cially of something within oneself; 1b: the state or fact of being conscious of an external object, state, or fact; 1c: concern awareness (as in race conscious-ness). 2: the state of being characterized by sensation, emotion, volition, and thought: mind. 3: the totality of conscious states of an individual. 4: the normal state of conscious life. 5: the upper level of mental life of which the person is aware as contrasted with unconscious processes." *Subconscious* is defined as the mental activities just below the threshold of consciousness. And *unconscious* is defined as the part of the psychic apparatus that does not ordinarily enter the individual's awareness and is manifested in overt behavior, especially by slips of the tongue or dissociated acts or in dreams.

In looking at the theory of the personal is political, what is personal? Is it only the conscious activity of the person that defines personal? Many argue yes. I suggest that the media and popular stereotypes would say that the personal must be conscious activity, though on further reflection, much of advertising is aimed at unconscious and subconscious images and reactions.

One level of consciousness is in "The Mother of the Groom," in which Mur-phy (1991) clearly made a conscious decision not to attend the wedding of the son she bore and then raised as a lesbian mother. Other examples she provides of very conscious acts that feminists can undertake are not wearing lipstick or not wearing high-heeled shoes. Murphy's position is clear that women should make and take those conscious decisions as personal decisions. Once taken, those personal decisions have political consequences.

What about actions or decisions taken because of the subconscious? Can the subconscious motive or reason for behavior be reached through talk and therapy? Sarachild (n.d.) would say that this would be psychology, and when that happens, the political is personal, not that the personal is political. Nevertheless, one can do both by examining one's subconscious for motives and then choosing to behave in a certain way. Yet if one engages in behavior even being unaware of the motive, it translates into concrete action, which has ramifications. One is conscious of the actions even though the reason may be subconscious.

What about the unconscious? Does the unconscious have ramifications that have an impact on the statement that the personal is political? Lorde (1984a) refers to Paulo Freire's (1970) *Pedagogy of the Oppressed* saying "The true focus of revolutionary change is never merely the oppressive situations which we seek to escape, but that piece of the oppressor which is planted deep within each of us, and which knows only the oppressor's tactics, the oppressor's relationships" (p. 123). What Lorde is saying is that all of us who are oppressed know well the oppressor's tactics and methods. Additionally, because we know the tactics, a part of each of us wants to exercise those tactics to retaliate against the oppressor or more likely, use that anger to oppress others, who are usually weaker or smaller than ourselves, or over whom we have some physical or emotional control and can thereby control and marginalize. In fact many do exercise those tactics in some way, often unconsciously.

Those oppressive unconscious acts are part of one's dark shadow. If the shadow is not recognized and dealt with and it remains in the shadow, it will come out as passive-aggressive behavior or some other form of acting out. Again we see concrete actions. The underlying reason may not be understood by the individual, but the behavior is clearly there to be observed (Bly, 1988). The failure of some feminists to deal with their shadow results in some of the negative costs previously mentioned.

There are various definitions of consciousness. One of these is "upper level of mental life." Some would say that spiritual experiences fit into this definition. Some would include cosmic energy and cosmic consciousness. In fact, some believe that as part of that cosmic consciousness, all humans are interconnected with all other living things. Native American spirituality is much like this. If a butterfly flaps its wings in China, according to chaos theory, the weather in North America is affected. That seems to be proof of the interconnectedness of us with all else on this planet working within a system.

So in this analysis of the personal being political, what level of consciousness warrants being considered personal? Another way of asking the question is whether any or all of these realms of consciousness are possible sources of personal action that can be considered political.

The Milan Women's Bookstore Collective (1990) said that "the personal is political" was "the little formula which, to many men, and women, summarized feminist thought" (p. 88). It then clarified this position: "Any [woman] can enter [the bookstore.] The women who enter are not asked who they are or what they believe. Here they can establish relations with others 'if they so wish.' The Bookstore is a political space because in it, women meet publicly and freely. 'To be women . . . is . . . the starting point of our politics' . . . The idea to be communicated is this: what is shared, and therefore important for the political struggle, that which every woman can make hers, is the will to be free" (p. 92).

This passage shows at least two levels of consciousness. First, the bookstore is defined as political. It is a statement that for women to meet publicly and freely in the bookstore is a political act. The bookstore has defined it as a political act. Second is the act of just being in women's space. If all the woman wanted to do was buy a book at the bookstore and have or feel some of the essence of the women-only space enter her being while she was there, was a different level of consciousness. The statement that awareness is not enough for a women's consciousness-raising is, at one level, an assumption, a value judgment. It also is a political statement and needs to be recognized as such. Perhaps a more useful statement is that there is a continuum. On one end, all personal actions are political; at the other end, all actions are personal choice, not political. This statement is also affected by the level of consciousness or awareness used in the evaluation of the actions on the continuum.

The bookstore was also a structural entity or structural force that the women created for women-only space. Important structural forces shape the experiences of all of us in many different ways that are affected by age, gender, race, socioeconomic status, sexual orientation, and others. Being so shaped creates different levels of consciousness and other factors. On the surface, those elements appear to be in opposition like personal and political. However, when analyzed at different levels about different phenomena, the different levels that appear oppositional in fact can be reconciled or at least explained. An example of common analysis is "that the personal is political" when analyzed at levels of human emotional work—men's healing work and women's healing work.

Regarding structural forces, Lorde (1984b) talks about whether the house of the master built under patriarchy can be changed by use of the tool that the master has developed. The legal system is another example of a system developed by the dominant culture, the master's tools. In Lorde's context, it can be argued that the use of the same political tools used by the master does not cause real change; it does not, cannot, build a new house. In this context, is it the white master's tools that she sees being used to attempt to change the white master's house? I believe she would say yes. Lorde (1984b) then says we must substitute the usual divide and conquer with define and empower: "I urge each one of us here to reach down into that deep place of knowledge inside herself and touch that terror and loathing of any difference that lives there. See whose face it wears. Then the personal as political can begin to illuminate all our choices" (pp. 112–113).

Is much of this fear of difference to which Lorde is referring subconscious or unconscious or both? It would seem that it is. She is referring to irrational fears that are sometimes unconscious, in denial, or as white persons, oblivious to the assumptions with which we live about our own whiteness (Frankenberg, 1993). (There is a lot of political rhetoric about the personal being political, causing it to be misunderstood by the "public.")

But there is still the question of what is personal and what is political. Though many might not see it this way, I suggest that going to church or not going to church is a political statement, a political act. Deciding not to participate in a policy issue, to vote or not vote in an election, abstain on a vote in a meeting or a dispute of some kind is each a personal decision with political consequences, not partisan, but political.

Following the theory of a cosmic connection whereby we are all interconnected, every act we do or every act we do not do is a choice. As a choice, that act is political. Everything we do is personal and therefore political.

In summary, every feminist act, every woman-centered act, every consciousness-raising act that is commonly considered personal is political. That is what is commonly understood as being political. My conclusion is that every act—conscious, subconscious, or unconscious—is connected with every other act in the cosmos, so every act, or every decision not to act, is a political decision. The personal is political. Thus, all personal is political, whether it is women's work or MPMW. Whether it is in a consciousness-raising group or a mythopoetic MPMSG, it is human's work. Being human work, it is personal work and therefore political. The personal is political.

Following the lead of feminist theory, many movement men would argue that the personal and political are intertwined: there are significant relationships between men's knowing their fathers (or knowing other men as intimate friends, or knowing their own feelings and how to express them without shame) and such things as 'women and children . . . being beaten and raped at home—by men.' Once one recognizes the way in which patriarchal gender roles and assumptions have formed all of us, it is inconsistent to trivialize the efforts of any group to face the truth about their own de-formation. That seems particularly clear when the group in question—white, male, privileged—is, from the feminist perspective, most thoroughly deformed, spiritually, by patriarchy. That group has a long way to go; even small steps toward transformation should be welcomed (Becker, 1993, p. 420)

Accordingly there are parallels between feminist theory and MPMW, mythopoetic MPMSG, and men's emotional healing work.

CONCLUSION

There has been a great deal of fear and animosity, often coming out as attempts to shame and ridicule the mythopoets, expressed by the women's movement and profeminist men. Yet the gulf between feminist and profeminist men and mythopoetic men is not as broad as it has been made out to be. Kimmel (1996) seems to be mellowing since his interactions with Bly in preparation for their debate in 1996 at the annual Men and Masculinity Conference in Portland, Oregon: "I am surprised to find allies among [some of] the mythopoets . . . in the struggle for gender justice (p. 362). He also acknowledges that there are two different and "distinct universes that each group relies upon for analysis. On the one side lies the world of spirit, the soul—poetry, myths, legends and non-European ritual: on the other side lies the world of political and intellectual engagement—history, social science, journalistic narrative" (p. 364).

There are differences in approaches between the two groups but also much more commonality than is usually presumed or understood. From the parallels and commonalities, it seems clear that mythopoetic men should receive more respect and support from feminists and profeminist men for the healing and transformative work they do to heal self, family of what ever configuration, relationships, and others. This healing can and will have a positive impact on healing and changing the negative aspects of social structures and systems that dominate our lives.

The chapters in Part IV in this book discuss some of these themes and commonalities, which may be a basis for starting to heal the rift between the feminists, profeminist men, and the mythopoetic branch. The intervening chapters explore in more detail mythopoetic theory and research that demonstrates the powerful impact on men of the mythopoetic perspective and mythopoetic men's healing work.

NOTES

1. Reference to newsletters of men's groups and other ephemeral materials are archived in the Changing Men Collections, Special Collections Division, of the Michigan State University Libraries. The archive contains 700 newsletters from all branches of men's work, worldwide, plus numerous topic headings for authors, subjects, men's centers, men's groups, and others, with over 800 cataloged entries under the subject of men's movement. The web site address for the Changing Men Collections is http://www. lib.msu.edu/coll/main/spec_col/radicalism/men.

2. Although Bly may have popularized the idea of the absent father's causing a father wound, the idea was not original with Bly. The following quotation comes from an undergraduate college textbook my mother, Caroline Read (Barton), used during her senior year in 1928 at Michigan State University (then Michigan State College):

The industrial revolution wrought a profound and fundamental change in the family life of the small workman. . . . Instead of plying his trade in his own home surrounded by his wife, his children and his apprentices, whose work he directed, he betook himself at the shriek of a whistle to the factory, where he labored with his fellows in crowded, unwholesome rooms until the evening. Instead of carrying through a piece of work to its end and thus experiencing the satisfaction that comes to the worker from the finished product, he carried on one simple mechanical process from morn till night, which, as division of labor became more and more minute, was but a small portion of the work necessary to a completed product.

This impacted his relationship with his family. "Absent from home the entire day, his influence over his children was necessarily weakened and he became distinctly less powerful a force in shaping the life and ideas of his family." (Goodsell, 1927, pp. 422–423)

REFERENCES

Alarcon, N. (1990). The theoretical subject(s) of this bridge called my back and Anglo-America feminism. In G. Anzaldua (Ed.), *Making face, Making soul, Haciendo caras* (pp. 356–369). San Francisco: aunt lute books.

Baldauf, G. (1995). Men's work. *Chicago Men, 4*(3), 2–4.

Barton, E. R. (1993). A gathering of men. *Manthem, 1*(2), 22, 23.

Becker, W. H. (1993) Gender, race, and the temptation of dualism. *Journal of Men's Studies, 1*(4), 403–425.

Bliss, S. (1986, November–December). Beyond machismo: The new men's movement. *Yoga Journal.*

Bliss, S. (1995). Mythopoetic men's movements. In M. S. Kimmel (Ed.), *The politics of manhood: Profeminist men respond to the mythopoetic men's movement* (and the *mythopoetic leader's answer*) (pp. 292–317). Philadelphia: Temple University Press.

Bly, R. (1988). *A little book on the human shadow.* New York: HarperCollins.

Bly, R. (1990). *Iron John: A book about men.* Reading, MA: Addison-Wesley.

Bray, L. H. (1992). *A preliminary exploration of the men's movement: Demographics and motivating factors.* Unpublished Masters Thesis, University of Alberta, Edmonton.

Christian, B. (1990). The race for theory. In G. Anzaldua (Ed.), *Making face, Making soul: haciendo caras.* San Francisco: aunt lute books.

Clatterbaugh, K. (1990). *Contemporary perspectives on masculinity.* Boulder, CO: Westview Press.

Clatterbaugh, K. (1997). *Contemporary perspectives on masculinity* (2nd ed.). Boulder, CO: Westview Press.

Coltrane, S. (1992). The micropolitics of gender in nonindustrial societies. *Gender and Society, 6*, 86–107.

Coltrane, S. (1994). Theorizing masculinities in contemporary social science. In H. Brod & M. Kaufman (Eds.), *Theorizing masculinity* (pp. 39–60). Thousand Oaks, CA: Sage.

Connell, R. (1987). *Gender and power: Society, the person and sexual politics.* Stanford, CA: Stanford University Press.

Ellis, K. (1994). Who's afraid of Robert Bly? Feminism, gender politics, and the mainstream media. *Masculinities, 2*(1), 8–20.

Estes, C. P. (1992). *Women who run with the wolves: Myths and stories of the wild women archetype.* New York: Ballantine Books.

Femiamo, S. D. (1986). *Advances in psychology: Implications for a curriculum in men's studies.* Unpublished doctoral dissertation, University of Massachusetts.

Frankenberg, R. (1993). *White women, race matters: The social construction of whiteness.* Minneapolis: University of Minnesota Press.

Franklin, C. W. II (1992). "Hey, home—yo, bro": Friendship among black men. In P. M. Nardi (Ed.), *Men's friendships* (pp. 201–214). Newbury Park, CA: Sage.

Freire, P. (1970). *The pedagogy of the oppressed.* New York: Seabury Press.

Goodsell, W. (1927). *A history of the family as a social and educational institution.* New York: Macmillan.

Grof, S. (1992). *The holotropic mind: The three levels of human consciousness and how they shape our lives*. San Francisco: Harper.

Hagan, K. L. (Ed.). (1992). *Women respond to the men's movement*. San Francisco: Pandora.

Hansen, K. V. (1991). "Helped put in a quilt": Men's work and male intimacy in nineteenth-century New England. In J. Lorber & S.A. Farrell (Eds.), *The social construction of gender* (pp. 83–103). Newbury Park, CA: Sage.

Hansen, K. V. (1992). "Our eyes behold each other": Masculinity and intimate friendships in antebellum New England. In P. M. Nardi (Ed.), *Men's friendships* (pp. 35–58). Newbury Park, CA: Sage.

Harding, C. (Ed.), (1992). *Wingspan: Inside the men's movement*. New York: St. Martin's Press.

Harding, S. (1991). What is feminist epistemology? In S. Harding (Ed.), *Whose science? whose knowledge?* (pp. 105–132). Ithaca, NY: Cornell University Press.

Hartsock, N. C. M. (1983). The feminist standpoint: Developing the ground for a specifically feminist materialism. In S. Harding & M. B. Hintikka (Eds.), *Discovering reality* (pp. 283–310). Dordrecht: Reidel.

Heuer, A. B. (1993). *Effects of family, society, and the church on men's self-image and their spirituality: approaching ministry to men*. Unpublished doctoral dissertation, Luther Northwestern Theological Seminary, St. Paul, MN.

Hollis, J. (1994). *Under Saturn's Shadow: The wounding and healing of men*. Toronto: Inner City Books.

Horne, A. M., Jolliff, D. L., & Roth, E. W. (1996). Men mentoring men in groups. In M. P. Andronico (Ed.), *Men in groups: Insights, interventions, and psychoeducational work* (pp. 97–112). Washington, DC: American Psychological Association.

Jastrab, J. (1995). *Sacred manhood, sacred Earth*. New York: Harper.

Jesser, C. J. (1996). *Fierce and tender men: Sociological aspects of the men's movement*. Westport, CT: Praeger.

Kaufman, M. (1994). Men, feminism, and men's contradictory experiences of power. In H. Brod & M. Kaufman (Eds.), *Theorizing masculinities* (pp. 142–163). Thousand Oaks, CA: Sage.

Kauth, B. (1991). *Men's friends: How to organize and run your own men's support group*. Milwaukee, WI: Human Development Associates.

Kauth, B. (1992). *A circle of men: The original manual for men's support groups*. New York: St. Martin's Press.

Kauth, B. (1997). *Warrior monk training retreat*. Jacksonport, WI: Human Development Association.

Keen, S. (1991). *Fire in the belly: On being a man*. New York: Bantam Books.

Kimmel, M. S. (1996). Afterword to M. S. Kimmel (Ed.), *The politics of manhood: Profeminist respond to the mythopoetic men's movement (and the mythopoetic leaders answer)* (pp. 362–374). Philadelphia: Temple University Press.

Kimmel, M. S., & Kaufman, M. (1994). Weekend warriors: The new men's movement. In H. Brod & M. Kaufman (eds.), *Theorizing masculinity* (pp. 259–288). Thousand Oaks, CA: Sage.

Kipnis, A. R. (1991). *Knights without armor*. Los Angeles: Jeremy P. Tarcher.

Lee, J. (1991). *At my father's wedding: Reclaiming our true masculinity.* New York: Bantam Books.

Lorde, A. (1984a). Age, race, class, and sex: Women redefining difference. In *Sister Outsider.* Freedom, CA: Crossing Press.

Lorde, A. (1984b). The master's tools will never dismantle the master's house. In *Sister Outsider.* Freedom, CA: Crossing Press.

McCartney, B. (1995). *From ashes to glory.* Nashville, TN: Thomas Nelson Publishers.

Messer, M. A. (1995). "Changing men" and feminist politics. In M. S. Kimmel (Ed.), *The politics of manhood: Profeminist men respond to the mythopoetic men's movement (and the mythopoetic leaders answer.* Philadelphia: Temple University Press.

Milan Women's Bookstore Collective. (1990). *Sexual differences.* Bloomington: Indiana University Press.

Millett, K. (1970). *Sexual politics.* Garden City, NY: Doubleday.

Murphy, M. (1991). Mother of the groom. In *Are you girls traveling alone?* Los Angeles: Clothespin Fever Press.

Robinson, N. (1995). Editorial. *Chicago Men: A Men's Journal,* 4(2), 1.

Sarachild, K. (n.d.). Consciousness-raising: A radical weapon. In *Redstockings.*

Schwalbe, M. (1996). *Unlocking the iron cage: The men's movement, gender politics, and American culture.* New York: Oxford University Press.

Sheehy, G. (1995). *New passages.* New York: Random House.

Smith, D. E. (1990). Women's experience as a radical critique of sociology. In D. E. Smith, *The conceptual practices of power* (pp. 11–28). Boston: Northeastern University Press.

Thompson, K. (1982, May). What do men really want? *New Age Journal,* pp. 30–51.

Tosi, C. (1992). State of the web. *Women Within Newsletter,* 4(1), p 1.

Walker, A. (1990). Definition of womanist. In G. Anzaldua (Ed.), *Making face, making soul: Haciendo caras.* San Francisco: aunt lute groups.

Winter, A. (1992). Men's groups—from a to z. In Merge (men's emergence resource guide). Portland, OR: Merge Publishing.

Wissocki, G. W., & Andronico, M. P. (1996). The Somerset Institute's modern men's weekend. In M. P. Andronico (Ed.), *Men in groups: Insights, interventions, and psychoeducational work* (pp. 113–126). Washington, DC: American Psychological Association.

Chapter 2
Beyond the Drum: An Exploratory Study of Group Processes in a Mythopoetic Men's Group

Steve R. Wilson and Eric S. Mankowski

The mythopoetic branch of the contemporary men's movement is an exploration of male spirituality and male psychology (Schwalbe, 1996). This movement encourages men to delve into their psyches through contact with literature, mythology, and art. Its adherents are typically heterosexual white men in midlife (Harding, 1992; Shiffman, 1987). For the mythopoetic branch, personal introspection and growth assume a far more significant role than the profeminist and men's rights branches. The mythopoetic perspective is not overtly political or interested in social structural change. Indeed, from the mythopoetic perspective, masculinity depends on uncovering and discovering deep psychospiritual patterns collectively known and understood by all men. These patterns or archetypes are best revealed through stories, myths, and rituals made relevant to men today.

The most significant part of the peer agenda of the mythopoetic branch pertains to the hundreds of ongoing men's mutual support groups (MPMSG) and weekend retreats. The goal of these groups and retreats is to initiate men into their archetypal masculinity. One target is the "soft male," who is out of touch with his animal instincts and does not have a direction to his life (Hillman, 1987). Through rituals involving wounding and healing, these "soft men" can come to embrace their full masculinity. Many of these ceremonial rituals have clear psychological incentives, which may fulfill certain developmental needs of the man, allowing him to experience his "initiation into manhood."

BASIS OF MYTHOPOETIC CONCEPTS AND PRACTICES

The mythopoetic branch of the men's movement draws heavily on the analytical theories of Carl Jung (Schwalbe, 1996). According to Jung, men start life as whole persons but, through wounding, lose their identity and become fragmented. Mythopoetic principles hold that if men probe the archetypes buried in their unconscious, eventually they will be able to heal these wounds and restore themselves to a state of wholeness and psychospiritual health (Clatterbaugh, 1997). The language between the conscious and the unconscious (expanding on Freud's notions of these same concepts) rests in communication through symbols (or archetypes) (Corsini & Wedding, 1989) that attempts to express something unexplainable but nevertheless existing and constant over time.

Most participants of the mythopoetic movement accept the Jungian belief that these archetypes are best discovered through participation in rituals, myths, and storytelling (Clatterbaugh, 1997). For example, Bly (1990) discusses the archetype of the "Wild Man" in his retelling of the 1815 Grimm brothers' fairy tale "Iron Hans" (Grimm, 1975). The story is about a wild man who comes out of a dark pond and imposes a series of tasks on a young prince, who through these initiatory tasks gains maturity as a man. Bly proposed that this Wild Man is clearly interpreted (using Jungian psychology) to be a mythical, symbolic representation of true masculinity, which, according to Bly, has been feminized, denied, and repressed in modern culture. Drawing from Jungian philosophy, Bly has asserted that in a symbolic sense, the Wild Man lies deep within all men's psyches. In order to evolve effectively from "soft men" (which men have become over time) to "wild men" (the new model of masculine authenticity), it is critical for men to identify and embrace their long-suppressed Wild Man.

The Freudian view of the father's role in the development of the boy is also seen as critical to the theoretical base of the mythopoetic branch. Freud postulated that the boy desires to have an exclusive relationship with his mother during the Oedipal period, which occurs when he is three to five years of age. Freud believed that the boy comes to see his father as an aggressive competitor for his mother's affection and to fear that his father will castrate him. The normal resolution of the Oedipus complex takes place when, in order to cope with his fear of castration, the boy identifies with his father and represses his desire for his mother. The boy's subsequent strong masculine strivings and desire to be like his father were seen as a by-product of his identification with his father (Freud, 1955).

Proponents of the mythopoetic perspective (e.g., Osherson, 1986) and other theorists (Pollack, 1995) have extended Freudian theory to suggest that developmental problems as well as psychopathology can result from the child's not having a vital father or father figure in his early masculine development who would provide appropriate, healthy modeling of masculinity (see Pleck, 1995, for an alternative view). Much of the mythopoetic branch of the contemporary men's movement appears to center around this ongoing separation-individuation struggle between men and their fathers.

MOTIVATIONS FOR THE MYTHOPOETIC BRANCH OF THE MEN'S MOVEMENT

Couched within these psychoanalytic theories, three more specific incentives emerge as potential motivators for the mythopoetic branch of the men's movement: father hunger, emotional inexpressiveness, and male friendship.

Father Hunger

A recurring theme that surfaces in popular literature relating to the mythopoetic branch is the concept of father hunger, a term that Herzog (1980) introduced to describe the affective state of longing for a male parent or surrogate experienced by the children of divorced parents whom he studied. Father hunger, resulting from paternal deprivation, includes various inadequacies in a boy's or girl's experience with the father: total father absence, as in perceived abandonment by the father as a result of divorce or death, temporary separation from the father for an extended period of time, or an emotionally absent father. An important consideration in relation to the mythopoetic branch is that paternal deprivation can occur when the father is available but there is not a meaningful father-child attachment bond.

Bly (1990) expanded on the notion of paternal deprivation and father hunger by stating that as a result of the onset of the Industrial Revolution, the unit most damaged was the father-son bond. According to Bly:

The traditional way of raising sons, which lasted for thousands and thousands of years, amounted to fathers and sons living in close—murderously close—proximity, while the father taught the son a trade: perhaps farming or carpentry or blacksmithing or tailoring. . . . The industrial revolution, in its need for office and factory workers, pulled fathers away from their sons and, moreover, placed sons in compulsory schools where teachers are mostly women. (p. 19)

Today Bly argues, many fathers work in business or industry away from the home; by the time they return at night, the children are often in bed and they themselves are too tired to do active fathering: "When a father, absent during the day returns home at six, his children receive only his temperament and not his teaching" (1990, p. 96). He has suggested that resolution of this father hunger can be accomplished only through the establishment of emotionally intimate relationships with other men who are similarly committed to embracing their "wild man." This, Bly has purported, is a motivating factor for men to gather with other men, separate from women. Key to men's gatherings is the territory of emotional expressiveness, an area in which men are traditionally not profi-

cient. Adherents to the mythopoetic movement consider this a vital part of healing men's wounds.

Male Inexpressiveness

The marked lack of expressive ability in the male child and, consequently,
the adult male is a consequence of father hunger. Men are not typically taught
to experience or recognize emotions similar to those of women (O'Neil, 1981),
and they have difficulty in emotionally communicating, establishing trust, and
being vulnerable (Levant, 1995). There is substantial evidence that male socialization discourages expressiveness, which is seen as a "feminine" trait (Levant,
1995). Social penalties exist for boys and men when they deviate from stereotypic gender role expectations (Pleck, 1981; Derlega & Chaikin, 1976). Social
learning of traditional male gender role definitions appears to result in a man's
belief that he is not supposed to be expressive of emotion (Levant, 1995; Winstead, Derlega, & Wong, 1984). However, through structured group intervention,
men can learn to express their feelings, given the proper conditions (Moore &
Haverkamp, 1989). Nahon and Lander (1992) have reported success in men
learning to express feelings in a group context.

Traditionally, men have been less able than women to relate in an open,
verbally expressive way to others of the same sex (Farrell, 1986). Homophobia
and competition are two aspects of male inexpressiveness that characterize masculine gender role development (Kilmartin, 1994). One aspect of homophobia
is the fear of feeling vulnerable and shamed when labeled a homosexual or of
having homosexual tendencies (Forstein, 1988; Herek, 1986). Generally, the
more secure a man is in his sexuality, the more open he can be in relating to a
member of the same sex. Competition can also be a barrier to the expression of
affection and love between male friends. From birth, boys are taught indirectly
to compete against one another—not only for girls but also for status and respect
(Franklin, 1984).

Mythopoetic men's gatherings are vehicles for the fostering of greater emotional expressiveness between men whose interactions have traditionally been
lacking in emotional content or superficial at best. Keen (1991) advocates men
gathering together in order to develop "a repertoire of their own emotions" (p.
241) and encourages them to "practice expressing rather than repressing their
feelings" (p. 242).

Male Friendship

Franklin (1984) attributed male sex role socialization to the traditional male
characteristics of competitiveness, dominance, and fears of emotional intimacy
with other males as primary reasons that males tend to form diffuse and instrumental friendships rather than emotionally expressive ones. Emotionally expressive friendships thrive on cooperation, sharing, and nurturing behaviors,

contrary to competitive, aggressive, and dominant traits valued in early male youth. The adult male who is "appropriately" socialized into masculinity is rendered nearly incapable of forming close ties with other males.

Generally men are attracted to other men who share similar ideas, values, and attitudes, and who like to engage in certain similar activities (e.g., sports, clubs) (Franklin, 1984). Since liking is not as expressive in male-male relationships as in male-female relationships and female-female relationships, mutual expressiveness does not seem to be as necessary in male-male interpersonal attraction. Because emotional sharing plays a lesser role, joint participation in activities seems to be the magnet that draws men together (Franklin, 1984). As is the case for early childhood friendships, heterosexual men are typically attracted to other men because of specific instrumental qualities, such as shared interests in sports and work, with their intimacy needs being met through their relationships with women (e.g., wives, lovers) (Pleck, 1975).

Consequently, men who live in a society in which the verbalization of such feelings has been neither modeled nor encouraged have difficulty expressing friendship. The mythopoetic branch can be instrumental in helping men to overcome this barrier by enabling them to become emotionally and physically close to other men. This can be done by allowing them to explore the psychological complexities of their father hunger and creating an arena for emotional expression of feelings that can be instrumental in the development of intimate, same-sex friendships.

STUDY PURPOSE AND METHODS

Despite research on relevant topics such as male friendship (Nardi, 1992a), traditional male inexpressiveness, and father hunger, there is a need for more detailed descriptions of mythopoetic men's mutual support groups, that seem to embody each of these vital components. In asking why men are attracted to the mythopoetic movement, as well as what benefits are gained by the men who align themselves with it, we provide a detailed description of an ongoing mythopoetic men's mutual support group, explore some of the underlying issues being addressed by this group and the mythopoetic branch of the contemporary men's movement, and discuss the implications for helping professionals by providing information on the efficacy of this nontraditional therapy for men.

Since little empirical knowledge was available in this area, participant-observation methodology (Chesler, 1991) was used at an ongoing mythopoetic men's mutual support group. In addition, background information on the men's movement was obtained through participation in a national men's movement conference, "Exploring Conscious Manhood," held in October 1992 in Austin, Texas.[1]

Fieldwork for this study was conducted at a men's center we refer to as the Arbor Center. We selected it because it conducted many fee-based therapeutic activities and groups for men, one of them a mythopoetic drumming group. The group met once weekly and was facilitated by a licensed social worker therapist, who will be called Adam.[2] Because this was an open group (a group open each week to all men who come), there tended to be a high fluctuation in weekly membership; regularly attending members did not come to every meeting. Consequently, the sample varied from a low of four members (the researcher, the leader, and two other men) to a high of sixteen. Average weekly attendance was seven members.

Over the course of ten months (June 1992–February 1993), S.R.W. (the first author) participated in this weekly support group, which was scheduled to meet for two hours but often exceeded this time frame through informal discussion following the formal group meeting. Considerable time was spent in personal interaction with the members. Following weekly participation, field notes were taken that focused on the activities conducted, themes or topics discussed that night, and interactions among members. In many instances, only the themes and content of the group were noted. At other times, emphasis was placed on general interaction patterns rather than specific content. These notes were examined and analyzed using content analysis procedures, looking for themes of discussion, characteristics of participants, and rituals utilized.

S.R.W. developed semistructured interview guides for participants of the weekly support group, with interviews conducted informally at various locations away from the Arbor Center where the group met. Researcher-developed interview guides included open-ended questions asking the men to describe their motivations for attending the group and participating in the mythopoetic men's movement as a whole. Members were requested to describe their perceptions of the movement, the extent of their personal involvement, and how they felt their lives had changed as a result.

FINDINGS AND DISCUSSION

To examine the existing patterns of the mythopoetic men's mutual support group, data were organized into two categories: the structure of the Arbor Center group, including a description of the site, its participants, a typical meeting, and the group's routine practices; and an examination of the extent to which the mythopoetic concepts are illustrated in the group studied.

Site

The Arbor Center is a professional suite of offices located in an office-park area in southern California. Numerous therapeutic activities are conducted for the public within the suite of five offices, including group therapy, individual therapy, and massage therapy.

The main room was the location of the Tuesday night open mythopoetic men's mutual support group. It is a large, open space with gray carpeting; a bookcase containing books, magazines, and art therapy supplies; and, on the north corner, a small brick fireplace with a large African tribal mask surrounded by similar tribal spears on the wall above it. There is no other art work on the walls, except for a framed cover of a 1991 magazine featuring a cover story on the mythopoetic men's movement. Elsewhere, small hand-held drums hang on nails hammered irregularly around the room.

The room is painted beige with a high, cathedral-type ceiling made of dark wood. The environment is that of a men's lodge, with natural woods used in the construction and free-standing wood drums placed around the room. Five fluorescent overhead lights illuminate the room. The air-conditioning has usually been left on, making the space very cold; however, when this has been turned off, the room quickly becomes quite stuffy and hot.

Prior to the group meeting, the room is often cluttered and disheveled, since it is used during the day for an addiction/recovery treatment program as well as for other group activities conducted by the therapists working at the center. Approximately twenty gray chairs are scattered about, as well as other therapeutic items, such as a chalkboard on one wall, beanbag chairs (for beating during anger work), stuffed animals, and assorted drums.

Group Members

Writers in the popular media have created a distorted image of the typical man attending a mythopoetic men's group (Hirshey, 1991). Although attendees cannot adequately be placed in mutually exclusive categories, this group has tended to be composed of men from three general life contexts, loosely adapted from categories described by Shewey (1992). One subgroup is recovering men who have a history of substance abuse of various types (e.g., food, alcoholism, drug dependency, and sexual addiction) and are working on overcoming these addictions. A large number of men attending this group have also been sexually abused as children. This is consistent with what has been found in similar types of men's groups around the country (Shewey, 1992). Probably 75 percent of the men attending are in recovery from addiction or abuse.

The second subgroup is wounded men who have been damaged by a history of divorce, bad jobs, bad relationships, and general misfortune. Often these men are working on improving their relationships with others, especially women. Approximately 15 percent of the participants fall into this subgroup.

The third subgroup is isolated men who are hungry to be around other men who are struggling with basic issues of masculinity and manhood, including fear and distrust of other men. These men are searching for the answer to the fundamental question: "What does it mean to be a man today?" Isolated men, who constitute about 10 percent of the group, may or may not be experiencing any of the above issues as well. A common theme that crosses all three subgroups is that most men in the group have had a fragmented or nonexistent relationship with their father in childhood. This was often accompanied by "too much mother," which, most believe, has negatively affected their adult relationships.

The weekly group has adopted the name the "Fire Walkers" (a pseudonym), which members informally use when referring to the collective group. Although the group has been in existence for over two years, currently only three members have been participating for more than a year. The average length of attendance for core members (participants who have long-term, regular attendance) is one year. Others who are not considered core tend to be excluded by the core members from outside activities, such as parties or other get-togethers.

The group participants range in age from thirty-six to over fifty years. The ethnicity of the members is primarily non-Hispanic white, although two members who attended periodically were Latino and one new member is Asian. Many of the participants are divorced or experiencing marital or relationship difficulties. All of the regular members attend at least one other form of therapy during the week (either with a therapist at the Arbor Center or elsewhere). From group discussion and informal interviews, it was found that nearly every member had belonged to at least one twelve-step recovery program (such as Alcoholics Anonymous or CODA, a codependency group modeled after Alcoholics Anonymous) either currently or recently. Occupations tend to be professional in nature, including an accountant, an air traffic controller, a high school teacher, a computer programmer, a registered nurse, an actor, and a firefighter. One member is gay, and the rest identify themselves as heterosexual, although two of the men have had homosexual relations with other men in their recent past. The ethnicity and sexual orientation mix does not seem to affect group interaction.

Members heard about the group from various sources. A local newspaper profiled the Arbor Center in early 1991, and many of the current core members came to investigate the group as a result. Some see one of the therapists working at the center for individual therapy and heard directly or indirectly about the group from that person. Promotional literature is distributed throughout the community, and some came as a result of reading a flyer or brochure about the group.

Consistent with what is expected in group dynamics (Levine, 1979; Johnson & Johnson, 1997), subgroups have formed: the core members; the regulars, who have attended for a while but have not been accepted into core membership; and members who are patients of an in-patient treatment program for childhood abuse trauma who know each other intimately through the therapeutic work but are relatively unfamiliar with the core or regular members.

Group Practices and Typical Meetings

Building the Container

Liebman (1991) stated that "the term 'mythological' refers to the realm of human experience that reveals itself in images and stories [which] depict themes of eternal concern to men and women" (p. 9). Of utmost concern to Adam and the participants is the mythological context in which the group is conducted. The preservation of a mythopoetic experience is crucial for identification with the mythological themes in the men's lives. This also is a vehicle for creating their own spiritual experiences, which are instrumental in reconstructing ideas of what is masculine or masculine behavior.

The actual mythological space or container for this group is the circle, which is created within the larger room. Several chairs (usually about six or seven) are taken from around the periphery of the room and placed in a circle at the south end of the room. This is often done by the leader or by any of the men who happen to arrive first.

Welcome and Drumming

The group is scheduled to run from 7:00 P.M. to 9:00 P.M. each Tuesday, but often it runs to 9:30 P.M. or later, depending on the intensity of the discussion and activities. The group experiences irregular attendance by some core members, and because new members are welcome at any time, it is difficult to project each evening's attendance and activities. Customarily, six to eight members are present, with at least five men attending faithfully from week to week. As the men arrive, a traditional greeting is for them to hug one another (Kauth, 1991), a behavior similar to that seen at twelve-step group meetings. Some light conversation serves to welcome one another. Members then proceed to select the drum that is most comfortable for them to use during the drumming session. These simple wood drums with shallow resonance are three feet tall. Adam brings his own large, resonant, African-style drum. Currently, only two members other than Adam bring their own drums.

As the men select drums and get seated (in no particular seating arrangement), Adam circulates a large manila envelope to collect the weekly fee, currently twenty dollars per member. Each participant writes his name and the amount paid (or owed) that night on a sheet attached to the envelope. Once this has been circulated to all the men, the last man turns out the overhead lights. Freeform drumming then begins by candlelight. Due to the limited light, faces can be only faintly identified, and most of the following activities are conducted in shadow.

Adam initiates the drumming by inviting the men to "enter a sacred circle of men, a time and space apart from our present reality." Of the many tools available to the mythopoetic branch, drumming is probably the most emblematic. As one member stated, the drumming "is a means for connecting with emotions." The beat of the drums seems to bring forth an emotional and spiritual connectedness among the men. As Adam speaks, he begins rhythmically drumming; the men may or may not imitate him. This seems to be a way for the men to feel together or part of a community without the use of words.

The drumming lasts about fifteen minutes and ends when Adam directs the drummers to stop "on 3," at which time he counts to 3. Immediate silence then ensues. There are a few moments of silence by the light of the candle (which Adam periodically refers to as "the fire"), broken when Adam speaks to invite the "outer check."

The Outer Check-In

During outer check, each man relates what is happening in his life. Adam always initiates this activity, often by suggesting that each man briefly tell the group "what you are bringing with you into the group tonight." This is a way for the members to let each other know at the outset what is uppermost in their minds. This has two benefits: it tends to put a boundary on what outside matters will be discussed and sets the tone for what might be discussed or conducted later in the evening in terms of therapeutic activities. Generally topics discussed reflect events of the day or week (e.g., difficulty at work, relationship problems, personal breakthroughs). This has not traditionally been a time-limited activity, and when some men choose to provide great detail of recent or past events, the outer check-in can take over an hour. Over time, the outer check-in evolved from a quick "feelings round" to an open forum with lengthy discussions of emotional concerns. Adam discourages interruption or feedback from the group during this time.

Once the outer check-in is completed, Adam provides a summary of the collective themes and the related feelings brought into the group that night. The next step is a dramatic shift from this traditional group model to activities that are experiential in nature and are based on the mythological focus of the group.

Rites of Initiation

An interesting characteristic of this mythopoetic group is the unofficial initiation that is conducted by the group members. Customarily, new men are not fully oriented to the customs of the group, including its nontraditional theme (that is, in relation to other standard forms of group therapy), since neither Adam nor the group members familiarize the uninitiated men with how the group is conducted. Following the outer check-in, there is often a sharp transition to the next experiential portion, again with little announcement or introduction by Adam, leaving new men confused and unsure of the group's norms. New members who adapt to this shift and are not put off by it tend to be more readily accepted by the core group and the regulars. Men who do not adapt or are noticeably frustrated by their unfamiliarity with the group's culture tend not to return after the first week.

A new man's reluctance to ask for clarification of the group format, as well as the group's less-than-nurturing introduction to the group culture, is consistent with stereotypic gender role expectations relating to male inexpressiveness and resistance to vulnerability (Levant, 1995). Adam and the core members deny that this is an informal initiation or hazing and are comfortable with the existing process. Regardless, a clear message has been communicated to the new member: there are insiders and there are outsiders, and he must somehow "prove" his worthiness to join the club.

Traditional male-only societies, such as Masonic organizations, fraternities, Boy Scouts, the YMCA, and the Catholic priesthood, require potential members to go through a trial or initiation rite. Garfinkel (1985) alluded to the fact that rites of initiation are "fraught with ambiguity" and include periods of isolation: "We must know how to make it on our own; we must be self sufficient. And yet, initiation rites require a man to humble himself and defer to the group. He must give up his individuality for the group ethos" (pp. 103–104). Initiation into the Fire Walkers' core membership is not unlike this ambiguous situation.

Experiencing the Mythological

The shift to mythopoetic experience in the group can be abrupt. Adam now directs the members to "stand up and move around the room, try to get in touch with your body." This is perhaps the most confusing portion of the group to the uninitiated. Entering the realm of the mythological is seen as crucial to conducting the work of the mythopoetic group. These activities, or rituals, are seen as sacred and mysterious to Adam and the group, who appear to hold the view that attempting to understand them intellectually can only serve to trivialize them or, worse, open the group to ridicule. This experiential portion of the group, which is often referred to as the mythopoetic portion, varies from week to week, with Adam spontaneously deciding which mythopoetic exercise is appropriate for that evening. Adam seems to have a broad repertoire of these activities from which to draw, and they are rarely duplicated.

The movement portion begins with some of the men performing tai-chi movements, while others move about the room as if performing a creative, interpretive dance. Not surprisingly, there is a certain amount of theatricality to this portion of the group. Adam drums rhythmically while everyone moves haphazardly around the room. The more conservative, self-conscious members quietly stretch, while the less inhibited take on the mannerisms of animals, such as bears, lions, or buffalo, with the appropriate sounds. The men engage in chanting and shouting as a way of unleashing pent-up frustration and doing something unconventional. Adam has identified the purpose of these exercises as providing a therapeutic way for the men to "get out of their head and into their feelings." As the men move about the dark room by candlelight, inhibitions lessen as Adam invites the men to let go of old ideas about what is proper and socially correct as a way of entering a liminal space. This activity, while a way to release energy, is also seen as a transformational process from the world of the present to a mythological time and space.

Although the activities vary, common exercises include those that involve physical exertion and a considerable amount of physical touching between men in a nonsexual context. Occasionally Adam tells the group to "move into each other's physical space, looking in the eyes of the men before you." Often he encourages the men to behave like animals, getting in touch with the earth, or to "leave your head and become a wolf or a bison." The men move freely around the room pawing the earth, growling, barking, and playfully interacting with each other. New members are customarily more restrained in these activities than are regular and core members. Informal interviews with some of the men revealed that this form of nonaggressive wrestling was frequently singled out as the most stimulating portion of the group. This rigorous exercise ends after about ten minutes, with all of the men collapsing on the ground as if exhausted. As one man stated, "To get past my head and into my body is what this is all about. Everything else is too analytical." Again, as with earlier activities, there is no introduction for the benefit of the uninitiated, and the new men are usually reluctant to abandon themselves completely to this unconventional activity without at least knowing the cultural norms of the group. This is reflected in their initially reserved movements around the periphery of the room, although they tend to be more playful and relaxed at subsequent meetings.

Often these exercises serve as a conduit to facilitate communication among members; however, many of the men characterize these movements as a way to get in touch with personal feelings they have long suppressed. Some of the Fire Walkers have suggested that the mythopoetic work conducted in group is a way of overcoming the cultural stigmatization they have felt as men. They appear to be combating a Eurocentric stereotype that requires them to behave in a tough, nonaffectionate, inexpressive manner. Although this portion of the group is couched in the mythological context that Adam encourages, the movements can be seen as a contemporary form of expressive therapy not traditionally experienced by men in a gender-specific group setting. Further, as confirmed through informal interviews, the Fire Walkers who long to conduct what they consider genuine mythopoetic work savor this physical portion of the group.

While these exercises are seen as therapeutically valuable, there seems to be a sharp similarity between some of the behaviors exhibited in group and those actions seen in contact sports (Messner, 1992). Love and intimacy among the men in this group are rarely expressed tenderly, but are easily displayed in hearty bear hugs and rough-housing. It is built into this culture that men who do not compete and need intimacy and emotional support from other men are, at best, weak or, at worst, gay (Nardi, 1992b). Similarly, the taboo of homosexuality seems to inhibit this group from openly expressing affection toward the other men, for fear that it will be "taken in the wrong way" (Ruben, 1985).

The Inner Circle

Upon completion of these ritualistic exercises, Adam calls on the group to reassemble "at the fire." Again, with no explanatory comments by Adam, the men return to the mesa area from wherever they ended up after the experiential portion of the meeting. They sit cross-legged on the floor while Adam invites them to "go inside and do some inner work," which is traditionally conducted during the inner circle. This is the time in which there is a more heartfelt discussion of feelings and emotions, particularly the feelings that the experiential exercises may have evoked. This discussion is preceded by the ceremonial smudging process, also initiated by Adam.

The smudging custom, taken from Native American traditions, is ceremonially performed each week and begins when Adam opens the box on the mesa that contains the smudge bowl and a small bundle of sage. He lights the end of the sage from the candle so that smoke rises from the smoldering herb. He places the sage into the clam-shell bowl and turns to the man on his left, so that they are facing each other, and reverently brushes the wafts of sage smoke toward him. The intent is to use the smoke to purify and momentarily cleanse the man of his outside cares. Adam frequently refers to "this tradition of our ancestral brothers" (specifically, the Chumash Indians, whose land is now southern California), while broadly explaining the spiritual cleansing that this process effects. After a few moments of having the sage smoke brushed over him, the man takes the sage and smudge bowl from Adam, turns to the man on his left, and repeats the process. This is done silently and reverently until the last man in the circle smudges Adam. Adam concludes the process by extinguishing the smoldering sage in the smudge bowl and invites each of the men to clasp each others hands and sit for a few moments in silence.

Adam then recognizes and acknowledges the sacred space of the inner circle by "calling upon the seven directions." The men are encouraged to visualize symbols that represent the powers of the directions that Adam reverently invokes in the forms of "the North, the South, the East, the West, Mother Earth, Father Sky, and the Deep Within." Adam has thus confirmed that the group has entered a mythologically important place for more rituals to be performed and that this space should be honored as such. While the preceding activities may have been more informal in nature, Adam clearly identifies this new space as consecrated.

The goal of the inner circle is to create a sacred space where honest and emotion-filled communication can occur. A secondary therapeutic goal is for the men to become more sensitive to their bodies and their feelings, or even their resistance to experiencing feelings. It is common for men to feel a loss of identity (or masculinity) when open emotions are displayed to other men (Balswick, 1988). Through the group, these men can learn to be supported by other men regardless of what they may be feeling.

As part of the process of edging away from the outer world, Adam takes out the "talking stick," inviting the men to conduct a second round of the check-in, commonly called the "inner check-in." This is a statement of "what things feel like" on the inside, apart from anecdotes, current events, and intellectualizations. The talking stick empowers the man to speak in a particular, focused way— briefly, honestly, from his own experience only, and "in the moment." Upon completion of this round, Adam replaces the talking stick in the box on the mesa and continues the work of the inner circle. Little time is spent discussing sex or women at these group meetings. Despite the stereotype of men's groups as engaging in "women bashing," the focus of this group is clearly more self-help in nature, with a primary interest in the self rather than in relationships with others, especially women.

Adam occasionally invites the men to read poems that they may have brought or to speak about a recent, vivid dream. Because the men rarely bring in poetry or speak of their dreams, Adam often recites poetry that he has brought or takes a few minutes to read a mythological tale rich in metaphorical imagery. Following this, Adam asks the men to place themselves in the context of the tale or the poem in order for them to speak about what was particularly significant for them.

One example was when Adam recited the tale of Iron John. According to the story, a golden ball belonging to the prince rolls into the Wild Man's cage one day. In exchange for his freedom, Iron John returns the golden ball to the prince, then lifts the boy onto his shoulders and carries him away into the forest. The boy goes through a series of initiatory tests and adventures that in time transform him into a man. In this context, the Wild Man represents the initiator who separates the boy from maternal comfort and exposes him to trials and tasks from which a masculine identity is forged.

While telling the story, Adam drummed a hypnotic rhythm at a low volume. He then directed the men to get up and "feel what it was like for the thing you identified with . . . become that thing." The men began to move around the room, experientially interacting with each other while "becoming" elements of the story that they had chosen. After a few minutes of nonverbal expressive movement, Adam called the group back together by the fire. Again without feedback from the other group members, the men took turns speaking about what was important symbolically for them. No particular order was followed, and some chose not to speak, although silence does not indicate that the man received nothing from the experience. He may instead have been processing the meaning of the story and activity at a nonverbal or nonconscious level.

Through a variety of methods, each man's specific material becomes a way for the group to comprehend the more general theme it contains. Each man's story moves from the individual, to the group, to the universal, using mythological themes, and he begins to think of himself mythologically instead of psychologically, even though many of the exercises that Adam used have clear psychological implications and could be viewed as traditional expressive therapy. Many of the men have had numerous years of conventional psychotherapy and see this nontraditional way of examining their lives as refreshing.

An example is one man's choice of "the castle" as the item in the story that particularly resonated for him. Adam therapeutically handled this by asking him to speak concretely but as descriptively as possible about his experience as the castle, and the impact it had on him. When Adam reflected on the universal "castle" quality of all men in terms of the Jungian collective unconscious, the castle was viewed differently. The metaphor now represented men's isolation and their "walled" access to feelings.

Closing Ceremony

Following these rituals, Adam brings the group to a close with the closing ritual known as the "naming circle." Adam invites the men to rise and stand in a circle with their arms around one another in a huddle over the candle. When the first man is ready (in no order), he says, "My name is _____." The group responds "Your name is _____" and repeats his name twice. The man next to him then states his name in the same way, the group responds, and so on, until the last man has spoken and been named. This is seen as a positive form of individual and group affirmation. Often the recitation of the person's name is accompanied by supportive pats on the back while each member looks at the individual being affirmed. Once the naming circle is complete, the group breaks, and the men talk among themselves freely as Adam turns on the overhead light and prepares to lock up the room for the night.

The men hug one another in farewell. Parting conversation is customarily a continuation of the topics discussed that evening; despite the late hour, many of the men exhibit a marked reluctance to leave. Once outside, core members often gather in the parking lot for continued talk about personal issues, gossip about the group, and ideas for the future of the group.

Mythopoetic Concepts Exemplified in the Group

Similar to the other factions of the contemporary men's movement, the mythopoetic branch does not speak with a single voice. However, Bly's book *Iron John* (1990) might serve as the central text from which much of the mythopoetic work springs. His book, as well as many of his related works, introduced men to an alternative way of examining masculinity and manhood. Additionally, the book embraced certain tenets that are now widely accepted throughout the mythopoetic branch of the contemporary men's movement: the "wound" that men and boys have experienced by the lack of a father resulting from the Industrial Revolution, the alchemical transformation that can occur at a men's gathering through the formal initiation into manhood, and the constructive use of mythology and archetypes, specifically the "Wild Man," as a metaphor for the authentic potential to which men can aspire.

Healing the Father Wound

In the early 1980s, Bly began discussing the empowerment of men that can occur when men gather together for a collective healing of the psychic wounds inflicted on them in their childhood. The wound to which he most often referred was the "father wound," which inhibits men from experiencing their masculine potential (interpreted as the integration of the lover, warrior, magician, and king archetypes; see Moore & Gillette, 1990). A common theme discussed almost weekly within the inner circle of the Fire Walkers' group was the phenomenon of the absent father. In retrospect, discussion surrounding relationships with fathers occurred about 50 percent of the time in group, with discussion of other personal concerns occupying another 40 percent. Only 10 percent of the time were women discussed.

Often the topic of fathers emerged spontaneously, even though Adam occasionally introduced it through poetry and stories. Little was ever mentioned about the impact of the mother, which is consistent with Bly's thesis that there is a distinct father hunger in American men today. It is important to note that most of the Fire Walkers men did not come from single-parent families; rather, their fathers' absence resulted from the distance created by the father's work outside the home and the general lack of his emotional involvement in their development.

The Fire Walkers men often spoke of the psychic and spiritual wounding that they experienced (along with the subsequent grief) because of a lack of emotional connectedness with their male parent (Hollis, 1994). This father absence also seemed to darken their current relationships with women, children, and other men. One man mentioned that his motivation for joining the group was to "test my ability to befriend [other] men." Bly stated that the boy who "learns feeling primarily from the mother [will] probably see his own masculinity from a feminine point of view as well" (Bly, 1985, p. 25). In that regard, some of the men assign blame to their mothers for their inability to relate effectively to other men. One of the members, raised primarily by his mother and other females, stated that he was involved in the group "to learn how to relate to men, my peers, from a male perspective as opposed to a female perspective." One of his goals was to work through his fears of other men, including his real or imagined fears of being "killed or rejected by other men." He believes that these fears, along with his general distrust of other men, resulted from an overabundance of "feminine energy." He later added that the group had been beneficial to him in addressing these fears.

Bly proposed that men have a set of underrecognized male modes of feeling, with grief being chief among them. Examples of father-hunger grief were often evident in the emotional expressions exhibited in the inner circle. For example, one member was recently unable to attend a weekly meeting due to the death of his father. This contextualized ritual had such a profound effect on the group that when the member returned the next week, almost the entire evening was spent allowing him to process this marker event in his life. For nearly an hour, he spoke uninterrupted about the events surrounding his father's death and the emotional impact it had on him. Bly stated, "You cannot become a man until your own father dies" (Morrow, 1991, p. 53). Through close identification with this trauma, the group members shed a considerable number of tears while offering him empathy, support, and nurturing, qualities not readily associated with traditional definitions of masculinity (Kilmartin, 1994).

As a way of showing sympathy for and honoring this core member and his father, the group decided to purchase a small pine tree for him to plant collectively in the back of the Arbor Center the next week. Prior to the planting, the group "smudged" the tree and gave it the name of the member's deceased father. This event was fondly recalled by many of the members interviewed and is occasionally referred to in the group. Such empathy was included in one member's statement (made on several occasions), "I come here for the nurturing I get from other men."

Finally, certain rituals are performed during the mythopoetic portion of the meeting that honor not only fathers, but other paternal ancestors as well. One of these is in the form of a song that periodically the men chant following the smudging process. As with many of the other rituals of this group, the song is neither explained nor fully introduced to the new members. Although Adam never invokes a deity, he calls on the gods in the form of "our grandfathers, fathers, and brothers" as a form of a spiritual "connection with the deep masculine." At every meeting, Adam initiates the song to celebrate this heritage, but the song is rarely received enthusiastically by the Fire Walkers. No one speaks openly of disliking the song; however, there always seems to be resistance to beginning the song following Adam's start, and the low volume at which it is chanted or sung is telling of how the men fail to find it meaningful. Further, while regular eye contact between members is noted during many of the other activities of the inner circle, the men typically look down or away from each other during the song.

Initiation into Manhood

According to Bly, men became separated from their families as a result of the Industrial Revolution. This has deprived boys of a form of apprenticeship with their fathers and, consequently, an imitative model from whom to draw conclusions about manhood. Bly (1990) stated, "Having abandoned initiation, our society has difficulty in leading boys toward manhood [which is why] we have so many boys and so few men" (p. 182).

Men in the 1990s and continuing into the 21st century sought out alternative ways to be introduced into manhood as a way of compensating for this developmental deficiency, particularly since culturally established ceremonies such as bar mitzvahs and confirmations are now only a vestige of a once-vital spiritual experience. Miller and others (1992), quoting mythologist Doug Gillette and Jungian analyst Robert Moore, stated that conscription into the military or into a street gang does initiate men, but through pseudorituals that produce a patriarchal manhood, which is skewed, stunted, and abusive of others. They call these initiations "pseudo" because "real men are not wantonly violent or hostile" (p. 172).

Jungian therapist Edith Sullwold stated that as adults, we can create personal rituals to finish growth processes from earlier periods in life (Miller, et al., 1992). The men of the Fire Walkers are creating their own rituals through the guidance of their "elder," Adam, who serves as a "spiritual guide" into the "mysteries of manhood." Adam does this in two ways: through the spontaneous experiential activities in which he invites the men to participate and through the filial brotherhood that occurs as a by-product of the men gathering together to share their personal stories of triumph and failure in the inner and outer check-in. An example was displayed when Adam led the men on a mythic journey through guided imagery.

With the men sitting cross-legged on the floor around the fire, Adam conducted a relaxation exercise and then suggested that the men visualize themselves in a hallway with four doors: a door to the room of the king, a door to that of the warrior, a door to that of the magician, and a door to that of the lover four archetypal images of the "mature masculine" (Moore & Gillette, 1990). Adam had the men visualize a symbol on each door and, upon entering the room of their choice, visualize the architecture and furnishings in the room. He then had the men envision a wise elder man coming before them and speaking. Adam paused strategically in order to allow the men to illustrate fully the scene that they were mentally constructing. The visualization concluded by this mythical elder giving the men a gift. The men were to create the message communicated as well as to visualize the gift that they were to receive. Adam then led the group out of this semihypnotic guided visualization exercise and suggested that the men "share the experience of your journey with the other men." One by one, each shared his vision, which clearly spoke not only of his personal values but also of his current priorities and concerns, while receiving emotional support through affirming comments and looks from the other men in the group. Most of the men seemed to choose the door of the warrior, and although the individual stories differed, a common theme reflected overcoming personal inadequacies through receiving a form of empowerment (in different shapes) from the mythical elder. The ritual proved to be another tool for constructive use of mythology in accessing feelings while noticing the collective fears and joys of all men. Notably, in contrast to the way in which archetypes were more often imposed on the group by Adam, archetypes in this activity were used organically, stemming from the context of the men's own experience.

It is important to note that the line between the techniques used in traditional group therapy and those used in this mythopoetic work can be blurred. Group therapy in various forms can be a technique for accessing members' feelings, developing trust between members, and fostering a sense of belonging (Burnside, 1986; Gitterman & Shulman, 1986). The Fire Walkers group attempts to achieve similar goals for a community of men. Nevertheless, the form does not carry the content, that is, the form may look different insofar as the Fire Walkers' work is couched in a mythological context, although the content may ultimately be similar to that of conventional group therapy.

Embracing the Wild Man

Bly draws on the Grimm Brothers' fairy tales to come up with Iron John, which he offers as an alchemical parable for modern men. In his view, Iron John (also known as the Wild Man) is the model of true masculinity, which is repressed and denied in modern culture. The Wild Man metaphor (not to be mistaken with "wildness" or, worse, a "savage man," both of which can be misconstrued as a new age form of patriarchy) is most appropriately seen as a mechanism by which to embrace forceful action in life, not with cruelty or with passivity, but with resolve. Hence, according to Bly, "finding" the Wild Man is an ongoing process for men.

The Fire Walkers are continually searching for Iron John. This is accomplished through having the courage to face the "shadow" side of their personalities during the therapeutic exercises (both experiential and mythological) and used as a form of exorcism of their dysfunctional past. Shadow is that part a person hides, denies, or represses. According to Bly (1990):

Welcoming the Hairy Man is scary and risky, and requires a different sort of courage. Contact with Iron John requires a willingness to descend into the male psyche and accept what's dark down there, including the nourishing dark. . . . Freud, Jung, and Wilhelm Reich . . . had the courage to go down into the pond and accept what is found there. The job of the contemporary man is to follow them down. (p. 6)

One man stated that part of his reason for attending the group was "to find my Iron John; to help me unlearn and then relearn what it means to be a man." At its best, this is what the mythopoetic movement can accomplish.

CONCLUSION

Mythopoetic groups raise the following issues for helping professionals and activists who work with men: the usefulness of groups as a source of referral for men who are experiencing life difficulties associated with masculinity and manhood, the conspicuous absence of men of color from the contemporary men's movement as a whole, and the absence of an agenda for social change implied in this collective mythopoetic activity called a "movement."

Referrals to a Men's Support Group

Professionals referring male clients to this kind of man's support group need to consider clients' resources as well as needs. Clients need to be emotionally ready for the nontraditional nature of groups that are heavily steeped in mythological ritual and healing work. Helping professionals have an additional responsibility to identify the theoretical framework of the group and to determine the extent to which the group can help particular clients move toward a more balanced and healthy masculinity.

It might further benefit clients to affiliate with groups or organizations that extend efforts not only toward helping men embrace their "warrior energy," but also toward exercising that same energy in working to improve conditions for both men and women on a global community level. The National Organization of Men Against Sexism advocates social action to change a system that is oppressive to women and, as a result, to all people, for example, and The National Congress of Fathers and Children advocates for fathers' and men's rights. The missions and structures of these organizations have clear social policy implications for helping professionals as well as for men with specific political and instrumental goals.

Men who are experiencing a spiritual deficiency and general emotional malaise could potentially benefit from involvement in a mythopoetic men's mutual support group similar to the Fire Walkers. Additionally, men who have a damaged or incomplete relationship with their fathers could also see these issues addressed in the arena of a mythopoetic group. The advantages of their participation in such a group could include examination of the "woundedness" that these men have experienced, while also exploring potential childhood abuse issues that may be unresolved. Those men who are initially interested in moving beyond the self into a larger form of social activism could be largely disappointed in this type of men's group.

Ethnicity and the Men's Movement

The notable absence of men of color in the contemporary men's movement is not surprising. Recruitment into the mythopoetic branch has been generally through word of mouth and new age periodicals, and although there may be a growing effort to bring men of color into mythopoetic men's gatherings (see, for example, Hoff & Dunsky, 1996), most meetings are still largely composed of white men (Schwalbe, 1996). Further, the issues that are being addressed, while perhaps ideologically generalizable to all men, are typically of concern primarily to men of privilege. Nevertheless, in Los Angeles, several Latino men gather weekly in a group called Hombres Latinos, which was formed a number of years ago in California and Texas out of a concern for what members perceived as a negative view of men in the Latino community. One of the group members has stated, "As soon as a group of Latino males get together, they think there is going to be trouble . . . all they think we are going to do is fight, drink, and talk about women." The Hombres Latinos do not affiliate themselves with the mythopoetic men's movement. "Once you mention Robert Bly in the same breath as us, people think they have us figured out. We are coming together as Latinos. Our history is different" (Heredia, 1992). Some of the rituals that the mythopoets use are recognized in Hombres Latinos—for example, their *compadrazco* system, a manner of getting together to listen to music, share ideas, burn sage as a form of spiritual cleansing, and exchange *abrazos* (embraces). In addition, they aspire to be "macho," which, by their definition, is "he who is dignified, a protector, responsible, nurturing, spiritual, faithful, respectful, friendly, caring, sensitive, and trustful, and he who provides" (Heredia, 1992; see also Valdes, Baron, & Ponce, 1987; Lancaster, 1992). Clearly, these are qualities shared by the mythological Iron John.

An additional concern related to ethnicity is an ethical consideration that arises regarding the appropriation of Native American rituals and religious ceremonies for purposes other than their intended use (e.g., talking sticks, chanting and drumming in a fashion imitative of Native American fashion) (see Schwalbe, 1996). This practice begs the question: Is all imitation flattery? The mythopoets seem to have used the globe as a ritual shopping mall, taking only those rituals considered suitable for men's gatherings or, worse, manipulating these traditions for their convenience. The unintended implications of taking or "using" rituals might be viewed as disrespectful to their culture of origin or as dishonoring the culture from which they were taken. Many European-American men may find it valuable instead to research and reclaim rituals and ceremonies that their European ancestors lost or were forced to give up during immigration or subjugation in Europe.

The fees charged for attending events can prohibit those with other financial priorities in life. Although related more to class than to ethnicity, financial considerations would disproportionately deter men of color from group participation. The Fire Walkers' group fee is twenty dollars per week, with no sliding scale, and mythopoetic weekend gathering retreats can be as much as five hundred dollars or more. Fee scales seem to imply that this introspective work is intended for the more financially privileged, even though others could potentially find benefit in such work. One member separated from the group because of the financial hardship created by the fee, as well as because of the moral issue of having to pay for this type of support group. Core members discussed forming an alternative group that would meet in someone's home each week, but stated their collective reluctance to do this, and some of the men see abandoning the group as a form of mutiny. Thus, the importance of this type of introspective work may vary across social and economic classes as well as among different ethnic groups.

Finally, the Fire Walkers often address issues pertaining to the emotional absence of the father and the residual effects of a perceived imbalance in their upbringing. However, many African-American and Latino men had literally absent fathers, often being raised by another family member, most often a female (e.g., a mother, grandmother, an aunt) (Perlmutter & Hall, 1985). Many women, particularly women of color, are raising children alone today, and the implication that somehow their single parenting is "not enough" for the appropriate development of the male child can have a chilling effect on them; it also blatantly disregards their experiences.

Social Activism and the Mythopoets

Earlier a distinction was drawn between the overtly political profeminist branch of the men's movement and the mythopoetic branch, which is more focused on intrapsychic work (Clatterbaugh, 1997; Wilson, 1993). Feminists and profeminist men have long been critical of the contemporary men's movement, mostly because of the narcissistic impetus of the mythopoets, while an agenda for social activism goes unrecognized (Hagan, 1992; Kimmel, 1995).[3] While profeminist and men's rights branches of the contemporary men's movement embrace a specific political agenda for mobilizing their causes, the mythopoetic wing, which seems to have partially evolved out of the recovery movement, has no well-articulated agenda for social change. As is the case for those recovering from chemical dependency, the emphasis is focused on healing the individual more than healing the world.

However, one could argue that the mythopoetic branch of the men's movement has made a political agenda out of breaking men's isolation. This work has provided an arena for men to talk about their feelings, learn to trust one another, and speak about their collective fears, such as the fear of being dominated and, most important, their fear of other men.

Many social activists sense a danger in the inward focus of the mythopoets. They seem to be concerned that by focusing on the interior life, mythopoets fail to attend to the social and political structures that dehumanize all people. However, mythopoets contend that the movement is not about changing others but about changing the self (Kimmel, 1995). As one member has stated, "It's [the men's movement] about finally settling in to focus on our emotional nurturing." Mark Muesse (1991) effectively wrote, "If our personal and spiritual empowerment does not lead us to rage and action in the face of male violence, substance addiction, war, rape, poverty and homelessness . . . then something is indeed wrong. Spiritual empowerment without social action is shallow, just as social activism without spiritual sustenance lacks depth and vitality" (p. 32).

Popular stereotypes of mythopoetic men's gatherings tend to deemphasize the therapeutic value of such events (see Rickabaugh, 1994). This study provided an examination of these stereotypes and a discovery of the value that mythopoetic men's mutual support groups can provide not only psychosocial development but friendships and improved social interactions. Some of the assertions regarding the movement include the assumption of "women bashing" (which was found to be unsupported for the most part) and the appropriation of Native American rituals for the purpose of accessing feelings (which was found to be supported, perhaps implying a distinct "ritual hunger" in this culture today). Another assumption is the considerable influence of twelve-step programs and traditional therapy on the mythopoetic branch of the men's movement—an assumption that was also found to be supported, implying that groups such as the Fire Walkers could be viewed as alternative form of social support, albeit more specialized in nature. Helping professionals should be aware of the potential benefits as well as the negative implications of these groups when referring their clients. These potential benefits may be best recognized by helping professionals who have done their own ritual, mythological, and spiritual work. In today's world of brief therapy and managed care, this type of open, facilitated, men's mutual support group can be a powerful forum for men's healing and a needed adjunct to traditional therapy.

NOTES

1. In choosing this qualitative technique, the intent was to generate insight and gain further information on the thought processes, characteristics, and motivations of movement participants. True to this method, variables were defined and hypotheses were formulated throughout the study (Lofland & Lofland, 1984). The aim was not to end up with a set of findings that could be generalized to other samples but to develop a thick, descriptive account (Denzin, 1991) of a particular group. The degree to which the account is applicable to other groups is an empirical question, answered by comparisons to investigations of other groups (Lincoln & Guba, 1985).

2. S.R.W. discussed the research proposal with Adam, who then allowed him to join the group as a fellow member and researcher. At the first meeting and regularly thereafter as new members joined, the researcher discussed his dual role in the group. This was never challenged or openly resisted by any of the participants.

3. It is noteworthy that Bly's (1990) critical analysis of masculinity begins by noting how the Industrial Revolution took men out of their homes and away from their sons. Ironically, despite this awareness of how social forces played a key role in creating problematic forms of masculinity, mythopoetic groups have focused their work much more on individual than social change.

REFERENCES

Balswick, J. (1988). *The inexpressive male*. Lexington, MA: Heath.

Bly, R. (1985). *Men and the wound* Audiocassette recording. Milwaukee, WI: Human Development Associates.

Bly, R. (1990). *Iron John: A book about men*. Reading: Addison-Wesley.

Burnside, I. (1986). *Working with the elderly: Group process and techniques*. Boston: Jones and Bartlett Publishers.

Chesler, M. (1991). Participatory action research with self-help groups: An alternative paradigm for inquiry and action. *American Journal of Community Psychology, 19*, 757–768.

Clatterbaugh, K. (1997). *Contemporary perspectives on masculinity*. 2nd ed. Boulder, CO: Westview Press.

Corsini, R. J., & Wedding, D. (1989). *Current psychotherapies*. Itasca, IL: F. E. Peacock.

Denzin, N. K. (1989). *Interpretive interactionism: Strategies of qualitative research*. Newbury Park, CA: Sage.

Derlega, V. J., & Chaikin, A. L. (1976). Norms affecting self-disclosure in men and women. *Journal of Consulting and Clinical Psychology, 44*, 376–388.

Farrell, W. (1986). *Why men are the way they are*. New York: McGraw-Hill.

Forstein, M. (1988). Homophobia: An overview. *Psychiatric Annals, 18*(1), 33–36.

Franklin, C. W. (1984). *The changing definition of masculinity*. New York: Plenum Press.

Freud, S. (1955). *The origin and development of psychoanalysis*. New York: Gateway Editions.

Garfinkel, P. (1985). *In a man's world*. New York: New American Library.

Gilbert, R. K. (1992). Revisiting the psychology of men: Robert Bly and the mythopoetic movement. *Journal of Humanistic Psychology, 32,* 41–67.

Gitterman, A., & Schulman, L. (Eds.). (1986). *Mutual aid groups and the life cycle.* Itasca, IL: F. E. Peacock.

Grimm, J. L. K. (1975). *The complete Grimm fairy tales.* London: Routledge & Kegan Paul.

Hagan, K. L. (Ed.). (1992). *Women respond to the men's movement.* New York: HarperCollins.

Harding, C. (Ed.). (1992). *Wingspan: Inside the men's movement.* New York: St. Martin's Press.

Heredia, C. (1992, November 8). Hombres Latinos tackles macho image. *Los Angeles Times,* p. E-4.

Herek, G. (1986). On heterosexual masculinity. *American Behavioural Scientist, 27,* 545–562.

Herzog, J. M. (1980). Sleep disturbance and father hunger in 18-month-old to 8-month-old boys: The Erlkonig syndrome. *Psychoanalytic Study of the Child, 35,* 219–223.

Hillman, J. (1987). The wildman in the cage: Comment. In F. Abbott (Ed.), *New men, new minds* (pp. 182–186). Freedom, CA: Crossing.

Hirshey, G. (1991, December). White guys with drums. *Gentlemen's Quarterly, 86,* 89–91.

Hoff, B. H., & Dunsky, H. (1996). Ritual and community: An interview with Michael Meade. *M.E.N. Magazine, 7*(8), 1, 15–20.

Hollis, J. (1994). *Under Saturn's shadow: The wounding and healing of men.* Toronto: Inner City Books.

Johnson, D. W., & Johnson, F. P. (1997). *Joining together: Group theory and group skills.* Reading, MA. Allyn and Bacon.

Kauth, B. (1991, Winter). Touching the masculine: Hugging in men's groups. *MAN! 12,* 60.

Keen, S. (1991). *Fire in the belly: On being a man.* New York: Bantam Books.

Kilmartin, C. T. (1994). *The masculine self.* New York: Macmillan.

Kimmel, M. S. (Ed.). (1995). *The politics of manhood: Profeminist men respond to the mythopoetic men's movement (and the mythopoetic leaders answer).* Philadelphia: Temple University Press.

Lancaster, R. N. (1992). *Life is hard: Machismo, danger, and the intimacy of power in Nicaragua.* Berkeley: University of California Press.

Levant, R. (1995). Toward the reconstruction of masculinity. In R. F. Levant & W. S. Pollack (Eds.), *A new psychology of men* (pp. 229–251). New York: Basic Books.

Levine, B. (1979). *Group psychotherapy.* Englewood Cliffs, NJ: Prentice Hall.

Liebman, W. (1991). *Tending the fire: The ritual men's group.* St. Paul, MN: Ally Press.

Lincoln, E. S., & Guba, E. G. (1985). *Naturalistic inquiry.* Newbury Park, CA: Sage.

Lofland, J., & Lofland, L. (1984). *Analyzing social settings.* Belmont, CA: Wadsworth.

Mankowski, E. S. (1997). *Community, identity, and masculinity: Changing men in a mutual support group.* Unpublished doctoral dissertation, University of Illinois at Urbana-Champaign.

Messner, M. A. (1992). *Power at play: Sports and the problem of masculinity.* Boston: Beacon Press.

Miller, R., and the editors of *New Age Journal*. (1992). *As above, so below: Paths to spiritual renewal in daily life*. Los Angeles: Jeremy P. Tarcher.

Moore, D., & Haverkamp, B. (1989). Measured increases in male emotional expressiveness following a structured group intervention. *Journal of Counseling and Development, 67*, 513–517.

Moore, R., & Gillette, D. (1990). *King, warrior, magician, lover: Rediscovering the archetypes of the mature masculine*. New York: HarperCollins.

Morrow, L. (1991, August 19). The child is father of the man. *Time*, pp. 52–54.

Muesse, M. W. (1991, Fall). The national dialogue. *Man!* pp. 31–32.

Nahon, D., & Lander, N. R. (1992). A clinic for men: Challenging individual and social myths. *Journal of Mental Health Counseling, 14*(3), 405–416.

Nardi, P. M. (Ed.). (1992a). *Men's friendships*. Newbury Park, CA: Sage.

Nardi, P. M. (1992b). Sex, friendship, and gender roles among gay men. In P. Nardi (Ed.), *Men's friendships* (pp. 173–185). Newbury Park, CA: Sage

O'Neil, J. M. (1981). Male sex-role conflicts, sexism and masculinity: Psychological men, women and the counseling psychologist. *Counseling Psychologist, 9*, 61–80.

Osherson, S. (1986). *Finding our fathers*. New York: Free Press.

Perlmutter, M., & Hall, E. (1985). *Adult development and aging*. New York: Wiley.

Pleck, J. (1975). Man to man: Is brotherhood possible? In N. G. Malbin (Ed.), *Old family/new family: Interpersonal relationships* (pp. 229–244). New York: Van Nostrand Reinhold.

Pleck, J. (1981). *The myth of masculinity*. Cambridge, MA: MIT Press.

Pleck, J. (1995). The gender role strain paradigm: An update. In R. F. Levant & W. S. Pollack (Eds.), *A new psychology of men* (pp. 11–32). New York: Basic Books.

Pollack, W. S. (1995). No man is an island: Toward a new psychoanalytic psychology of men. In R. F. Levant & W. S. Pollack (Eds.), *A new psychology of men* (pp. 33–67). New York: Basic Books.

Rickabaugh, C. A. (1994). Just who is this guy, anyway? Stereotypes of the men's movement. *Sex Roles, 30*, 459–470.

Ruben, L. (1985). *Just friends: The role of friendship in our lives*. New York: Harper & Row.

Schwalbe, M. (1996). *Unlocking the iron cage: The men's movement, gender politics, and American culture*. New York: Oxford University Press.

Shewey, D. (1992). *In defense of the men's movements*. St. Paul, MN: Ally Press.

Shiffman, M. (1987). The men's movement: An exploratory empirical investigation. In M. Kimmel (Ed.), *Changing men: New directions in research on men and masculinity* (pp. 295–314). Newbury Park, CA: Sage.

Valdes, L. F., Baron, A., Jr., & Ponce, F. Q. (1987). Counseling Hispanic men. In M. Scher, M. Stevens, G. Good, & G. A. Eichenfield (Eds.), *Handbook of counseling and psychotherapy with men* (pp. 203–217). Newbury Park, CA: Sage.

Williams, R. C., & Myer, R. A. (1992). The men's movement: An adjunct to traditional counseling approaches. *Journal of Mental Health Counseling, 14*, 393–404.

Wilson, S. R. (1993). *Beyond the drums: An exploratory study of the men's movement and its impact on men*. Unpublished master's thesis, University of California, Long Beach.

Winstead, B. A., Derlega, V. J., & Wong, P. T. (1984). Effects of sex-role orientation on behavioral self-disclosure. *Journal of Research in Personality, 38*, 541.

Chapter 3
Warriors and Fathers: *Once Were Warriors* and the Mythopoetic Understanding of Men's Violence
Chris Bullock

In his discussion of mythopoetic men's retreats, Shepherd Bliss claims that he and other mythopoetic leaders "work more from the heart, body and soul than from the head, though there is a clear theory behind what we are doing" (1992, p. 97). It is true that men influenced by mythopoetics, including me, have usually been influenced by reasons more to do with the heart than the head. However, here I focus on the other half of Bliss's comment and discuss mythopoetics as theory. There are dangers in this focus, notably the danger of making a bloodless abstraction of an approach that emphasizes the local detail of story, image, and archetype in understanding masculinity. But there are benefits too. Much of the hostile discussion of mythopoetics in collections like *Women Respond to the Men's Movement* (Hagan, 1992) and *The Politics of Manhood* (Kimmel, 1995) by profeminist authors has personalized the issues, treating mythopoetics as if it were a collection of the personal foibles of Robert Bly. To counteract this personalization, it seems valuable to explore the value of mythopoetics as a way of understanding key contemporary social and psychic phenomena. The phenomenon I focus on is that of men's violence against women in domestic settings.

My interest in men's domestic violence came into focus in 1995 not as the result of the notorious O. J. Simpson trial, but because of a less publicized case. On December 21, 1995, the *Dallas Morning News* reported the shooting of Kara Phillips by her former live-in boyfriend, Don Wallace. Their relationship portrayed a pattern of violence, attempted earnest reconciliations, then more violence. During one of his attempts at reconciliation, in a letter postmarked December 9, Wallace apologized for his actions and wrote: "You're my heart

and without a heart a person can't survive, so please help me. I love you!!!"
(p. A26). In her pathbreaking study, *The Battered Woman*, Lenore Walker derived, from interviews with numerous battered women, the concept of the battering cycle—the idea that many abusers go through repeated cycles of building
tension, battering, and then apologies and loving contrition. Wallace would appear to be a cyclical abuser of this kind. My intuition that examining cyclical
abuse would provide insights into the structure of masculinity seemed confirmed
when I later learned that cyclical abusers form a substantial part of the population of male batterers (Dutton, 1995).

Here I explore the distinctive contribution of mythopoetics as theory by com-
paring mythopoetic understanding of cyclic domestic violence to the ways of
understanding domestic violence developed in other theoretical approaches. My
testing ground for evaluating approaches to understanding men's violence is
Once Were Warriors, a novel about domestic violence by New Zealand Maori
author Alan Duff; *Warriors* was published in New Zealand in 1990, in Hawaii
in 1994, and in the United States generally in 1995.

My assumption that Alan Duff's novel can provide a useful testing ground
for theories of men's cyclic violence is based on Raymond William's argument
in *Marxism and Literature* that literature can be a source of genuine insight not
only into "dominant" social structures and ideologies but also into "emergent"
cultural elements, that is, meanings and values "substantially alternative or oppositional" to those dominant structures (1977, p. 123). My argument is that
social and psychological theories of men's violence explain important features
of cyclical violence evident in the text, but that a mythopoetic approach explains
other features that social and psychological theories tend to miss. However, there
are also features of violence in *Once Were Warriors* that challenge the mythopoetic theory of violence and from which mythopoetics could and should learn.

THEORIES OF MEN'S DOMESTIC VIOLENCE

Alan Duff's *Once Were Warriors* is mainly set in a decaying urban housing
project in which Jake and Beth Heke and their family live. Jake revels in going
to the bar to talk with his mates and display the superiority of his fighting skills;
Beth has an ineffective yearning for better things and a fighting spirit that gets
her beaten up during regular late-night drinking parties. In the earlier part of
the book, the delinquent behavior of their second son, Mark, nicknamed Boogie,
gets him sent to a boys' home; the eldest son, Nigel, goes through a brutal
initiation ritual to join a Maori street gang, and Grace, their thirteen-year-old
daughter, who has largely taken over the role of mother and storyteller to the
younger children, is raped by Jake's friend, Bully, at one of the late-night parties
and commits suicide.

For the funeral, Beth takes Grace back to the meeting house of her traditional
Maori relatives, and this funeral launches three parallel plot lines. In the first,
Beth invites the traditional Maori chief to talk to the young people of her neigh-

borhood so they can, through encountering the ideals of Maori warriorhood, transform their violence and hopelessness into a new pride in themselves. In the second plot line, Jake spirals down into homelessness and shame, but finally becomes a good "father" to a homeless street kid. In the third, Nigel's death concludes the long, grim process of his disillusionment with the street gang as a vehicle for manhood.

What theories of men's violence can we draw on to understand Jake's behaviour and associated developments in *Once Were Warriors?* The first grouping of theories on men's violence I discuss come from the universalist or essentialist position: that men's violence is caused by innate or universal characteristics of men as a gender. This position informs biological theory concerning male hormones (usefully reviewed by Turner, 1994), early feminist theory concerning the link between rape and male anatomy (Brownmiller, 1976), and theory concerning the inevitability of male dominance developed on the right wing of the men's movement in books like Steve Goldberg's *The Inevitability of Patriarchy* (1974). The universalist theory most pertinent to domestic violence comes from sociobiology, with its claim that men's intimate violence is designed to ensure their reproductive advantage. The sociobiological case is summarized by Martin Daly and Margo Wilson, for example, as follows:

We propose that the particular cues and circumstances which inspire men to use violence against their partners reflects a domain specific masculine psychology which evolved in a social milieu in which assaults and threats of violence functioned to deter wives from pursuing alternative reproductive opportunities, which would have represented substantial threats to husbands' fitness by misdirecting parental investment and loss of mating opportunities to reproductive competitors. (1994, p. 269)

Whatever the general virtues or voices of the universalist and essentialist perspective on violence, it seems clear that they have little application to *Once Were Warriors*, largely because the book introduces Jake, who appears to prize masculine culture far above issues of reproductive advantage. The first extended example of violence in the narrative occurs when Jake beats Beth because she has refused to cook a meal for one of his party-going male friends. While he lives at home, Jake consistently chooses the masculine culture of bar and party over family: he drinks in the pub rather than visit Boogie in the boys' home, and insists that his daughter kiss one of his male friends she is visibly repelled by. However, if factors emphasized by universalist interpretations do not seem key to Jake's behavior, there are many indicators of his social and class subordination, which seem to suggest examining social factors as causes for his violence.

The sociological position on violence presents some variant of the premise that men's violence is a product of specific social situations or of long-standing practices of gender socialization. There are a number of sociological theories of domestic violence, but sociopolitical theories associated with current versions of feminism highlight the issue of gender. The basic feminist case is put clearly by Emerson Dobash and Russell Dobash in their influential book, *Violence Against Wives*: "Men who assault their wives are actually living up to the cultural prescriptions that are cherished in Western Society — aggressiveness, male dominance and female subordination — and they are using physical force as a means to enforce that dominance" (1979, p. 24). This view — that violent men are the shock troops of patriarchy — is still the dominant sociopolitical perspective on the issue. In their synthesis of contemporary research on "doing violence to women," Neil Websdale and Meda Chesney Lind (1998) conclude with the "framing of that violence as just one weapon in the patriarchal arsenal" (p. 80).

An interesting variant of feminist theory that introduces the issue of class is developed by Lynne Segal (1990) in *Slow Motion: Changing Masculinities, Changing Men*. She argues against the biological and transcultural interpretations of men's violence — what I call the universalist position — and in favor of an interpretation that links men's violence to class and culture. Speaking of family violence, for example, she argues, "In a culture which constructs masculinity around ideas of dominance, social power and control over others, but then denies to some men any access to such prerogatives, it is not surprising that subordinated men may be likely to resort to violence as the one form of power they can assert over others" (p. 256). Thus, although neither the fantasy nor the enactment of violence is confined to lower-class men, it still tends to be "the sharp and frustrating conflict between the lives of lower working class men and the image of masculinity as power which informs the adoption and, for some, the enactment, of a more aggressive masculinity" (p. 265). In my view, Segal's argument is valid; it is supported by, for example, research showing the predominance of unemployment and low educational achievement among men who batter (Hastings & Hamberger, 1988).

Unlike essentialialist theories, feminist sociopolitical theory offers solutions to violence. For Segal, the macrocosmic solution is an obvious one: for men to "join women in fighting against the exploitation of women at work and at home" (p. 319). On a microcosmic level, the feminist solution seems to be to promote criminal justice system involvement and cognitive-behavioral retraining of offending men. These are also solutions supported by the profeminist wing of the men's movement, such as the White Ribbon Campaign Against Men's Violence (*What*, 1994).

Links among cultural prescription, social class, and men's violence seem everywhere evident in *Once Were Warriors*. Jake lives out the economic subordination involved in being an unemployed laborer in an increasingly technological society, and the political subordination involved in being a full-blood Maori in a colonialist country. To deal with this situation he adopts the cultural prescription to be "tough, manly" (p. 95) because violence is "the only taste of victory [Maoris] get from life" (p. 112). In this way, he is, as Beth reflects, "just another of the wild ones, the Maori wild ones, who can see things not equal, not balanced, that you can't put into words and so you do the only thing you can do—strike out" (p. 94).

Once Were Warriors thus suggests that the feminist sociopolitical theory of violence is accurate and helpful concerning men's violence. But does this theory tell the whole story? Why, for example, do men respond to apparently similar socialization in utterly different ways? This difference is reflected in *Once Were Warriors*, where growing up in the Heke household leads one brother, Boogie, to "hat[e] fighting" (p. 17) and the other brother, Nigel, to join the battle-oriented Brown Fists. As to solutions, while forced modification of violent behavior and cognitive retraining have an obvious ethical and practical value for women and men, I think these solutions miss out a significant aspect of the problem. I agree with counselor Jerry Fjerkenstadt when he argues that "a man . . . may strive to meet feminist ideals of behaviour and temperament by becoming 'good' and controlling his behavior. But . . . the end result is a man who is trained, corrected, treated and 'loved,' but who continues to harbour enormous potential for violence without any way of working with it" (1989, p. 30).

What is missing from feminist sociopolitical theory is attention to the inner life of the batterer. Profiles of batterers suggest that they share this inattention. In *Once Were Warriors*, Jake has endless nightmares and grinds his teeth continuously, but this "didn't bother him as, say, a sure giveaway of his inner turmoil. . . . It was just . . . how a man is. So he'd always ask Beth, Whassa big fuckin deal about teeth and dreams?" (p. 44). The inadequacy of socialization theory by itself, problems with purely behavioral treatment, and a desire not to share the inattention of batterers themselves should lead us to pay attention to inner life, however contested that term has become, and thus to psychological theories of men's domestic violence.

In *The Batterer: A Psychological Profile*, Donald Dutton (1995), a pioneer in the study and treatment of men who batter, claims that "the psychological seeds of abusiveness . . . come from three distinct sources: being shamed, especially by one's father; an insecure attachment to one's mother; and the direct experience of abusiveness in the home. No one factor is sufficient to create the abusive personality; these elements must exist simultaneously for the personality to develop" (p. 76). Dutton's account of the causes of men's violence synthesizes a number of psychological theories. The view of batterers as shame-prone personalities comes from personality variables research, where a survey instrument helps establish personality themes and tendencies. By using such an instrument, Dutton was able to establish that while violence from their fathers was a significant factor for batterers, "the scales measuring rejection were more important than were those measuring physical abuse alone" (p. 83).

The second source of abuse, insecure attachment to mother, belongs to a framework developed by the object relations school of psychoanalysis, originated by such researchers as Melanie Klein and David Winnicott, and by the attachment theory developed by John Bowlby (Dutton, 1995). Through reference to these theories and his research instruments, Dutton develops a picture of the batterer as the boy who did not gain a secure sense of identity and had both an intense need for his mother and an angry reaction against her. In adulthood, the batterer is a man who

> needs the other person to provide an emotional glue that keeps his self intact . . . His rage fuses the self; the anger overrides the feeling of coming apart. However, its aftermath and the woman's threat to leave recreate this feeling. At the same time, being socialized into a male culture where such feelings are unacceptable, his terror is submerged and stifled. . . . This is the psychological basis for the sleep disturbances, the nightmares . . . [usually] blotted out by alcohol or drugs. (p. 103)

The third source of abuse, the experience of abusiveness in the home, is explored in social learning theory (Bandura & Walters, 1963), which assumes that children who have observed or experienced abuse in their childhood homes are likely to practice abusive behavior in adult relationships. This effect has been widely researched; one researcher calls the link between childhood and adult abuse "the most agreed upon finding in family violence research" (Lewis, 1987).

Dutton's account of the causes of abuse is quite convincing. His discussion of the effects of shame and insecure attachment on identity start to explain why Don Wallace can both make someone be his heart and then beat and shoot her. Most important, Dutton's depiction of causes speaks to key elements in *Once Were Warriors*. Like many other batterers, Jake has little access to his past and no interest in exploring his feelings and fears. But he does reveal that shame has played a major role in his violence. During a trip near Beth's home village, he reveals that his branch of the Heke family was descended from a man captured in battle and enslaved, and that the shame from this fate, the most shameful in the traditional Maori view, descended on him and his siblings in the village he grew up in. In this story of Jake's origins, we learn nothing of his mother, but his teeth grinding, nightmares, and incessant drinking very much fit the symptomology of Dutton's model of insecure attachment.

However, Dutton's perspective and *Once Were Warriors* start to diverge over the issue of solutions. Dutton supports tougher measures to restrain and incarcerate violent men in cases where nothing else will work (Chisholm, 1995), but he sees group therapy as the treatment of choice for reachable offenders. In *The Batterer* he offers an inspiring picture of groups that work not through shame but through "bonding [not] based on anti-female feelings" (1995, p. 168) to get "men to acknowledge the violence and be accountable for it" (p. 166). Dutton's solutions seem valuable, but they are not the solutions developed in the second half of *Once Were Warriors*. There, solutions seem to involve rejection of a false kind of warriorhood in favor of a truer kind and an odd kind of descent into fatherhood. To speak to these solutions, I need to turn to the mythopoetic approach to men's violence.

MYTHOPOETIC THEORY

My discussion of mythopoetics as theory focuses on two key mythopoetic claims concerning men's violence: a claim concerning inner life, which also involves discussion of descent, fathers, and shame, and a claim concerning true and false warriorhood.

The mythopoetic claim concerning inner life and violence involves three points: that masculine socialization in Western cultures promotes a devaluation of inner life, that this devaluation leads to violence, and that the solution to violence involves rededication to inner life. Jerry Fjerkenstadt (1989) argues the first point in "Renegades or Tribesmen: Exploring the Inner Aspects of Male Violence," which I consider the keynote article of the mythopoetic approach to violence. In the West, Fjerkenstadt claims,

Men are trained to be strong, obedient, willful, good, and driven. But the inner life of a man often requires introspection, depth or vulnerability, any of which may be seen as being in conflict with the qualities for which men are trained. When the two are in conflict, one must be sacrificed. And because it has no honor in our society, it is the inner life, the life of the soul, that is usually lost. (p. 30)

The link between loss of inner life and violence, according to Fjerkenstadt, is that the loss leads to "a strong sense of inner deadness" (p. 30). Men look to the external world, to women, children, and others to fill the void, and develop a fury when nothing external will fill it.

How can men regain contact with inner life as an alternative to violence? Part of the mythopoetic answer is that men need to acknowledge the pain of inadequate fathering and descend deeply into that pain, which is often the pain of shame. Mythopoetic writers have focused extensively on the concept of the absent father (see Corneau, 1991). This refers not only to the father who has disappeared but also to the father who is distant from or plays only a small role in his family and the shaping of his sons. Robert Bly (1990), who sees this distance and lack of respect for fathers as characteristic of our era (not an argument that originates with him, I should add), claims that many men deal with this situation by soaring upward into the realms of high achievement, spiritual enlightenment (pp. 100–102)—or of violence, I would add, since, as Dutton so clearly points out, violence too is a way of avoiding personal pain. The solution Bly sees to avoidance is the descent into the wound, the going down into the very point at which one was hurt, with the result that the "descender makes an exit . . . through the wound. The wound is now thought of as a door. If his father abandoned him, he now truly becomes abandoned; during this time he has no house, no mother, no woman. If shame wounded him . . . this time he lives the shaming out" (p. 72).

This work of descent might seem like purely individual work, but some mythopoetic writers emphasize its collective character. For Jerry Fjerkenstadt, the solution to domestic violence lies in men "taking responsibility for [their] unconscious" (1989, p. 37) through the collective telling of honest stories; he argues that "men need to form communities that honor stories, stories that weave together men's physical, sexual and emotional powers. This is the greatest hope for decreasing male violence" (p. 37). Such communities are clearly not simply therapeutic groups but are closer to the old concept of the tribe, and in the tribal context ideals like warriorhood, the second focus of the mythopoetic position, become pertinent.

The idea that the mythopoetic branch of the contemporary men's movement dedicates itself to an uncritical worship of warrior ideals accounts for some of the hostility toward it in feminist and profeminist circles. To be exact, though, mythopoetic writers generally claim that there is both validity and great danger in warrior ideals, and this mixture is usually expressed in the metaphor of true and false warriorhood. Robert Bly, in *Iron John*, treats the warrior as a mode of being with inner, outer, and sacred dimensions. Access to this mode of being helps a person resist the invasion of boundaries (as in sexual abuse, or inappropriate criticism), discriminate between what is worthwhile and what is not, and make a commitment to the worthwhile. For Bly, "when a warrior is in service . . . to a true King—that is, to a transcendent cause—he does well" (p. 151) but "if the King he is serving is corrupt, as in Ollie North's case, or if there is no King at all, and he is serving greed or power, then he is no longer a warrior, but a soldier" (p. 150).

For Robert Moore and Douglas Gillette, the positive qualities of the warrior, which they regard as an archetype of mature masculine psychology, include alertness, awareness of death, physical and mental self-control, a "worthy transpersonal commitment" (1990, p. 82), and the ability to maintain emotional distance. They argue, though, that these qualities also involve dangers, which are accentuated in the shadow warrior—the man who serves nothing but his own fear and greed, who is afraid of the feminine, and who is responsible for "the appalling statistics of wife beating and child abuse" (p. 92). To avoid these dangers, "we need to be leavening the energies of the Warrior with the energies of the other mature masculine forms: the King, the Magician, and the Lover" (1990, p. 95). As an old Celtic motto goes: "Never give a sword to a man who can't dance" (quoted in Bly, 1990, p. 146).

In the mythopoetic view of men's violence, then, there is a claim concerning inner life and a claim concerning warriorhood. Of these claims, the second seems to speak more immediately to *Once Were Warriors*, for it appears obvious that in Duff's novel, we are encountering precisely the same discrimination between true and false warriorhood that we find in mythopoetic writings.

Representing false warriorhood in the first part of the novel are Jake Heke and his son Nigel. Although Jake, standing at the bar, feels "like a chief, a Maori warrior chief" (p. 5), Beth has a correct assessment of this pretension when she tells him and the other party-goers that "the Maori of old had a culture and he had pride, and he had warriorhood, not this bullying, man-hitting-women shit, you call that manhood? It's not manhood, and it sure as hell ain't Maori warriorhood" (p. 22). Nigel's route to a warrior manhood is to join the Brown Fists, a Maori gang. His disillusion comes in finding that Brown Fist warriorhood consists of beating up helpless Maori householders to repossess white-owned appliances. The way that false warriorhood replicates colonialist relations is obvious, and just as obvious to Nigel is that this work seems "like being back home, you know, with his old man beating Mum up" (p. 152). For Nigel, the false warriorhood of the Brown Fists becomes a "nightmare" (p. 153) from which he is unable to escape.

The positive vision of warriorhood, in which manhood and resistance to violence can coexist, is conveyed in *Once Were Warriors* mainly through Duff's portrayal of Boogie, the second son, and of Beth Heke herself. As to Boogie, the social worker teaches the boys at the boys' home the war *haka*, or *peruperu*, the Maori war ritual that involves disciplined movements designed to bring the ancestors down into the bodies of the participants. Beth, when she sees Boogie after this training, is moved by "how proud, how ramrod straight this teaching had made her boy . . . and . . . [how] *free*" (p. 126). When she decides to bring in the "paramount chief," Chief Te Tupaea, regularly to address the young people of her neighborhood, her aim is to bring them their "rightful warrior inheritance. Pride . . . Not attacking violent pride, but heart pride" (p. 161).

Regaining a "rightful warrior inheritance" is not the only solution envisaged by Duff's novel. The route by which Jake Heke moves away from being a cyclical batterer has nothing to do with true or false warriorhood and everything to do with the mythopoetic claim concerning inner life, descent, fatherhood, and shame. It is evident that Jake has what Robert Bly calls "father hunger" (1990, p. 94), from the yearning for physical contact evident when the old Maori men in the pub "touched his face, *stroked* a man (like his daddy never did) [and] made him feel humble. And warm all over. Sentimental" (p. 58). There is shame in father absence, shame in being from a "slave" family, and Jake descends into this shame when he is living on the street and associating in the pub with those most shamed of people, the old confirmed alcoholics. In this life he feels the "hurt comin' on . . . except this time without the surge of power. Of violence come rushing up to the rescue of this hurt person inside of him" (p. 166).

It is out of the acknowledgment of vulnerability — that "he's hurt and lonely and wanting company" (p. 170) — that Jake is able to invite a street kid who has been the victim of domestic violence into his makeshift hut, and to find that, as a result, "his dreams were alright. Not mad violent. For once" (p. 182). There is no sensational denouement, with Jake becoming, for example, an ally of Chief Te Tupaea and Beth Heke. Instead, at Nigel's funeral he is simply "this fulla [*sic*] with this equally bedraggled boy, over in the pines, concealed, peeping out like thieves, or shamed children of slaves. . . . And tears trickling from him — Him. He who they used to say was toughest in all Two Lakes. Bad as. Mean as. Jake Heke" (p. 192). Thus in the concluding scene of *Once Were Warriors* we have the two mythopoetic solutions to men's violence embodied in two separated groupings: in the center, the collective of true warriorhood; on the periphery, and much less visible, the man who has healed inner life and father wound.

PROBLEMS AND CONCLUSIONS

At first glance, the outcome of *Once Were Warriors* would seem to endorse the value of mythopoetic theory, and it does do this to some extent. Yet there is surely something disquieting and unresolved in the book's final scene. If warriorhood and descent are compatible solutions, then why are the figures representing each solution set so distinctly apart? My concluding argument is that although *Warriors* does demonstrate the value of mythopoetic theory, it also points to a problem in that theory that mythopoetic writers would do well to take note of.

Let us first look at what examining *Once Were Warriors* has shown about the value of mythopoetics, as compared to competing theories of men's violence. First, it should be clear that despite descriptions in *Women Respond to the Men's Movement* (Hagan, 1992) of mythopoetics as a conservative and essentialist perspective (for example, Brown, 1992), the mythopoetic approach to men's violence has little in common with universalist approaches to the issue. The emphasis that mythopoetics want to place on inner life and the distinction between true and false warriorhood is quite at odds with biological and sociobiological explanation, which assumes men's warriorhood as a reproductive or hormonal reflex (Daly & Wilson, 1994). As *Once Were Warriors* shows, a consciously chosen, ritualized, and deliberately modified warriorhood can be seriously entertained as a solution to men's violence, while warriorhood regarded as reflex offers no such possibility.

The second general implication is that mythopoetic explanation is not as incompatible with sociological explanation as is sometimes assumed. Both Fjerkenstadt's article on the inner aspects of violence and the feminist sociopolitical perspectives on violence start from the social training of men. It is true that Fjerkenstadt paints the social world in broad, simplifying brushstrokes, and sociological commentators are equally reductionistic about men's inner lives. But it should be clear that both sociology and mythopoetics have useful things to say about Jake Heke's violence and that their relation, as theories, could be one of complementarity, not hostility.

Third, with psychological theories of men's violence, at least in the intelligent form in which they are synthesized by Donald Dutton, the case is more one of convergence than complementarity, since both Dutton and mythopoetic writers share an interest in the inner life of men. Nevertheless, the two claims that I saw as basic to mythopoetic theory distinguish it from even the progressive currents of contemporary psychology. If it is true that both Dutton and the mythopoets respect the inner life of men, it seems to me that mythopoetics takes the further step of identifying particular features of individual masculine experience—in the case of *Once Were Warriors*, father wound and father-hood—and seeing them not only as a source of problems but as a potential source of healing. And the same is true on the level of collective experience, represented by archetypes like the warrior.

The strengths of the mythopoetic theory of men's violence, and by extension, I would suggest, of mythopoetic theory in general are that it poses solutions that are not as conservative and essentialist as they might appear (Ellis, 1994), which are indeed compatible with social approachs and show ways of transforming men's distinctive problems and paths into men's healing.

All this being true, there is nevertheless a slippage in the solutions proposed by the mythopoetic approach to men's violence that also extends to mythopoetic theory in general. It seems fair to say that what both *Warriors* and mythopoetics propose as a solution to men's violence is an ideal of tribal community and warriorhood made relevant to contemporary times by their openness to inner life. *Warriors* shows a community in which Chief Te Tupaea and his traditional beliefs combine with Beth Heke's very untraditional support for male crying and self-expression to make what Bruce Harding calls a "revivified Maoridom" (1992, p. 151). Fjerkenstadt proposes a tribal, storytelling community that "supports men by developing rituals and ceremonies that display and channel totem energies" (p. 35) but also encourages the quite untraditional need for men to take "responsibility for their own contradictions" (p. 35) and "responsibility for [their] unconscious" (p. 37).

In "Renegades or Tribesmen" Fjerkenstadt never suggests that there might be incompatibility between traditional and nontraditional tasks. However, in *Warriors*, it is this potential incompatibility Duff is pointing to by keeping Jake and his "son" separate from the community represented by Te Tupaea and Beth. Indeed, for the attentive reader, incompatibility is evident within that community itself. For example, Beth's message to the young men of the community is to "have yourself a damn good cry" (p. 162), while Chief Te Tupaea emphasizes the traditional value of self-control, so that it should never "occur to the warrior to show in sight or sound his terrible pain" (p. 174).

With *Once Were Warriors* as guide, we can return to "Renegades or Tribesmen" and see the same kind of incompatibilities there. Fjerkenstadt focuses on men's "train[ing] to be strong, obedient, willful, good and driven" (p. 30) and argues that the "bias towards believing each individual has only one set of characteristics prevents people from taking responsibility for their own contradictions" (p. 35). Yet he then goes on to claim that "aggression, competition, and force are deep instinctual structures in men" and that being given "a totem . . . provides [a man] with a way to study and observe his own nature" (p. 35). The slippage here between social perspectives and essentialist ones, between the view of inner nature as multiple and inner nature as unitary enough to be represented by a totem, throw into doubt Fjerkenstadt's concluding claim that a men's community which tribally "cares for men" can also "hono[r] men's inner nature" (p. 37).

What we are seeing in the mythopoetic theory of men's violence (and I believe the same is true of mythopoetic theory as a whole) is a fissure between traditional and contemporary, collective and individual perspectives. Curiously, though, what seems to be a weakness could also, if consciously recognized, be a strength. It seems clear that what is not needed to understand and deal with men's violence is a single theory, however worthy. We should not choose among behavioral retraining, group therapy, community building, or individual and inner work but instead examine the complex interplay by which these solutions might be related to each other. Mythopoetics is not incompatible with some of the other theoretical possibilities from which this multiplicity of solutions spring. A mythopoetics that could recognize the difficult interplay between individual and collective in its own positions—rather than simply reiterating collective solutions like warriorhood as if they were unproblematic—would constitute theory of a particularly helpful kind.

REFERENCES

Bandura, A., & Walters, R. H. (1963). *Social learning and personality development*. New York: Holt, Rinehart & Winston.

Bliss, S. (1992). "What happens at a mythopoetic men's weekend?" In C. Harding (Ed.), *Wings pan: Inside the men's movement* (pp. 95–99). New York: St. Martin's Press.

Bly, R. (1990). *Iron John: A book about men*. Reading, MA: Addison-Wesley.

Brown, L. S. (1992). Essential lies: A dystopian vision of the mythopoetic men's movement. In K. L. Hagan (Ed.), *Women respond to the men's movement* (pp. 93–100). New York: HarperCollins.

Brownmiller, S. (1976). *Against our will: Men, women and rape*. New York: Bantam.

Chisholm, P. (1995, October 30). The scourge of wife abuse. *Maclean's*, 47–49.

Corneau, G. (1991). *Absent fathers, lost sons*. Boston: Shambhala.

Daly, M., & Wilson, M. (1994). Evolutionary psychology of male violence. In J. Archer (Ed.), *Male violence* (pp. 253–288). London: Routledge.

Dobash, R. E., & Dobash, R. P. (1979). *Violence against wives: A case against the patriarchy*. New York: Free Press.

Duff, A. (1995). *Once were warriors*. New York: Vintage.

Dutton, D. (1995). *The batterer: A psychological profile*. New York: Basic Books.

Ellis, K. (1994). Who's afraid of Robert Bly? Feminism, gender politics, and the mainstream media. *Masculinities, 2*, 8–20.

Fjerkenstadt, J. (1989). Renegades or tribesmen: Exploring the inner aspect of male violence. *Inroads, 2*, 30–37.

Goldberg, S. (1974). *The inevitability of patriarchy*. New York: Morrow.

Hagan, K. L. (Ed.). (1992). *Women respond to the men's movement*. New York: HarperCollins.

Harding, B. (1992). Wrestling with Caliban: Patterns of bi-racial encounter in *Colour scheme* and *Once were warriors*. *Australian and New Zealand Studies in Canada, 8*, 136–155.

Hastings, J. E., & Hamberger, L. K. (1988). Personality characteristics in spouse abusers: A controlled comparison. *Violence and Victims, 3*, 31–48.

Kimmel, M. (Ed.). (1995). *The politics of manhood: Profeminist men respond to the mythopoetic men's movement (and the mythopoetic leaders respond)*. Philadelphia: Temple University Press.

Lewis, B. Y. (1987). Psychological factors relating to wife abuse. *Journal of Family Violence*, 2, 1–10.

Moore, R., & Gillette, D. (1990). *King warrior magician lover: Rediscovering the archetypes of the mature masculine*. New York: HarperCollins.

Segal, L. (1990). *Slow motion: Changing masculinities, changing men*. London: Virago.

Turner, A. K. (1994). Genetic and hormonal influences on male violence. In J. Archer (Ed.), *Male violence* (pp. 233–254). London: Routledge.

Walker, L. E. (1979). *The battered woman*. New York: Harper & Row.

Websdale, N., & Chesney-Lind, M. (1998). Doing violence to women: Research synthesis on the victimization of women. In L. H. Bowker (Ed.), *Masculinities and violence*. (pp. 55–81). Thousand Oaks, CA: Sage Publications.

What every man can do to end men's violence against women (1994). Toronto: White Ribbon Campaign.

Williams, R. (1977). *Marxism and literature*. Oxford: Oxford University Press.

Chapter 4
The Mythopoetic Interpretation of Texts: Hermeneutical Considerations
David B. Perrin

Robert Bly is considered the father of the "mythopoetic men's movement" (Ola-veson, 1996, p. 27). According to E. R. August (1994, p. xviii) *mythopoetic* refers to "a branch of the men's movement that combines myth and poetry in a search for archetypal patterns of masculinity." Elsewhere August (1995, p. 1) describes this search as "a struggle to propagate a positive masculine spiritual-ity.... While the popular media and academic feminists were insisting that men's ways of thinking were limited to linear, rational logic, mythopoetic men were demonstrating the potency of archetypes, myth, and poetry in the lives of men." The mythopoetic branch is at the service of facilitating the initiation and training of men to live out a healthy form of masculinity. Emphasis is placed on getting in touch with one's own feelings, improvement of self-image and esteem, development of a sense of trust in other men, relating in a more mature fashion to women, and being an agent of change, hope, and betterment. The mythopoetic branch has as its goal the replacement of debilitating and destruc-tive models of masculinity characterized, for example, by rationalism, oppressive power, and individualism with models of masculinity that value feelings, see power as empowerment (of self and others), and emphasize interdependent autonomy.

Examples of texts used for mythopoetic interpretation include Homer's *Od-yssey* and Virgil's *Aeneid*. The Iron John myth taken from the Grimm Brothers' collection of fairy tales, as used by Robert Bly, is another example of the type of narrative that is being used as a source of personal and communal transfor-mation in men's groups.[1] Robert Bly, Michael Meade, James Hillman, and oth-ers show that the mythopoetic interpretation of texts has sometimes replaced the role of male mentors in the absence of healthy male models in the family or the population at large. The idea that many males grow up "fatherless" has been well documented (Blankenhorn, 1995; Corneau, 1991; Thomas, 1993). This raises the question of how the mythopoetic interpretation of texts by men's groups can add light to and become an important consideration for scholarship in the area of men's studies today.

This chapter asks what kind of methodological framework can help account for the personal and communal transformation that men are happily experiencing in the mythopoetic reading, interpretation, and appropriation of texts such as those mentioned above. Of particular interest is the healthy masculine energy that becomes available to the contemporary male in the interpretation and appropriation of these quasi-religious myths, legends, and fairy tales. But how is this healthy masculine energy made available? What access do men have today to the vital energy of manhood portrayed in these ancient and contemporary narratives? What are some of the methodological issues, from the perspective of reading theory and interpretation, that must be considered in the use of these narratives by individuals and groups of men? William Doty (1996, p. 191) indicates that he is aware of the importance of the need to pay attention to methodological issues in the mythopoetic interpretation of texts:

Mythic figures and images as well as their many contemporary literary transformations can provide models in an imaginal, psychological, and interrelationally based discipline by which we decide to configure masculinities and friendship patterns appropriate to our own politics and histories. However, it is important to think critically about some of the methodologies and attitudes with which we approach literary and mythological materials as we construct our toolkits. Such hermeneutical reflection is crucial insofar as influential decisions about appropriation are made daily and usually unself-consciously or ideologically.

Charles Upton (1993) has also indicated that there are methodological considerations that must be taken seriously in the mythopoetic interpretation of texts. He provides a lively and sensible critique of the mythopoetic interpretation of texts by examining Bly's use of the Iron John story. Upton notes that to a large extent, the mythopoetic interpretation of texts is based on the groundbreaking work of Carl Jung and company. In *Hammering Hot Iron*, Upton (1993) focuses on the distortions of archetypal psychology that have entered the mainstream of popular culture and thought by the mythopoetic movement. Upton recognizes the importance and value of the mythopoetic interpretation of texts but believes that the "incomplete and sometimes contradictory intellectual framework" for the mythopoetic interpretation of texts needs to be assessed.

This chapter contributes to the intellectual framework that underscores the validity and value of the mythopoetic interpretation of texts without falling into the pitfalls of archetypal psychology signaled by Upton. It assesses the mythopoetic interpretation of texts from the perspective of current studies in textual hermeneutics, particularly from the work done by Paul Ricoeur (1973, 1974, 1986/1991a; Dicenso, 1990).

RICOEUR'S HERMENEUTICAL APPROACH TO NARRATIVES

The Value of Ricoeur's Theory for Mythopoetic Interpretation of Texts

Ricoeur's hermeneutical approach to the interpretation of myths, legends, and fairy tales can provide a theoretical framework for the explanation and understanding of the transformative power of these narratives in the lives of men. This approach is valuable because Ricoeur does not understand hermeneutics as the search for the absolutely objective and univocal message of the narrative.[2] Rather, he views it as an approach to the interpretation of texts that shifts the emphasis from the investigation of the objective message of the text to the *actual* meaning of the text in the life of a person (Ricoeur, 1991a, 1991b). The overt sense of a narrative gives way to another reference, the covert world of the self in its current existential possibilities (Ricoeur, 1977a). Ricoeur's hermeneutical theory suggests that in order to say that we have "interpreted" a text, the ideal meaning of that text must be engaged as real meaning grounded in the life of the reader. This is to suggest that to receive, interpret, and appropriate texts is a movement toward deepening one's understanding of oneself and of the world in which one lives. This is done by way of the preoccupations and questions of one's life. The life of the reader therefore contributes to the meaning of the narrative.

Ricoeur thus adopts a post-Heideggerian approach to interpretation theory. Hermeneutics, in its post-Heideggerian expression, holds that the understanding or appropriation of a text is the dialectic operative when an imagined, possible way of living in the world shaped by the text, is made actual in the life of the reader-interpreter (Ricoeur, 1991b). The pre-Heideggerian approach to interpretation is concerned with the singularity, the acumen, of the author's message (Ricoeur, 1973). It seeks to pass along information or some message presented by the author in the text.[3] The post-Heideggerian approach views interpretation as leading to an increase in self-understanding in one's existential situation. Consciousness of the self is not a given. Transformation, an increase in self-understanding, and new ways of being in relationship are mediated by the text according to Ricoeur.

Ricoeur thus presents the interpretation of a text as an exploration of new existential possibilities for oneself. Accordingly the text is perceived as capable of opening up a new dimension of life for the reading subject. Because of this self-involvement of the reading subject, Ricoeur's hermeneutical approach makes the interaction of today's reader with a text central to interpretation. To interpret these narratives is to insert oneself more fully in the meaningful world constructed by the text, and to appropriate a text is to make one's own the creative possibilities configured in the narrative. In so doing one is more intimately immersed in one's own world. In hermeneutical reflection, the constitution of the individual in his or her life circumstances is contemporaneous with the constitution of meaning (Ricoeur, 1991a).

Presupposed in this type of textual hermeneutics is the capability of written texts to produce a world, the world of the text (Ricoeur, 1981). The world of the text refers to proposals by the text that indicate new existential possibilities for life. This world may suggest new ways of being in relationship with self and others, may emphasize particular values, or may challenge one's current ways of doings things. In short, the world of the text presents a specific vision of the way it is possible to live in the world. This might be described as a new myth to guide decision making for the interpreting subject. Shepherd Bliss describes the function and purpose of mythopoetic work to be exactly this: " 'Mythopoetic' is not 'myth and poetry.' It is the creation of new myths in our own lives" (quoted in Whyte, 1996, p. 1).

What the reader receives from the text is not just the materiality of the text (the sense of the text or what the text says in general); the reader receives an epiphany, a meaningful way of being in the world for *this* reader (Ricoeur, 1974). The full meaning of these epic narratives can appear only within the context of a life. They are epiphanies only at the point where the world of the text interacts with the actual life of a reader. The value of Ricoeur's hermeneutical interpretation of texts lies in the fact that he views interpretation as an effort to discover the world of the text as a possibility for oneself.

Ricoeur holds that the meaning of the text is a mix of what the text presents and what the reader-interpreter brings to it. The concerns of the text and the concerns of the reader can thus be taken into consideration in the interpretive process. Ricoeur avoids the pitfalls of suggesting that the appropriation of some absolute objective truth or archetypal reality that originates from within the text is the object of the interpretive process.

Reading and the Active Reception of Narrative

Several components of Ricoeur's theory of reading (1991b) are important to show why the mythopoetic interpretation of texts potentially leads toward transformation and change in the lives of the men using these texts during mythopoetic retreat experiences.

First, Ricoeur's hermeneutical program abandons the primacy of the cogito in order to suggest that all reflection is mediated—that there is no immediate self-consciousness. Appropriation of a text occurs when someone's world is enlarged and self-understanding moves beyond the actual limitations of the ego subject. The dynamic of transformation and conversion is effected by otherness, whether this be a life event, a sudden crisis, or the world of possible living afforded by literary works of fiction. Everyday reality is imaginatively presented and metamorphosed by literature. Great literature stands the test of time because it affords the possibility for men and women, in various cultural and historical settings, to enter into the imaginative variations for life that it presents.

Second, Ricoeur analyzes the aesthetic experience of the reader that gives rise to a catharsis of the reader, which opens the door to consider new possibilities for life. This catharsis is proportionate to the self-availability that the reading subject brings before the text. Catharsis, launched by an active reception of the text, is what effects the work of the text. New norms for life proposed by the text may shake current customs or norms. In this way the text "teaches." Therefore, the mythopoetic interpretation of texts is not first a subjective appropriation whereby the reading subject or community possesses the key to the text. The mythopoetic interpretation of texts, as has been witnessed by countless men, is the intentional letting go (catharsis) of destructive attitudes, practices, and values in order to embrace a more hopeful and enlivening vision of life. To the extent that readers enter into the text and become "unreal" within the norms prescribed by the work of fiction, reflection takes a pause and the ego-self relinquishes itself. Whether consciously or unconsciously, the reader's vision of the world and of the self may shift or become renewed according to the prescription of the text.

Third, Ricoeur's hermeneutical theory and practice propose that written language (the poems, myths, fairy tales, and so forth used by men's groups) are not diminished representations of reality (Plato's concept of mimesis), but rather are intensifications of reality (Ricoeur, 1984, 1991b), a position arrived at through a reconstruction of Aristotle's concept of mimesis. Mythopoetic texts are presented as the basis for the transformation event effected in the life of the reader because of the surplus of meaning displayed in the world of the text. Writing is the fixation of the expansion and meaning of life. Ricoeur's hermeneutical theory and practice suggest that the narratives that men's groups use are equivocal not by default, but by an excess of meaning. These narratives are overly determined linguistic models of reality that dispose of the self existentially and ontologically. This is to say that they have ontological import. Fiction intends being, not as a given that is complete but as a potentiality of being.

Fourth, and as we know already, Ricoeur's research in textual hermeneutics attempts to expand the understanding of self in the reality within which the self is immersed. This task is never complete. His hermeneutics presents the possibility of a cyclical approach to explaining and understanding texts used in mythopoetic work. This cyclical approach moves the reader back and forth between the text and the givenness of one's own life. As the text is understood more deeply, so is one's life. The opposite is also affirmed by Ricoeur: as one's life is understood more deeply, so is the text.

In presenting this dialectic, Ricoeur (1991a) states that hermeneutics encompasses both the methodic moment of interpretation (explanation) and the nonmethodic moment (understanding). For Ricoeur, when we first read a text, we understand it at a certain level. The text cannot fail to be about something. By reading the text, we have already interpreted it at some level. However, our initial understanding can be modified, authenticated, and deepened by recourse to a methodic explanation of the text. We can describe the historical and cultural climate in which the text was written, talk about the life experiences of the author reflected in the text, research the meaning of the symbols and images used in the text, and so on. But all of these approaches to the text do not yet suggest the *actual* meaning of the text. They explain the text, and these explanations *contribute* to the meaning. The actual meaning of the text occurs only when the text interacts with the life of a person and presents new possibilities for one's life. This is the nonmethodic moment when the text is actually understood because the subject has received something personally through the text. The hermeneutical reader receives from the text a new mode of being that is always becoming because as the reader knows more about the text (explanation), he or she allows the text to question his or her life in new and different ways (understanding). This self-understanding is then used to get "more" from the text.

Fifth, it is the received paradigms of the text that structure the reader's expectations concerning the text:

[Reading] is the process by which the revelation of new modes of being—or if you prefer Wittgenstein to Heidegger, new "forms of life"—*gives* the subject new capacities for knowing himself. If the reference of a text is the projection of a world, then it is not in the first instance the reader who projects himself. The reader is rather broadened in his capacity to project himself by receiving a new mode of being from the text itself. (Ricoeur, 1981, p. 192)

The text itself participates in directing the reading subject by the way it tells the story through plots and subplots. It guides the reader along in the way, for example, the characters are brought into relationship with each other, crisis situations are resolved, or pieces of information are left out of the text in order for the reader to fill these in with his or her own imagination. Ricoeur therefore moves away from a complete psychological understanding of interpretation that subjectifies the meaning of the text by emphasizing that the text itself guides the reader.

All of this happens within the actual existential situation that the reader brings before the text, and that always includes others. The act of reading is always within the context of a reading community that conditions the current meanings of texts because of a common understanding given to words in any one historical and cultural situation. Through readings of the text, the reading subject follows the movement of the text from what it may have said to its audience in the past to what it actually says to its audience today. Ricoeur's interpretation theory includes a role for the text: the tradition of the meanings of the text passed on down through the ages and the current meaning of the text in today's historical moment. This approach to interpretation keeps the text alive and relevant in order to meet the challenges confronting readers of the text today.

Reading as Playful Production

Ricoeur's theory of reading and reception makes the confrontation between the possible world of living presented by the text and the world of the reader at once a stasis and an impetus, that is, an alteration between moments of stepping back from the text and other moments of losing oneself in it. This synergetic alteration affords the opportunity to play, or try on, different possibilities for life. The transformative power of the text lies in its ability to prefigure an experience yet to come in the life of the reader, but the reader can experiment with this future possibility in the here and now. Hence the paradox surfaces: the reader becomes unreal with the unreal of the text and subsequently enters more profoundly into the authentic depths of human reality.

It is this understanding of play that helps us appreciate how playful reception of the epic narratives used by men's groups affords them the opportunity for personal conversion. The category of play is particularly important for men's groups since, frequently, during mens' retreats, the participants play the text in a various number of ways.

I am referring here to the mythopoetic interpretation of texts during men's retreats that brings the text into contact with the participants in concrete and dramatic ways. Retreats that do dramatic reenactment of epic narratives have sprung up across North America. They are advertised in many of the mythopoetic journals, flyers, and newsletters. For example, issues of *Wingspan* contain an abundance of retreats held throughout North America. During these retreats, the mythopoetic interpretation of narratives is frequently used as a source of personal and communal transformation.

During mythopoetic retreats, the text is "played," for example, by wearing styles of dress suggested by the text, reenacting various types of male-male confrontation, living in conditions similar to those described in the text, and using musical instruments—mostly drums and other primitive percussion instruments. All of this activity is directed toward the playful appropriation of the masculine energy offered by the text. The metamorphosis of the reading-receiving subject initially takes place through the playful reenactment of the text in various ways, whether through reading it silently or out loud or reenacting it in some fashion. This active and conscious reception of the text has the potential to mediate metamorphosis of the receiving subject. Play is transformative as reading is transformative because play allows a certain distancing from the conscious self. Self-understanding, which is not immediate, can be enhanced by the kind of mediation afforded by the playful reception of the epic narratives used by men's groups.

Ricoeur describes play in the following way: "Play is not determined by the consciousness which plays; play has its own way of being. Play is an experience which transforms those who participate in it. It seems that the subject of aesthetic experience is not the player himself, but rather what 'takes place' in play" (1981, p. 186). The playing subject is removed from his or her immediate conscious self to be engaged in play by the game. Play momentarily shatters the utilitarian, and thus limiting, preoccupations of the subject. The shattering of illusions about oneself, others, and life in general is made possible because of the alternative vision for life presented by the text. New possibilities of the real are proposed by the text, and the reader enters into these by "playing" with them, thus opening himself or herself to new values and new possibilities for life, or regaining hitherto parts of the self that have never been engaged. For example, the player may act out particular emotions (anger, remorse, joy), be involved in some reconciliation suggested by the text (with oneself or with another significant person in his life), or experience physical closeness to other men in a way never experienced before. These various movements are tried on in a safe environment and in so doing appropriated at some level. Reading and playful reception of texts used in mythopoetic retreats thus afford the opportunity for a renewed subjectivity.

The playfulness of reading can shatter illusions because in reading, we set free our imaginations and temporarily live in an imaginary world. We live in an "as if" mode, which breaks down our defenses and makes our imagination dwell in possible new ways of being in the world. As Ricoeur (1981, p. 187) states:

The player is metamorphosed "in the true"; in playful representation, "what is emerges"; but "what is" is no longer what we call everyday reality; or rather, reality truly becomes reality, that is, something which comprises a future horizon of undecided possibilities, something to fear or to hope for, something unsettled. Art only abolishes nonmetamorphosed reality. Whence the true *mimēsis*: a metamorphosis according to truth.

The essential and true being potentially emerges through playful reception of epic narratives. The subject is invited to undergo an imaginative variation of the ego that is created by the text in order to participate in the world in a new way. To enter into the text is to divest oneself of the former self in order to receive a changed self, albeit temporarily, conferred by the text. But this temporary metamorphosis leaves a trace. Textual hermeneutics for Ricoeur is securely linked with fundamental ontology. Something is left behind from the game, such that the otherness of the text can become a real possibility for one's own life, either now or sometime in the future.

CAUTIONS IN MYTHOPOETIC INTERPRETATION OF TEXTS

Certain cautions need to be taken into consideration in the mythopoetic interpretation of texts. These cautions are the flip side of what has already been affirmed concerning the life-enhancing mythopoetic interpretation of epic narratives and texts used by mythopoets.

Meaning Is Not Limited to Strict Literal Interpretation

Implicit in Ricoeur's hermeneutical approach to interpretation is a critique of the literal reception of mythopoetic narratives that might limit their meaning. A literal reception of epic narratives by mythopoets may be limiting even though the potential of the text may be initially launched with a literal reception of the text. John Lee alludes to this potentially shallow reception of men's lives in *At My Father's Wedding*. Lee (1991, pp. 76–77) states:

Reclaiming the body is one of the main goals of the men's movement. It is the only way we can fully move into our wounds and out into the world less wounded than we began. Many men—and women—may not understand how to get their bodies back. Some ways to experience the body are through movement—dance, drumming, pushing, pulling, beating a pillow, pounding the earth with a tree limb; and sound—screaming, crying, shouting, speaking out, singing. While many men have screamed or pushed or even beaten drums, they've done so without focusing on their rage, anger, grief, and guilt. Without consciously using these movements to rid the body of repressed emotions, the movements do little to heal.

A greater effort than mere repetition of actions literally suggested by the text is required before the text becomes living discourse in the life of the reader.

From Ricoeur's hermeneutical theory we see that the fullness of the meaning of the text cannot be lived directly. Men participating in the mythopoetic retreats need to know that there is much more work that needs to be done beyond the few hours or days invested in the actual retreat. The interpretation and appropriation of texts cannot be limited, for example, to the re-creation of "masculine" practices or emotions portrayed by figures in these narratives during the actual retreat. The appropriation of masculine energy presented by these narratives by literally reenacting the lifestyle or characteristics of the characters is but a step in the appropriation of the text. Until the text is brought into confrontation of the real issues of one's life—for example, the repressed emotions that Lee refers to—the work of the mythopoetic interpretation of the text has not been accomplished.

Ricoeur's hermeneutical theory suggests that there is no immediate and intuitive entry into the meaning of the text that does the text justice. Reality is not immediately available, that is, immediately intuited in the Husserlian sense (Klemm, 1983). Rather, reality is subject to the process of interpretation mediated through language. The life-transforming potential of the mythopoetic interpretation of texts is available to the reader only through the detour of interpretation and the self-availability one brings to the text. Interpretation takes a lot of work. It presupposes some familiarity with the text and with one's own life, requires an openness to the values suggested by the text, and requires an openness to change, to look reflexively at life in a new way over the course of an extended period of time.

Not a Historical or Psychological "Return"

Ricoeur's hermeneutical theory suggests that ultimately it is the work of the text itself that is at work in the reading subject, that is, that effects personal and communal transformation. The text does reference reality not directly but indirectly through metaphoric and symbolic representation (Ricoeur, 1977a). The narratives are not, in the end, direct historical descriptions of the world in which the characters lived. Joseph Campbell (1986, 1990b) shows that he is well aware of this in his many works on mythology. The task for men today is not to attempt to reenter the world of the ancients in order to tap their life-giving energy. This is not possible, or even desirable, since all historical and cultural distance from a text is not alienating (Ricoeur, 1981; Pellauer, 1979).

In fact, Ricoeur's hermeneutical theory holds that it is *only because* of our historical and cultural distance from the text that it becomes enriching for us. Therefore, though older texts may have lost their meaning for us and that meaning needs to be recovered, recovery is not first of all a project of cultural and historical proximity to the text. Mythopoetic interpretation of texts needs to be open to the past tradition of the interpretations of the text as well as to present and future avenues of meaningfulness that are new. It is true that change is possible when texts are appropriated because interpretation renders familiar what was foreign. However, while at one level, interpretation suppresses cultural and temporal distance, at another level it preserves cultural distance in order to propose a different perspective that may challenge one's current vision of life (Ricoeur, 1974).

This approach to mythopoetic interpretation draws the subject into the heritage of the past as an act of recovery only in order to project the possibility of new meanings that illuminate the present and future moments of one's life (Klemm, 1983). Recovery of the meaning of ancient or contemporary texts is, in the end, the construction of possible new ways of living in the here and now. The fullness of this moment can be useful for discerning helpful ways of living for the future.

The Choice of Texts

Not all narratives are appropriate for mythopoetic work. According to W. G. Doty (1996) critical choices must be made as to which texts are suitable for mythopoetic interpretation and which ones may not: "Reflection on attitudes for approaching mythic resources involves evaluating how there may or may not be appropriate connections between their originating cultures and our own; hence ethical reflections ought to precede conscious choices of particular models we would replicate today." There is much discussion that could take place concerning what criteria would be helpful to discern the appropriateness of a particular text for a particular group or purpose. The purpose here, however, is simply to indicate that a discerned choice should be made concerning the appropriateness of texts for mythopoetic work.

From another perspective, Upton (1993) signals the need for the discerned use of particular images or mythic figures presented in texts. Further problems arise when mythopoetic images or figures are summoned without due critical reflection. For example, in *Iron John* Upton (1993) remarks that Bly makes the following clear: "Bloody violence and healthy wildness are not the same thing." Upton continues:

> But when the archetype of the underworld male comes up, it doesn't arrive neatly divided into positive qualities to be adopted and negative ones to be avoided. The things we need to integrate and those we had better get rid of dawn upon us as a single complex; and only through a long course of shadow integration can they be clearly separated. Thus when Bly calls us to worship the spontaneous, the unexpected, he is invoking appropriate wildness and destructive savagery at the same time. (p. 202)

Clearly there is work to be done on the choice of texts and appropriate images to be used for mythopoetic reflection. This reflection must be approached with a critical attitude toward the values referenced and constructed by the complete text and by particular images or characters within the text.

The Impact of Romanticism

A hermeneutical reception of narratives dispels the naivefe that suggests it is possible to recover a text completely by living the text directly. Appropriation of texts is not a form of congeniality with the time and cultural place of an author of a work. This is to say that we do not want to return to a romantic naivefe of "recovering" that leads us to believe we are capable of rendering the text relevant by literal coincidence. Nor do we wish to coincide with or attempt to identify with the original audience. This can be the tendency because of the influence of romanticism on our culture.

Romanticism, largely a product of the post-Enlightenment period of the eighteenth century, is one of the most influential and powerful forces that has shaped our contemporary world. Art, architecture, politics, music, literature, and, to a very large extent, The western world vision, has been shaped both positively and negatively by different Romantic movements. In general romanticism rejected the Enlightenment with its emphasis on human reason and instead exalted intuition, feeling, inspiration, and the genius of human creativity. It emphasized the exotic, stories of strange and foreign lands, the allure of other cultures, and the fantasy world of the imagination (Barzun, 1964; Creighton, 1965).

A romantic understanding of texts implies that it is possible to "return" to some lost, idyllic world portrayed by the text. A nostalgic "return" or search for a virtual world that this one is not is sometimes reflected in the mythopoetic interpretation of texts during men's gatherings. A few examples from recent literature seem to indicate that the mythopoetic interpretation of narratives has been influenced by romanticism.

Referring to the mythic characters known as the "Companions," Meade (1993, p. 18) says: "The weird companions are at the root of all male initiation groups, from street gangs to music groups to sacred brotherhoods. They also carry the message that what will shatter this world more certainly than anything else is the loss of the threads that connect the here and now to the 'other world.' Only when these ancestral figures of unity and inclusiveness are found will the Old Queen of the psyche release her daughter to the world." We see here an allusion to some other world that needs to be sought in order for life to continue in the here and now.

The cover story of *Newsweek* of June 24, 1991, features an article by Gerry Adler on the men's mythopoetic movement. This article enthusiastically praises the search for some lost world through the use of mythopoetic texts. Adler states: "The men's movement also has a more profound strain, a romantic assertion of primitive masculinity in all its innocent strength and virtue. This is at the heart of Bly's 'mythopoetic' approach to male malaise. He analyzes contemporary American culture in terms of pre-Christian fables and concludes, unsurprisingly, that we are sadly lacking in kings, wizards and enchanted forests" (p. 49). Roger Kose (1991), a photographer very much involved in the study of the masculine through his photography, says "I want to explore the timelessness of the masculine; to see my connection to my ancestors; to avoid, as much as possible, any connection to a particular time in history" (p. 13).

David Shackleton (1996) presents this idyllic and romantic notion of a "return" to some lost innocence from another perspective with a model of the interior journey that describes the transformative process. This new model of spirituality consists of four stages: (1) innocence (unconscious monism), (2) denial (spirituality lost), (3) recovery (spiritual childhood), and (4) wisdom, wellness (spiritual maturity; conscious monism). It is stage 4 that reflects this idyllic return to some lost innocence. Shackleton states, "It seemed to me that mature spirituality must resemble in some ways the value-free, non-dualistic perception that we are undoubtedly born with, but lose fairly quickly. . . . Mature spirituality must represent a return to that state of oneness, of monistic and mystical unity, but in some fashion embracing the power of knowledge and understanding, rather than the powerless of infancy" (p. 6). He continues, "The essence of the transition is to enter again the mystical unity and perfection of the Universe. . . . In stage 4, I am free of value judgements of any kind, powerful and free to act" (p. 24). This notion of a return on the interior level to some value-free and thus "innocent" state is not possible. No matter where we are at in our journey in life, we are awash with values, conceptual frameworks, and baggage that we have collected in our lifetime and are at the basis of our search for an ever-deepening personal freedom. They form the grist for the mill that shapes the reader's current involvement with the texts that he or she may be using for personal work at this time.

Therefore, attempts to return to some "original purity" may restrict the self-understanding of the reader's life because this "return" may not adequately take into consideration the current sociopolitical, cultural, economic, and spiritual climate of the reader's life. This can be a fundamental problem overlooked in the mythopoetic interpretation of narratives. Any method used to understand and appropriate texts needs to take into consideration the current life experience of the reader and community in which the text is received.

CONCLUSION

Ricoeur's hermeneutical interpretive approach to the legends, myths, and fairy tales currently used by mythopoetic men's groups can help explain why these narratives are capable of being the place of a transformative event in the life of the male subject and the male community. For Ricoeur, written texts are overly determined models of reality that are capable of breaking open and enhancing the current meaning of one's life. The interpretation of texts has full meaning only when the texts are restored to the time of action and of suffering. Their surplus of meaning is contingent, however, on the mix produced by the current questions of one's life brought into interaction with the text.

Therefore, Ricoeur's hermeneutical theory suggests that the reception of narratives used by men's groups must not be exclusively or even predominantly literal. Hermeneutical interpretation allows narratives to be brought *from* their place of production *into* the production of the contemporary world of men's lives. The mythopoetic interpretation of texts does not fold back on the texts themselves but ultimately references new existential possibilities for the attuned reading subject. What needs to be worked out for the productive use of texts during retreats conducted for men is a practical psychology that will take contemporary hermeneutical concerns into consideration. A recent study that might be helpful toward this goal is Schwalbe's book (1996) about his three-year participant observation of the Raleigh Men's Center and his analysis of mythopoetic men's work.

The issue at stake is not to determine how we can become contemporaneous with past geniuses by a "return" to some other world (the romantic reception of mythopoetic texts); rather, the issue is nothing else than an attempt to make these texts productive in our current life situation where the project of the text may ultimately succeed *or* fail.

The reader receives a new way of being in the world through the meeting of the world of the text and the world of the reader. A helpful approach to understanding mythopoetic interpretation of narratives includes how *they* become operative in the life of the reader through the detour of interpretation. This process of interpretation includes playful reception of the text as well as a serious commitment to work with the text, subsequently taking into consideration the way it manifests itself in a particular life. This is what Ricoeur's hermeneutical approach offers: a way to interpret texts that values and takes into consideration the current life experience of the reader. After mythopoetic retreats, there is still much work to be done in the life of each individual participant in order to continue the life-giving thrust that was launched by the mythopoetic reception of the texts done during the retreat.

For the man who is struggling to be open, honest, and loving or who is striving for authenticity, the mythopoetic interpretation of texts offers the possibility to reach these goals. The temporary breakdown of controlling patterns of thinking offered by the work done during retreats allows men to restructure their outlook in life and themselves. During the playful mythopoetic interpretation of texts, there may be new information about one's life that needs to be considered or old information that needs to be remembered. With a flood of painful tears or the sigh of relief spontaneously breathed from unexpected joyful realizations, the experience offered by the mythopoetic interpretation of texts may launch and build on the personal transformation sought by men struggling to construct more meaningful lives today.

NOTES

1. Contrary to Olaveson's (1996, p. 27) remark which cites Shepherd Bliss as the originator of the term "mythopoetic," Bert H. Hoff (1996, p. 1) reports that Shepherd Bliss denies coining the term "mythopoetic," but "simply had applied the term to Men's Work." For an interesting note on the history of how Jacob and Wilhelm Grimm (1785–1863 and 1786–1859) collected the various tales often used in the mythopoetic men's movement. See Joseph Campbell (1990a, pp. 9–15).

2. There are many different approaches to hermeneutics. I have used Paul Ricoeur's hermeneutical theory for the framework of this article. A survey of other approaches can be found in Ormiston (1990). See also, for example, DiCenso (1990) and Jeanrond (1991).

3. In general, a post-Heideggerian, and thus a post-Romantic approach to interpretation involves two fundamental shifts in the way texts are interpreted. The first is a shift from epistemology to ontology, that is, before there is any consideration of the human subject knowing, there is a more primordial level, that of Being which is to be considered: "Instead of asking 'how do we know?', the question will be 'what is the mode of being of that being who only exists through understanding?' . . . What we are interpreting is the *meaning* of being." (Ricoeur, 1973, pp. 120–121) The second major shift is from the understanding of another person to the understanding of the world as it is brought to us through texts: "The foundations of the ontological problem are to be sought in the domain of the relation to the world and not in the domain of relation with another person. It is in relation to my situation, in the fundamental understanding of my position within being, that understanding in its principle sense is implied. . . . In making understanding 'worldly,' Heidegger 'depsychologizes' it." (Ricoeur, 1973, pp. 121–122).

REFERENCES

Adler, G. (1991, June 24). Drums, sweat and tears: What do men really want? *Newsweek*, pp. 46–51.

August, E. R. (1995, November). Bringing us together: An elder statesman contends mythopoetics and activists share more than they think. *MenWeb—M.E.N. Magazine*, p. 1. Available at: http://www.vix.com/menmag/august.htm.

August, E. R. (1994). *The new men's studies: A selected and annotated interdisciplinary bibliography* (2nd ed.). Englewood, CO: Libraries Unlimited.

Barzun, J. (1964). Romanticism. In *Collier's Encyclopedia* (Vol. 20, pp. 162–167). New York: Crowell-Collier.

Blankenhorn, D. (1995). *Fatherless America: Confronting our most urgent social problem*. New York: Basic Books.

Campbell, J. (1986). *The inner reaches of outer space: Metaphor as myth and as religion*. New York: Harper & Row.

Campbell, J. (1990a). *The flight of the wild gander: Explorations in the mythological dimensions of fairy tales, legends, and symbols*. New York: HarperCollins.

Campbell, J. (1990b). Myth as metaphor. In J. M. Maher & D. Briggs (Eds.), *An open life: Joseph Campbell in conversation with Michael Toms* (pp. 21–53). New York: Harper & Row.

Corneau, G. (1991). *Absent fathers, lost sons: The search for masculine identity* (L. Shouldice, Trans.). Boston: Shambhala. (Original work published by Editions de l'Homme. No date given.)

Creighton, J. E. (1965). Romanticism. In *Encyclopedia Americana international edition* (Vol. 23, pp. 655–657). New York: Americana Corporation.

Dicenso, J. J. (1990). *Hermeneutics and the disclosure of truth: A study in the work of Heidegger, Gadamer, and Ricoeur*. Charlottesville: University Press of Virginia.

Doty, W. G. (1996). "The manly love of comrades": Mythico-religious models for an athletics of male-male friendship. In B. Krondorfer (Ed.), *Men's bodies, Men's gods: Male identities in a (post-) Christian culture* (pp. 181–210). New York: New York University Press.

Hoff, Bert H. (1996, September 9). Poetry and personal passion: The ecology of mind and heart. Available at: http://www.vix.com/menmag/whytemyt.htm.

Jeanrond, W. G. (1991). *Theological hermeneutics: Development and significance*. Crossroad: New York.

Kipnis, A. R. (1991a, October–December). The green man reawakens. *Wingspan*, pp. 1, 4.

Kipnis, A. R. (1991b). *Knights without armor: A practical guide for men in quest of masculine soul*. Los Angeles: Jeremy P. Tarcher.

Klemm, D. (1983). *The hermeneutical theory of Paul Ricoeur: A constructive analysis*. Toronto: Associated University Presses.

Kose, R. (1991, October–December). How come your pictures feature naked men or else hooded figures like monks? *Wingspan*, p. 13.

Lee, J. (1991). *At my father's wedding: Reclaiming our true masculinity*. New York: Bantam Books.

Meade, M. (1993). *Men and the water of life: Initiation and the tempering of men*. New York: HarperCollins.

Olaveson, T. (1996, September–October). Academic arguments. *Everyman*, pp. 21, 27.

Ormiston, G. L., & Schrift, A. D. (Eds.). (1990). *The hermeneutic tradition: From Ast to Ricoeur*. Albany: State University of New York Press.

Pellauer, D. (1979). The significance of the text in Paul Ricoeur's hermeneutical theory. In E. Reagan (Ed.), *Studies in the philosophy of Paul Ricoeur* (pp. 98–114). Athens: Ohio University Press.

Randall, M. (1992). " 'And so she walked over and kissed him . . . ' Robert Bly's men's movement." In K. L. Hagan (Ed.), *Women respond to the men's movement: A feminist collection* (pp. 141–148). San Francisco: HarperCollins.

Ricoeur, P. (1973). The task of hermeneutics. *Philosophy Today, 17*, 112–128.

Ricoeur, P. (1974). *Interpretation theory: Discourse and the surplus of meaning.* Fort Worth: Texas Christian Press.

Ricoeur, P. (1977a). *The rule of metaphor: Multi-disciplinary studies of the creation of meaning in language* (R. Czerny with C. McLaughlin & J. Costello, Trans.). Toronto: University of Toronto Press. (Original work published 1975)

Ricoeur, P. (1977b, January–April). Towards a hermeneutic of the idea of revelation. *Harvard Theological Review, 70*, 1–37.

Ricoeur, P. (1981). *Hermeneutics and the human sciences* (J. B. Thompson, Ed., Trans.). Cambridge: Cambridge University Press. (Original articles published 1970–1979).

Ricoeur, P. (1984). *Time and narrative* (Vol. 1) (K. McLaughlin & D. Pellauer, Trans.). Chicago: University of Chicago Press. (Original work published 1983)

Ricoeur, P. (1990). Hermeneutics and the critique of ideology. In G. L. Ormiston & A. D. Schrift (Eds.), *The hermeneutic tradition: From Ast to Ricoeur* (pp. 298–334). Albany: State University of New York Press.

Ricoeur, P. (1991a). *From text to action: Essays in hermeneutics II* (K. Blamey & J. B. Thompson, Trans.). Evanston: Northwestern University Press. (Original work published 1986)

Ricoeur, P. (1991b). *A Ricoeur reader: Reflection and imagination* (M. J. Valdés, Ed.). Toronto: University of Toronto Press.

Schwalbe, M. (1996). *Unlocking the iron cage.* New York: Oxford University Press.

Shackleton, D. (1996, September–October). A new model of spirituality: My journey with litter. *Everyman, 21*, 6.

Thomas, D. (1993). *Not guilty: The case in defense of men.* New York: Morrow.

Upton, C. (1993). *Hammering hot iron: A spiritual critique of Bly's* Iron John. Wheaton, IL: Quest Books.

Chapter 5

A Proposed Model for Comparing Writers in the Mythopoetic Branch of the Contemporary Men's Movement

Thomas M. Brunner

Since the Enlightenment, psychologists—competing with priests—have had an ever-increasing influence on how humans view their interior and exterior lives. In the United States since the beginning of the twentieth century, professional psychology has fared as well as or better than in any other country in the world. Today it is estimated that one in three Americans will seek some form of psychological help during their life course. A *U.S. News and World Report* news poll reported that 81 percent of respondents agreed that if they had a problem, they believed some form of psychological counseling could help them (Goode & Wagner). In times of mental distress, Americans increasingly turn not just to a priest, but to a psychologist. Not surprisingly, anyone surveying The *New York Times*'s Best-sellers' List, for the past ten years will have noticed that books which integrate psychology and religion consistently rank highly. One prime example is F. Scott Peck's *The Road Less Traveled* (1978), on this best-sellers' list for the past ten years.

American mainstream society's receptivity to Peck as well as others who integrate psychology and religion (e.g. Robert Bly, Clara Pinkola Estes, Thomas Moore) may represent a hunger for a kind of healing beyond that offered by contact solely with priests of institutionalized religions. The integrative writer I will most centrally focus on here is Robert Moore, a leading member of the mythopoetic branch of the contemporary men's movement. Other members of this men's movement branch (James Hillman, Robert Bly) as well as a mythopoeticist who has widely influenced mainstream culture in general (Thomas Moore) will be compared to Robert Moore to exemplify the usefulness of this proposed model. The four-celled grid in Figure 5.1 may be used to reveal dif-

Figure 5.1
The Theoretical Grid. The vertical line represents the typical tone of the writer,
and the horizontal line represents the typical medium used for delivery of the
message.

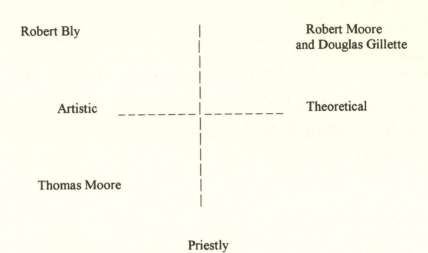

Prophetic

Robert Bly   Robert Moore
                                         and Douglas Gillette

Artistic   Theoretical

Thomas Moore

Priestly

ferences and similarities among these four (Bly, Hillman, Robert and Thomas
Moore) writers and others.

By the end of this chapter it should become clear why these mythopoetic
writers have been placed in particular locations on the grid. As the process of
locating these writers ensues, the following threefold argument will be posited:
(1) these four writers exhibit distinguishable modes of thinking, (2) this grid is
useful toward hypothesizing why these writers have been absorbed into the
center of American mainstream society to differential degrees and (3) this grid
is useful toward understanding the intellectual and social tensions in the mythopoetic branch of the contemporary men's movement.

What is meant by *mythopoetic* will be analyzed more from an empirical rather
than an essentialist viewpoint. A common indication of the essentialist attitude
is an obsessive concern with defining terms and concepts before the search for
knowledge begins (Stanovich, 1996). Discerning the true essence, if there is
one, of the term *mythopoetic* is not a task I accept here. Rather, of higher interest
is the exposure of what appear to be distinctive intellectual styles used by (and
at the disposal of) mythopoetic (as well as other) writers. In short, the explanation of the phenomenon of mythopoeticism, not the analysis of language, is
the leading goal of this chapter. Thus, instead of chasing the term *mythopoetic*
linguistically, the effort here will be to operationalize the term by examining

some systematic intellectual characteristics (and dynamics) exhibited by those reasonably considered mythopoeticists.

The term *reasonable* does not imply that any randomly selected author may be called mythopoetic. If the author's writings are outside poetry and mythology yet would change to the degree such that one of their regular readers would immediately notice, the writer may be considered part of the mythopoetic group. As will become apparent, the term *mythopoetic* represents not simply a class of writers but also a method with discernible stylistic derivatives.

By the 1990s, several of these integrative thinkers had become nationally acclaimed writers, at least in terms of literary popularity among mainstream society, while others had not. Although he writes for the mainstream, Robert Moore, coauthor (with D. Gillette) of *King, Warrior, Magician, Lover* (1991), has not become as popular to the mainstream, though his theory of masculinity has become widely influential in the mythopoetic branch of the contemporary men's movement. Unlike Robert Bly, Robert Moore's books have never become best-sellers. Yet both integrate mythology and poetry into their writing as they address men's issues. Why is Moore not more popular with mainstream readers?

Even if one is uninterested in the possibly superficial question of mainstream popularity, there is an underlying question: Why is it that the ideas of these writers, though they all draw from mythology and poetry to present a message to culture, are absorbed by mainstream culture (as indicated by book sales) at seemingly differential paces? These questions become more perplexing if one notices how Thomas Moore freely admits that his teacher-mentor—the one he draws many ideas from—is James Hillman. But Hillman's books have never reached the level of sales that Thomas Moore's have, though he has published a series of books, and is as active as a lecturer. This is where the grid is useful: it seeks to explain how these writers may be examined as quite different, though in content area—their mythopoeticism—they are similar.

DIFFERENT FOCUSES: THE PROXIMITY OF SACREDNESS OR OF EVIL

A significant difference between Thomas Moore and Robert Moore becomes apparent by observing their respective focuses as writers: Thomas Moore on the proximity of sacredness and Robert Moore on the proximity of evil. Thomas Moore locates it close by, as he talks about the closeness (or immanence) of "sacredness" or "soulfulness" in everyday life (T. Moore, 1992, 1994a, 1994b). Conversely, one of Robert Moore's main purposes is to elicit in the reader a sense of the ubiquity of the presence of evil, especially if the human "shadow" is not accounted for consciously.

Why Robert Moore spends more time and energy on explicating the dark side of the human psyche becomes understandable after hearing about the experiences he considers indelibly etched in his memory. Robert Moore specifically talked about what he called a "foundational experience" while riding in a cab through the streets of a city in India. As he rode along, he says he realized how real the presence of evil is as he noticed how casually his cab driver accepted the reality of young prostitutes being bought and sold. "I realized just how real the presence of evil is on earth," Moore said (Brunner, 1995).

That Thomas Moore's work focuses more on the nearby existence of sacredness, is illustrated in what he entitled his best-seller: *Care of the Soul: A Guide for Cultivating Depth and Sacredness in Everyday Life* (1990). Thomas Moore's book reads like a poetic collection of meditations, as have his later books (1994a, 1994b). As a former Catholic monk, Thomas Moore uses his book as a magnifying glass; in small secular things he finds profound sacredness hidden. He says, "You can see already that care of the soul is quite different in scope from most modern notions of psychology and psychotherapy. It isn't about curing, fixing, changing, adjusting, or making healthy, and it isn't about some idea of perfection or even improvement. . . . Rather, it remains in the present, close to life as it presents itself day by day, and yet at the same time mindful of religion and spirituality" (T. Moore, 1992, p. xv).

In contrast to tranquil pondering, Moore issues a diagnosis of what has gone wrong—a twofold idea of what needs to be fixed: (1) the disappearance of meaningful ritual processes and (2) the consequential rise of patriarchy. As he says in his introduction, "Along with the breakdown of masculine ritual process for masculine initiation, a second factor seems to be contributing to the dissolution of mature masculine identity. This factor, shown to us by one strain of feminist critique, is called patriarchy" (R. Moore & Gillette, 1990, p. xvi).

One might argue that the two Moores simply differ in how they talk about the sacred. Some truth is captured in this statement. But beyond their content, they substantially differ in terms of their tones, something not as easily seen by simply looking at content. To flesh out this subtle difference between the two Moores, it becomes essential to invoke another distinction: the priest versus the prophet.

THE PROPHET AND THE PRIEST

How the priest is to be distinguished from the prophet may be a question that was addressed even before biblical times. Sociologist Robert Bellah (1980) draws this distinction when he speaks of politicians who use the presence of a "civil religion" in America to influence the masses. Bellah suggests the role of the priest is more as a communicator of the sacred, who talks *with* the people about the presence of the divine. This is the role Thomas Moore seems to have filled according to the reviews his readers have given him on talk shows across the country; he has served as a divine writing correspondent. In contrast, the prophet, according to Bellah, speaks more from an aloof position. The prophet does not so much talk *with* the people as talk *to* the people. The tone of the prophet's message goes beyond that of the priest's claim to special knowledge;

to the prophet their answer is the only answer, not simply a commodity in the marketplace of ideas.

Robert Moore's writings concentrate on how sacredness, if it is to be found, must involve a confrontation with the darker aspects of the male psyche. In this way, Robert Moore calls not just for a shift of focus from the material to the spiritual (as Thomas Moore does), but also for a moral accounting for the darker aspects of the male psyche. Robert Moore, as he writes about this darker aspect of the male psyche, highlights the presence of a shadow (R. Moore & Gillette, 1992). In doing so, Robert Moore writes in the spirit of Jung, who believed one becomes enlightened by making the darkness (i.e., the shadow) conscious.

As Bellah points out, both prophets and priests traditionally have claimed to have some special knowledge to pass on to audiences. Thus, prophets often assume that the fate of a people hinges on the acceptance of their ideas. That Robert Moore casts himself in the role of the prophet is illustrated in one of the closing sentences of *King, Warrior, Magician, Lover*: "If contemporary men take the task of their own initiation from Boyhood to Manhood as seriously as did their tribal ancestors, then we may witness the *end* of the *beginning* of our species, instead of the *beginning* of the *end*" (1990, p. 156).

Furthermore, Robert Moore in his 1995 speech to the New Warrior Network, "Masculine Initiation for the 21st Century: Facing the Challenge of a Global Brotherhood, amplifies the urgency of his message: "We are in a time that is more subtle but the forces of chaos and destruction on our planet are far greater at this moment than they were in 1942, and most people are in massive denial about it" (Brunner, 1995). Robert Moore also says this regarding the series of books (1993a, 1993b, 1994, 1995) he published, which explicate the archetypally based theory he proposed in *King, Warrior, Magician, Lover* (1990): "The fact that I have published these five books to a popular audience was a political act; because I see the situation as so serious, I felt that to simply continue working in a much more circumscribed scholarly debate would be really immoral—it would be my own declaration of [moral] bankruptcy" (Brunner, 1995).

THE SACRAMENTAL AND PROCLAMATIONAL USE OF SYMBOL

The priest-prophet distinction may also extend into different ways of using symbols. The priest, such as Thomas Moore (1992), uses symbols to view life in a sacramental way—that is "with the belief that there is some sacred significance or mysterious reality allowing the observer some degree of accessibility." A quotation from *Care of the Soul* illustrates this: "There are two ways of thinking about church and religion. One is that we go to church to be in the presence of the holy, to learn and to have our lives influenced by that presence. The other is that church teaches us directly and symbolically to see the sacred dimension of everyday life" (1992, p. 214). By using poetical and mythological references, Thomas Moore's main idea seems to be that trivial events in life can be symbolically representative of more significant realities.

In contrast, prophets like Robert Moore often use symbols in a more politically edged way. The sacramental use of symbol may be nested within this approach, but ultimately the symbol is used for much more than simply seeing what is already present. The proclamational use of symbol emphasizes what is missing but yet must be present, else the world faces a dire fate. This sense of urgency is commensurate with the role the prophet places himself in, since she or he believes it is his or her symbol on which the fate of a people hinges.

Robert Moore approaches some symbols sacramentally, such as religious symbols from various historical periods, but he uses one symbol to define his stance on masculinity, the diamond body, and he uses it proclamationally (R. Moore & Gillette, 1990). This diamond body model is not just a symbol to Moore; it is a reality that must be accepted by culture. Enhancing the reader's sense of mystery is clearly not his ultimate mission, though it may be for Thomas Moore. Robert Moore's mission is to invade the center of culture with this symbol, as prophets often do. That he has approached mythopoetic branch associates such as the New Warrior Network, with a message of urgency, while proposing his diamond body model of the human psyche, is an example of his wish to carry his message into organized groups.

While Thomas Moore's books may be sifted down into the maxim, "The sacred is closer than you think," Robert Moore's books exhibit the central idea that "the demonic is closer than you think." In other words, as Thomas Moore addresses the question of healing by addressing how to take care of that which is immortal, the soul, Robert Moore sends out a much more mortal message: We are a species that is aggressive by nature, and society and individuals need to have these primal energies regulated through ritual (R. Moore & Gillette, 1990). In this way, the division between what may be called the "sacred-mindedness" of the priest and the more "evil-focusedness" of the prophet extends to a division between the sacramental and proclamational use of symbols. A pattern develops.

What this grid also helps to point out is that sometimes "the medium becomes the message, insofar as the message may be judged based as much (or more) on the medium than the content of the message. This is to say the prophet in society may be thwarted in his purpose to invade the center of culture because of his tone, not merely (and sometimes unrelated to) the accuracy of their idea. The prophet may be received as a visionary, or merely a proselytizer, depending on how the message is connected with currently prevailing ideas the mainstream holds.

In saying this, a theoretical priest might be someone who, rather than offering a new model for the masses, might instead justify or examine a contemporary belief system by creating a descriptive model. The difference, then, between the prophetic and priestly theoretician is that the priest's model may simply be descriptive of something already present, while the prophet's would be descriptive of something absent yet believed to be necessary. Of course, since various sectors of society may have different belief systems, they may have different priests. But these priests do not, like the prophet, seek to invade the center of culture with a politically edged idea. This is not to say they would block efforts to disseminate their ideas, but the prophet more aggressively seeks to invade the polis with an idea.

At issue is not simply the degree of a writer's popularity in mainstream culture. The distinguishable tones and thinking styles these writers use also factor into the intellectual and social tensions present in the mythopoetic branch of the contemporary men's movement.

CONTEXTUALIZING ROBERT MOORE

There are two basic types of mythopoetic men's writing: theoretical (e.g., Robert Moore) and artistic (e.g., Robert Bly). These types can be in tension or in alliance. If tribalism exists, then factions within the mythopoetic branch of the contemporary men's movement may believe that only one kind of thinker can be considered their leader.

Many other options exist as to how to view more artistically laden ideas versus more theoretically laden ideas. From this grid, ways to view the mythopoetic branch of the men's movement include seeing Bly and Robert Moore as different wings of the mythopoetic branch of this movement, or two halves of the same wing of the mythopoetic branch. Bly and Robert Moore may be considered similar since they could both be part of the center, but they are also different in many ways. Robert Moore is more like Freud, in that institutionalization is his ultimate goal, and he speaks from a prophetic voice based on a theory, while Bly has no one model of humans or men. In this way Bly is more like Thomas Moore, in that both of them are significantly less theoretical than Robert Moore. As Robert Moore says,

I am more systematic than Bly, in that I believe there is a sense of the need to confront the shadow in a much more comprehensive and in-depth manner based on the best in contemporary psychoanalytic theory. Bly does not have training to go to those levels. I am trying to work on masculine psychology at the species-specific level to understand why—particularly now—the male of our species is the most dangerous creature on Earth. So when I speak of masculine spirituality and initiation, I am not referring to any indigenous or tribal spirituality however profound—but to a human spirituality which can help contemporary men face their narcissism and relate to their archetypal grandiosity in constructive and creative ways. In this I am an heir to C. G. Jung's *Answer to Job* and Edward Edinger's *Ego and Archetype*, as well as to many other scientific theorists. (Brunner, 1995)

How Robert Moore can be compared with others within the mythopoetic branch of the contemporary men's movement becomes clearer as he speaks of how people disagree with and even try to negate what he has to say. The following quotation further reveals how this grid can be said to be a place of tension: "That is why I get a lot of criticism from some of the guys like Shepard Bliss [another major figure in the mythopoetic branch of the men's movement], who really are rather antagonistic toward me because they see me as too interested in organization, too interested in institutions" (Brunner, 1995). The tensions of the two lines of this grid are felt from what Moore has to say. One way to think about the reason behind these tensions is the different goals the writers have for their ideas. The reality of differing goals is exhibited as Robert Moore speaks about a tension he perceives within the mythopoetic branch of the contemporary men's movement:

Part of the problem in building an effective men's movement which might respond adequately to the masculine crisis of our time can be traced to the early impact of founding personalities. Without Robert Bly there would be no men's movement as we know it today. We are deeply indebted to him as a founder. It is important for us to note, however, that when the founder is a poet—even a great one—the archetypal lover energy is privileged. Lover energy does not understand or value organization—in fact, it is highly distrustful of any institutional forms. Mid-life men make up the core of the men's movement—and they are ineffectual enough without having the lover energy privileged over other archetypal potentials. Even the New Warrior Network, which at least struggles with the challenges of adequate institutionalization, is hampered by an uncritical privileging of lover energy. Without more balance at the archetypal level the mythopoetic men's movement can never realize its potential or meet its critical challenges. (Brunner, 1995)

Moore fleshed out the reality of tensions within the men's movement by also voicing his perspective of Hillman's influence on the men's movement:

James Hillman, another key early figure in the men's movement is in my view a brilliant postmodern philosopher of the soul, but he does not have a serious psychological theory, of personality in general or of masculinity in particular. Many in the men's movement do not have the philosophical or psychological sophistication to understand this. There is nothing in Hillman's work on which to ground an adequate understanding of masculine maturation or initiation. In my view, in spite of the obvious luminosity of his mind, his real impact has been to lead men in the movement away from a serious engagement with the specifically masculine shadow or with the enormous task of masculine maturation in our time. (Brunner, 1995)

In terms of this grid, one might say that Thomas Moore and F. Scott Peck (1978) are on the lower left corner. Robert Moore, James Hillman, and others are more on the upper right-hand corner. One might also say they are intellectual compensations for the others, as Bly is for Robert Moore and Thomas Moore is for James Hillman.

The usefulness of this grid in understanding the disparity between the popularity levels of Thomas Moore and James Hillman is suggested by Emily Yoffe author of the *New York Times Magazine* (1995) who asks how Thomas Moore becomes a best-selling author overnight, and James Hillman remains considerably less popular and yet is similar in terms of the content of the ideas. Yoffe explains that it is a matter of packaging, of how the ideas are presented. Hillman's writing is denser, harder to follow, and less accessible to everyday readers. Thomas Moore writes in a gentle, flowing manner and is more accessible.

IMPORTANCE OF CONTEXTUALIZING THE MYTHOPOETIC WRITERS

Historically, movements that have splintered into tribalistic sectors (Hilgard, 1987), each adhering to one sole method of examining a phenomenon, often die more quickly than if an attitude of critical multiplism pervades. Critical multiplism is a research strategy whereby heterogeneous methods are used to examine a phenomenon. The mythopoetic branch of the men's movement, as this grid shows, is at a point where several intellectual methods are differentiating themselves from neighboring methods. The grid offers a visual image of how any of these four intellectual styles complements the weaknesses of the others. This realization may transform any attitudes of tribalism into attitudes of inclusiveness in the name of strengthening the mythopoetic branch, as well as the whole men's movement. This evolutionary transformation seems necessary for the men's movement to be optimally influential in the twenty-first century.

To be sure, other models delineating different systematic dynamics among mythopoetic writers are necessary. Assuredly, this grid will fall short of "cutting Nature at her joints," the goal of any empirical theory worth its salt. This assumption has been integrated into the grid; the dotted lines denote how these rough boundaries are able to be traversed. However, insofar as authors exhibit some consistency in their intellectual style, the lines signify that they are distinguishable. Flexibility also enters the picture as there is room for degrees of allegiance; the further along a writer is from the center, the more allegiance they may have toward the emphasis at the end of that line. This grid, as a kind of template, may become not simply a lens to contextualize the various mythopoetic methods of analysis, but also those intellectual styles of the profeminist and men's rights thinkers

How these quadrated intellectual styles may be differentially affected by the needs of mainstream society may have been partially answered by cultural historian Philip Rieff (1966), who suggested that the seller of products is parodied by the preacher of psychology since both may have something to sell. What Rieff fell short of realizing, but writers like Robert Moore cannot, is that the buyers—those shopping for an alleviation of their suffering—may prefer, with their purchase, to be located closer to the sacred than to evil. This may translate into the desire for a gentle sermon given by a priest. And what is unmistakably true is that the failures of a prophet may be more precisely understood in the context of a successful priest.

CONSILIENCE: A PRINCIPLE FOR GUIDING THE MYTHOPOETIC BRANCH

One purpose of this model is to offer a holistic vision of how various intellectual styles that mythopoetic writers use may be seen as complementary and yet distinguishable. Nested within this first purpose is a derivative purpose: to encourage communication among the various quadrants. A key issue for those trying to meld this movement into an integrative force will be how to engender interanimation between its more scientific or theoretical types and its more artistic types. The goal is more than trying to get the rival camps to shake hands. A more future-oriented question asked on a global level is, Can the mythopoetic branch seek to create a third culture—one further evolved than the traditionally opposed cultures (or communities) of the scientist and the artists, who often draw mainly from the humanities? Addressing this divisiveness, C. P. Snow noted in his classic book, *Two Cultures* (1959), how serious the nonrelationship seemed to be: "I believe the intellectual life of the whole of Western Society is increasingly being split into [these] two polar groups." And, he lamented, "There seems to be no place where the cultures meet" (pp. 11, 21).

In this way, the tensions in the mythopoetic movement may be seen as tensions echoed across a significant span of human history. This sort of polarization is a sheer loss to us all. This is one reason that the number two is a dangerous number; it may create unnecessary tribalism. In this way, any attempts to divide anything into two ought to be regarded with suspicion, as Snow pointed out.

Fifty years ago, Snow intimated the coming of a third culture: "When [the third culture] comes, some of the difficulties of communication will at last be softened; for such a [common] culture has, just to do its job, to be on speaking terms with the scientific one" (p. 67). Snow prophesized the coming of what Pulitzer Prize–winning Harvard biologist E. O. Wilson (1998) argues has arrived: a spirit of united efforts at knowledge he calls "consilience." Wilson speaks to those dissatisfied with the current fragmentation of knowledge by saying, "The ongoing fragmentation of knowledge and resulting chaos in philosophy are not reflections of the real world but artifacts of scholarship" (p. 8). To Wilson, the key to a unification of knowledge is consilience, literally a jumping together of knowledge by the linking of facts and fact-based theory across disciplines to create a common groundwork of explanation. Optimistically, Wilson sees our time as more opportune than any other in terms of possibilities for collaboration between kinds of thinkers, where they meet in the borderlands of biology, the social sciences, and humanities. In some ways, Robert Moore serves as an exemplar of how one might account for data from biology and the social sciences because he also integrates in accounts of the human garnered from the humanities. In looking at his work, data from all three of these areas are utilized. But Robert Moore and others could go much further toward integrating their perspectives.

Anyone viewing the proposed four-celled model must be aware of certain caveats. One is the danger of the dialectic presented from the bipolar lines. Yet to account for the necessity of bipolarity to map the current mythopoetic branch, all those enlisting themselves in the collective effort to envision the future of the mythopoetic branch might ask themselves the following question: What is the relation between science and the humanities, and how is it important for advances in our understanding of what it means to be man?

Like all other profound questions, this query may be broken up into smaller questions. One more specific question is this: How may the various strains of the mythopoetic branch be integrated so as to account for what is best about both the artistic endeavor (the expression of the human condition by mood and feeling) and the scientific tradition (the explication of logic and order)? Clearly, there is a need not simply for loose integration, but rather, systematic synthesis.

Will the mythopoetic branch take advantage of the collaborative opportunities the sprouting third culture affords? Will various strains of the contemporary men's movement join and even synthesize into multidisciplinary examinations of masculinity? On which side the majority falls may prove to be one of the most decisive events for the history of the men's movement. The contemporary men's movement may be enhanced through a collective strength or weakened by divisiveness, as has already happened in the profeminist and men's rights/father's rights branches.

Regardless, no doubt may be cast on the fact that as our culture evolves, social movements that integrate the humanities and the sciences will most powerfully wake up the human race from what will be looked back on as its twentieth-century, fragmented worldview. This time of consilience may indeed prove to be another Renaissance. The question is how well the mythopoetic branch will celebrate and participate in its growing spirit.

REFERENCES

Bellah, R. (1980). *Varieties of civil religion*. San Francisco: Harper & Row.

Bly, R. (1990). *Iron John*. Reading, MA: Addison-Wesley.

Brunner, T. M. (1995, June 10). Tape-recorded interview with Robert Moore.

Edinger, Edward (1972). *Ego and archetype: Individuation and the religious function of the psyche*. New York: G. P. Putnam's Sons.

Estes, C. P. (1992). *Women who run with wolves*. New York: Random House.

Goode, E., & Wagner B. (1993, May 24). Does psychotherapy work? *U.S. News and World Report*, pp. 57–65.

Hilgard, E. R. (1987). *Psychology in America*. Orlando, FL: Harcourt Brace Jovanovich.

Hillman, J. (1991). *A blue fire*. New York: Harper Perennial.

Jung, C. G. (1951). *Aion* (R.F.C. Hull, Trans.) Princeton: Princeton University Press (Original work published in 1951).

Moore, R., & Gillette, D. (1990). *King, warrior, magician, lover*. San Francisco: Harper San Francisco.

Moore, R. (1993a). *The king within*. New York: Avon Books.

Moore, R. (1993b). *The warrior within*. New York: Avon Books.

Moore, R. (1994). *The magician within*. New York: Avon Books.

Moore, R. (1995). *The lover within*. New York: Avon Books.

Moore, R. (1995). *Masculine initiation for the 21st century: Facing the challenge of a global brotherhood*. Speech presented to the New Warrior Network summer meeting, Windsor, Ontario, subsequently published in 1997 in *The new warrior handbook*. London: New Warrior, pp. 10–15.

Moore, T. (1992). *Care of the soul*. New York: HarperCollins.

Moore, T. (1994a). *Meditations*. New York: HarperCollins.

Moore, T. (1994b). *SoulMates*. New York: HarperCollins.

Peck, M. S. (1978). *The road less traveled*. New York: Simon & Schuster.

Rieff, P. (1966). *The triumph of the therapeutic*. New York: Harper & Row.

Snow, C. P. (1959). *The two cultures: And a second look*. New York: New American Library.

Stanovich, K. E. (1996). *How to think straight about psychology*. New York: Harper-Collins.

Wilson, E. O. (1998). *Consilience*. New York: Knopf.

Yoffe, E. (1995, April 23). How the soul is sold. *New York Times Magazine*, pp. 44–50.

Chapter 6
Silencing the Men's Movement: Gender, Ideology, and Popular Discourse
Joel Morton

The popular, media-driven rise and fall of the contemporary men's movement occurred within a span of less than five years. Although one may trace the movement back to the early 1970s, when antisexist men's consciousness-raising groups as well as men's and fathers' rights and divorce reform groups began to appear, as a term of popular discourse the phrase *men's movement* emerged only after the 1990 public television airing of Bill Moyers's interview of Robert Bly, called *A Gathering of Men*.[1] The documentary catapulted Bly into the national spotlight as leader of the "movement," thus initiating popular misrecognition of mythopoeticism as the whole movement. The Moyers piece also served as the best possible advertisement for Bly's forthcoming "book about men," *Iron John*. Published in 1990, *Iron John* was an immediate and major success, its lengthy run at the top of the best-seller list establishing the (now popularly misrecognized) men's movement, and Bly himself, as commercially viable.

In the few years hence, network television, mainstream magazines, and local (but not necessarily locally owned) newspapers seized on the opportunity to sell the movement in its mythopoetic guise. Network television news magazine shows, talk shows, and sit-coms featured segments or episodes devoted to it. Popular national magazines ran several cover stories as well as dozens of shorter pieces. And newspapers across the country reported on and editorialized about it.[2] Thus, for a brief period in the early 1990s, "men" and the "movement" were very big news indeed, yet by 1993, the number of mass media representations of the men's movement, packaged primarily as mythopoeticism, had dwindled to a trickle. Presuming that the men's movement (in all its variety) is something more than a mere fad or trend, how can this silencing of the movement be explained?

Consider, for example, *Newsweek*'s treatment of the popularly emergent movement on the cover of its June 24, 1991, issue—a date that corresponds with *Iron John*'s run atop the best-seller list. In a calculated reversal of Freud's famous question about women, *Newsweek* (Adler, 1991) asked, "What Do Men Really Want?" In boldfaced text, the cover of the weekly news magazine announced a national debate on masculinity. The ideological import of this question, thus displayed, should not be overlooked. However, the cover immediately answered its own question by its depiction of a man holding a smiling infant in one arm and a drum in the other.

Given the cover's configuration of word and image, the term *men* is made to signify by the visual representation of a handsome adult caucasian male. Clad in blue jeans, the "man" is bare from the waist up, except for the power tie draped around his neck and partly covering his hairy (one might say manly) chest. Not to be confused with fems, fags, or any other sort of wimp, "men" are further signified by the wedding band on the model's left hand. Thus, even a casual glance at the cover confirmed what "men" are and are not. "Men" combine enlightened fatherhood and family values with something of the primitive (the drum) and a dash of the counterculture (the blue jeans). However, "men" are not black, red, or yellow or gay, impotent, or working class. Instead, "men" are white (obviously), middle class (the tie), heterosexual (the wedding band), and sexually potent (the baby). While marking off through silence and exclusion those adult males who are not "proper men," the cover fuses the businessman with the "wild man" in an apparent resolution of the question of "what men really want."

Thus replete with culturally dominant social, sexual, and racial messages about masculinity, the *Newsweek* cover is designed to "make sense" of, and money off, the newly emergent mythopoetic men's movement, which it refers to directly with the phrase "Now They Have a Movement of Their Own" and indirectly with the words "Drums, Sweat and Tears." The complete text works not only to identify "men" and to suggest what "men" "really want" (to father, to cry, to sweat, and to make noise, money, and women), but also to represent the "movement" as "men's" physical and emotional effort (via "sweat" and "tears") to attain the things they want. While the cover humorously parodies mythopoetic men's work of dredging up the "deep masculine" within, it also celebrates that work by displaying "man" in a moment that combines fatherly and fiscal responsibility with manly emotion and playfulness. The decentering of national manhood acknowledged by the cover's question is thus ideologically recentered by the complete text. Paradoxically, then, the effect of the cover is to acknowledge, contain, and thus neutralize the destabilizing question about manhood it asks the nation.

According to Stuart Hall (1977), "The media serve, in societies like ours, ceaselessly to perform the critical ideological work of 'classifying out the world' within the discourses of the dominant ideologies" (p. 346).[3] This, I suggest, is precisely the work performed by early 1990s popular media representations of the men's movement. The mainstream magazine coverage discussed here works especially to frame the men's movement within dominant discourse on gender, embracing those aspects of the movement that replicate the taken-for-granted assumption of "natural" sexual difference, while excluding those that question that hegemonic or "commonsense" assumption.[4] Dominant discourses on race and class permeate the texts as well, so that the texts' construction of masculine "difference" draws on stereotypes that reinforce the economic, political, and cultural power of straight, middle-class, white men.

Of course, the great irony of the mythopoetic branch is that it is just such men who largely fill out its ranks. Thus, one pressing ideological task of the popular media in the early 1990s was to quell the disturbance from within this most privileged group so that business might proceed as usual. The perceived threat was not so much *from* the movement itself as *to* the gendered subjectivity of individual consumers, precisely that consuming desire that the disciplinary power of popular texts is meant continually to reproduce and regulate. Thus, as a term of popular discourse, the "men's movement" mattered ideologically to the extent that its use decentered popular understanding of what it meant to be a "man." In response, popular representations of the movement somehow had to account for this decentering, explain it in "commonsense" terms, and thereby produce in readers a consensus about masculinity that allowed for the movement itself without allowing the movement to upset prevailing gender relations.

As Hall (1977) points out, "The [media's] role of shaping and organizing *consensus*, which is necessarily a complex not a simple entity, is critical here. What constitutes [the media] not simply as a field, but as a field 'structured in dominance,' is the way its limits operate—to rule certain kinds of interpretations 'in' or 'out,' to effect its systematic *inclusions . . .* and *exclusions.*" Among the systematic "exclusions" used by the media to produce "consensus" are "those groups, interpretations, positions, aspects of the reality of the system which are regularly 'ruled out of court' as 'extremist,' 'irrational,' meaningless,' utopian,' impractical,' etc." (p. 346). In the case of mass media print representations of the men's movement in the early 1990s, such "exclusions" fairly leap out at one. Most obvious is the exclusion of the movement's explicitly political branches, whether reactionary or progressive, in favor of the broadly apolitical mythopoetic branch. Consider, for example, the erasure of profeminism from popular discourse. Despite having held national meetings every year since 1975, the movement's profeminist wing receives almost no ink in these articles. When they are mentioned, profeminists are not "real" men, but, in the words of the *New Republic* (Gross, 1990), "masculine squishes" or "a gang of man-haters trapped in men's bodies," or, in the words of *Fortune* (Men in trouble, 1991) "feminist fellow travelers, mainly concerned with promoting ideas that seem indistinguishable from the National Organization for Women."[5]

In addition, the articles almost fully exclude any men's groups, gatherings, or organizations that are anything but white and middle class. The *New York Times* (Clines, 1993) provided perhaps the single prominent exception to this rule with an article (and photograph) on what it suggested "may be the first chapter of the men's movement in an American penitentiary." While this exception suggests that the movement reaches beyond lines of race and class, it also works to maintain hegemonic consensus about African American men as dangerous and deserving of incarceration. If coverage of men of color in the movement was rare, media discussion of sexual tension and pleasure among movement men was completely excluded, as were the voices of effeminate, gay, straight, bisexual, or transgendered men. Finally, the articles largely ignore feminist response to the movement, an exclusion that reinforces popular consensus on who and what counts as "woman." Thus, while feminists are ignored, "women" do respond to the men's movement in mainstream "women's" magazines, an "inclusion" that serves to reinforce the continued white patriarchal rule of the commercial media.[6]

"Inclusions," or "those 'definitions of the situation' which regularly, of necessity and legitimately 'have access' to the structuring of any controversial topic," work in tandem with "exclusions" to construct the commercial media as a field "structured in dominance" (Hall, 1977, p. 346). As consensus-producing "definitions of the situation," mainstream magazine articles on the men's movement took many different forms, though nearly all of them reduced the movement to its mythopoetic branch. Consequently, popular confusion of the movement's mythopoetic branch as *the* movement should come as no surprise. Between 1990 and 1993, there appeared many seemingly straightforward news reports on mythopoetic gatherings, such as the *Newsweek* cover story of June 1991, nearly always reported as encompassing the men's movement. Dozens of reviews of mythopoetic texts and profiles of mythopoetic leaders also appeared, often accompanying other articles on the mythopoetic branch of the movement, as in the case of the set of articles (including cover story) in the *Christian Century* of May 1991 by Dittes, Schmidt, and Baumgaertner. Editorials or commentaries on the movement, uniformly reducing the scope of the movement to its mythopoetic branch, appeared in magazines as diverse as *Maclean's* What Is It That Men Really Want?" (Gordon, 1991), *Psychology Today*'s "Why the Men's Movement Isn't So Funny" (Pittman, 1992), and *Seventeen*'s "The Guy's Movement" (DiPrima, 1992). Several women's magazines ran articles that also defined the movement by exclusion of its profeminist and men's rights branches. Examples include *Working Women*'s "Warning: Vikings in the Office" (Collins, 1991), and *McCall's* "The Men's Movement Is Here . . . But Where Is It Taking Us?" (Hedegaard, 1991), which gauged the effect of the mythopoetic branch of the men's movement on women both in romance and at the workplace. Men's magazines ran their stories as well, including, for example, *GQ*'s "White Guys with Drums" (Hirshey, 1991), the title itself stereotyping the broader movement according to a single aspect of mythopoetic practice.

Finally, some magazines ran first-person, participant-observation accounts of movement events, all of which were mythopoetic gatherings. In what follows, I focus on three such narratives: the *New York Times Magazine*'s "Call of the Wildmen" (Gabriel, 1990); *Esquire*'s "Inward, Ho!" (Stanton, 1991); and the *American Spectator*'s "America's New Man" (Ferguson, 1992). Offered as a specific illustration of the hegemonic silencing of the men's movement between 1990 and 1993, these narratives help answer particular questions that may be asked of all popular representations of the movement during this period. How and why is the mythopoetic branch routinely made to stand for the movement itself? Precisely what constitutes the "men's movement" in these texts? Precisely who or what constitutes a "man"? How do the texts call on readers to identify certain bodies and acts as "male" or "masculine," and thereby compel readers to exclude other bodies and acts from that "natural" designation of sexual difference? What contradictions, exclusions, and silences arise in popular textual definitions of "men" and the "men's movement," and how is the "movement" itself (including, of course, its mythopoetic branch) finally erased from popular discourse?

First-person narratives are a good place to begin a consideration of popular print representations of the contemporary men's movement because they highlight the obvious impact of Moyers's 1990 PBS documentary, *A Gathering of Men*, on all subsequent representations. Moyers's largely sympathetic and noncritical interview of Robert Bly, coupled with frequent shots of Bly leading a rapt gathering of men, initiated popular definition of the movement as mythopoetic by fully excluding any discussion of its reactionary or progressive wings. Popularly speaking, this is the first and, because of its repeated national exposure, the most important instance by which the cultural identity of the movement was produced by the exclusion of its explicitly political elements. *A Gathering of Men* offered an ahistorical definition of the movement that focused national and commercial attention on the private or "inner" problems of (particular) contemporary men. Henceforth, the glaring contradictions in popular usage of the term *men's movement*—especially its erasure of differences among men along lines of class, race, and sexuality—were concealed by the greater market appeal of the psychic travails of white, middle-class, middle-aged, heterosexual males. In this way, popular discourse reduced the movement to its mythopoetic wing, with its easily sensationalized, largely nonthreatening, mostly apolitical search for the prediscursive, natural "wild man within." Thus, unsurprisingly, all subsequent first-person print narratives concerning the contemporary men's movement describe visits to mythopoetic men's gatherings.

If the ideological work performed by the media is, as Hall says, "to classify out the world," then any attempt to understand how that classifying works must consider the point of view of the classifier. For instance, in "Call of the Wildmen," a feature story of the October 14, 1990, *New York Times Magazine* narrator Trip Gabriel is careful to establish his distance (emotional and otherwise) from the ritual proceedings he encounters. Gabriel presents himself as a well-adjusted, normal, and objective man. Unscarred by "men's problems," he is one

whose inability to conjure up mistreatment at the hands of his own father marks
him as an adult male whose masculinity poses him no particular difficulty. He
is "different" from those he encounters—men in "their 30s and 40s, healthy and
presentable looking guys"—for whom the "traditional rites of passage for American males" had "left them somehow uncertain of their masculine identity" (p.
42). Thus, Gabriel's narrative positioning interpellates readers as normal,
healthy, well-adjusted male subjects.[7] Through him, readers may "objectively"
observe the otherwise "regular" guys attempting to "discover an earthier, more
self-assured version of themselves" (p. 37). This objective pose the narrator
takes up and instills in his readers is precisely the point of view necessary for
the construction of mythopoetic practice as a kind of aberration among privileged men. It marks off those involved as a minority of majority men, whose
problems are to be understood as personal and idiosyncratic, rather than as
indicative of middle-class American masculinity more generally. Used this way,
"objectivity" deflects readers away from the history of gender, class, and race
contradictions from which the men's movement, including its mythopoetic
branch, actually emerges.

Nonetheless, like Moyers, Gabriel treats his subjects with some empathy atypical of later representations of mythopoetic men. He acknowledges the value of
men gathering to discuss their experience as men and yet dismisses the ritual
exercises performed at the gathering as "silly" (p. 47). In this text, then, one
finds in Gabriel's voice the hegemonic legitimization of adult male uneasiness
combined with a flat rejection of new cultural practices designed to assuage or
address that uneasiness. On the one hand, Gabriel's experience of the three-day
gathering affirms the desire of men to "just talk" about their lives: "What most
men seem to want are more forums in which they can talk directly to one
another, a kind of recovery program for victims of errant notions of masculinity,
a sort of Men's Anonymous" (p. 47). Such phrasing acknowledges the short-
comings of conventional masculine inexpressiveness and the lack of formal or
informal means by which men might break with that convention. Yet on the
other hand, mythopoetic ritual practices as manifested at the gathering are "pat-
ent foolishness." Gabriel articulates his ambivalence as follows: "The men
around the fire had seemed at times ridiculous, but they were ridiculous and
real" (p. 47).

As in Moyers's *A Gathering of Men*, Gabriel's "Call of the Wildmen" renders
the men's movement as exclusively mythopoetic. Furthermore, the narrative's
silence on questions of sexual difference, class, and ethnicity reinforces dominant assumptions about masculine identity: the middle-class, white, heterosexual
"regular guy" remains the norm against which masculinity is measured. Perfectly
normal "guys," like Gabriel himself, not only reject the "movement's" cultural
practices, but also have no need to "just talk" about being a man. In this way,
this early print representation of mythopoetic events begins the work of "classifying out" the men's movement, demarcating it well within the popular discursive field "structured in dominance." Thus, although popular representations

of the movement would continue to appear for at least two more years, "Call of the Wildmen" reflects the ironic process of silencing the men's movement through a profusion of words about it.[8]

If the ambivalence of "Call of the Wildmen" grudgingly legitimates the exploration of male subjectivity among certain privileged men, two subsequent narratives, *Esquire*'s "Inward, Ho!" (Stanton, 1991) and the *American Spectator*'s "America's New Man" (Ferguson, 1992), capitalize on mythopoeticism's new-found legitimacy (to sell magazines) and seek strictly to regulate or control the discussion so that "masculinity" cannot escape the parameters of dominant discourse. Published well into *Iron John*'s run on the best-seller list, these articles' cover story status reflects the commercial viability of the mythopoetic branch of the men's movement as of late 1991. Yet as these two narratives attest, the selling of the movement went hand in hand with the silencing of it.

As a nationally distributed, self-styled "magazine for men," *Esquire*'s profit depends on the sophisticated marketing of an image of confident, monied, masculine difference, an image that beckons readers to buy their way to genuine manhood by consuming the products advertised in its pages. As the name indicates, *Esquire* hails its readers as royal male subjects who may enjoy the power proper to their state only by fashioning themselves after the male models and celebrities featured in each issue. Thus, the magazine's cover for the "special issue" story on "Wild Men and Wimps" presents a head shot of unshaven, long-haired, black-tied leading man Jeff Bridges staring hungrily out at the reader.

As part of the "Wild Men and Wimps" special issue, "Inward, Ho!" (Stanton, 1991) is a comic, hyperbolic, and sardonic narration of a New Warrior Training Adventure weekend. Writer Doug Stanton secretly posed as one of "twenty-three middle class spiritual searchers" who paid $550 apiece to become "New Warriors: Nineties Real Men who growl and yodel to protect what's theirs (their balls, among others things), weep and moan over what they've lost (their minds, it seems), and kick the world's ass without apology while smiling at feminists" (p. 113).[9] The narrative works by Stanton's presenting himself as a knowing outsider willingly "kidnapped" by "a gang of merchants in the therapy trade dressed up like Boy Scouts on steroids." Over three days he undergoes "interrogation," "surrender" to "elders" in the "Pit o' Grief," a "ritual bonding game of Capture the flag," "guided visualization" to "Meet the Wildman," the "psychodramatic process" of finding the "shadow," and finally an "initiation ceremony" as a New Warrior. The experience comes off as a kind of prolonged, intensive adult male hazing ritual conducted in paramilitary style and designed to humiliate, cajole, and otherwise compel initiates to confront their deepest fears about being men. Of the weekend's "central moment . . . the exploration of your Shadow," Stanton asks, "Who will freak out next? Those who haven't imploded, like me, nervously pace the carpet, fighting tears, pausing to stare at the contortions of our brethren. Where are my tears coming from? Is this what I've always wanted, to spew my guts out all over the walls?" (p. 120). Depicting himself as heroically resistant, Stanton remains at ritual's end the single initiate not to "implode," and "for the rest of the weekend my newfound pals are guarded strangers. So much for brotherhood" (p. 122).

Like "Call of the Wildmen," "Inward, Ho!" is a narrative that defines the men's movement strictly according to one version of the mythopoetic search for the "deep masculine." Like Gabriel, Stanton remains wholly silent on the explicitly political practices of other wings of the movement. Thus, he characterizes the movement as an "inward" turn by alienated middle-class white men. Yet for Stanton, "to talk about the men's movement" is "to talk about how American men—white, educated American men—are spending money to make themselves feel good" (p. 113). While one may say essentially the same thing of those men who buy *Esquire* magazine, it remains that the men's movement, as defined here, is an elaborately staged commercial venture designed to take advantage of men who should know better.

Even more dismissive of the movement than Stanton, Andrew Ferguson (1992) defines the men's movement as a crass, shallow, and cynical marketing scheme perpetrated on white middle-class male dupes and losers. In "America's New Man," the *American Spectator* cover story of January 1992, Ferguson presents himself as a normal, healthy American man—fully distinct from the "bunch of patheticos . . . drum-bangers, poem-shouters, and Dad-haters" he encounters at the First International Men's Conference at the Stouffer Aboretum Hotel in Austin, Texas.[10] Indeed, the only "real" man to be found in "America's New Man" is the author, Ferguson himself.

Realist narrative such as Ferguson's works by implicitly forcing the reader to identify with the storyteller's point of view.[11] For readers who would resist that "normal" point of view, the alternative in this piece is to become "Chuck," Ferguson's unknowing informant, an unflattering likeness of whom appears on the magazine's cover. "Chuck," Ferguson writes in his opening paragraph, is overweight. "His jeans are cinched a good distance below his waist, down there where his stomach descends into his pubic bone. His jeans have been ironed. The crease touches the top of his Nikes, which look brand new. Chuck is getting a divorce, his third. Too, he is a drunk, as he told me last night, or rather a recovering alcoholic, also a sex addict. These are the two addictions he has so far been able to acknowledge and process through. He is worried there might be more. Plus his life is littered with co-dependencies" (p. 26). Ferguson, the reader's unseen model of manhood, depicts "Chuck" as the rank-and-file men's movement man. Such men, writes Ferguson, share certain characteristics. "All, clearly, have way too much time on their hands. Many of the men I spoke with had been divorced twice or more. 'It's beginning to dawn on me what's so odd here.' a woman journalist told me one evening. 'There are no—I mean no— good-looking men here.' New Men tend to be paunchy, with much facial hair to compensate for the diminishing crop up top. Calling the Austin gathering of men the First International Losers Conference would have been more accurate" (p. 33).

The point, for Ferguson, is that the "New Man" of the men's movement is a failed man. In this way, "men" are defined according to what they are not. Those who violate the cultural standard for masculine heterosexual beauty do not count; those who fail to attract women or sustain a marriage do not count; those who take time away from "productive" work do not count; those who succumb to addiction do not count.

According to Ferguson, who makes no distinction among movement branches, these are the nonmen of the men's movement, whose desperate but privileged self-absorption is all the more open to exploitation at the hands of movement hucksters Bly, Shepherd Bliss, John Lee, and Marvin Allen. Through Ferguson's first-person filter, we meet each of these mythopoetic leaders (as always in these narratives, the movement equals mythopoeticism) except for Bly. Bly's absence from the weekend event becomes the narrative's central conflict and primary evidence for the movement's commercial basis. "Bly had of course been invited, but had declined. . . . He faxed to many movement leaders a letter denouncing [conference organizer] Marvin Allen as a media hound, a sensationalizer, who was using the conference to further his own career" (p. 32).

If, as I suggest, the ideological work performed by these popular representations is to silence the contemporary men's movement, then Ferguson plays out his role as conservative ideologue intent on emasculating and thus dismissing the movement's mythopoetic men. Published in early 1992, his piece disparages not only the movement itself but also, ironically, previous popular representations of the movement, including Moyers's, *Newsweek*'s, and *Esquire*'s, each of which Ferguson sees as taking part in the greedy commodification of white male anxiety. Of course, the accusation of crass commercialism rebounds on Ferguson's head, too, in that the *American Spectator*'s cover story is itself a cynical effort both to sell, and to silence, the men's movement. Indeed, in pieces such as Ferguson's, it becomes increasingly difficult to separate the selling from the silencing. As a late addition to the wagon train of popular representation of mythopoeticism as the men's movement, "America's New Man" concludes that "the men's movement doesn't exist in any definable sense, and certainly not as we have been led to believe" (p. 33).

Given the texts under consideration here, by 1993 "men" were no longer in crisis, and the "men's movement" was no longer on the move. The texts suggest that what had been in 1990 and 1991 a tentative yet popular legitimization of the felt need among some middle-class white men to stretch the boundaries of masculinity became, by 1993, an object of popular ridicule and stereotype. Early on, the media operated to strip the movement of its counterhegemonic potential, producing a narrow definition so that its explicitly political branches could be lopped off and discounted entirely. In a matter of months, having focused attention exclusively on the mythopoetic branch, so that it was popularly misunderstood as *the* men's movement, the media proceeded to define mythopoetic leaders as cynical capitalists and movement participants as failed men. The potentially positive social aspects of mythopoeticism—engaged fathering, increased emotional availability, reduced violence, decreased competition, deepened spirituality—were effectively ignored. Thus, by 1993, mythopoeticism, popularly defined as the men's movement, ceased to be of public concern, and was rendered silent.

Silence, as used here, should be understood as the ideological effect of media representation of the mythopoetic branch of the men's movement in the early 1990s. While acknowledging a degree of variation in the performance of middle-class masculinity, the media nonetheless succeeded in producing a definition of the contemporary men's movement devoid of threat to the reigning social order. While explicit profeminism was ruled "out of court" from the beginning and wholly excluded from popular definition of the movement, mythopoeticism was highlighted but effectively drained of its subversive elements, and finally dismissed as the last bastion of an aging, pathetic, and impotent new age masculinity. Whether this popularly produced definition of mythopoetic masculinity will remain unchallenged is yet to be seen. In effect, the ideological work of the media has been to drive mythopoeticism underground, where rituals of personal transformation continue to be practiced in private, separatist settings away from the media spotlight. The challenge to mythopoetic men now is to make public their personal transformations, combining the personal with the social in a collective effort—in alliance with feminist, profeminists, gay and lesbian activists, and progressive men and women of color—to resist the continued reproduction of hegemonic masculinity.

This is not merely another call for public alliance between mythopoeticism and other progressive elements in America's gender wars. The mass media have, I suggest, effectively disciplined mythopoetic men to accept silence as the alternative to shame by popular ridicule. The continued acceptance of this silence marks mythopoetic men as complicit in the media-fed, hegemonic reproduction of a white middle-class, American masculinity too timid, complacent, and satisfied to make gender trouble. If the point of mythopoeticism is to help men break away from the trappings of media-controlled definitions of manhood, it must do so publicly, loudly, and in league with others who share that general aim.

NOTES

1. Videocassette copies of *A Gathering of Men* are available for sale through Mystic Fire Video or may be borrowed from public libraries. One might compare *A Gathering of Men* to the *Murphy Brown* parody of the men's movement, complete with a Robert Bly-ish clone, a talking stick, and even Murphy's own chance to speak of her father. While sometimes considered a complete disparagement of mythopoetic men, the episode's conclusion, with Murphy clutching the talking stick and movingly recalling her father's memory, in fact speaks to the potential power of mythopoetic ritual in reconnecting children—and not only boys—to their fathers.

2. This chapter considers only the nationally prominent print media representations of the men's movement. One crucial aspect of ideological analysis not dealt with here

is the reception of popular representations among movement participants themselves, for which ethnographic research on men's groups is ideally suited. My own fieldwork on men's peer mutual support groups in the Kansas City region suggests that participants often felt misrepresented by the media's coverage. For example, one man said that the media were "making fun of the men who were in search of their feelings. . . . I can remember reading several articles that made fun of the warrior weekends and things that men were going to. And the people who were writing them had no idea what essentially was going on, or were not able to grasp what the men were looking for out of that."

3. Stuart Hall has been the leading light of British cultural studies since the 1970s, and his "Culture, the Media, and the 'Ideological Effect' " (1977) is a classic statement on the role of the media in reproducing the structure of domination in advanced capitalist democracies. Interested readers should also see his "Encoding, Decoding" (1990).

4. As Hall (1977) points out, the appeal to "common sense" is both ideological and unconscious: "You cannot learn, through common sense, *how things are*: you can only discover *where they fit* into the existing scheme of things. In this way, its very taken-for-grantedness is what establishes it as a medium in which its own premises and pre-suppositions are being rendered *invisible* by its apparent transparency" (pp. 325–326). The media's deployment of "common sense" about gender difference is basic to its role (among other ideological tasks) of helping to reproduce hegemonic masculinity.

5. During the course of 1991, *Fortune* seems to have changed its tune regarding the men's movement. While the December issue (Men in trouble, 1991) states that "the men's movement is dumber than the women's movement" (p. 184), another brief *Fortune* article from earlier that year (In search, 1991, January) concluded this way: "But if the new-model male remains blurry as yet, men have at least begun to ask seriously what the social revolution that has moved women so far over the past two decades means to them" (p. 48). Here, in separate issues of the same magazine in the same year, one sees the hegemonic acknowledgment of the movement's social potential followed by hegemony's condescending foreclosure on the issue.

6. See, for example, *Madamoiselle* (Harrison, 1991), *Working Woman* (Collins, 1991), *McCall's* (Hedegaard, 1991), *Ladies' Home Journal* (Lowry, 1992), and *Seventeen* (DiPrima, 1992). Not to be confused as a "women's" magazine or even as a "popular" magazine, *Ms*, the well known liberal feminist magazine, ran one response to the men's movement (Doubiago, 1993).

7. Louis Althusser (1969) illustrates interpellation through the analogy of a police officer hailing an individual: "Hey, you there!" When the hailed individual responds, she has been interpellated, that is, she has become a subject of, and subject to, the police officer's ideological discourse. Thus, she has been constituted as a subject in ideology. (See especially the section, "Ideology Interpellates Individuals as Subjects," pp. 170–177.) As in realist narrative generally, Gabriel's interpellating or hailing of readers as subjects of *his* ideological discourse operates implicitly so that they identify with him as normal, healthy, well-adjusted men, *unlike* the men about whom Gabriel writes.

8. Eight photographs by Danny Turner accompany Gabriel's text. The largest, spread over most of the two facing pages that open the article, depicts an early morning group massage. The opening photo spread also includes a close-up shot of two men tightly embracing. Thus, the reader turning to the article's opening pages encounters visual representations of male-to-male physical and emotional tenderness, which may, to a degree, undercut Gabriel's textual rejection of mythopoetic cultural practices. Essential to mythopoetic masculinity, such practices are, for the most part, private, occurring during

meetings, gathering, or conferences. Indeed, one mythopoetic informant told me that when his "brothers" visit him at his home, their ritual exchange of hugs always occurs inside the front door, so that the neighbors "don't get the wrong idea." Nonetheless, it is intriguing to imagine the potential effect if such clearly counterhegemonic practices were to be publicly displayed. Imagine, for example, a contingent of majority straight mythopoetic men marching in a gay pride parade, deploying group massage as a potent symbol of their support for their male-identified brothers.

9. Prior to the weekend, all would-be New Warriors must sign an agreement to the effect that their experience on the New Warrior Training Adventure will remain strictly confidential. Obviously, Stanton's word was not good; he broke his agreement of confidentiality.

10. Readers unfamiliar with mythopoetic events should understand that this event is quite different from the outdoor men's gathering described by Gabriel, or the New Warrior Training Adventure, an initiatory experience, described by Stanton. In some ways like a typical academic or professional conference, the First International Men's Conference, organized by Marvin Allen, occurred in a hotel with scheduled speakers and workshops. The setting of this semipublic, gender-inclusive conference contrasts sharply with the private, men-only camping experience of the men's gathering (described by Gabriel) or the private, initiatory experience of the NWTA weekend (described by Stanton).

11. For a discussion of the interpellative power of realist narrative, see, for example, Belsey (1988), especially chapter 3, "Addressing the Subject."

REFERENCES

Adler, J. (1991). Drums, sweat and tears. *Newsweek*, pp. 46–47.

Althusser, L. (1969). *Lenin and philosophy and other essays*. London: Verso.

Belsey, C. (1988). *Critical practice*. London: Routledge.

Bly, R. (1990). *Iron John*. Reading, MA: Addison-Wesley.

Clines, F. X. (1993, February 23). Men's movement challenges machismo in prison. *New York Times*, p. C18.

Collins, G. (1991, October). Warning: Vikings in the office. *Working Woman, 116*, 114.

DiPrima, D. (1992, September). The guys' movement. *Seventeen, 51*, 86.

Dittes, J., Schmidt, S., & Baumgaertner, J. (1991, May–June). Being a man. *Christian Century, 108*, 588–596.

Doubiago, S. (1993, March–April). Enemy of the mother: A feminist response to the men's movement. *Ms, 2*, 82–85.

Ferguson, A. (1992, January). America's new man. *American Spectator, 25*, 26–33.

Gabriel, T. (1990, October 14). Call of the wildmen. *New York Times Magazine*, pp. 36–39, 42, 47.

Gordon, C. (1991, November 18). What is it that men really want? *Macclean's*, p. 13.

Gross, D. (1990, April 16). The gender rap. *New Republic*, pp. 11–14.

Hall, S. (1977). Culture, the media, and the "ideological effect." In J. Curran, M. Gurevitch, & J. Woollacott (Eds.), *Mass communication and society* (pp. 315–348). Beverly Hills: Sage.

Hall, S. (1990). Encoding, decoding. In S. During (Ed.), *The cultural studies reader* (pp. 90–103). London: Routledge.

Harrison, B. G. (1991, October). Campfire boys: Why the men's movement is hot. *Mademoiselle, 97*, 94, 96.

Hedegaard, E. (1991, November). The men's movement is here . . . but where is it taking us? *McCall's, 119,* 98, 100, 209.

Hirshey, G. (1991, December). White guys with drums. *Gentleman's Quarterly, 61,* 86, 89, 90, 91.

In search of masculine mystique. (1991, January 14). *Fortune,* pp. 46, 48.

Lowry, T. (1992, January). What men can't get from women. *Ladies' Home Journal, 109,* 77–81.

Men in trouble. (1991, December 2). *Fortune,* p. 184.

Moyers, B. (1990). *A gathering of men.* New York: Public Affairs Television.

Pittman, F. (1992, January–February). Why the men's movement isn't so funny. *Psychology Today, 25,* 84.

Stanton, D. (1991, October). Inward, ho! *Esquire, 116,* 112–122.

Chapter 7

Reconstructing Masculinity: Role Models in the Life Stories of Men's Peer Mutual Support Group Members

Eric S. Mankowski

Feminism and changing economic conditions have challenged the viability of dominant, hegemonic definitions of masculinity as a basis for men's identity (Connell, 1990; Segal, 1990). Increasingly, a masculinity based on expectations of physical strength, toughness, aggression, emotional suppression (with the exception of anger), and dominance in relation to women (Pleck, 1981) is untenable. In response to these threats to the structural sources of hegemonic masculinity, some men are attempting to "re-create" (Betcher & Pollack, 1993), "re-vision" (Kupers, 1993), and "reconstruct" (Levant, 1995) healthier and less conflicted forms of masculine identity.

Men's peer mutual support (MPMS) groups are one setting in which these reconstructions are occurring (Andronico, 1996; Sternbach, 1990). Men who participate in such groups are taking an active step in understanding and changing how gender affects their lives. In the groups, men exchange stories about their experiences of growing up male and offer each other emotional support and encouragement in their efforts to redefine the imprint of masculinity on their lives and lessen gender role conflict (O'Neil, 1991).

The social processes in these groups include several forms of discourse and interaction that may facilitate redefinitions of masculinity (Gilbert, 1992; Schwalbe, 1996): the exchange of personal stories, histories, and instructive myths and participation in ritualized forms of physical and social interaction. By exchanging stories in a supportive context, men can develop a shared understanding of what it means to be male that differs from oppressive and self-destructive meanings that typify traditional forms of masculinity (Brannon, 1976; Eisler, 1995).

MEN'S GROUP NARRATIVES

This shared understanding takes the form of a narrative that describes the lived experience of men in the group (Mankowski & Rappaport, 1995). The narrative of a MPMS group might describe experiences (e.g., first sexual encounter) that characterize what it is like growing up as a male and common aspects of men's relationships (e.g., physical violence). Basic features of such narratives include events and characters that move through time and are set against a backdrop of beliefs and values (McAdams, 1988). The meaning given to these events, however, depends on the masculinity ideology (Pleck, Sonenstein, & Ku, 1993) that characterizes the group's narrative. Mythopoetic men's group narratives are based in a particular set of ideological beliefs and expectations about what men are like and should do (Schwalbe, 1996).

Generally mythopoetic groups are inspired by Jungian personality theory, which describes an archetypal, spiritually based masculinity that can be accessed through the exchange of myths, stories, and guided, nonverbal interactions among men (Williams & Myer, 1992). Through these interactive forms, the MMS group creates a narrative that participants can use to revisit their personal histories, reinterpret or restructure that history based on the implications of the narrative, and develop new goals, sense of purpose, or life mission.

One component of a group narrative is a set of role models, or *imagoes* (McAdams, 1988, 1993)—"idealized and personified images of the self which play the role of characters in the life story" (McAdams, 1988, p. 210). Imagoes take the form of role models, mentors, or heroes. Two imagoes commonly described in mythopoetic texts are the warrior (McCarthy, 1994; Moore & Gillette, 1990) and the mentor (McAdams, 1993, p. 189). The New Warrior is an international organization of mythopoetic men's groups that is even named after the warrior imago. According to one author, the warrior "represents focused energy (in the service of a noble mission), accountability, integrity, and the embracement of one's own feminine" (Jesser, 1996, p. 29). The mentor is used to represent an older man, sometimes called an elder, who is needed to initiate younger men into an authentic and mature masculinity. The mentor guides, blesses, and challenges the younger men in their psychological development. The warrior and mentor imagoes may function as possible selves (Markus & Nurius, 1986) for men's identity development and give alternatives to the provider and protector imagoes that commonly characterize masculine identity.

In addition to the texts of the mythopoetic branch of the men's movement, relevant imagoes might be found on television, in film (Jeffords, 1994), and in the life stories of other men in men's groups. While the warrior and mentor have been advanced as guides to the reconstruction of masculinity, the questions of whether and how individual participants in MPMS groups are drawing on these models or other imagoes to redefine masculinity and reduce gender role conflict is not well understood. As a step toward that knowledge, I present findings from a study of an MPMS group that documented the sources and functions of imagoes in the group's narrative and analyzed how long-term participants used these imagoes to describe and interpret their histories as men.

STUDY PURPOSE AND METHODS

The data reported here were obtained as part of a six-year naturalistic study (Mankowski, 1997) that used participatory action-research methodology (Chesler, 1991) to describe members' life stories and the transactional relationship between those stories and features of the group's narrative. At the time of the study, the group had been meeting for nearly six years, usually every third week for three hours. Although the group did not explicitly identify itself as a mythopoetic group, it used many of the forms of discourse and group process that characterize such groups (Kauth, 1992; Schwalbe, 1996), for example, the exchange of personal stories and storytelling, the ritual creation of a closed space or container for group interactions, and the use of art, music, and drumming, plus physical and nonverbal interaction.

All five members of the MPMS group participated in the study. The men ranged in age from twenty to fifty-five, were highly educated (all had at least a bachelor's degree), and most had grown up, and were currently living, in middle- or upper-middle class families. They were predominantly white (one was East Indian), married (four of five), and fathers (three of five). Three of five had previous involvement in other men's groups.

I conducted semistructured interviews with all participants about their life history and their involvement in and evaluation of the men's group. The life history protocol was based on a similar interview developed by McAdams (1988) in his research on life stories. Participants were asked to describe what it was like for them to grow up as a man in this society and to discuss several aspects of that experience, including possible themes, critical or key events, and role models or heroes that characterized their history, important beliefs about masculinity, and future goals or plans related to being a man. They were also asked to describe what they considered to be important about the men's group and how they had changed as a result of their participation in it.

All members were given a copy of their interview transcript to read and evaluate and asked to edit it in any way that was necessary to make it a more complete and accurate representation of their views. Later, at the participants' own request, all the transcripts were circulated among the group and read by all participants. Their reactions to each other's interviews served as part of the basis for a subsequent focus group interview (Hughes & DuMont, 1993) designed to elicit their shared and common understanding of the group and of their masculinity. The group discussed the process of a typical group meeting, the history of the group, ongoing themes of the group, key events or turning points that strongly influenced or shaped the group, role models or important individuals who influenced the group, beliefs about men and masculinity that were important to the group, and the overall plan, dream, or future vision of the group. Finally, an audiorecording of a group meeting made by the participants one year previously and an interview of the group on a local radio program two and a half years previously were also used to understand the group's process, shared knowledge, and development over time. Transcripts of the individual and group interviews and recorded meeting were analyzed with the aid of a qualitative data analysis computer program (Richards & Richards, 1991).[1]

FINDINGS AND DISCUSSION

Role Models in the MPMS Group

The group members modeled noncompetitive, trusting, and intimate forms of masculinity for each other through open and extensive self-disclosure of their feelings and desires and through expressions of physical intimacy and care such as touching, holding hands, hugging, massaging, and kissing. This modeling of a gentle, emotionally expressive, vulnerable man provided an alternative to culturally dominant representations of masculinity and inspired members' development of identities consistent with this alternative. In addition to the comfort of this intimacy, the process was also quite challenging to fears of closeness that stem from homophobia (Kimmel, 1994).

Consider the following segment of the focus group discussion in which the members talked about being male, the models they had for being male, and how they now use the stories in each other's lives as models for their own life story. In the first quotation, a member named Evan[2] talks about how he dealt with his father's death and the way in which his behavior at his father's funeral was strongly shaped by his gender role:

From my standpoint, the stuff that I work on as a group came about because male role models that I find are no longer applicable to my life and maybe haven't been for a long time. A men's group to me has to do with dealing with those role models, whether they were realistic or unrealistic. As a male, my role model said you dealt with death by going to the funeral and you carried the casket and you lowered this thing that went down in the ground and you turned around and you walked away. Real men don't cry. Those were the role models that I grew up around and they don't work for me.

At this point, Jeff entered the discussion and indicated how the cultural sources of role models available to him and to the other men in the group were unsatisfactory:

There are cultural expectations, whether we got them from school or from mother and father, but somehow they got internalized and now we're trying to break out of that. I feel like I need to have encouragement and support from men to do that, to be the person that I am as a male and not feel restricted by some kind of cultural box. There's some shared understanding of what that expectation is even though it may change from one family to another. I think my work in this group is breaking out of that box that says this is what you should be as a man: strong, silent, nonemotional.

He then elaborated:

The Clint Eastwood kind of model of you achieving and realizing every challenge and overcoming, but not having any kinds of softer feelings, no sadness, no tears, no weakness; just being silent and strong.

Although these men now hold a generally critical view of these masculine role models, the power that the models remains partly attractive. As Kaufman (1994) has suggested, men have ambivalent, even contradictory experiences of the power that accompanies masculinity. Consider Marty's response to Jeff's description of masculinity as typified by Clint Eastwood. Marty describes his admiration of Jeff's father's response to suddenly being laid off his job, and likens it to the toughness and stoicism of the Terminator, a recent cinematic version of the masculine ideal long portrayed by Eastwood:

It's interesting how powerful that is. I think of your story of your dad after he's been laid off, the story of him sitting there for three days then suddenly getting up and announcing that the family would move across the country and that he would open a new business. What's so interesting to me about that, if I'm really honest, is part of me admires that. Part of me almost thinks, "I want to be that way," which is just so crazy. Where is that coming from? [laughs] There's part of me that almost likes that mythic idea. You sit on the porch for three days, don't talk to anybody, and then you go out and you're like the Terminator, you rise up from your ashes and you start a business, and it's just weird that part of me identifies with wanting to be that way.

Jeff replied:

I'd admire that too and yet it's my admiration of that that I've had to work really hard to kind of break through because my father is a very nonemotional, nonexpressive man. He's a successful businessperson, and well-to-do, retired and all of that. And now I see him struggling immensely with my mother's illness. He doesn't know what to do with that on a feeling level, so it comes out through all these illnesses on his part—physical kinds of problems that he has.

Until this point in the focus group discussion, I had not specifically asked the group to discuss role models. Their discussion of them without solicitation indicated that the topic was a component of their group narrative that existed independent of my interview. However, I later asked the group specifically about role models and their importance in the group. Donald responded by commenting on the way in which Bert, the founder of the group, established a norm for mutually appreciating each other when they noticed something they liked in another member:

I think Bert was a role model for this group because he came in and really set a tone about it. Saying what you appreciated about other people in the group really mattered because it set a sense of really looking for the value and respect of the people that came here. And, at least for me, I came to this group, particularly in the early days of this, feeling what it meant to me a man was to be total shit. It meant to me you are violent, you are abusive; that's what I brought to this group. And people would sit across from me and say, "That's not what you are; I see this other thing in you. And you, if you choose to, can nurture and become that; you don't have to be this other thing." So, that was one of the first times of my life that somebody had said, "I want to embrace this part of you that you care about and want to develop." Bert said that it's important for us to appreciate each other as men from day one. And it wasn't so much he said it— that's what he did—that's what he brought. And that became a value that I think still goes on in this group today.

Jeff spoke next:

As far as models, it just seems like to me each person in the group is a model for what being male can be and also the struggles of being male. And I agree, that Bert kind of modeled tremendously how we could be authentic and try to be authentic without being threatening. No, that's not a good word, 'cause it was threatening to be pushed, to be authentic, but without the violence. We can push our edges without being violent about it. A few weeks ago you were talking about it, and somebody mentioned it in their individual interview, how much admiration I think we each felt, how much admiration I felt when you [looking at Marty] were talking about your relationship with your partner and the difficulties of that over time and how you had chosen to stick that out. There's a sense here for me that I'm sitting with models of how I can be a better man.

Clearly, the other men in the group are an important source of role models for these men. Members used the lives and stories of other men in the group as templates for redefining masculinity in their own lives.

Incorporation of Group Role Models into Members' Life Stories

How do men's group participants use the stories and characters in other men's lives to begin retelling their own stories? A wide range of characters and role models populated the life stories of the men's group participants. Some of the imagoes were based on specific characters or persons in the men's lives: famous men or fictional characters from the mass media and sports world (e.g., Willy Mays, Clint Eastwood, the Terminator), actual persons in the men's lives (e.g., "my father," "my father-in-law"), and more general types of characters (e.g., the Liberator, a writer, a "social-justice-Christian"). The life stories of Donald, Evan, Dilip, Jeff, and Marty show how these three types of models were used to resolve conflicts in their experience of masculinity and to construct more positive alternatives.

Imagoes in Donald's Life History

Donald's life story contained three imagoes that were personalized representations of different themes in his life story: Willy Mays (an idealized sports hero), the Terminator, and Gandhi. Each image was centrally linked with a different period of Donald's life story. According to Donald, "There was the baseball hero era, where [Willy Mays] was my hero and there's the era of Gandhi being my hero and in between there's the Terminator [laughs]."

A major function of Donald's life story at this point in his life was to integrate these three different imagoes into a unified whole. Gandhi functioned as the imago for the recent parts of Donald's story in which he strives for nonviolence, while the Terminator character functioned as an anti-imago—a repressed character or a character in conflict with the main themes in the life story (McAdams, 1988). In this case, the Terminator represented the violent and emotionally angry or repressed character from Donald's past that he was trying to escape. Even so, he continued to place some value in the Terminator's qualities:

The Terminator gets shit done at any cost. There is a goal, there is a mission, there is an objective and you do whatever it takes to get it done. The only way I completed that Ph.D. was to just say: "I'm going to fucking do it no matter what happens. You are not going to let these emotions get in the way of what you have to get done. You're going to somehow get them out of the picture enough that you can accomplish what you've got to accomplish or do what you've got to do." That's an important part of who I am, and where I've been, and what I've done. That's part of that notion of being violent. Violence is okay if you've got to do it to get whatever it is done that you got to get done.

The theme of never-ending achievement and competitive hierarchy that characterizes normative, hegemonic forms of masculinity (Connell, 1987, 1990) is represented in Donald's story by the Terminator imago. This character was an enduring presence in Donald's life story. More than two years earlier, in October 1993, when the group was interviewed on a local radio station, Donald used the Terminator image to describe the importance of his participation in the group: "A lot of what this group has been is forcing me to stop being the Terminator in the sense of going through my day to day life in a mechanistic way largely divorced from my emotional life. This group has been an opportunity for me to force me to be attentive to my emotional life, and that has been one of the most positive forces in my life over the last year and a half." Donald's use of the Terminator character in his life story at different points spanning two and a half years indicates its central and enduring position.

Donald recognized the struggle and division within himself represented by the contrasting imagoes of the Terminator and Gandhi. The conflict between them corresponds to that between the two basic ideologies about the inherent nature of men commonly represented in discourse about gender and masculinity (Clatterbaugh, 1996). In the essentialist view, men are inherently violent, and the strictures of masculinity are a social invention necessary to control this violence. From the social constructivist view, masculinity is an unnecessary social invention that encourages men who are inherently peaceful to commit violence. Donald found support for his struggle to resolve the conflict between these two ideologies in the life story of Gandhi and in the role models provided by other men in the group:

Deep in my heart, for a long time, I believed all men are violent. That what it meant to be male was to be violent. And I really sought and read about trying to find role models that weren't violent. And Gandhi's the one that is the best image of that for me—of how to deal with conflict nonviolently. He repeatedly had to deal with conflict and did it in nonviolent and effective ways. And that's how I want to live my life.

Part of what convinces me now that not all men are violent is meeting with the same group of guys for three years and knowing they couldn't be faking it that long. There are men in the world who aren't violent, and increasingly I'm one of them. That's part of that support system that we have for one another. We are learning skills in this group that feed into understanding myself, understanding other people, understanding how to manage relationships, how to understand and manage my own feelings, empathy. Those things help me cope with anger in ways that are not abusive and violent.

Imagoes in Evan's Life History

The major imago in Evan's life story was the mentor, a key figure in mythopoetic men's writing and one of the prototypical imagoes found in life stories (McAdams, 1988). The image of a mentor as a kind of older, wiser teacher has often been discussed within mythopoetic men's writing as a missing but needed presence in the lives of men. In this view, younger men require the presence of older men in their lives to initiate them into a mature masculinity. The mentor imago characterized many of the events in Evan's life story. For example, he hopes to become a mentor and has self-consciously adopted this role by beginning a men's group composed of his son and his son's friends.

Evan's father-in-law provides a specific example of the mentor imago in Evan's life story. In Evan's words, "My father-in-law, who was older, would take me by the hand and be the mentor about life." Evan's father-in-law exemplified a resolution of the conflict between a strong, virtuous masculinity and a close, affectionate, and sometimes physically intimate masculinity between men. This conflict between intimacy and fear, rooted in homophobia, is central to the construction of traditional, hegemonic masculinity and its oppressive nature (Kimmel, 1994).

Evan's father-in-law taught him how to be a "very manly" man while at the same time being physically intimate, close, and affectionate with other men. The following key event in Evan's life story illustrates how he used the imago of his father-in-law to personalize and resolve the conflict between these two supposedly opposing images of masculinity:

He was what they call a man's man. He liked to hunt and fish and all that crap, but he was comfortable around other men. I remember one day I was driving the car. This guy who worked for him as his auctioneer, he and this fellow were great friends, and they were sitting next to each other, side by side, in the back seat of the car. Now I'm not talking about with a distance in between them, I'm talking about side. You know, RIGHT NEXT TO EACH OTHER [in a loud voice]. There wasn't three people in the car. In the back seat, THERE WERE TWO PEOPLE. They were great chummy and they could touch each other and they could . . . you know. You could tell this was a caring relationship. This was not a lover relationship, it was a caring relationship, and I remember seeing that, and actually, I didn't think it was odd. I thought it was great. But we are talking about a VERY male person. Not macho male, not guarding his masculine identity, but a very MALE person. That was a good influence. I think it helped me a lot.

Evan continued, describing another key event involving his father-in-law:

I remember one night, I took him in and put him to bed, got him to bed. And he said: "Aren't you gonna kiss me goodnight?" [long pause]. I'd never had a male [laughs] say to me: "Aren't you going to kiss me goodnight?" Now, he had five daughters. I'd seen his daughters kiss him goodnight. But him asking me was something that was totally alien to me. But, I never missed kissing him goodnight from there on out.

The implicit message in Evan's story is that it is normal and expected for men to be kissed by women but not men: "I'd seen his daughters kiss him goodnight," but kissing and being asked to kiss another man "was totally alien to me." The contrast that Evan established highlights the apparently unique ability of his father-in-law to integrate being loving, affectionate, and manly. His father-in-law provided an image of the kind of man Evan wants to be and helped Evan develop a less homophobic masculine identity.

By comparison, Evan's longtime friend David was not viewed as a mentor: "David is not as demonstrative. He had no one to learn it from. This is something you could learn from an older person and not feel threatened by. Like my father-in-law who was older to kind of take me by the hand and be the mentor about life." David's character functioned as an anti-imago, enabling Evan to establish his sense of masculinity by what he is not as well as what he is.

Imagoes in Dilip's Life History

Dilip also drew on the lives of people in his family who courageously fought for justice or personal change and inspired similar changes in his own life. For example, the transformations that Dilip's father made in his life gave Dilip the confidence to attempt similarly radical changes in his own life:

My dad was an alcoholic businessperson in a very white supremacist arena, which was advertising. He quit his job, and he quit drinking, and he bought a couple of businesses, and now he's a substance abuse counselor. Ultimately, what that did for me was the sense of, my dad changed. At forty years old, my dad decided that he wasn't going to live this life any more [hits hands together]. And at twenty years old, I can decide that I don't want to be racist, I don't want to be sexist, I don't want to be homophobic, I don't want to be a successful lawyer, I don't want to be a powerful politician. I need to change my life too.

Dilip was also inspired by the more distant lives of men such as Gandhi and Malcolm X. These heroic figures coalesced into a more general imago of a Liberator with whom Dilip identified. Dilip became very motivated to change the way in which sexism and racism had affected his life and the hierarchical, competitive model of masculinity on which these oppressions were based.

But the Liberator imago was too perfect for Dilip to attain himself. Like the version of masculinity it sought to replace, the Liberator became another way in which Dilip could measure his achievement, while ignoring his and others' feelings, desires, and limitations. He had returned to the same dynamic that originally motivated his changes:

Being the Liberator was part of this whole sense of like, "I need to perform and I need to carve out an identity for myself." My new identity was like being a radical activist. As I lost this sense of, "I need to be David Dillinger, I need to be Gandhi," as I lost that kind of status, I also lost the sense of, "I need to be antioppressive." So maybe it was all just a status thing. Now I'm trying to be much more genuine. Like, "what can I do in my own life and in the community around me and in my relationships to be as nonoppressive as possible?" And it's no longer a status thing. I have to deal with myself. The man in the mirror kind of thing.

Imagoes in Jeff's Life History

Jeff spoke most explicitly about characters who were once imagoes in his life but later seemed to function as anti-imagoes: Clint Eastwood, men he knew who were in the military, and his father's imago, John Wayne, who was also influential in Jeff's story: "My experience in being a male was the modeling that my father gave me. He owns like every John Wayne movie [chuckles] there is. There's a poster of John Wayne he has hanging in his garage. He emulates, kind of looks up to, that kind of male figure. And I think that that certainly had an influence on me."

Another of Jeff's models was similar to his father's hero, John Wayne, in terms of the characteristics the imago represented and the medium in which the imago was presented. Both were famous movie actors who represented a stoic, masculine character:

My model was Clint Eastwood. The strong silent type. I've grown past that now, but certainly that was the image that I had. He might say five or six lines in the whole movie [chuckles] and no expression of the emotion. In *The Line of Fire* he plays this old, old secret service agent, and actually tears up, and has some tears, and wow! That was amazing to me. I thought to myself, This is not Clint Eastwood! [laughs]

As a young boy, Jeff spent many hours at his father's service station, where he met older men who influenced his sense of masculinity:

Some of the men, I really idealized. There was a lot of hero stuff going on. For example, the head mechanic. When I was about nine or ten, I always had kind of a militaristic interest. My father was in the military. My brother went off and was in the air force for six years and in the military police. And that was kind of attractive to me. This head mechanic, he had done two tours in Vietnam, and he was this incredibly handsome guy [whom Jeff described as "incredibly strong, very quiet, no sharing of emotion, very self-contained, very self-reliant, doesn't need anybody else"]. I idealized him, I mean he was kind of a hero to me. He showed me how to whittle, and when there weren't cars to work on we did things like making sling shots and rubber-band guns. He taught me things about cars too. I always thought: "I want to be a marine" 'cause he was a marine and it just seemed cool.

Just as changes in the characters that Eastwood has played over time correspond to popular changes in masculine ideals (Jeffords, 1994), Jeff's imago changed over time. When Jeff was a boy, the silent, stoic Clint Eastwood was his hero. As he grew older, Jeff became interested in the expressive forum of music, and his imago changed. In Jeff's words, "Being a musician is not being the John Wayne type, and it did give me a real chance to get in touch with some kind of feeling of the things that were going on inside."

Again, as with the other men in the group (Donald's Gandhi versus Terminator; Dilip's Liberator versus more genuine self), there was an ongoing conflict in Jeff's life between a feeling and expressive masculinity and numb action. This conflict is illustrated in Jeff's description of a struggle he had in his early adult years as a school teacher trying to cope with unruly students:

There was the John Wayne part of me that said: "I should be able to handle this and kick them into shape and make 'em straighten up." And the more sensitive musician, spiritual part of me was saying: "Come on, you know, what they need is some compassion and some love and some understanding and some empathy." And I think that those two parts of me have always kind of struggled with each other. I feel like now the more feeling side, the more empathic side, is the stronger voice, but I can still. . . . Sometimes with our dog, I can get gruff and drill sergeant like and yell at her, and I know that doesn't do any good logically. But it still comes up. Those are remnants of the masculine model or image that I had, that I should be that way.

Jeff is now studying to be a counselor and has continued making similar changes in his life:

I feel like I've grown tremendously in the area of being more expressive, more comfortable with the more sensitive side of myself, and much, much, much more comfortable with being more open and more honest and more direct and disclosing.

Imagoes in Marty's Life History

Marty's life takes several turns that can also be described in terms of the imagoes that characterize his life story. His imagoes were similar to Dilip's in that they drew on a general category of persons who write about and work for social justice. For example, guidance was offered by the feminist writer Mary Daly, whom Marty credits as being particularly influential in transforming his understanding of being male and masculine from a Christian-based to a feminist-based ideology:

I trace it back to becoming radicalized in my freshman year of college, and to really starting to see the world in different ways, and the end of my life as a Christian. I owe very much to feminism, particularly to Mary Daly, if I'm honest. In her book, *Gyn/ecology* [1978], she talks about the paradigms of Christianity—God the Father who comes down and basically rapes this woman, takes her, and she does his will. What a sick, perverse way of looking at the world. It was a good antidote. It rang true with a lot of what I knew about men and guys and the world.

As others have noted, having a close relationship with a feminist can be a key factor in becoming an antisexist man (Christian, 1994). Marty spoke about his partner's role in his changing sense of masculinity and his desire to have closer relationships with other men:

Most guys who arrived at some kind of antisexist, profeminist view of the world have been pushed or challenged by women. It did not pop into my head by myself. Kay [his wife] was a big influence. That got me interested in reading, thinking about it, realizing some things in my own life. One of the things that was most troubling to me was to realize that I didn't have any men friends, really. A lot of guys I knew just didn't have close male friends. And that seemed real weird. When I went to Indiana, a group of us started a men's group.

SUMMARY AND CONCLUSIONS

Men's peer mutual support groups are a setting in which men are redefining masculinity and their relationships with other men. By documenting the source of role models and idealized characters in men's lives and describing the functions of these role models in their life histories, we can see how such characters are used in men's groups to transform the meaning of masculinity and reduce gender role strain (Pleck, 1995).

Sources of Imagoes

Potential role models in men's life stories are depicted in the cinema, sports, and books, but most importantly in the lives of other men they know. Although the concept of mentor was influential in Evan's life story, imagoes based in mythopoetic men's movement writing appear to be not as influential as the other men in the group. The warrior character, for example, was not specifically used by men in the group. However, characteristics ascribed to the warrior by some mythopoetic writers (e.g., focused energy, accountability, integrity; Jesser, 1996) are also descriptive of group members' imagoes. For example, Donald noted some of these characteristics in the Terminator when discussing the focus required to complete his dissertation and in Gandhi when describing his own struggle to live a nonviolent life with integrity.

The primary and most influential source of role models for the group members' lives appears to be the other men in the group, as indicated by the men in the focus group discussion. This suggests that the relationships formed among participants in a men's peer mutual support group have a greater impact on the group narrative and on the way in which masculinity is redefined than the idealized characters and role models presented in men's movement literature. The real work of men's groups may be creating intimacy with other men in the group and addressing barriers to it (e.g., homophobia), rather than an abstract or intellectualized image or archetype of this work.

Functions of Imagoes

Imagoes can be used to reconstruct masculinity in several different ways. First, characters can function as ideal, possible selves in childhood recollections of being a boy. In the men's group, these characters were generally positive, nonviolent images of power or ability and were present in their life stories before major difficulties or crises related to masculinity had been experienced (e.g., Willy Mays, military figures).

Other characters function as negative or feared self-images in the life story. These anti-imagoes were used by the men to describe times when it was necessary to deny emotion or get work done (e.g., the Terminator, John Wayne).

A third group of imagoes functions as positive models and are developed later in adult life, often in the context of a men's group, and they contradict oppressive anti-imagoes. These characters guided the liberation of group members' stories (e.g., Gandhi, the Liberator, Evan's father-in-law, Christian working for social justice) and the reconstruction of masculinity toward gentler, more expressive, or more creative forms in the men's lives.

Using Role Models to Resolve Gender Role Strain

Gender role strain stems from men's attempts to live up to contradictory and damaging demands of their gender role ideal (Pleck, 1995) and has been associated with a range of negative outcomes (McCreary, et al., 1996). For example, recall Jeff's struggle with being punishing versus empathetic in his relationship with his students. On the one hand, the ideal represented by Clint Eastwood demanded that he act tough and unforgiving. On the other hand, a part of himself, represented by other men in the men's group, felt he should be more understanding and considerate of the students' needs. Jeff experienced a conflict between these two role models and struggled to reconcile them in his life. His resolution of this narrative conflict may translate into reduced gender role strain.

Suppression of feelings and emotions is another self-destructive consequence of fulfilling men's gender role ideals. Donald's suppression of feelings and emotions when writing his dissertation became a normative part of his masculinity. At the time, Donald may have viewed this suppression uncritically. Through identification with other group members as role models, however, Donald created a story that takes a more critical view of emotional suppression and self-mockingly relates it to the image of the Terminator. While the emotional suppression may have helped him to finish the dissertation in the short term, it was damaging and partially contributed to harmful angry and violent outbursts later in his life.

These aspects of gender role conflict highlight how men feel both powerful and powerless in the face of conflicting demands made by masculine ideology and feminism. Situated between these conflicting ideologies, men experience a sense of threat to their identity (Breakwell, 1983; 1986). In peer mutual support groups, men struggle to find a voice to faithfully describe their experience, particularly as it relates to gender. Growing up, men have damaging experiences of isolation and violence that are coded in and justified by the language of hypermasculinity (Pleck, 1981; Connell, 1990). In describing these experiences, the group members are allied with feminist critiques of hypermasculinity. On the other hand, as they grow older, the apparent power, control, and reward that accompany male status lurk as a tempting and comforting trade-off for the pain of isolation, competition, and violence.

The imagoes in the narrative of this men's peer mutual support group suggest ways of resolving this conflict by offering new possibilities and contradicting old presumptions about their masculinity. The men revisited their individual pasts with the accompanying strength and support of the other members of the group. Returning to the scenes in which they were isolated, neglected, or violated and those in which they have isolated, neglected, or violated others or themselves, they became able to tell stories about healing from these experiences. This ability was at least partially related to the group's facilitation of new interactions and experiences that precisely contradicted the old ones. For example, being intimate and connected in the group contradicted isolation, receiving attention contradicted neglect, and being touched gently contradicted violence.

The group's contradictions assisted the men in their attempts to resolve the problematic and contradictory experience of pain and power associated with masculinity (Kaufman, 1994) and to reduce gender role strain. On the one hand, the men experience themselves as unalterably male. On the other, they find aspects of their masculine experience and roles to be quite troublesome. The sharing of stories in the group created a common narrative about being male that enabled them to construct a tenable masculine identity. The narrative contains role models that lessen or resolve the conflict between being male and critical views of masculinity.

Critical Contextualization

Two concerns about the theoretical framework used in this chapter merit further discussion. First, basing my inquiry into the men's group on McAdams's (1988) life story model of identity, structures the account in several ways that obscure as well as enlighten the meaning of the group and the participants' lives. The intellectual roots of the concept of imago are found in the soil of Jungian psychology. Use of McAdams's framework in studying men's groups makes sense because Jungian psychology has strongly influenced beliefs about gender endorsed in and the activities of mythopoetic men's support groups (Schwalbe, 1996). However, by asking specifically about role models in their lives, I ensured that the men's group participants would tell stories relevant to the theory. The fact that several of the men spontaneously discussed the importance of role models in their lives before being asked does, however, suggest that role models are an integral part of the men's understanding of their lives.

Second, from the context of feminism and women's responses to the men's movement (Hagan, 1992), it might be asked whether the men in the group have really changed or challenged the ways in which power and gender are intertwined in social structures. The men have established a safe space for themselves and in their group process come to feel better about themselves as men. However, these gains were possible in part because most of them have a privileged status in society as white, educated, financially secure, heterosexual males. They are not personally affected as men by structural inequality and injustice on a daily basis. Because of this, men in mythopoetic groups may be less motivated to create group ideology and practices that address these structural forces. Further still, they do not need such an ideology or practice in order for them to make personal changes or improve the quality of their lives with respect to these structural forces.

Profeminist men view the problem of masculinity in structural terms and believe that it is not possible for gender justice to be achieved through MPMS groups alone (Clatterbaugh, 1996; Stoltenberg, 1993). Individual men may work to end the negative effects of masculinity on their own lives, but ignore the negative impact of masculinity at structural levels of society, such as unequal pay for women who do the same work as men, differential rates of employment for men and women, and the existence of economic classes that result in competition between workers regardless of their gender.

Limitations and Future Research

Methodological limitations in this research prevent closer analysis of several important questions about the men's reconstruction of masculinity in mutual support groups. First, because the individual interviews were conducted at one point in time, only retrospective but no prospective developmental trends could be described (or observed). To analyze such trends, life histories could be collected from new members as part of the process of joining a group.

A second way in which studies of identity construction in MPMS groups could be improved is to include the voices of men who participated in but subsequently chose to leave their group. The information these men could provide might be crucial for understanding how and why group narratives are established, preserved, and ritualized or institutionalized. One question to be asked from this standpoint is why men seek participation in a support group but elect not to join, or join but subsequently decide to leave groups, and what role the group narrative plays in these decisions. In other words, why is the narrative a useful resource to some men but not others, or at one point in their lives but not later?

Finally, it would be interesting to see whether the social and psychological processes observed in this group also characterize men's groups with different ideological and substantive views about men and masculinity (e.g., conservative men's groups such as Promise Keepers, socialist men's groups, gay men's groups, profeminist men's groups). Information from such comparative studies is necessary to determine the implications of this case study for men's wide-ranging efforts to challenge (or preserve) hegemonic forms of masculinity.

NOTES

1. As with other scientific methods, the reliability of the data generated from these procedures is attributable to careful recording of observations repeated over time with the same instrument (in this case, an interview protocol and tape recorder). The validity or trustworthiness of the interviews and their analysis can be attributed to several aspects of the procedure used to generate them: extensive development and piloting of the protocol, checking with members about the accuracy of the resulting transcripts, my long-term and extensive participant observation of the group, and numerous consultations that I had throughout the data collection and analysis about the meaning of the interviews and my observations of the group with colleagues who were not members of the group (Lincoln & Guba, 1985).

2. All participants were assigned pseudonyms.

REFERENCES

Andronico, M. P. (Ed.), (1996). *Men in groups: Insights, interventions, and psycho-educational work.*

Betcher, R. W., & Pollack, W. S. (1993). *In a time of fallen heroes: The recreation of masculinity.* New York: Guilford.

Brannon, R. (1976). The male sex role: Our culture's blueprint for manhood and what it's done for us lately. In D. David & R. Brannon (Eds.), *The forty-nine percent majority: The male sex role* (pp. 1–48). Reading, MA: Addison-Wesley.

Breakwell, G. M. (1983). *Threatened identities*. New York: Wiley.

Breakwell, G. M. (1986). *Coping with threatened identities*. London: Methuen.

Chesler, M. A. (1991). Participatory action research with self-help groups: An alternative paradigm for inquiry and action. *American Journal of Community Psychology, 19*, 757–768.

Christian, H. (1994). *The making of anti-sexist men*. London: Routledge.

Clatterbaugh, K. (1997). *Contemporary perspectives on masculinity: Men, women, and politics in modern society*. 2nd ed. Boulder, CO: Westview Press.

Connell, R. W. (1987). *Gender and power: Society, the person and sexual politics*. Standford, CA: Stanford University Press.

Connell, R. W. (1990). A whole new world: Remaking masculinity in the context of the environmental movement. *Gender and Society, 4* (4), 452–478.

Daly, M. (1978). *Gyn/ecology: The metaethics of radical feminism*. Boston: Beacon Press.

Eisler, R. M. (1995). The relationship between masculine gender role stress and men's health risk: The validation of a construct. In R. F. Levant & W. S. Pollack (Eds.), *A new psychology of men* (pp. 207–225). New York: Basic Books.

Gilbert, R. K. (1992). Revisiting the psychology of men: Robert Bly and the mythopoetic movement. *Journal of Humanistic Psychology, 32*, 41–67.

Hagan, K. L. (1992). *Women respond to the men's movement*. San Francisco: HarperCollins.

Hughes, D., & DuMont, K. (1993). Using focus groups to facilitate culturally anchored research. *American Journal of Community Psychology, 21*, 775–806.

Jeffords, S. (1994). *Hard bodies: Hollywood masculinity in the Reagan era*. New Brunswick, NJ: Rutgers University Press.

Jesser, C. J. (1996). *Fierce and tender men: Sociological aspects of the men's movement*. Westport, CT: Praeger.

Kaufman, M. (1994). Men, feminism, and men's contradictory experiences of power. In H. Brod & M. Kaufman (Eds.), *Theorizing masculinities* (pp. 142–163). Thousand Oaks, CA: Sage.

Kauth, B. (1992). *A circle of men: The original manual for men's support groups*. New York: St. Martin's Press.

Kimmel, M. S. (1987). The contemporary "crisis" of masculinity in historical perspective. In H. Brod (Ed.), *The making of masculinities: The new men's studies* (pp. 121–150). Cambridge, MA: Unwin Hyman.

Kimmel, M. S. (1994). Masculinity as homophobia: Fear, shame, and silence in the construction of gender identity. In H. Brod & M. Kaufman (Eds.), *Theorizing masculinities* (pp. 119–141). Thousand Oaks, CA: Sage.

Kupers, T. A. (1993). *Revisioning men's lives: Gender, intimacy, and power*. New York: Guilford.

Levant, R. (1995). *Masculinity reconstructed: Changing the rules of manhood: at work, in relationships, and in family life*. New York: Dutton.

Lincoln, Y. S., & Guba, E. G. (1985). *Naturalistic inquiry*. Beverly Hills, CA: Sage.

Mankowski, E. S. (1997). *Community, identity, and masculinity: Changing men in a mutual support group*. Unpublished doctoral dissertation, University of Illinois at Urbana-Champaign.

Mankowski, E. S., & Rappaport, J. (1995). Stories, identity, and the psychological sense of community. In R. S. Wyer, Jr. (Ed.), *Advances in social cognition: Vol. 8. Knowledge and memory: The real story* (pp. 211–226). Hillsdale, NJ: Erlbaum.

Markus, H., & Nurius, P. (1986). Possible selves. *American Psychologist, 41*, 954–969.

McAdams, D. (1988). *Power, intimacy, and the life story: Personological inquiries into identity.* New York: Guilford.

McAdams, D. P. (1993). *The stories we live by: Personal myths and the making of the self.* New York: Morrow.

McCarthy, B. (1994). Warrior values: A socio-historical survey. In J. Archer (Ed.), *Male violence* (pp. 105–120). London: Routledge.

McCreary, D. R., Wong, F. Y., Wiener, W., Carpenter, K. M., Engle, A., & Nelson, P. (1996). The relationship between masculine gender role stress and psychological adjustment: A question of construct validity? *Sex Roles, 34*, 507–516.

Moore, R., & Gillette, D. (1990). *King, warrior, magician, lover.* San Francisco: Harper San Francisco.

O'Neil, J. M. (1991). Male sex-role conflicts, sexism, and masculinity: Psychological men, women and the counseling psychologist. *Counseling Psychologist, 9*, 61–80.

Pleck, J. H. (1981). *The myth of masculinity.* Cambridge: MIT Press.

Pleck, J. H. (1995). The gender role strain paradigm: An update. In R. F. Levant & W. S. Pollack (Eds.), *A new psychology of men* (pp. 11–32). New York: Basic Books.

Pleck, J. H., Sonenstein, F. L., & Ku, L. C. (1993). Masculinity ideology and its correlates. In S. Oskamp & M. Costanzo (Eds.), *Gender and social psychology* (pp. 85–110). Newbury Park, CA: Sage.

Richards, L., & Richards, T. (1991). The NUDIST Qualitative Data Analysis System. *Qualitative Sociology, 14*, 307–324.

Schwalbe, M. (1996). *Unlocking the iron cage: The men's movement, gender politics, and American culture.* New York: Oxford University Press.

Segal, L. (1990). *Slow motion: Changing masculinities, changing men.* New Brunswick, NJ: Rutgers University Press.

Sternbach, J. (1990). The men's seminar: An educational and support group for men. *Social Work with Groups, 13*, 23–29.

Stoltenberg, J. (1993). *The end of manhood: A book for men of conscience.* New York: Dutton.

Williams, R. C., & Myer, R. A. (1992). The men's movement: An adjunct to traditional counseling approaches. *Journal of Mental Health Counseling, 14*, 393–404.

PART II
THERAPEUTIC APPLICATIONS

Chapter 8
The Use of Myth and Quasi-Myth in Therapy
Ross Thomas Lucas

Myth has been used as an adjunct for therapy for a considerable time, recently as an effective way of getting at material that might otherwise be inaccessible to the client. There are times when there is a need for a particular myth subject, but when the therapist does not know a myth to fit the need, it may be helpful to create a quasi-myth to meet the specific need.

It is a generally accepted fact that women are more likely to come for therapy than men. A common hypothesis is that men are more hesitant than women to talk about their feelings. Due to this hesitance to share feelings, one difficulty a therapist faces is getting men to move beyond their intellectualizations and rationalizations. To be successful in therapy, one has to move beyond the intellectual smoke screens. Myth provides one way of moving beyond the smoke screen and into the male psyche. A case study approach will be used to illustrate how quasi-myth works in a particular therapy case.

The client is a middle-aged man. He has been somewhat successful in life but is now experiencing a depression that saps his energy and leaves him feeling unfulfilled. As a result, he has entered therapy. Now, after several sessions where there appears to be little or no progress, the therapist is frustrated and thinking of making a referral. The stalemate in therapy is that no matter how the man is approached, change does not seem to occur. The man's psychological defense structures are such that he cannot see a different way of relating to the world than what he has always done. What can the therapist do to help this man see new possibilities?

Men are accomplished at defending themselves from change. They have an elaborate process of rationality and rationalizations to keep them from looking too closely at painful material. In part, this comes from the attitude of competition that is taught to so many men by our society. For a man to admit that his way is not necessarily the best way may be very risky. Related to this competition is the need for many men to be right. To admit to being wrong or to not already knowing the best way of living is seen as dangerous. A less threatening approach is needed.

Using myth, storytelling, or fantasy as a means of getting beyond rational defenses is not a new approach. Men have been storytellers for untold ages. As they listen to stories, they can stand outside the story with their defenses apparently intact. However, the story can go beyond the intellectual defenses and have an impact on the man, his perception of himself, and his world.

In years gone by, men would sit in a hypnotic setting around a campfire and share stories that had been passed from generation to generation. The ones that taught about significant aspects of life and endured have become known as myths. These myths have changed people's lives and still have the power to change lives.

A myth is more than just a good story; it is "also made of the stuff of the world" (Schwartz-Salant, 1992). A myth is not something told just for fun, although entertainment can be one reason for the telling. Ultimately the myth exists and is told because it represents a very real part of life. A myth is simultaneously a teaching tool, a diagnostic tool, and a healing tool. It can be all of these things because, like a dream and a metaphor, it can draw the listener or reader toward something that is inherently familiar (Bolen, 1992).

The images in myth do more than express an individual's psyche; they are part and parcel of the experience of the whole human race. Myths teach basic human truths, providing insight into living (Flowers, 1988) and facilitating change in people (Campbell, 1972). Without any claim to factuality, they tell us the truth in the language of metaphor and symbol (Bolen, 1992).

One of the values of a myth is its universal nature. The myth allows a backdoor entrance into understanding one's self and the world. "Myths bypass the mind's effort to divorce emotion from information" (Bolen, 1992). According to Singer (1990), "The secrets of the psyche come to light in myth, metaphor and ritual. Metaphor is the word, myth is the story, and ritual is the enactment of the story that is built up of words."

Myths are not individual creations. They arise out of the "collective unconscious" of the human race. According to Carl Jung, there are two aspects of the unconscious: the "personal unconscious," which is what Freud and much of modern psychology focuses on, and the "collective unconscious." Although awareness of the material contained in the collective unconscious will vary from person to person, it is part of the entire human race. It is within the collective unconscious that myth is born. In a similar vein, Joseph Campbell (1972) refers to myths as "public dreams."

Myth has probably been with us as long as humankind has been around (Campbell, 1972). In different cultures in widely separated areas of the world, similar myths arise. The exact details may be different, but the substance is the same from place to place and from time to time. The implication is that there are universal themes associated with being human (Flowers, 1988). These themes emerge in public as myth.

MYTH IN THERAPY

Psychotherapy has become an important aspect of healing. In psychotherapy, an individual confronts thinking, feeling, spiritual elements, and behaviors in his or her life and is then able to enhance life in ways she or he desires.

Myths can be a particularly potent force in the psychotherapeutic process. In fact, they may have been the first psychotherapeutic interventions. There are times in psychotherapy where a client does not seem to improve in spite of a stated desire for change in behavior. Many times that stalemate is a result of the client's not being ready or able to face certain truths about herself or himself.

Another way of conceptualizing the lack of readiness to face himself or herself is to understand that the client does not yet feel safe to change. One of the major needs in life is physical, emotional, and spiritual security. It matters little if the security is real or only apparent. "In exchange for the promise of security, many people put a barrier between themselves and the adventure of consciousness" (Singer, 1972). Other terms used to describe the client's lack of safety are *resistance* and *denial*. I do not claim that real security and false security are the same thing. If the security is false, there will be a part of the person that is aware of that and still live in anxiety and fear. The difficulty is sometimes that false security is more familiar than the real security a person might have and thus held onto tightly.

One task of the therapist is to move the client beyond fear. Myth is one way of doing this. The appropriate and timely use of myth can be the difference between progress for a client and a stalemate in therapy. The key is in timing and in selecting the right myth.

Myth can be used to approach threatening material symbolically. People have long used symbols as a way of dealing with material that is beyond their comprehension in one way or another. One way the personal unconscious attempts to deal with threatening materials in a symbolic way is through dreams. Starting long before Sigmund Freud and continuing into the present, dreams have been seen as part of the healing of the mind and soul of people. Joseph Campbell refers to myths as "collective dreams." The dream is the expression of the individual unconscious, and the myth is the expression of the collective unconscious. Myths and dreams are both symbolic creations, and the symbol-making capacity is a part of the healing process (Jung, 1964).

Denial is a type of self-imposed blindness. Because of fear of discomfort, a client may choose to remain in the blindness. When this happens, a different pain is substituted for the one that is feared. In therapy, it is essential to find a way of aiding the client to move beyond the denial and understand what is happening. First, the client must "see" what is happening in life. Otherwise the client can do little to change. To "see" something one has to conceive of the possibility of whatever it is existing. Rollo May (1969) said, "I cannot perceive something until I can conceive." Once the client has conceived of something, it must then be fit into a context that can be understood. Myth provides a way for the client to perceive something that might not be seen in another way. It also provides a context within which what is seen can fit.

Myths are valuable assets to the therapy process because they "make an impression, are remembered, and nudge us to find out what they mean" (Bolen, 1992). Whitmont (1969) points out that the "symbolic approach can mediate an experience of something indefinable, intuitive or imaginative, or a feeling-sense of something that can be known or conveyed in no other way."

Jungian psychologists have perhaps made the most extensive and efficient use of myth lore. A particular myth will be used to give a client a point of identification related to a particular issue. As the client understands the substance of the myth, she or he will have an opportunity for learning (i.e. change). The myth may give insight into the client's current situation and may also provide a vision toward which the client may work. The important thing is that it promotes growth.

The therapist does not always need to know how the client is going to make use of a myth. By attending to the client and connecting what is said to a myth, the therapist may help the client to make connections that the therapist is not even aware of needing to be made. The key is attending to the client.

Although Jungian analysis is usually a long-term psychotherapeutic process, myth is also useful in short-term therapy. In order for therapy to be successful, the client must first come to some understanding of what the issues are. When the amount of time is limited, it is crucial to get that understanding as quickly as possible.

The right myth can help an understanding of the issues to develop in a shorter time. Because myths arise out of a common understanding of life, they provide a context for the client. Within that context, the client will be able to grasp a whole series of meanings within a myth which, with other techniques, might have to be teased out one at a time.

Cognitive psychology puts considerable emphasis on the concept of a schema—a collection of patterns of thought that give meaning to life. The goal of therapy is to identify those schema that are helpful and those that are not. The client may then work to alter less helpful schema so as to provide a better overall adjustment to life.

When a client is stuck in therapy, there may be the cognition that he or she is the only person who has ever had or faced a particular situation. This client may have developed a "schema" that places him or her in a unique, and often impossible, situation. The goal is to correct distorted schema that direct the client's life in ways that are less than helpful. Because of the universal nature of myth, the right myth may illuminate the schema and the distortions associated with it, and offer corrective options for the client. At that point the negative schema can change.

CREATING MYTH AS A PART OF THERAPY

There is an extant lore of myth that is diverse and meaningful. There are myths that can be applied to many, if not most, life situations. Just because the myth is set in a different culture or time does not make it less effective. Jung (1964) points out in *Man and His Symbols* that "we read the myths of the ancient Greeks or the folk tales of American Indians, but we fail to see any connection between them and our attitude to the 'heroes' or dramatic events of today. Yet the connections are there. And the symbols that represent them have not lost their relevance for mankind."

We can also use fairy tales as sources of myth. "In most cultures, there is no clear line separating myth from folk or fairy tale, all these together form the literature of preliterate societies" (Bettelheim, 1975). Indeed, the combined mass of literature from both myth and fairy tale is sizable. Nevertheless, despite the abundance of material, a particular therapist may or may not know the myth that will fit a particular situation. What may then be helpful is to create a myth or a quasi-myth to address a particular situation.

In actuality, no one can create a myth. "You cannot predict what a myth is going to be anymore than you can predict what you're going to dream tonight. Myths and dreams come from the same place. They come from realizations of some kind that have then to find expression in symbolic form" (Flowers, 1988). True myth arises out of the collective unconscious or out of a common human schema over a long period of time. A particular myth evolves within a particular culture and instructs about the "values, patterns and assumptions on which the culture is based" (Bolen, 1992). Because one cannot say what will be myth or not, I refer to these creations of mythlike stories by the therapist as quasi-myths.

Although the exact mixture of the components of a quasi-myth may vary, the substance is usually there in one form or another. A quasi-myth needs some mixture of three elements in its creation: distance, generalizability, and power.

Distance appears to be part of most of the myth literature. Myths are usually set in distant lands or distant times or both. Common beginnings for myths are "Long ago . . ." and "In a land far away . . ." Distance is important so the client can view the myth with some degree of detachment. In creating a quasi-myth, there is a temptation to place the story in a context that is too close to the client. If the myth is too close to the client, the fear that is blocking growth will be harder to overcome. The usefulness of the intervention will be greatly diminished.

Another component needed in therapeutic myth is generalizibility. Myths by their nature are specific about a situation, but can be applied generally to many different situations. If the quasi-myth is too specific, it will lose its effectiveness, and if it is too general, the client may not make the needed connections.

Finally, the myth is about a being who has or is overcome by power or who loses power or finds power. The element of power says that there is something that is happening or can happen. Life does not just remain the same.

A CASE STUDY

A case can illustrate the use of quasi-myth in therapy. The subject is a white male in his mid-thirties who has been professionally successful but has struggled with issues of self-esteem for many years. He was in therapy once before for a period of two years and came to this therapist because his attitude toward himself was not changing.

In the process of therapy it became apparent that he was fixated on the idea of his being unworthy and unlovable, and he was constantly searching for the answer of how he could be more lovable. A major theme was that he had never felt important in his father's eyes. Rather, he felt rejected and saw all his fear of rejection as being related to his father.

At about the sixth session, it became apparent that the client had long ago built strong intellectual defenses. He was able to understand the dynamics of therapy and could explain the etiology of his problems yet could not get beyond his belief system, which resulted in his low self-esteem. At this point it appeared appropriate to use a myth to help him move beyond the intellectualization and negative schema.

What seemed to be needed was a myth that had to do with a person not seeing what was apparent to others. When none of the myths that came to mind seemed to fit, the therapist developed a quasi-myth that contained an element of distance and an element of power and was generalizable rather than specific:

A long time ago in a land far away there was a kingdom. The kingdom was a wonderful place to live. There were beautiful lakes, great forests, majestic mountains, and picturesque villages. The people who lived there were happy and loved their life, their kingdom, and their king.

The king was a wise and good king. He sought to care for his people in the best way he could. He listened to their concerns and tried to meet their needs. He was loved and respected by all the people of the kingdom.

The king had a son. He and his son would play together often. They would climb trees together, swim in the lakes together, and explore the wilderness together. The father loved his son, and the son loved his father, and they were good friends.

One day the boy went all by himself to explore in the nearby village. He walked the streets, sampled the food, and played with the children of the village. The children of the village, nor the adults for that matter, did not recognize that the little boy stranger was actually the king's son. And the little boy did not think of his father as the king, but rather as his father and his friend.

For several days, the little boy went to the village and played with his new friends. Each evening, long before dark, he would return to his house, the king's castle, by a round-about way.

One day he and his friends were playing in the village square where some of the men gathered to talk. He overheard them talk about a great king who was very wise and just. He heard them say what a wonderful man this king was and the boy's image of the king was of someone larger than life. He decided that the great king was someone he would like to see.

The boy was used to talking to grown-ups, so he did not hesitate to ask where they had seen the great king. One man said he had seen the king in the forest. Another man said he had seen the king down by the lake at the foot of the mountains. They all agreed that the king lived in a great and marvelous castle. They talked about the beauty of it and the great tapestries that hung on the walls and the great statues in the courtyard and the great throne where the king sat. The castle was the grandest thing any of the men had seen.

The little boy was fascinated and decided he had to meet this king. He sat in the square alone thinking and planning how he would go about finding the great king. The boy was so lost in thought that he forgot about the time, and soon it was dark, yet he still sat in the village square thinking and planning. He forgot all about getting back to his home before dark. Long after the others had gone to bed, he still sat lost in thought.

His thinking was interrupted when the Captain of the King's Guard came up and spoke to him. "Your father is very worried," the Captain said.

The boy felt terrible when he realized the time, and he quickly joined the Captain, whom he had known all his life, and together they returned to the castle.

He went through the castle gates, the gates he had seen all of his life. Together he and the Captain entered the grand hall. He paid little attention to the wall hangings; they were something he had always lived with. The statues were familiar and were like old friends.

The Captain stopped as they entered the hall, and the boy ran the length of the hall to the chair where his father often sat. The chair was raised off the floor and was very ornamental and valuable, but the boy noticed none of this. He noticed none of it because he was looking at the eyes of his father, eyes that still held traces of tears but which were now filled with a look of relief.

As the son ran toward the father, the father sprang from his throne, and they met in a great embrace. The father cried tears of relief, and the son shed tears of sadness that he had worried his father.

However, the excitement the boy had felt upon hearing of the wise and great king was still burning in his heart. He began to tell his father of the wise and great king that the people in the village had spoken about. He went over all the things he had heard and all the plans he had made for finding the great king and talking to him.

The king, in his wisdom, listened to his son. When the son finished, the king stood and put his arm around his son and walked with him toward the sleeping quarters. He told his son how proud he was of him for wanting to know people who were wise and just.

At the door to his son's bedroom, the king stopped and hugged his son. He smiled at him and said, "Some day soon, if you want, I will go with you to look for this great and wise king."

With that statement from the king, the quasi-myth ended.

The effect on the client was interesting. At first he simply sat quietly. When he did start to talk, he identified himself with the boy and his father with the king. This was disturbing to him because of the way his father had been when he was growing up. In no way was his father like the great and wise king. The therapist remained silent, waiting for the man to process his own thoughts. After a few more moments of silence, the man spoke again. He looked up and smiled. He then said something to the effect, "You know, I am both the boy and the king." He went on to say what other people say about him. It was the first time that he acknowledged that at work and with friends, he is respected and appreciated. In many ways, it was as if he were seeing himself for the first time. On that note, the session ended.

Note that the power of this quasi-myth does not lie in its rationality. It is not rational that the boy would be allowed to go off alone, that people who lived near the castle would not recognize the king's son, or that the boy would not know that his father was king. The lack of rationality did nothing to lessen the impact of the story. "The unrealistic nature of these tales . . . is an important device, because it makes obvious the fairy tales concern is not useful information about the external world, but the inner processes taking place in an individual" (Bettelheim, 1975).

What is particularly interesting is that the myth continued to work beyond the initial telling. The client continued having insights about himself. In several subsequent sessions, he related some new insight coming from the story.

Over the course of the next two months the man changed the way he viewed himself. The therapist did not refer to the story again; however, on at least three occasions the man referred back to the story. Once he indicated that he had been thinking about the story and was coming to understand that he was a good man and had just not seen it. He was able to see things about himself that he had blocked in the past.

In what was a surprising twist for the therapist, one time he identified his father with the little boy in the story, always searching and never finding himself. It was the first time that he had begun to see the dynamics at work in his father that indicated that the father's action toward him may have been the father's issues and not something actually about the client.

The third occasion that the story was referred to was just before closing therapy. He commented that he was hoping to teach his children the story so they could understand that they were great people.

The story has been reused with a variety of persons, both men and women, and although it has varied some from telling to telling, the results have been similar in each case. Each client has come to see the significance of the story for her or his life and has grown because of the connections he or she has made.

CONCLUSION

All therapy techniques pose inherent and unique risks, and this is no less true of the use of myth or quasi-myth. One of the dangers is that the therapist may project personal material into the selection of the story. It is incumbent on the therapist who is using a myth to be aware of his or her own projections. One signal that a myth may be part of the therapist's projections is that the therapist becomes overly invested in the story. If the therapist has to make the story fit the client, then it may be more of a story about the therapist.

Another indicator of the possible misuse of myth is when a myth is used in every session. An unskilled or inexperienced therapist may try to use myth to cover a limited repertoire of interventions. Myth is only one of many therapy tools. A therapist who relies on myth to work without understanding the psychological dynamics risks doing injury to the client.

REFERENCES

Bettelheim, B. (1975). *The uses of enchantment*. New York: Vintage Books.

Bolen, J. S. (1992). *Ring of power*. San Francisco: Harper.

Campbell, J. (1972). *Myths to live by*. New York: Bantam Books.

Flowers, B. S. (1988). *Joseph Campbell: The power of myth with Bill Moyers*. New York: Anchor Books, Doubleday.

Henderson, J. L. (1964). Ancient myths and modern man. In C. Jung (Ed.), *Man and his symbols* (pp. 95–156). New York: Dell.

Jung, C. (Ed.) (1964). *Man and his symbols*. New York: Dell.

May, R. (1969). *Love and will*. New York: Norton.

Schwartz-Salant, N., & Stein, M. (Eds.). (1992). *Gender and soul in psychotherapy*. Wilmette, IL: Chiron Publications.

Singer, J. (1972). *Boundaries of the soul*. New York: Anchor Books.

Singer, J. (1990). *Seeing through the visible world*. San Francisco: Harper.

Whitmont, E. C. (1969). *The symbolic quest: Basic concepts of analytic psychology*. New York: Putnam.

Chapter 9

Working with Men from a Mythopoetic Perspective: An Integrity Therapy Framework
Nedra R. Lander and Danielle Nahon

Throughout the journey of life, human beings have sought rituals by which to celebrate its various stages and explain its mysteries. In early society, rituals provided men and women with the social structures needed in order for them to engage in this process. The Industrial Revolution, however, tore most men away from the earth and from the rituals that bound them to the rhythms of nature, the seasons of harvest, and hence the cycle of life. Consequently, many men have strived to find more conscious means to reach out and bond with other men and renew this relationship with earth and nature through communities aimed at understanding and celebrating life's stages and the integrity of their own life journeys. The mythopoetic branch of the contemporary men's movement seeks to provide men with the opportunity to engage in this reconnecting with the self, other men, and the planet. As Bliss (1995) says, the term *mythopoetic* "refers to remythologizing. It means re-working, so the mythopoetic approach means revisioning masculinity for our time" (pp. 292–293).

Although there is no official spokesperson for mythopoetic groups in North America and beyond, the popularization of the mythopoetic branch is often identified with the work of Bly (1990). Williams and Myer (1992) review the aim of the mythopoetic approach as that of bringing forth the "healing energies" of men, using ceremonies, drumming, storytelling, and other experiential approaches in order to allow participants to bring forth their innate or archetypal—a term derived from Jungian psychology—sense of masculinity. Bly emphasizes the use of ancient stories and myths in providing "a reservoir where we keep new ways of responding that we can adopt when the conventional and current ways wear out" (p. xi). He focuses on the story of Iron John—credited to the brothers Grimm as Iron Hans, but possibly many thousand of years older—and presented in translation by Bly (1990). Bly uses the symbolism of the story of Iron John to illustrate the process whereby a young man undergoes a journey of personal growth and personal transformation in order to integrate the deeper aspects of his masculine archetypes—in other words, his underlying sense of masculine identity—into his personality. In keeping with the theme of the mythopoetic branch, Moore and Gillette (1990) suggest that all human beings strive to become initiated into adulthood, including adult responsibilities, duties toward self and others, plus spirituality. They suggest that in order for men to reconnect with what they term the powerful archetypes of masculinity—the lover, the warrior, the magician, and the king—one can use several techniques: active imagination dialogue; invocation (defined as a conscious process of calling up desired images of the self); contact with older men whom one admires, possibly possessing older energy; and "acting as if," in other words, behaving like the archetype which one wishes to access.

There is little hard-core scientific research previously published in the arena of the mythopoetic branch, and more specifically about the process of personal change that occurs as a result of the mythopoetic journey. *Unlocking the Iron Cage* (Schwalbe, 1996) is a sociological participant observation case study of the process of a long-term mythopoetic group coupled with observations and interviews. Williams and Myer (1992) suggest that mythopoetic men's groups comprise an experientially based approach that can serve as an adjunct to traditional forms of psychotherapy. They note that "the use of myth and metaphor in this process is a powerful tool to sidestep the hesitancy that men typically exhibit toward the process of becoming affectively vulnerable during counselling" (p. 402). Guarnaschelli (1994), founder of On the Common Ground, a mythopoetic men's organization in New York City, articulates the goal of mythopoetic groups as that of enabling men to undergo a personal initiation through increased personal authenticity, contact with other men, and nurturing of society.

Although Williams and Myer (1992) have suggested that the mythopoetic group approach serves as a useful adjunct to traditional therapies for some men, no previously published study has systematically explored the relationship between the process of change inherent in the mythopoetic journey and the process of change inherent in traditional therapies.

In this chapter, we explore the connections and complementarities between integrity therapy (Lander, 1986; Lander & Nahon, 1992a; Mowrer, 1953) and the mythopoetic branch. It is our thesis that integrity therapy—an existential framework of psychotherapy that has been developed to include a unique focus in working with men (Nahon, 1986; Nahon & Lander, 1992)—is compatible with the mythopoetic framework.

INTEGRITY THERAPY

Philosophical Perspective: Integrity Therapy as an Existential Framework

Integrity therapy is an existential therapeutic framework in terms of both substance and form. The existential framework aims to clarify, reflect on, and understand life, focusing on the process of living (van Deurzen-Smith, 1988) and the uniqueness of individuals, their values, and the search for meaning in their lives (Coleman, 1976; Lowe, 1969). Following its existential basis, a major assumption underlying integrity therapy is that human beings have the capacity to choose between good and evil (Lander & Nahon, 1989). Existential therapy stands in stark contrast to the rationalist school of thought, which has tended to dominate psychology and psychotherapy, and argues that only through science and the empirical process can truth be known. Furthermore, the rationalist, cognitive-behavioral, and emotional perspectives of the process of therapy are based on the belief that the therapist has to do something to or for the other in order to get the other to change. In contrast with these perspectives, integrity therapy, based on the existential position, purports that truth is subjective and that the discovery of truth comprises a major life goal for human beings. Integrity therapy views the process of therapy as unique to each individual and to each context, and thus as one that cannot be "manualized"—in other words, cannot be presented in a cookbook approach. Integrity therapy stresses the client's equality to the therapist and the client's role in the therapeutic process (Lander & Nahon, 1992b, 1995). The process of change in therapy is seen as being the task and responsibility of the client rather than that of the therapist. From the integrity therapy framework, the therapist does not guide the client; rather, the client takes the lead, and the therapist follows.

In contrast with the reductionistic basis of other therapies, integrity therapy does not seek to translate psychotherapy into quantifiable constructs. Rather, it offers an operational definition of integrity as comprising honesty, responsibility, and increased emotional involvement with others. Its aim is to challenge individuals to examine and enhance their level of integrity within their relationships with both self and others, being sensitive to the context in which they occur. Each situation and each individual is viewed as unique, and the level of integrity of each encounter is viewed as reflecting the existential moment. Integrity therapy offers a simple yet comprehensive perspective, which one of our postdoctoral interns described as being profound in its Zen-like capacity to provide a simple yet mega-encompassing and universal framework with a remarkable tolerance for divergent views (H. de Groot, personal communication, 1997). The simplicity of integrity therapy can present the professional with a challenge because there is no lexicon or set of cryptic meanings to be mastered, thus belying the view that complexity implies credibility. Integrity therapy asks that the therapist use the language of the other rather than have the other learn the therapeutic jargon. Rather than using an artificial lexicon and destroying individuals' own voices by asking them to adopt the voice of the therapist, integrity therapy adopts everyday simple language in the context of therapy. In this chapter, we use poetic language, reminiscent of the lyrical nature of the story of Iron John, rather than attempt to emulate the sometimes antiseptic jargon of articles on therapy.

How does integrity therapy differ from other therapies that focus on the individual's unique search for the self (e.g., Rogers, 1992), or the genuineness of encounter characteristic of Gestalt therapy (Perls, 1989)? Could one not argue that in fact most therapies aim to allow for individuals to increase their level of honesty and involvement with others? And how does integrity therapy differ from the constructionist view of therapy (e.g., Rosen & Kuehlwein, 1996) or "therapy as narrative" (e.g., Russell & Wandrei, 1996)? Are we rediscovering the wheel? No. In its early roots based on the work of Mowrer (e.g., Mowrer, 1953), Integrity therapy has had a profound influence on other schools of thought. Examples of key integrity therapy concepts that have later been incorporated by other schools of thought include the importance of values and value clashes in psychotherapy, therapist authenticity, therapist self-disclosure, the importance of contracts in psychotherapy, and the role of religion and spiritual concepts in psychotherapy. The importance of using the client's own language has since been incorporated by feminist therapy in its focus on a consciousness of women's voices, women's perspectives, and women's ways of knowing.

Integrity therapy stands in contrast to the humanistic therapies that characterize the Rogerian (Rogers, 1992) and Gestalt (Perls, 1989) approaches. Lander and Nahon (1992b) have argued that the basic tenets of the humanistic therapies are potentially lacking in integrity and may set up a covert disempowerment of the client. Integrity therapy is distinct from all other therapeutic modalities, including other existential therapies, such as logotherapy (Frankl, 1992; Gerwood, 1998), in its overt and deliberate focus on integrity, as our organizing umbrella, to understand self as a being-in-the-world as well as a framework to guide and provide meaning to one's life; its belief that mental health arises from living with integrity and mental illness from a crisis of integrity; and its focus on value clashes and conflicts as the source of intra- and interpersonal stress. Furthermore, integrity therapy is unique in that it can either stand alone or complement other therapies.

Integrity Therapy: Foundations

Integrity therapy views mental illness as resulting from a personal lack of integrity with self and others (Lander & Nahon, 1988a, 1988b; Mowrer, 1961a). Integrity is operationally defined as comprising three necessary elements: honesty, responsibility, and increased emotional involvement with others (Mowrer, 1964a; Mower & Vattano, 1976), also known as closure of the emotional space with others (Lander & Nahon, 1995b).

Honesty means being open and truthful about one's feelings, attitudes, and actions—past, present, and future. It involves acknowledging past or present wrongdoings that may have caused problems in one's life or another's life and being willing to own 100 percent of one's "50 percent" in contributing to a dysfunctional interaction with others as the first step in resolving the conflict. In dealing with a personal or interpersonal transgression, this type of honesty becomes critical. After a person has been radically honest within a relationship, a strange and wondrous experience begins to take place: the very secrets hidden in fear of rejection from others have instead helped to draw others close. Past defensive behaviors and facades are no longer necessary. One can relax, be oneself, and begin to work on problems as they now exist.

Responsibility means making amends or setting things right once the acknowledgment of wrongdoing has been made. According to Mowrer (personal communication, 1970), it is not enough "to dump one's garbage," one must then do something about it. A person who has "gotten into a mess" must assume the responsibility for getting out of it. This approach, integrated with the honest accountability for one's transgressions, goes a long way toward ensuring that the others in a conflictual situation will be willing to listen. When one individual has been willing to become responsible to the other in this manner, the other will more often than not come forward nondefensively and risk becoming accountable and responsible in return.

Increased community and increased emotional involvement with others is perhaps the unique component of integrity because it is so rarely a natural ingredient of most human interactions. Emotional involvement requires that the ultimate intent of a conflict resolution or, for that matter, of any other meaningful interpersonal interaction be one of "closing the psychological space" between two or more individuals—in other words, increasing one's sense of community with the others (Lander & Nahon, 1992a).

From the integrity therapy perspective, guilt is viewed as a healthy response to "an inner awareness of dishonest or deceitful behaviours toward self and others" (Lander & Nahon, 1995a, p. 81). Most stresses in life are seen as stemming from a clash of values. Difficulties with life and living result from interpersonal conflicts rather than intrapsychic conflicts (Lander & Nahon, 1986; Mowrer, 1964a). Stress and anxiety arise not from the dread of hypothetical events, but from the well-justified fear of the consequences of past behaviors (Mowrer, 1961b, 1976). What psychotherapy calls for is not new or different values, but rather an increased fidelity to one's value system (Mowrer, 1953, 1964b). Integrity therapy stresses that one's own unhappiness, angst, mental illness, and "dis-ease" with the self, as Mowrer described it (personal communication, 1969), reflect the degree of violation of one's personal value systems. It is the integrity to become true to one's very own values and one's fidelity to these values that gives one the capacity to transcend difficulties with living.

Integrity Therapy and Psychotherapy With Men

Empirical research on psychotherapy with men is in its infancy. Nahon and Lander (1992a) were among the first to challenge the prevailing belief in the literature that men would not be likely to enter therapy and, once in therapy, would not be likely to do well, due to the widely held belief that men somehow possess an inherent defect in the ability to express their feelings. This chapter was based on the early clinical finding of the Men's Clinic, which opened in 1986, the first clinic in North America (if not the world), located in Ottawa, Ontario, to focus on addressing men's physical, emotional, and spiritual health care needs (Nahon & Lander, 1993b, 1993c). The counseling work carried out in the Men's Clinic was based on the integrity therapy philosophy, and more specifically on the belief that only through an existential, integrity therapy perspective would men be likely to do well in therapy (Nahon & Lander, 1994). Over four hundred men took part in the counseling programs at the clinic; over twenty-five groups were run by a female and male cotherapist dyad that operated on integrity group therapy principles.

The effectiveness of the integrity therapy approach in working with men was evaluated by an empirical study (Nahon, 1993; Nahon & Lander, 1993a) that measured the outcome of sixty-one men who had been separated from a marital or common-law relationship for less than two years. Subjects were randomly distributed into one of six treatment groups—three gender-focused groups offering a gender-role reevaluation component and three non-gender-focused Groups—that offered a traditional group psychotherapy approach. Both treatment modalities were based on integrity therapy principles. A pregroup evaluation phase indicated no significant changes in psychological functioning over the natural waiting period before the start of the group. Results indicated that significant therapeutic gains were made in the areas of psychological well-being, self-disclosure, and the capacity for emotional contact. Noted changes were maintained over a six-week follow-up phase.

INTEGRITY THERAPY: A PARALLEL PROCESS WITH THE MYTHOPOETIC JOURNEY

We propose that integrity therapy is a compatible companion process for men who follow the mythopoetic journey. Based on the work of the Men's Clinic, integrity therapy has proved viable for many men undergoing challenging or stressful life transitions and resulting in long-term positive therapeutic outcomes. Our clinical observations suggest that regardless of race, age, socioeconomic status, diagnosis, or sexual orientation, men have consistently responded well to an integrity therapy–based framework. Working within this framework—in the context of individual, couple, and group psychotherapy—has allowed men to unfold the hidden parts of themselves, to repair their historical and recent wounds, and to begin to heal. Our focus is one of sharing how integrity therapy interacts and interfaces specifically with men who follow the tradition of Iron John, the archetypal warrior, and the new warrior. (The reader's familiarity with Bly's *Iron John* is essential as a background for this material.)

Men's Discovery of Their Personal Power

We have found that men enter therapy because of an aching sense that they feel abandoned, betrayed, alienated, and somehow at fault for the agony, angst, and unhappiness that engulf them like a black hole from deep within. For these men, the integrity therapy framework provides a sense that they can "see the light at the end of the tunnel." No one has had an idyllic childhood; consequently, each of us carries wounds and scars as part of our human experience. Integrity therapy asks us as human beings to look at our personal power and the way that, even as children, we have used it as our means of survival. It is this personal power that, despite unimaginable horrors, has allowed us to evolve toward becoming an adult struggling to be free of the iron cages we initially created to protect ourselves but now have acted to entrap, confine, and confuse us as adults (Lander & Nahon, 1994).

The men we have worked with in groups have come from diverse socioeconomic backgrounds, cultures, education levels, and sexual orientations. Despite these differences, they were able to sit in the group circle and share their wounds, past and present; look at their dreams, lost and found; explore their own selves honestly, owning their parts in the interactions with others, past and present; and look at ways to close the spaces with others in their lives, giving and offering no excuses for being a participant in the tapestry of their lives. They were able to cry, laugh, rage, hug, and begin the repair work necessary for healing to occur. Despite their differences, they discovered that what they held in common was that they were hurting inside, with a very deep sense of pain that threatened to consume them. Thus, a man who was a blue-collar worker was able to see that the man who was an executive or a university professor shared similar fears, hurts, and vulnerabilities. This was one of the major therapeutic factors of the group. It became a great equalizer and was very healing because it allowed the men to transcend the usual power hierarchies and values of society and to discover that they belonged in these groups and were accepted because of their humanness and their suffering rather than being shunned, as they might have feared. When they were contacted for follow-up several months later, it became evident that this process of healing and repair continued, as measured by a follow-up study (Nahon, 1993; Nahon & Lander, 1992, 1995). Many of these men called the clinic over the succeeding months, and sometimes several years later, to let us know about the positive changes in their lives after the therapeutic contract was finished.

Women Working with Men

Another aspect of the role of integrity therapy in working with men is illustrated by our groups' response to having their men's work guided by a man and a woman as cotherapists. Out of four hundred men, only two or three had initially voiced surprise that a female therapist would work with men. The rest really had no problem with this. In fact, many spoke of the importance and value of having a female present to prevent them from getting into "bitch sessions" and to prevent generalizing their rage to other women, when only one woman had hurt them so deeply, and become able to enjoy and begin to trust women again.

One man described the presence of the female cotherapist as being "like a bookend," which keeps the books from falling off the shelf, yet can expand or contract to accommodate them. He also related that her presence helped him discover a richer vocabulary to enhance and discriminate nuances in emotional states; for example, instead of being "f———ing angry" he felt that he could now begin to talk about the painfulness of his rage, thereby avoiding mixing sex and rage, and added that he now felt better about himself. As these men continued to accept the challenge of exploring their own issues of integrity, they began to speak of a deep sense of hunger to find, claim, and protect their selves.

Respecting the Voice of the Other

As we examine the process of integrity therapy in relation to the story of Iron John we see a parallel journey that attests to the fact that these therapeutic processes are highly compatible and complementary. The mythopoetic journey for men is laden with its own unique culture, language, values, images, rituals, metaphors, and meanings. The metaphor becomes the essence of the warrior's journey; it is the voice of the *NEW Warrior* as he undergoes the journey of self-discovery, self-affirmation, and self-proclamation. Similarly, integrity therapy allows individuals to speak to others within the frame of reference of others, without losing their own personal boundaries of self or their own sense of integrity.

Therapy as a Rite of Passage

Integrity therapy offers men a guide in asking them to examine the levels of integrity in their lives and the values that they themselves have violated. It challenges them to become more faithful to themselves and to honor their own values. In the context of the integrity therapy groups, men have been able to reach a sense of shared community with others, as they have worked on personal authenticity and integrity. The divergent paths that have led them to the group culminate in a sense of shared journey and brotherhood of spirit. Within the circle of the group, there is a repairing process that occurs as members are able to talk, yell, cry, laugh, touch, hug, and trust themselves and others to have the capacity to heal from within. As Nahon and Lander (1992) suggested, this going around the circle comprises a "rite of passage" that may find a deeper archetypal meaning as a traditional dance of entry into the circle of adult manhood, especially in this culture where there are few or no meaningful rituals initiating men into manhood.

Integrity Therapy and Daring to Face the Narcissistic Injury

We see integrity as the pursuit and heartbeat of the man who pursues the mythopoetic path. Integrity therapy asks all men (and all women) to examine themselves with a sense of radical honesty, daring to own what belongs to them as well as daring to refuse to own what does not belong to them. This requires a sense of courage that is dredged up from deep within the self and is needed to overcome the fears and anxieties of anticipated pain or wounding. Only through this courage can men dare to look at their dark side and the dark side of human nature, often referred to as the shadow by Jung and in the mythopoetic branch. This is a difficult human task, for it requires that one dare to face both one's power and one's wound. It is the realization that one has access to a deep well of personal power for choosing good over evil and for choosing a part of the self in which to invest. The wound is one of a narcissistic injury inherent in the realization that one is neither flawless nor perfect.

Integrity Therapy and the Battle of the Dark Side Versus the Health Side

In order to access the power to choose good over evil, one must go down deep within the self, the psyche, and the soul, and in doing so risk seeing one's capacity to do evil, own it, and choose not to invest in it. This is ultimately a process that is under the control of the self, and not of anyone else. As one dares to make this choice, one experiences a sense of release that enables one to face one's own dark side and to bring the elements of the shadow out of the darkness so that they can be acknowledged, dealt with, and reintegrated under conscious control.

Through this process, one comes to the realization that this dark side is allowed entrance into the real world of action and thoughts only through a process of personal choice. This is followed by the self-discipline that arises from learning how to resist operating from the framework of the dark side or shadow—in other words, how to resist being ruled by one's dark side—and how to deny others access to it. The concept of the dark side of human nature has been explored since antiquity, starting with symbols of early cultures and followed by (for example) the Bible and continuing with Greek and Roman mythology. Its use precedes both Freud and Jung. In integrity therapy, the concept of the dark side versus the health side is used as a simple therapeutic metaphor to which we have found men to be very intuitively receptive. Most men easily comprehend the notion of the dark and health sides and are able to begin owning these within themselves. As they become aware of the fact that their unacknowledged dark side has been the source of their turmoil, they are able to acknowledge it and use it as an ally in the process of repair and healing.

Integrity Therapy and Working with the Shadow

Integrity therapy views the shadow as being an integral part of the self. From the integrity therapy perspective, the basic human struggle or task is to move from the narcissistic position to the altruistic position by daring to base actions and behaviors on the perspective of the health side rather than the dark side. Some call this shadow work; for us, it is a part of integrity therapy in terms of the challenge to own the less positive potentials of human nature and choosing to invest in health, harmony, peace, goodness, creativity, and generativity rather than stagnation or descent into evil and destruction.

Integrity Therapy and Personal Accountability for Change

As men continue working with the concepts of integrity therapy, their desire to get on with the therapeutic work of repair and healing continues. They become increasingly motivated to heal the wounds, past and recent, that have caused their suffering. In other words, they begin to search deeply and find the pain and rage of the angry man (Allen, 1994) within. They bring out this pain in order to repair it through the process of integrity therapy. They begin to explore the boundaries of their selves, their values, and their own integrity violations; examine how they had used and misused their personal power over the years; and appreciate how and to whom they had given away their personal power. They begin to look at and find their own sense of integrity through a "tough love" (O. H. Mowrer, personal communication, 1969) process of being denied their victim stance, being held accountable, discovering that their self was not as bad as they feared it to be, and beginning to face and own their capacity to do evil. This initial process of discovering the boundaries of "the me and the not-me"; becoming more honest, more responsible, and more closing of the psychological space with self and others; and then reclaiming power that had been given away becomes the process of reclaiming the self by finding the key under the pillow—not their mother's, but their own. They come to understand that integrity, much as one's personal power, cannot be given to them; it must be reclaimed from within and thus cannot be stolen either from or by someone else. One must openly announce to the self that one's level of integrity and one's personal power are exclusively one's own.

The integrity therapy perspective views the process of change in therapy as the domain and responsibility of the client, not the therapist, and thus the client takes the lead. This is analogous to the process in the story of Iron John whereby Iron John does not tell the boy where to go or even how to get there, but rather waits and is available when the boy seeks out his support. With the integrity therapy approach, it is the men themselves, and not the therapists, who are doing the healing; the therapist is important in this process in challenging the men to be scrupulous in looking at their own level of integrity. Increasingly, as the men are able to do this for and to themselves, there is less and less need for the therapist. One young male client in individual therapy, having just terminated a short-term process of therapy (about nine sessions), remarked, "What I have learned here is really a self-help model. You have given me the tools with which to use my own resources creatively."

For us, the key that unlocks all of our iron cages, our armor, and our emotional shields as human beings is to behave with integrity. It is the key that challenges us to discover who we are, what our own personal values really are, and, most of all, whether we will have the courage to be true to these values. To follow the values of others and not one's own is to be in an integrity crisis, leading to a betrayal of both the self and our relationship to others. To know oneself is to behave with honesty, responsibility, and always with the intent of creating a sense of community and increased emotional involvement.

Integrity Therapy and the Pricking of the Finger

As men begin to explore the wounds from the past, they are challenged to own their part in the interactional dynamics even if this means facing the wounds that they experienced—even in childhood—and own their 50 percent of the responsibility in these dynamics. Here the finger is pricked (as in Bly's retelling of the story of Iron John), and one must own one's part—yet resist the temptation to take on the entire culpability for the situation. One can own only one's 50 percent, the other involved in the dynamic must own the other 50 percent. Ironically this becomes a narcissistic injury, for it reflects the interactional nature of the wound and the part that one plays in the wounding and the healing. It is not solely in one's own hands, nor is it solely in the hands of someone else. In accounting for the process of wounding, we believe that there are no victims, because no participant can be absolved of his or her share of the accountability.

This narcissistic injury plays an important role in the discovery of the shadow and the deep passions of one's inner and authentic wild man. Through this journey, one also discovers that all is not so bad as previously feared and defended against. Inherent in the pricking of the finger is the discovery of gold in the wound, which comprises the good and valuable parts of the self. Evil is only a potential, and yet it is only a choice away from becoming real rather than being an immutable reality.

Integrity Therapy and Doing the Kitchen Work

The discovery of the capacity to choose between good and evil is followed by the work of an exploration of integrity with reference to the men's current lives and relationships. Here the challenge is for them to be radically honest and responsible by offering no excuses or alibis. They are challenged to own themselves fully, including the health and dark sides (Lander & Nahon, 1994), as well as the hard work inherent in growing and resisting the temptation to engage in a hierarchical relationship with others, based on rank and entitlement. This is the "kitchen work" (from the story of Iron John in Bly, 1990) of daily life, which reminds individuals that there is no integrity in the idea of being better than others. Individuals may have one talent or many, but ultimately one remains of equal value to others. Consequently, one can "own the gold" while maintaining the sense of being of equal value to others, of living in community with others like the "tarboosh" (a symbol from Bly, 1990, defined as a caplike head covering, worn alone or as part of a turban; Sykes, 1982) of humility rather than grandiosity. Through this process, one is therefore able to convert the pain of the narcissistic wound into gold to be shared with others.

Integrity Therapy: Claiming the Golden Apple

As a man progresses along the journey of integrity, he grows more and more into facing the difficult challenges inherent in daily life and relationships. Choosing to behave with integrity becomes a battle of life and death about maintaining the boundaries and integrity of one's very self, thus becoming analogous to the metaphor of the threat to the king's kingdom (in the story of Iron John). As a man faces the threat to his identity, he must draw on the three components of integrity—honesty, responsibility, and increased emotional involvement—to explore the path of integrity for the self within a given context. In this process, he is asked to seek deeply within himself with honesty, responsibility, and the intent of closing the space with others to define his path of action and his voice. This is analogous to calling for Iron John three times and receiving the three colored suits of armor, which can be likened to the three components of integrity on which to guide one's journey securely and safely. Integrity has been portrayed as a suit of armor (Lander, 1986; Lander & Nahon, 1986), based on the awareness that owning, respecting, and using one's vulnerabilities are one's greatest strengths. It is hard to lose one's way or lose sight of one's goals when traveling this path. Daring to live with integrity allows for an increasing sense of harmony and relatedness with self, others, and nature.

In this manner, integrity therapy follows the pattern of the story of Iron John and unlocks the iron cage in which most contemporary men find themselves trapped due to socialization. Through this process, the various facets of the self are discovered to have the potential for good or evil, with the added—and critical—realization that the choice between these is one's own. The men who have worked on their journeys with us, both individually and in a group context, have been able to claim the key that was theirs all along. The fact that we were women did not seem to matter. Human being to human being, wild man to wild woman, priest to priestess, warrior to warrior, student to mentor, man to woman really became an encounter of equal with equal. The myth that they had harbored was the belief that this key had been taken from them and hidden. Their discovery of gold was the discovery that the key was theirs all along and that they could now own it openly and with integrity, for it had not been obtained through deceit but rather through rightful ownership and proclamation.

Integrity therapy is an existential framework of therapy that allows men to discover the unique keys with which to unlock their iron cages and begin a process of repair, healing, discovery, and growth. By exploring their fidelity to their value systems, men who travel on the mythopoetic journey are able to find a safe haven in which to understand and secure their unique identities as males and as human beings. Through this process, they can begin to rework their relationships with others. Integrity therapy allows each man to find his own way and to discover his own beingness, his own authentic wild man, his own male shadow (Kipnis, 1991), his own anima, his own priest, his own warrior, his own dark side, and ultimately his own potential to choose good over evil. Through daring to struggle for a higher level of integrity, he becomes true to himself, and becomes able to follow the mythopoetic path of the human journey with integrity and with a sense of wellness and well-being in community with other men and with women.

REFERENCES

Allen, M. (1994). *Angry men, passive men: Understanding the roots of men's anger and how to move beyond it.* New York: Fawcett Columbine.

Bliss, S. (1995). Mythopoetic men's movement. In M. S. Kimmel (Ed.), *The politics of manhood: Profeminist men respond to the mythopoetic men's movement (and the mythopoetic leaders answer)* (pp. 292–307). Philadelphia: Temple University Press.

Bly, R. (1990). *Iron John: A book about men.* Reading, MA: Addison-Wesley.

Coleman, J. C. (1976). *Abnormal psychology and modern life.* Glenview, IL: Scott, Foresman.

Frankl, V. (1992). *Man's search for ultimate meaning.* New York: Insight Books/Plenum Press.

Gerwood, J. B. (1998). The legacy of Viktor Frankl: An appreciation upon his death. *Psychological Reports, 82*(2), 673–674.

Guarnaschelli, J. (1994). Men's support groups and the men's movement: Their role for men and for women. *Group, 18*(4), 197–211.

Kipnis, A. (1991). *Knights without armour.* Los Angeles: Jeremy P. Tarcher.

Lander, N. R. (1986, October). *Hobart Mowrer's integrity (therapy) groups.* Paper presented at the annual meeting of the Canadian Group Psychotherapy Association, Gray Rocks, Quebec.

Lander, N. R., & Nahon, D. (1986). *Treating the "untreatable" patient: A case study in unlabelling.* Paper presented at the American Psychological Association annual meeting, Washington, DC.

Lander, N. R., & Nahon, D. (1988a, August). *Mowrer's integrity therapy: An old concept revisited.* Paper presented at the American Psychological Association annual meeting, Atlanta, GA.

Lander, N. R., & Nahon, D. (1988b, August). *Integrity therapy: A vision for the nineties.* Paper presented at the 24th International Congress of Psychology, Sydney, Australia.

Lander, N. R., & Nahon, D. (1989, August). *Values of the therapist: Reformulating the therapeutic impasse.* Paper presented at the American Psychological Association annual meeting, New Orleans, LA.

Lander, N. R., & Nahon, D. (1992a). Betrayed within the therapeutic relationship: An integrity therapy perspective. *Psychotherapy Patient, 8*(3–4), 113–126.

Lander, N. R., & Nahon, D. (1992b). Betrayed within the therapeutic relationship: An integrity therapy perspective. In E. M. Stern (Ed.), *Betrayal in psychotherapy and its antidotes: Challenges for patient and therapist* (pp. 113–125). New York: Haworth.

Lander, N. R., & Nahon, D. (1994, June). *Myths, men and meaning: The magic of being male.* Paper presented at the 1994 Conference on Men and Health Care, University of Alberta, Edmonton, Alberta.

Lander, N. R., & Nahon, D. (1995). Danger or opportunity: Countertransference in couples therapy from an integrity therapy perspective. *Journal of Couples Therapy, 5*(3), 72–92.

Lowe, C. M. (1969). *Value orientations in counseling and psychotherapy.* San Francisco: Chandler.

Moore, R., & Gilette, D. (1990). *King, warrior, magician, lover: Rediscovering the archetypes of the mature masculine.* New York: Harper.

Mowrer, O. H. (1953). *Psychotherapy: Theory and research.* New York: Ronald Press.

Mowrer, O. H. (1961a). *The crisis in psychiatry and religion.* Princeton, NJ: D. Van Nostrand.

Mowrer, O. H. (1961b). The rediscovery of responsibility. *Special Supplement on Psychiatry in American Life, Atlantic Monthly, 7,* 88–91.

Mowrer, O. H. (1964a). *The new group therapy.* Princeton, NJ: D. Van Nostrand.

Mowrer, O. H. (1964b). Freudianism, behaviour therapy and "self-disclosure." *Behaviour Research and Therapy, 1,* 321–337.

Mowrer, O. H. (1976). Changing conceptions of neurosis and the small-groups movement. *Education, 97*(1), 24–62.

Mowrer, O. H., & Vattano, A. J. (1976). Integrity groups: A context for growth in honesty, responsibility, and involvement. *Journal of Applied Behavioral Science, 12*(3), 419–431.

Nahon, D. (1986, October). *An outpatient psychotherapy group for men.* Paper presented at the Seventh Annual Meeting of the Canadian Group Psychotherapy, Gray Rocks, Quebec.

Nahon, D. (1993). *The effectiveness of "masculinist" group psychotherapy in the treatment of recently separated men.* Unpublished doctoral dissertation. University de Montreal, Montreal, Quebec.

Nahon, D., & Lander, N. R. (1992). A clinic for men: Challenging individual and social myths. *Journal of Mental Health Counseling, 14,* 405–416.

Nahon, D., & Lander, N. R. (1993a). Clinic addresses unique counseling needs of men. In American College of Physician Executives, *Innovations '93: Models for cost management and health care quality* (pp. 299–303). Tampa, FL: ACPE.

Nahon, D., & Lander, N. R. (1993b). The masculine mystique. *Canadian Pharmaceutical Journal, 126*(9), 458, 479.

Nahon, D., & Lander, N. R. (1993c). *The "Men's Clinic": Widening horizons for scholarship, meaning and change.* In *The men's movement: Widening the horizons*, symposium presented at the 101st Annual Meeting of the American Psychological Association, Toronto, Ontario.

Nahon, D., & Lander, N. R. (1994, June). *Widening the circle: The Men's Clinic, life force and metamorphosis.* Plenary presentation at the 1994 Conference on Men and Health Care, University of Alberta, Edmonton, Alberta.

Nahon, D., & Lander, N. R. (1995, July). Men's psychotherapy groups: Challenging the myth of the "emotionally defective male." In *Men and psychotherapy*, symposium conducted at the First International Multi-Disciplinary Congress on Men, Ottawa, Ontario.

Perls, F. S. (1989). Theory and technique of personality integration. *TACD Journal*, *17*(1), 35–52.

Rogers, C. R. (1992). The necessary and sufficient conditions of therapeutic personality change. *Journal of Consulting and Clinical Psychology, 60*(6), 827–832.

Rosen, H., & Kuehlwein, K. (1996). *Constructing realities: Meaning-making perspectives for Psychotherapists* (pp. 307–335). San Francisco: Jossey-Bass.

Russell, R. L., & Wandrei, M. L. (1996). Narrative and the process of psychotherapy: Theoretical foundations and empirical support. In H. Rosen & K. Kuehlwein (Eds.), *Constructing realities: Meaning-making perspectives for psychotherapists* (pp. 307–335). San Francisco: Jossey-Bass.

Schwalbe, M. (1996). *Unlocking the iron cage: The men's movement, gender politics, and the American culture.* New York: Oxford University Press.

Sykes, J. B. (Ed.). (1982). *The concise Oxford dictionary of current English* (7th ed.). Oxford: Clarendon.

van Deurzen-Smith, E. (1988). *Existential counselling in practice.* London: Sage.

Williams, R. C., & Myer, R. A. (1992). The men's movement: An adjunct to traditional counseling approaches with men. *Journal of Mental Health Counseling, 14*(3), 393–404.

Chapter 10
Object Relations Perspectives of Masculine Initiation
Wesley R. Goodenough

Traditional dominant masculinity emphasizes external qualities such as intellect, action, and competition among men. The notion driving much of mythopoetic men's work is that men are looking for greater development of internal qualities such as soul and spirit. It raises the question, "What does it mean to be a man?" and answers that masculinity begins in the core of a man's being (rather than in socialization) and reveals itself in many diverse forms.

The thesis proposed by Robert Bly (1990) in his best-selling book *Iron John* is that modern society does not have an adequate answer to this question. Our culture, he says, offers two alternatives: the "John Wayne" macho model of masculinity, or the "naive" antimacho model. The first rides roughshod over women, children, the earth, and other men. The second, looking expectantly to women for approval by mimicking "feminine" qualities, forfeits his masculine energies and locates virtue outside himself. Men of mythopoetic orientation believe that these models are polar caricatures of an authentic masculinity. They believe that a new paradigm is needed that balances masculine soul energies with intellectual and competitive energies in a way that is generative, protective, nurturing, creative, and constructive. Initiation plays a key role in establishing this new paradigm.

MASCULINE INITIATION AND AUTHENTIC MASCULINITY

Masculine initiation, as seen by men of mythopoetic orientation, is about essential masculine maturation. Interest in masculine initiation among mythopoetic men is reflected in *Iron John* (1990), where Bly writes, "The ancient

societies believed that a boy becomes a man only through ritual and effort—
only through the 'active intervention of the older men' " (p. 15). A prominent
feature in this book is the notion that sons must be broken out of their union
with mothers in order for them to move toward masculine fullness.

The notion is that boys arrive in the world from the bodies of women and
are nurtured at their mother's breast, where they make their first and lasting
bond. Even when their father is present and engaged in the family, children's
primary attachment is with their mother. For boys to make a proper transition
to manhood, they must separate from the world of women and find their place
as a man among men.

The notion of a transitional initiation is compatible with the work of Erik
Erickson (1963) who postulated seven crises of human development, including
the crisis of identity versus confusion that takes place in adolescence. The dangers of failing in this crisis may be delay in entering adulthood, regression to
childish behaviors, or making poorly conceived choices with long-term consequences.

For Erickson (1963) and other modern thinkers, this process of identity formation encompasses questioning, reevaluation, and experimentation. Among
mythopoetic thinkers, this transition for males requires the agency of an initiatory experience. Specifically, initiation is an identity-orienting transition that
places a boy squarely in the world of men. That it is critical for entering into
the fullness of masculinity is emphasized by Robert Bly (1996) in his book, *The
Sibling Society*:

In many ways, we are now living in a culture run by half-adults. Fraternities used to be
the main exhibit of half-adults with their half-realized pornography. In the computer
Usenet news group, where digital images are stored, 83.5 per cent of the pictures are
pornographic. The half-adults, twenty to thirty years old, don't try to protect children
from these files. Serious participation in politics is at an all-time low; Congress allows
corporations to meet air quality standards by lowering the standards. We are always
under commercial pressure to slide backward, toward adolescence, toward childhood.
With no effective rituals of initiation, and no real way to know when our slow progress
toward adulthood has reached its goal, young men in our culture go around in circles.
Those who should be adults find it difficult or impossible to offer help to those behind.
That pressure seems even more intense that it was in the 1960s, when the cry "Turn on,
tune in, drop out" was so popular. Observers describe many contemporaries as "children
with children of their own." (p. 44)

Although men and women experience many kinds of informal initiations in
their lives, the issue here is about creating a clear masculine identity. Other
events in men's lives, whether formal or informal, are limited in their scope.
For example, fraternity hazing, military boot camps, and street gang initiations
are limited to initiating individuals into their respective circles.

Recognizing the lack of substantial initiatory opportunities in modern society,
some men have sought ways to provide it. They found that the groundwork had

been done in the field of cultural anthropology and psychology. Mircea Eliade (1975) provided insight into the specific processes of initiation, Joseph Campbell (1968) traced the motifs of the "hero's journey" in art and literature around the world and through all ages of human culture, and the work of Carl G. Jung and his followers provided the clue to the universality of such motifs by postulating a collective unconscious, a racial memory, that lies under and structures human experience and personality development.

Eliade and Campbell

The practice of masculine initiation among tribal cultures around the world is the subject of work by Mircea Eliade (1975). He identifies the common elements of these initiations. First, there is a clear separation from parents where the boy goes away from the village into the forest or remote parts. The second element, the ordeal, is a wound given by the initiating men—a cut, a tattoo, a subincision of the penis, circumcision, or other scarification. Further elements of initiation include teaching by elders and being welcomed back into the community as men. These elements harmonize with the hero cycle described by Joseph Campbell (1968).

Campbell's work provides mythological and soul-oriented foundations for the initiatory practice. His groundbreaking work on the hero cycle (Campbell, 1968) roots initiation in eons of human history and culture. Briefly, Campbell's hero cycle begins with a separation from normal, customary dimensions of life. The hero may blunder into an enchanted forest or may ask for an adventurous assignment as in the Iron John story. Leaving home, he enters a rarified, dangerous dimension—perhaps a forest, a cave, or a distant land. He may meet guides or allies, but eventually he must perform a heroic deed such as slaying a monster or stealing fire. Campbell refers to this part of the cycle as initiation. Having successfully performed the task, the hero receives gifts or treasures that he carries back into his home world, where they become a blessing for his community.

That this motif can be seen in literature, art, and cultural pieces from every age and from every part of the globe speaks to its being fundamental to human life and experience. Masculine initiation is a metaphor of the hero cycle where the initiate is taken from the world of women into the wilderness to confront severe challenges in the circle of initiating men. By meeting these challenges, the initiate is transformed; he is taught the ways of men and subsequently returns to his home as a man ready to assume the role his family and community depend upon. He brings back a new sense of himself as a man among men.

Jung and Moore

The work of C. G. Jung has become foundational for much of men's work in the mythopoetic quarter. It provides for connections among humans in all places and times at the deepest, soul-oriented levels of human experience. Jung's idea of collective unconscious postulates a kind of racial memory where the meaning of masculine and feminine experience in the earliest dawn of human existence is part and parcel of what it means to be human today. This notion of collective unconscious underlies modern interest in old hearth stories, folk tales, and poetry among mythopoetic men. It is this subconsciously recognizable theme work that captures the public imagination in modern adventure tales from *Star Wars* to *The Karate Kid*. Such stories are said to represent in social and cultural forms the same material that individuals experience in dreams. It is material from the deep unconscious parts of the human soul. In short, the stories inform us of the basic substance of being human, in both masculine and feminine form.

It is no surprise that Campbell should have been enamored of Jung, for they shared a fascination with world mythology. As Campbell reports in his Editor's Introduction to *The Portable Jung* (1971), Jung realized as early as 1911 that "in the traditions of any specific folk, local circumstance will have provided the imagery through which the archetypal themes are displayed in the supporting myths of the culture" (p. xxii). Jung's work gave Campbell a viable answer to the question of how the same motifs appeared repeatedly in diverse cultures and times throughout the world.

For Jung there are two realms of unconscious (Campbell, 1971). One is the personal unconscious composed of complexes and introjections, as well as "shadow" material that has been forgotten, hid, repressed, and denied. Of particular interest in this part of the unconscious is the shadow. Moore and Gillette (1990) describe the shadow as "an autonomous complex which holds opinions, expresses feelings, and generally wills an agenda radically different from the Ego's" (p. 39). It is created by the constant process of hiding, repressing and denying parts of the self. Bly (1988) refers to the shadow in the metaphor of a huge sack we each carry over our shoulder into which we toss every piece of ourselves that is uncomfortable. The other realm of the unconscious is the collective unconscious—a kind of racial memory. This is the realm of archetypes, unseen patterns, and prototypes of human identity and behavior. They are analogous to instincts among animals.

Due to the connections between the human psyche, culture, and mythology, Jungian language is commonly used among those doing mythopoetic men's work. They speak of archetypes and of the shadow. Psychologists and writers of the Jungian approach; Moore & Gillette 1990; Hillman, 1991; Estes (1992) inform them. Schwable (1996) notes the extent to which this is true: "I found that it was only after reading Jung and Hillman that I could see how mythopoetic activities in which I'd participated grew out of their thinking" (p. 37). It is this archetypal material that is believed to allow men to access authentic masculinity.

Robert Moore, a noted Jungian analyst and teacher, along with Douglas Gillette, has prepared an evocative view of masculine psychology that identifies a four-sided archetypal structure as a "hard-wired" masculinity (Moore & Gillette, 1990). In this model, mature masculinity is characterized by full realization of

Table 10.1
Moore and Gillette's Archetypal Forms

Mature Archetype	Passive Shadow	Active Shadow
King	Abdicator	Tyrant
Lover	Impotent Lover	Addicted Lover
Warrior	Masochist	Sadist
Magician	Manipulator	"Innocent"

the four main archetypal energies: the king, the lover, the warrior, and the magician. Immature masculinity is characterized by either the boyish forms of the four main archetypes or among adult men by their shadow forms (see Table 10–1). Masculine initiation is seen by mythopoetic men as a vital process to aid in accessing the full archetypal energies and mature masculinity.

OBJECT RELATIONS THEORY

The importance of object relations theory for the work of masculine initiation is its ability to inform the microprocesses of contemporary masculine initiation. It is compatible with Jungian language, the Gestalt, and psychodrama processes that are used in creating the initiatory ordeal.

The key principle of object relations theory is the notion that human development is driven by relational needs rather than by drives and urges and that the human psyche is by nature fundamentally relational. Melanie Klein was the original theorist, and William Fairbairn, Otto Kernberg, and Heinz Kohut were among the principal developers of this approach.

In Kernberg's (1976) model of object relations theory, early interactions with mother and, eventually, interactions with a world of objects are internalized as representational relational items (identification systems), which are transformed (metabolized) over time into a sense of self. One key element of this theory is the notion of splitting—the polarization of good (satisfying) and bad (unsatisfying) in both the inner and outer worlds. The process of idealization involves repression and denial of whatever is considered bad in order to emphasize the good.

Object Relations Theory and Jungian Concepts

While Jungian notions of personality vary significantly from object relations theory, there are some critical areas where they can be said to parallel or overlay each other. This is particularly true of Jung's notion of the collective unconscious and the shadow.

Jungian theorists explain the collective unconscious as an innate set of material common to all human beings arising out of our common human racial history. Object relations theory suggests that human behavioral patterns arise out of the relationally constructed internal identity objects that have receded from our awareness in the process of integration into the self. Our self is created out of a myriad of self-object-affect constructs that originate in relational experiences, which function much like Jung's archetypes. We are able to act and react in our social environment according to what each situation requires and according to an internal relational model. Rather than being instinctual, these role patterns have been formed out of a multitude of interactions and relationships and are equally unconscious.

The second Jungian idea of interest to masculine initiation, the shadow, also has important correspondence to object relations theory. While Jung used the term *shadow* in a very broad sense to indicate the whole of unconscious, Moore and Gillette, as well as other depth psychologists, view it as a kind of "contra Ego" (Moore and Gillette, 1993) that takes an active stance quite different from that of the ego. It is the realm of the personal unconscious composed of and created by repression and denial of parts of ourselves we believe to be bad or unacceptable, as well as complexes, preconscious material, and forgotten material. It is our shadow that we project out on others or transfer to others so that while we believe we are seeing that other person, we are actually seeing a projection of our shadow qualities and reacting emotionally to them.

Although the term *shadow* is not a part of object relations theory, the notion of split-off and repressed parts of the self is fundamental to it. The central theme of the object relations developmental process is the use of splitting to cope with parts of the world that are acceptable and unacceptable. The process of splitting begins in earliest infancy and continues through life so that each progressive stage produces a higher level of splitting. In the end, the human personality is composed of many subidentities appropriate for any situation but inseparably bound with the notion of "good" and "bad." The process of idealization depends on the repression of the "bad" to enable the individual to maintain the illusion of being "good." Although maturation resolves some of this "good" and "bad" splitting in a process of integration, in practice the process continues throughout life, and at any time there remain pieces of repressed "bad stuff" in the unconscious.

While the object relations notion of multiple subidentities is far from the Jungian notion of archetypes, the two concepts are parallel enough in function that we can correlate one notion with the other. The object relations idea of splitting and repression is quite similar to the notion of shadow in Jungian theory. While Jungian thought is effective in supporting the broader notions of masculine development, it does not give us tools to create a decisive process in a time-limited environment. To process twenty or thirty men through an initiation on a single weekend as in a NWTA requires quick, aggressive techniques that are beyond the capacity of typical Jungian tools. Object relations theory provides an effective cognitive map for the Gestalt and psychodrama processes that can be used to give each initiate a powerful and meaningful initiation ordeal.

Object Relations and Gestalt Initiatory Processes

The work of Mircea Eliade (1975) and Joseph Campbell (1968) indicates that certain motifs and models of the initiatory process have existed around the world and through time. The work of Carl Jung draws a connection that suggests that the process of separation, ordeal, and return is part of the racial memory of our species and therefore essential to the process of masculine development. How do these works, along with object relations theory, inform modern masculine initiation?

CREATING A VALID INITIATION

Masculine initiation generally conforms to the motif of the hero cycle (separation, ordeal, instruction, and return) Moore and Gillette (1993) point out that a valid initiatory experience must take place in sacred (or liminal) space and time. This extraordinary space and time, the place of ritual and ceremony is also the realm of transformation.

Creating sacred space and time for a valid masculine initiation is accomplished when the initiators exercise their intent to do so, retreating to a remote site away from normal life activity, perhaps carrying out ritual practices to declare the place and time as sacred, and performing exercises to create sacred community among the men assembled.

Another component of the initiatory experience is a significant task to be accomplished or an ordeal to be survived. There is a test of the inner stamina, and sometimes of the physical stamina of the initiate. Ultimately the initiate must confront his inner limitations to meet the outer challenge. This also corresponds to Campbell's hero cycle.

According to Eliade (1975), indigenous societies used privation and physical challenges as well as physical wounding in their initiations. An extensive initiatory process might include challenges on both physical and spiritual dimensions. Malidoma Somé (1994) recounts in detail his initiatory experience as a young man in Burkina Faso, West Africa. Clearly the process was rigorous enough that some hopefuls did not survive the experience. Challenges were laid out that required movement between ordinary and nonordinary realities and called up great courage in the young initiates, as well as physical stamina.

In our society today, practices that would create physical wounds or that carry significant risk to health would have serious ethical as well as legal concerns. However, we can provide relatively safe ordeals of significant challenge involving personal intrapsychic encounters. Confronting our shadow and the deep wounds that we have put away there can be a task of great courage and strength. These are encounters with personal material that is unacceptable and frightening. Such a task can be a significant ordeal for an initiation process and quite possibly represents the true psychic meaning of all initiation. Campbell (1960) has spoken famously about the true nature of the hero's journey. It is an inward journey more than an outward one. He says, "The labyrinth is thoroughly known; we have only to follow the thread of the hero path. And where we had thought to find an abomination, we shall find a god; where we had thought to slay another, we shall slay ourselves; where we thought to travel outward, we shall come to the center of our own existence; where we had thought to be alone, we shall be with all the world" (p. 25).

The process under consideration here provides a real challenge for initiates and is compatible with modern society since it is founded in psychological terms. Specifically, the initiate is asked to confront some self-selected portion of his own shadow. This is accomplished using Gestalt and psychodramatic technique in a group setting with the aid of trained facilitators. What is described here is based on my experience of a model taught by Shadow Work Seminars (Barry & Bilgere, 1995). A similar process is used in the New Warrior Training Adventure Weekend. This process is carried out only in the strong container of a well-developed supportive group context. Extensive effort and time are expended to engender the group bonding and trust necessary to create a container sufficient to support this kind of process.

Initiation Using the Object Relations Map

The process is conducted with all participants, initiates and facilitating staff men, standing in a circle. The imagery of a circle has meaning on several levels of understanding. It is a vessel to contain the process and the energies released as the process unfolds; a stage on which the drama is enacted; and the life sphere of the man who is working; and the underworld place where the hero's journey takes place.

Each initiate, when he is ready, steps out into the center of the circle to begin his own work. The intent of the facilitators is to help the man encounter a piece of his own shadow—one of his split-off identities. The nature of this split-off material is such that a person expends much energy to maintain the repression, and so by definition, this material is frightening to the individual. Truly to encounter it, face it, and own it, is a task of courage and represents a significant initiatory ordeal. In object relations terms, such a confrontation integrates that piece of split-off self. In Jungian language it is bringing the shadow into the light of acceptance and healing.

The process may go in almost any direction as dictated by the initiate himself. The facilitators may ask the initiate to make a statement about how he would like his life to be, and then by a series of questions attempt to lead him to identify the incongruence between his wish and his life. At some point the initiate will identify a situation in his life, or a person, or event that is instrumental in blocking him from what he wants in life.

When a point of conflict has been identified, the facilitator opens the process of dramatic role play, inviting the initiate to choose someone from the circle to play a role. Following is a brief hypothetical example of such a process (greatly simplified for illustrative purposes):

Facilitator:	Tell me an affirmation of yourself?
Initiate:	I am a success in all I do.
Facilitator:	Is that true for you?
Initiate:	I've really messed up some things. Sometimes I can't seem to do anything right.
Facilitator:	I want you to pick someone here to play you being successful. [The initiate picks someone to play the role.]
"Success":	I am a success! I am successful! I always get it right!
Facilitator:	Now what is your reaction to this when you see yourself as successful?
Initiate:	I want to wring his neck!

This process is Gestalt in nature. It is very here-and-now in character and engages unconscious material. It is metaphorical in that the situation is generalized around the participant's wishes for success, but it is also real in that the subject matter belongs to the initiate's life experience. Object relations concepts are at play here. The initiate has overtly picked someone to play himself as "successful," but most likely he is projecting an internal object of another sort onto the role player and is beginning to interact with the projection. This is evident in his reaction; he is clearly becoming angry. The next step might be to focus on the projection to enhance it, bring up its intensity, and develop the individual's relationship with it:

Facilitator:	Is he playing this right? What should be his tone of voice, his facial expression, his gestures.
Initiate:	[Gives some more cues.]
"Success":	[Repeats the lines using the suggested embellishments]
Initiate:	[Starts to become more animated and intense.]
Facilitator:	Who is this person?
Initiate:	That's father! Always so perfect. Never made a mistake. And he never let anyone forget it either!

Here the individual is projecting a split-off and repressed internal object onto the player. All of the emotional meaning connected to this object is being accessed. Nor is it his true father. It is an internal object identified as one aspect of his father, and it is a part of the initiate himself. In Kernberg's (1976) terminology, this "identification system" contains an image of self, and on image of the father, and an affective coloring. The internal object is brought out and concretized in the role play, and all three elements of this internalized system show up. The facilitator now begins to develop the relationship:

Facilitator: Who *did* make mistakes?

Initiate: [Begins to weep] I never did anything right for him. I could never do well enough to suit him.

Facilitator: I want you to pick someone to play you." [Initiate picks someone to play himself.] Now, tell me about you here [points to role player]. How old are you here?

Initiate: I'm about eight.

The initiate is beginning to exhibit the affective component of this internal object system, which is the behavioral traits of an eight year old. The facilitator has concretized the self component of the internalization system by having someone else play the role. The scene is becoming clearer. Each role on the stage represents an internal object of the initiate, an introjected component of some person in his life, himself at an earlier age, a repressed emotional state, or a part of himself he has split off.

As this process continues, it will be the facilitator's intent to guide the role play in such a way that the individual will confront one of his split-off or repressed objects where there is a high level of emotional energy. Here the eight-year-old object needs to confront the father object:

Facilitator: [Switching the initiate back into the role of the eight-year-old.] What is it you want from father?

Initiate: I want him to see me as I am.

Facilitator: Can you tell him that?

Initiate: [In a pleading voice, with tears.] Dad, don't you see me? I just want you to see me and love me like I am.

Father Role: I'm a success! I'm a success!

Facilitator: How is this working?

Initiate: [Weeping] He still doesn't see me.

Facilitator: [Switching the initiate out of the eight-year-old role again.] I want you to watch this and tell me how you react to it. [Instructs the role players to enact the same scene with the language the initiate has just used.]

Initiate: [After viewing the role play.] I'm pissed at that. A man should pay attention to his child's needs. [Begins to show anger. His demeanor is no longer docile but animated and powerful.]

Facilitator: So what do you want to do here?

Initiate: I need to get his attention and make him notice me.

Facilitator: Then I want you to switch back into your place, but before you do, I want you to tell me what you are going to do.

As this scene plays out, there are a myriad of possible directions it might follow. Resuming the role of the eight-year-old, the initiate may immediately confront the father object in a powerful way until he is satisfied that he has gotten the attention he wants. Or he may fail to summon the anger (energy) to make the confrontation happen. If he becomes blocked, the facilitator might help him to identify what is blocking him and what he might do to resolve it. A further dramatic scene may be created for the initiate to work out his heroic confrontation. In each case, the process concretizes the nonmaterial inner objects on the floor, allowing the initiate to process through the relationships in metaphoric ways.

What makes the process powerful is that the objects underlying the metaphors are real within the initiate and bind huge amounts of affective energy. The initiate is dealing with the reality of his internal objects in the metaphor of the psychodrama.

However it is resolved, the initiate will have had to call on his inner resources of courage, will, and stamina to bring the confrontation to a conclusion. The integration of split-off objects occurs when the initiate recognizes that all the roles of the drama, even those that are despicable to him, are himself, and he takes ownership of all the identities and energies so exposed.

In the metaphoric world of the process, the inner world of the initiate has become integrated at one more place. The initiate has met and confronted an old enemy that has likely blocked his life's path in many ways. He has overcome in the subterranean world of shadows and now brings treasures of released energy and insight back to his world. And he has completed the initiation ordeal that he has come to experience.

SUMMARY AND CONCLUSION

What in Jungian terminology is called shadow in object relations theory is characterized as containing countless inner identities and relational complexes. By concretizing these inner objects into roles on the psychodrama stage, the initiate is able to interact with them, clarify them, and ultimately own them. Kernberg (1976) would call this metabolizing them. Object relations theory provides the cognitive map for the initiatory ordeal by specifying the internal objects and their nature.

While mythopoetic men's work is generally informed by Jungian theory, the use of object relations theory parallels it because both theory sets recognize the reality of a personal unconscious and the projection of unconscious material on others in interpersonal relationships. While Jungian thought and language serve in the broader context for men's work, object relations theory provides enlightening detail for the process of the initiatory ordeal.

There is an important issue that has not been addressed here. Although it is not pertinent to the purpose of this chapter, it does bear on the greater question of the nature of masculinity and the role of initiation in masculine maturation. Jung's theory of the collective unconscious, including the archetypes, presumes that authentic masculinity and feminity are "hard-wired." That is, we become truly human in masculine form by accessing and fulfilling the archetypal blue-prints within us. Object relations theory, on the other hand, assumes that the internal objects are socially and interpersonally derived. They are not "hard-wired" but "software." The impulse that drives personality development is not libido but our need for relationships.

Whether accessing innate archetypal patterns, as in Jungian thought, or inte-grating split-off socially defined internal objects, we are nonetheless co-creating new ways of being men. Deep in the heart of many men who participate in mythopoetic men's activities is the conviction that the ultimate product of mas-culine initiation will be a changed world. It is no longer acceptable for men (or women) to rampantly consume the earth, women, children, and other men. Men may seek healing from their own wounds, but in the end, an initiated man returns to his community as a man of service. He possesses recovered treasure destined to heal and nurture his family of whatever construction, his community and the world.

REFERENCES

Barry, C., & Bilgere, D. (1995). *Shadow work: Carpet training manual.* Mt. Horeb, WI: Shadow Work Seminars.

Bly, R. (1988). *A little book on the human shadow.* San Francisco: Harper.

Bly, R. (1990). *Iron John: A book about men.* Reading, MA: Addison-Wesley.

Bly, R. (1996). *The sibling society.* Reading, MA: Addison-Wesley.

Campbell, J. (1968). *The hero with a thousand faces* (2nd ed.). Princeton, NJ: Princeton University Press.

Campbell, J. (Ed.). (1971). *The portable Jung.* New York: Penguin Books.

Eliade, M. (1975). *Rites and symbols of initiation.* New York: Harper & Row.

Erikson, E. H. (1963). *Childhood and society* (2nd ed.). New York: Norton.

Estes, C. P. (1992). *Women who run with the wolves: Myths and stories of the wild woman archetype.* New York: Ballantine.

Hillman, J. (1991). *A blue fire: Selected works of James Hillman.* New York: Harper & Row.

Kernberg, O. (1976). *Object relations theory and clinical psychoanalysis.* New York: Jason Aronson.

Moore, R., & Gillette, D. (1990). *King, warrior, magician, lover: Rediscovering the archetypes of the mature masculine.* San Francisco: Harper San Francisco.

Moore, R., & Gillette, D. (1993). *The magician within: Accessing the shaman in the male psyche.* New York: Avon Books.

Schwable, M. (1996). *Unlocking the iron cage: The men's movement, gender politics, and American culture.* New York: Oxford University Press.

Somé, M. (1994). *Of water and the spirit: Ritual, magic, and initiation in the life of an African shaman.* New York: A. Jeremy P. Tarcher/Putnam Book.

Chapter 11

The Therapeutic Status of the Mythopoetic Approach: A Psychological Perspective

Daniel J. Richard

I am not a mechanism, an assembly of various sections.
And it is not because the mechanism is working wrongly, that I am ill.
I am ill because of the wounds to the soul, to the deep emotional self
and the wounds to the soul take a long, long time, only time can help
and patience, and a certain difficult repentance
long difficult repentance, realization of life's mistake, and the freeing oneself
from the endless repetition of the mistake
which mankind at large has chosen to sanctify.
   (D. H. Lawrence)

One of the well-kept secrets in our society is that men suffer (Elchler, 1989, in Meth & Pasick, 1990; Kaufman, 1994). Traditional masculinity dictates that men be independent, strong, self-reliant, competitive, powerful, adventurous, and emotionally restrained (Levant, 1990a). To live this role is not without cost, however, as the "suffering" that men endure may result in an inability to identify or find the safety to express emotions, have pleasure, be creative, balance the demands of work, communicate, deal with intimacy, and ask for help (Levant, 1990b; Freudenberger, 1990; Nahon & Lander, 1992). The more subtle and cumulative effects of these behaviors may account for men's higher rates of incarceration, completed suicide, childhood learning disabilities, antisocial personality disorder, substance abuse, and mortality (Wicks, 1996). Being male may indeed be dangerous to men's health.

What it means to be a man in the early twenty-first century is changing, and as a result many men are experiencing increased psychological turmoil, part of which may result from misunderstanding the impact of the midlife developmental transition. Men are being asked to behave in ways that are more different than ever before, prompted by merging gender roles, work stress, and increased responsibility. The pressure men experience has caused them to question their value and beliefs in their masculinity and left many feeling confused and helpless. In accordance with masculine ideology, however, the shame and inadequacy men may feel in seeking help restricts them from using traditional counseling services. A common myth is that men do not benefit from therapy (Scher, Stevens, Good, & Eichenfield, 1987).

To gain a broader awareness of the benefit or loss men might receive from such an encounter, it is important to understand the behavioral, affective, and cognitive coping strategies men bring to the therapeutic context. Fine (1988) states that "once a man is honest enough to admit that he needs help, it often turns out that he has problems in many, if not all areas of his life" (p. 47). If this is indeed true, the crucial question becomes how to inspire this "honesty" or, more practically, how to connect men to the process. North American culture has a difficult time accepting the suffering that men endure, since the injuries are hidden, shrouded by denial, heroism, and isolation. For these reasons, clinical literature suggests that men represent a unique challenge in therapy. With the difficulty that the traditional therapeutic encounter presents for many men and the limitations created by the increasing demands of health care, it is incumbent on therapists to seek other resources and alternate approaches to treatment that address the masculine gender's particular brand of suffering.

THE THERAPEUTIC CHALLENGE

The concept of therapy itself poses a formidable challenge to masculine ideology. Men may erroneously see the efforts of a therapist as an overfocus on his "weaknesses" (Bergman, 1995), an experience too revealing and shameful. Self-esteem may be further damaged by the belief that to receive help means the seeker is inadequate, unable to solve his own problems, and too diminished in the face of the therapist to whom he feels or fears he must relinquish "control." To experience this deluge of negative emotions in addition to the presenting problem may reflect why the mechanism of denial is a first-line defense in the therapeutic setting (Fruedenberger, 1990). This denial is so pervasive that Goldberg (in Pasick, Gordon, & Meth, 1990) believes it may account for higher mortality rates and maladaptive coping: "As men learn to deny emotional and physical pain, they develop methods which insulate them from their pain: rationalization, intellectualization, and logical thinking" (p. 70).

Men with increased scores on the Gender Role Conformity Scale (GRCS) show a more positive attitude toward a cognitively oriented therapy videorecording than a similar video with an affective approach (Levant & Pollock, 1995). Other researchers would agree that men usually change through cognitive interventions (Scher et al., 1987) but point out that although it provides symptom relief, it reinforces cognitive detachment from others: "The process of self-awareness and self-exploration are narrowly defined by the cognitive-behavioral orientation and it may be harmful to reinforce dysfunctional patterns by attending only cognitively" (p. 220). Similarly, Fine (1988) felt that although cognitive approaches will initiate the process, unless deeper feelings are brought out, the results will be less effective in the long run. These data suggest that although connecting with men on a cognitive, intellectual level will address conflicts, it reinforces traditional coping methods and fails to affect the suppressed, emotional component of men's behavior.

THE CONTEMPORARY MEN'S MOVEMENT

Men's liberation or the "men's movement" grew from a limited number of publications in the mid-1970s on men's changing roles (Lewis, 1981). This movement developed different branches and seemed to address different concerns of the male predicament. The profeminist branch concerns itself with political and philosophical issues pertaining to women's continued oppression by patriarchal society. Men's rights largely focuses on changing laws and the public perception of men. The mythopoetic branch, identified and most widely recognized as the men's movement, emphasizes literature, mythology, ritual, and personal healing. The Christian branch incorporates other branches and celebrates male identity through Christianity (Mathews, 1996). There are also others blurring the distinction between the political, therapeutic, and spiritual branches such as the profeminist, gay-affirmative, and promen's and antifeminist (Hearn, 1993).

IMPACT OF FEMINISM

Not all men are in denial over the difficulties they are experiencing as products of the masculine ideal. In fact, the impetus for men's change may have been, to some degree, in response to women. In the quest for fundamental liberation rights, feminist criticism of flaws in the male-dominated society and patriarchy as a whole caused what might be considered a "crisis of confidence" in men (Schwalbe, 1996). Because some factions of radical feminism viewed all forms of masculinity as morally corrupt, men experienced a different kind of injury in the sense of being "defective" or "inadequate" and the shame and resentment of needing to apologize for being men. This paradigm shift prompted some men to reexamine their roles not only in the context of oppression but also by questioning the unrealistic and flawed model of masculinity that they followed. Men began to gather together in small groups and found themselves undergoing experiences similar to those of women who discovered their identity some two decades ago. Some of these groups, however, seemed to view this "liberation" in a less political and more personal context, as the realities both

genders experience are considerably different. Scher et al. (1990) suggest that
"women are oppressed by their roles, while men are restrained and constrained
by theirs" (p. 322). With this in mind, Bly (1990) posits that both genders
embrace different modes of feeling as women's predominant experience with
pain and devaluation has influenced feminism to concern itself predominantly
with the "outer work" of social change, while men's experience with grief and
denial has prompted their liberation toward an "inner work" of spiritual and
personal growth and healing. Although this idea may tend to understate the
plight of feminism, it seems to illuminate both the unique forces that bear on
the genders and the different paths needed to promote change.

THE MYTHOPOETIC APPROACH

The mythopoetic branch seemed to emerge as a result of growing dissatisfaction with the available models and attitudes toward adult masculinity and
from a realization that because of their socialization, men are often kept from
becoming complete human beings. Brannon's (1985) four components traditionally associated with (U.S.) attitudes about masculinity—men should not act
feminine ("no sissy stuff"); men should strive for success and respect "the big
wheel"; men should be strong and devoid of weakness ("the sturdy oak"); and
men should seek danger, risk, and adventure ("give 'em hell")—seemed to
create a caricature of the male role and offer limited expression of male energy.
The traditional male characterized by Clint Eastwood or the film character
Rambo seemed to possess a sense of vitality and energy but was harsh, competitive, and limited in his capacity for intimacy. Conversely, the "soft male"
of the 1970s and 1980s characterized by Alan Alda was better able to express
vulnerability, compassion, and closeness; however, this increased sensitivity is
often associated with a diminished sense of vitality, decisiveness, radiance, and
sexuality (Gilbert, 1992). In this atmosphere of dissatisfaction, the mythopoetic
branch emerged as an environment where men could safely reexamine masculine
dynamics and, as Graham (1992) states, "recover [their] lost manhood by escaping the confines of contemporary culture to redefine the masculine identity"
(p. 317).

Mythopoetic groups of men began to gather informally to explore and advance
their inner development. Although there is no official organization that governs
the many mythopoetic groups and experiential workshops in existence, the key
architect of the movement is considered by many to be the poet Robert Bly. In
Iron John (1990), Bly relates the story of Iron Hans, an archetypal model for
men who mentors a boy through the mythic journey and trials of becoming a
man. Bly advocates recovering the healthy and natural aspects of masculinity
that were lost and have consequently diminished the male presence. It is proposed that men sustained these losses through the transformation of the father's
role from a source of moral teaching in the colonial age to the "distant bread-
winner" of the mid-twentieth century (Pleck, 1987), the oedipal relationship that

ties boys to their mothers, and the failure of men to provide opportunities for initiation of their sons (and other men's sons) into manhood (Williams & Myers, 1992).

That there are "wounds" to the psyche caused by other men develop the notion that male influence (or lack thereof) has as great or greater implications toward male psychological development than maternal care. The idea of violence and other unhealthy behaviors being related to the absence of (male) role models or initiators serves to dispel the psychoanalytic view that all dysfunction can be traced back to the mother-child relationship. Developmentally, research suggests that low father involvement in nurturant parenting and rigidly traditional fathering restrict the development of children's self-esteem, frustration of tolerance, impulse control, cognitive functioning, and interpersonal relationships (Pasick et al., 1990). Few would disagree that the opportunity to examine and evaluate father-son relationships is a critical need for men (Scher et al., 1987). An ideal forum to support this and other examinations might be found in the gatherings that stimulate men to rediscover many of the lost dimensions of their identity that, for a variety of social and personal reasons, have been denied, suppressed, or distorted (Kaufman & Timmers, 1983).

THE PSYCHOTHERAPEUTIC PROCESS

The mythopoetic approach refers to a process of ceremony, drumming, readings of poetry, mythic storytelling, music, physical movement, personal testimonials, imagery, didactic instruction, and enactment of ritual to explore the psychology of men (Gilbert, 1992). Functionally, the mythopoetic gathering may resemble consciousness-raising and growth groups, both defined as nonpathological in orientation and fostering a supportive climate whereby participants examine their personal experience with the focus on interpersonal relations among members. The therapeutic effectiveness of these approaches would indicate that positive consciousness-raising group outcome is associated with factors in successful outcomes in traditional group therapy (Warren, 1976; Wong, 1978), while growth group outcome studies would suggest it facilitates positive, enduring change in interpersonal relationships (Berman & Zimpfer, 1980). In further support of connection between consciousness-raising groups and men's issues, Scher et al. (1990) suggest that the nonpathological orientation makes consciousness-raising groups more appealing to traditional men, who are typically reluctant to consider psychotherapy. This might present a "face-saving" means to talk about difficulties and share feelings, while avoiding the threat of vulnerability. Moreover, Levant (1995) suggests that the benefit of consciousness-raising groups may facilitate men's relating differently to other men, while overcoming the reliance on women to perform expressive socio-emotional tasks. By logical extension, the mythopoetic group might also facilitate similar growth and enduring changes in its participants by virtue of its nontraditional and phenomenological approach.

MYTHOPOETIC PHILOSOPHY AND TECHNIQUE

The theoretical foundations of the mythopoetic are deeply rooted in the principles of Jungian psychology (Shwalbe, 1996). These concepts are used to explore and explain the male psyche as feminists long before had used them to illuminate principles of female psychology (Bolen, 1984). Jung (1964) theorized that this collective unconscious consists of powerful primordial images called archetypes that predispose people to perceive, experience, or react to the world in certain ways. Jung believed that through societal and other intrapsychic pressures, these male archetypes or representations of mature masculinity are fragmented and unbalanced (Hjelle & Ziegler, 1992). These archetypes are sought to be discovered and reintegrated into the masculine consciousness, and with this process a sense of mature, healthy psychological development (such as the acceptance and expression of both female and male energies) might be realized.

This interpretive approach may function on various levels of meaning for the mythopoetic participant. On a practical level it allows men to "own" their troubles safely, and see their difficulties as part of the "exaggerated myth" (Pedersen, 1991) in which they are caught. On a more spiritual level, it awakens a sense of the sacred, universal, mysterious, and powerful connection to others and to the world (Schwalbe, 1996) that might challenge men to explore and liberate themselves from old perceptions and beliefs rather than to feel imprisoned by their predicament. Jung believed that the ultimate aim of therapy was neither curing nor alleviating patients' unhappiness but increasing self-respect and self-knowledge (Douglas, 1995). Support for Jungian psychotherapy would show that it is singularly beneficial for people who are undergoing a midlife crisis concerned with problems of the second half of their life (Diekmann, 1991, cited in Douglas, 1995). It is not surprising that a large number of participants in mythopoetic gatherings fit this profile.

Another key concept in applying the mythopoetic approach is the sensitivity to the "male mode" of feeling. Men may have a way of interpreting, feeling, experiencing, and relating that is different from that of women (Thompson, 1991). Allen and Gorden (1990) believe those working with men need to recognize and use the "male model" of communication to be effective rather than the "female model" that most therapy emulates. Proxemics—the study of interpersonal distance—may also be related to this mode. In traditional therapy the client and therapist sit facing each other. Direct eye contact is virtually unavoidable, which is extremely difficult if either individual experiences the shame of mistrust. At a men's gathering, the male mode is to sit in a circle facing a fire or symbol, a grouping that allows men to be with one another side by side. Bly (1990) identifies this mode of relating as more natural for men, reflecting the (socialized side-by-side work) relationship of father-son, elder-to-younger tribesmen, teacher-apprentice, or mentor-mentee.

The all-male gathering itself would seem to intrinsically possess the therapeutic qualities of acceptance, sharing, and transference of story, poem, or myth.

The experience is, as Bly states, "not a desire to separate from women [but where] men are drawn together by a sense of loss, grief, and a shared confusion" (Moyers & Bly, 1990), which might be fully experienced and worked through. The ability to access deeply seeded grief, which Fine (1988) believes is the "doorway to a man's feelings" (p. 324), may lend a strong cohesion and productivity to the gathering. The group process itself enables men to discover that their self-doubt and sense of isolation is not unusual. This realization provides considerable relief and enables men to face difficulties with their "dignity intact" (Meth & Pasick, 1990), a situation that is much more difficult to attain in a one-on-one counseling situation.

The mythopoetic groups activities are designed to allow the embrace of the mythical and the sacred in what Bly (1992) calls "ritual space," or an area, usually in a natural setting, where men can meet free from the influences of civilization. In this context, the gathering represents a separation from ordinary reality and a return to a more basic, primitive, uncomplicated way to relate, feel, and express emotions. A rationale for the primitive gatherings is proposed by Wicks (1996): "Separated from the structures of society that supports our identities, we are forced to confront a deeper, truer self" (p. 64). For some, as Schwalbe suggests (1996) primitive gatherings "may represent a loss of faith in science to solve human problems" (p. 14). In any event, the quest for ritual and its connection to the psychospiritual may speak of an older, deeper need nourished by this process.

The ritual process used in the mythopoetic approaches has been used in a religious context for thousands of years as a very powerful method to enact change (Wikstrom, 1990). The setting, reflected in both the religious and mythopoetic context, is carefully selected and organized to represent "a complex whole of environmental elements, affecting all the sense organs of the participants construct this behavioral setting into a lituragal one" (Vanderlans & Geerts, 1990, p. 88). Erikson (1966) believed that ritual helps form an achievement of basic trust, which is essential to well-being, as well as a need for "sameness" and coherence, facilitated growth of the identity. In the development of the self-consciousness, R. L. Moore argued that "contemporary psychotherapy might be considered a ritual process through which a segment of modern society finds a form of leadership in a time of crisis" (Boudewijnse, 1990 p. 15). To harness the power of ritual in a therapy setting is to be transformed by means of the ritual into someone who, in the eyes of his own ego, is felt to be more satisfactory (Vandermeerch, 1990).

The particular language used in the mythopoetic gatherings may also facilitate change and be conducive to the male mode of understanding and feeling. The use of poetry, myth, and stories, as Bly suggests, is "a way men can experience problems of men past. The terms to describe conflicts are easier for men to relate to than within the context of therapy" (Moyers & Bly, 1990). This idea is supported by the understanding that social dialogue that is concrete, vivid, and rich in specific illustrations and metaphor might enhance the therapeutic process (Epstein, 1994). As a symbolic medium, language can be used to develop narrative explanations about one's life, culture, and relationships that are the reference point of understanding and generating meaning (Gergen, 1985). The resonating metaphors used in the mythopoetic gatherings may relate to the way in which many men process their inner emotional life. As men are "heroes" in their own life stories, the integration of poetry, literature, myth, psychology, and culture may create images that are helpful in their own life's dramas.

Despite the information provided, the questions still remain: How might the mythopoetic experience affect the psychology of men? How does the unlikely synthesis of ancient practices and modern principles inspire or empower men to address their unique brand of suffering, and how does this experience translate into everyday life? If indeed the mythopoetic holds some special significance for men, an equally important question might be: How can those working with men harness these concepts and use them as an adjunct to traditional therapy? In the end, is the mythopoetic approach more shadow than substance or does it contain at its core, ideas, concepts, and techniques that many men can embrace toward a process of growth and change?

THE RESEARCH STUDY

Methodology

Published quantitative research on the therapeutic effectiveness of mythopoetic groups is limited, aside from Hartman (1995), Levin (1997), and Dunn (1998). Much of what is available has typically taken a qualitative approach using structured interview or participant observation to collect data. These include studies to determine rates of group formation and disbandment, individual participation and retention, and factors associated with durable and effective groups (Mankowski, Maton, Burke, & Hoover, 1997, and Chapter 12); and those describing reasons for contact, continued involvement, and processes within a men's support group (Richter, 1994). Other studies have investigated more thoroughly the types of issues discussed and resolved (Wilson, 1993, and Chapter 2) as well as explored the clinical implications and utility of the mythopoetic to the field of mental health (Lesser, 1995). Combined, these data, Bray (1992), and Shulz (1997) would suggest that mythopoetic gatherings tend to draw predominantly white, middle-aged, middle-class men who are experiencing a sense of isolation, crisis, desire for male friendship, or difficulty with interpersonal relationships. Participants continue with these groups because of the new experience of intimate connection and for the most part have experienced a new transition in the male-male mode of feeling and relating. These studies indicate the therapeutic value of male support group process, the utility of a novel approach to addressing role strain, and the value of using mythopoetic gatherings as an adjunct to traditional counseling.

The purpose of the study that I report was threefold. (1) to investigate and explore participants' subjective experiences and reactions to mythopoetic-type gatherings, (2) to develop a comparative analysis of mythopoetic experiences with that of a more traditional men's therapy groups, and (3) to gather information from the leaders or facilitators of the respective groups to clarify theoretical and technical approach and to further define their "role" in therapeutic change.

Participants

The participants were drawn from three different groups. The first group contained fifteen men who had been or continue to be involved with mythopoetic-type gatherings. All but two of these participants were associated with the ManKind Project (MKP), formally known as New Warrior Network (NWN), an international nonprofit corporation offering New Warrior Training Adventure (NWTA) weekends held throughout Canada the United Kingdom and the United States. This experience is defined in an advertisement as a "highly structured, physically oriented weekend experience incorporating tribal ritual, competition, psychodrama, guided imagery, and confrontation to help each male reclaim his deep male power and live up to a high level of personal integrity" (advertisement, Wingspan vol. 10, no. 2, 1996; Pentz, 1997). The program is facilitated by group leaders and staff (who are members) who have completed the NWTA, participated in a graduation ceremony, and attended eight to ten weeks of facilitated follow-up in an integration training, used to process and integrate the NWTA experience. The men often continue in the same groups after the facilitated eight to ten weeks when the I-groups become a closed men's peer mutual support (MPMS) group.

In the second group of participants were six men who had recently completed a men's therapy group (MTG). The focus of this group, a brochure stated, was to "provide a non-competitive, confidential, and safe setting for men to explore ways to connect and achieve greater intimacy in their relationships." This group met weekly for one and a half hours for twelve weeks and was cofacilitated by two therapists.

The third group of participants contained five men who were identified as leaders of the respective groups: one therapist from the MTG and four from the MKP.

Group Experience Survey

The group experience survey used for the mythopoetic and MTG was designed to gather three types of data. The first section's purpose was to collect demographic and other information, such as involvement in a relationship and prior treatment in counseling, to lend a broader perspective on precipitating events as well as implicit and explicit reasons for seeking a given group. The second section assessed functioning associated with strict gender role adherence and areas that may typically cause male distress. This section was designed to tap the individuals' subjective experiences and how it affected relationships with men and women, emotional expression, issues of power, achievement, spirituality, and masculinity. The last section allowed the participants to compare and contrast their group or gathering with other therapeutic experiences and to elaborate on the practical applications of and personal reactions to the group.

Group Leader's Survey

This instrument also gathered demographic data and was designed to make explicit the role of the leader—his theoretical assumptions, goals, processes, and perceived mechanisms of change within a given group experience.

Procedure

In the fall of 1996, after contacting American Psychological Association's Division 51 (the Society for the Psychological Study of Men and Masculinity) and NWN, a request was posted (on their respective Internet 'listservs') for participants of mythopoetic-type gatherings in an anonymous group experience survey. Individuals interested in participating in this research were asked to e-mail an address and in turn would be mailed a survey and a self-addressed stamped envelope in which to return it. Twenty-five surveys were mailed, and fifteen were returned. All returned surveys were complete and used in the study.

The MTG participants were solicited through an agency in the South Shore Boston area. After speaking with a coleader of the group, it was agreed that the surveys would be offered to interested group members. Fifteen surveys were distributed, six were returned. All returned surveys were complete and used in the study.

Finally, the group leaders data were collected in a similar fashion. The NWN Internet home page provided nineteen training centers throughout the country. Center Directors of these centers were sent e-mail requests to participate in a study by contributing a leaders' perspective on theory and application behind the approach. Twelve messages were sent via the Internet to training centers; six responded, and four surveys were returned. All were used. Only one of the MTG co-leaders completed the survey.

Findings

After completion of the data gathering, the data was analyzed. The findings are summarized below.

Mythopoetic Group

Demographics. The participants of this group ranged in age from twenty-five to fifty-eight, with the median age of forty. All except one (left blank) identified themselves as Caucasian and involved in an intimate relationship. The majority might be considered middle class by occupations listed. Of the respondents, 94 percent (fourteen) participated in the NWTA; two participants engaged in other mythopoetic gatherings at the time of survey completion. The date of original exposure to the groups ranged from 1991 to 1996, with the median year being 1995. All participants had follow-up meetings ranging from two months after the gathering to ongoing contact. Of these men, 70 percent (eleven) have also attended counseling ranging from four months to ten years, with the median time of eight months. Of this group, 82 percent (nine) identified the presenting problem as depression or relationship difficulties.

Particular Approach. Common themes that drew the men to this approach were grief regarding family relationships, struggling with ambivalent feelings toward male connection, and seeking a higher spiritual component and a less cerebral approach to growth. One participant responded: "I was spiritually adrift. The mythopoetic approach appealed to me because it tends to be nonintellectual and has a spiritual element. It's an experiential process."

Relationships with Men. How this experience affected their relationships with other men seemed to reflect movement from a place of distrust, fear, aggression, and detachment regarding other men to stronger, more meaningful, and trusting relationships: "Relationships with men did not mean much to me. I had friends, but I did not trust them very much. They were like me: competitive, aggressive, did not share feelings. After my experience, I found that I could relate to men and enjoyed talking to them."

Relationships with Women. With women, general themes seem to reflect the idea that self-analysis prompted a clearer, more honest, and respectful approach. These men also mention a sort of "demystification" of women: "Less dependent on women for my emotional needs. I look for them less for validation of my masculinity and can be more comfortable and love them in a mature fashion."

Emotional Expression. Generally the meaning of emotional expression seems to have been transformed from something that was avoided and degraded to a valued process that is more authentic, or at least more comfortable. These men might accurately be categorized as having been repressed and constricted and now have embraced a personally acceptable way of expression: "Emotional expression was something 'weak people' did. After my weekend experience I found that it was not only acceptable to show emotions, it was actually necessary. By feeling free to express myself, I have been able to relieve a lot of stress and turmoil."

Spirituality. How the gatherings affected the participants' concept of spirituality seems to vary widely. Some had a profound redefinition of spirituality; while others mention "no change." Overall, the experience seems to have prompted a clarification regarding religion and spirituality: "I have moved from a weekly churchgoer, flaccid, an audience member, letting others decide what a ritual should be and what is personally significant. The ritual work that I was a participant in through the men's group accessed a dormant and entombed veridicality that revealed the vastness of my spiritual gifts and qualities."

Masculinities. Responses suggest that the men have struggled to redefine themselves and have been most successful in the presence of other men. Using the language of the gatherings, men speak of the need for models, the power that comes with sharing emotions, and the joy that results from this rediscovery: "I had no models previously, or poor ones. Now I am able to form and develop my own definitions, which are evolving." Another member states: "If I had to sum up masculinity, I would say 'able to cry in public.' There is a lot more risk involved in public displays of emotion; being willing to face that risk means having a lot more strength than those who choose to hide it. A man that can do that is a 'real man'; he is very masculine."

Most Important Aspect of the Experience. The strongest responses concerning the most important part of the experience reflect the closeness and sharing among the men. Other ideas reflected the safety that men had discovered with other men, which allowed them to explore their inner self, their past, and their shadows (unrecognized, usually negative parts of the personality). This response is self-explanatory: "Learning that I am not alone."

Least Important Aspect of the Experience. Most of the group found flaws in the MKP or were disappointed with some aspect of their experience, although a few stated "it was all important" or "I can't think of one part that didn't help me." Ironically, the components that in some ways defined these gatherings were mentioned as the least helpful by a minority of men: "Ritual stuff . . . the male ritual stuff was just macho bullshit" or "the drumming—give me a Brahms piano trio any day."

Personal Application. Each man seems to have taken something different from the experience. A common theme in how they will use what they have learned was to "honor" the wisdom of their feelings and a sense of personal responsibility and integrity that is carried into the world: "I see myself clearly as a man. I've touched the importance of forgiveness in my life. I come more from feelings than my familiar head." Another states: "It is all right, and even necessary, to freely express how I feel. Events in my past caused me to interact badly with people. I can now recognize these problems and avoid them. I am more willing to expect integrity from other people and will encourage them to have it."

Other Therapeutic Experiences. Forty-four percent (seven) of the respondents listed other helping-type experiences. These ranged from personal-growth workshops and weekend experiences to twelve-step programs, ongoing therapy, and spiritual practices.

Comparison of Experiences. Of the seven who listed other helping experiences, five compared them to their mythopoetic experiences. The positive aspects of the gathering, identified as an "experiential" and "physical" process, the inclusion of ritual, a communal sense, and the postweekend integration groups, suggest a very potent experience: "This was the most powerful because it is not about reading a book or taking notes at a seminar, but experiencing yourself in new ways. This is an adventure, not a cerebral experience."

Men's Therapy Group

Demographics. The participants of this group ranged in age from twenty-nine to forty-eight, with the median age of forty-four. All identified themselves as Caucasian, and all but one was involved in an intimate relationship. The majority might also be considered middle class, indicated by their occupations. All participated in the MTG. This experience consists of one meeting per week (one and a half hours) for a twelve-week cycle. At the completion of the cycle, men may enroll in additional 12-week cycles. The date of original exposure to the group ranged from 1993 to 1997, with the median year being 1996. Experience in the group ranged from 12 weeks (one cycle) to 144 weeks (twelve cycles). All but one participant had completed more than one cycle. All of the men who responded have also attended individual or couples counseling ranging from two months to eight years, with a median time of one year. The presenting problems in all these cases were listed as depression or unhappiness and relationship difficulties.

Particular Approach. Many of these participants became involved in the group after suggestions by a therapist or a close acquaintance or by experiencing groups in a context unrelated to psychotherapy. Overall, it seems the men had a long-standing curiosity about group work and finally became involved after a combination of finally seeking a novel approach to their difficulties and prompting from another: "I was experiencing acute depression and overwhelming confusion and an inability to simplify my life. This group was recommended by my individual therapist."

Relationships with Men. How the group affected their relationships with men reflected experiencing a higher quality of connection and emotional expression between both genders. Although some reflect the difficulty of extending these relationships outside therapy, most speak of a more honest, open, and less traditionally socialized male interaction: "I can be more intimate and can discuss intimate topics. I have made connections with men like I haven't before."

Emotional Expression. These men generally expressed the idea that they are learning to understand, cope with, and express emotions within the group and hint at the difficulty of overcoming traditional views of emotionality: "I considered myself numb—'the walking dead' as I called it. I still need to validate my feelings more." Overall, it seems that the participants identify themselves as spiritual beings. Although many of the participants relate these experiences as originating outside the group, it seems significant to their overall self-perception and level of awareness in therapy: "I'm not sure if the group affected my spirituality, but overall I have become more spiritually aware."

Masculinities. The participants' view of masculinity did not seem to be strongly affected by the group. Some reflect no change (or no need to change)—"not a priority"—while a minority of the men hint at the need to reexamine the personal meaning of this term: "I still have trouble expressing and being around strong masculine behavior."

Most Important Aspect of the Experience. All of the men identified experiencing a sense of connection to others as being most important. The desire and ability to express feelings, to trust, and to share in the safety of the group is most evident: "Meeting and getting to really know my good friends. Trusting in them and sharing my feelings and emotions with them."

Least Important Aspect of the Experience. As a group, the men did not relate any substantial drawbacks or areas of diminished importance in this experience. Typical responses reflected cost, reaction to other members, or various "grades" of importance: "It feels as if all of it had some importance, just a difference in degrees."

Personal Application. The men essentially gave general but pragmatic responses to how they will implement what they had learned. The themes were varied: "I will try to build trust with others, try to identify situations that come up and work on the opportunities then and there." Another states; "I will be more connected in all relationships and be able to deal with messes in a positive way without withdrawing. I will be more assertive and get more of what I want out of life."

Mythopoetic Group Leaders

Demographics. The leaders of this group ranged in age from thirty-nine to fifty, with a median age of forty-four. All participants categorized themselves as white and were involved in an intimate relationship. The entire sample was drawn from the NWN. Time involved with this organization ranged from three to ten years, with a median time of five years. A typical profile of an NWN certified leader or co-leader would reflect someone college educated, with formal and/or informal training in various modes of counseling or therapy (workshops, seminars, or institutes) and/or training in education or personal growth areas.

Theory. Although there seemed to be no strong corroboration among leaders' perspectives on the theory behind their approach, there did seem to be a general pattern of concepts. The majority made reference to Jungian theory and shadow work as a foundation, and the necessity of the connection and integration of various aspects of the personality, psyche, and body: "A combination of Jungian, shadow work, psychotherapy, drama recreation . . . basis is for men to connect body, emotion, and head."

How It Helps. A common theme among how the leaders believe the NWTA "helps" is the cultivation of insight. The utility of this approach seems to suggest that with increased awareness comes increased opportunity and alternatives to behavior: "helps men to rescript their choices made in earlier life . . . brings a new perspective from a more mature place."

Effectiveness. Generally the leaders mentioned their own experiences, reactions from other participants, and observations to support how they know it "works": "Men report consistently that the changes are persistent and ongoing."

Leader's Role. The leaders frequently mention mentoring and guiding the men in reference to their role in the group. The idea of holding a broader understanding of the interaction between the men and to create a cohesiveness is also frequently stated.

Group Process. The training (or what "happens" in the group) seems to follow a formal structure, which includes screening activities and reenacting and working through past emotional experiences in a safe and controlled environment: "Men are encouraged and prepared through experiential sequences to recreate and reformat past emotional trauma . . . and create a life mission with intermediate goals."

Follow-up Gatherings and Importance. The integration training of eight to ten weeks of continued weekly meetings after the NWTA seems to be an important adjunct to the NWTA. Here participants are able to process what they have experienced in the group and apply it to their lives: "The weekend is a doorway to a new life experience, and the ongoing group provides a positive community for continued learning, growth, and self-discovery."

Greatest Impact on Members. The overall themes seem to be both general and specific: the caring support of a large staff and an environment that nurtures the men. The technical aspects of working through old issues and the liberation and empowerment that results seem to be evident: "It is the cadre of twenty-five to thirty-five men [staff] that sets the tone of an entrusting, loving environment" and "the discovery that the men can go back and revisit the past, make new choices about the present, and have it change their future."

Men's Therapy Group Leader

Demographics. This leader is a forty-one-year-old white male involved in an intimate relationship and co-leader of the men's group for five years. A summary of background and experience would reflect graduate education in psychology, licensing and certification in various subspecialties, and experience with various populations representing twenty years of experience in the field of mental health.

Theory. The assumptions in theory seem to be that past conflicts or maladaptive ways of coping in relationships will surface in the group, where men can be guided to interact more effectively: "Focus on the 'here and now.' Guiding men to interact with one another around cognitive and emotional experiences that happens in the group. The notion is that what goes on in relationships will show up in the interaction with the group."

How It Helps and Effectiveness. How this approach helps is reflected in the idea of an increased choice of behaviors will have an empowering effect: "The men are able to achieve greater connection and intimacy in important relationships. Men feel more empowered around learning they have choices."

Group Process. After a brief screening and statement of guidelines and expectations, the general goals of the group are to improve intimacy and connection: "Strictly therapy centered, no other activities. The general goals are to improve intimacy and communication in important relationships, increase connection."

Greatest Impact. In this leader's view, the greatest impact on the participants of this group is "men connecting with other men and realizing the experience of safety and acceptance."

Discussion

The findings of this study generally support the current literature on the mythopoetic men's movement. The typical participant in this study fits the profile (Bray, 1992; Wicks, 1996; Schawlbe, 1996) of the white middle-class male entering middle age and coming to terms with certain losses, transitions, and unfulfilled aspects of his life. Of the men who responded to this study, a large portion had been or are still involved in some form of counseling to address issues of depression or relationship difficulties.

The motivating factors of this group in some ways extend from these difficulties and are also closely aligned with concepts familiar to the mythopoetic groups. Common themes included feelings of isolation and disconnection from themselves and from others (Osherson, 1992), the desire for male friendship (Bly, 1990), the grief experienced from a lack of parental nurturance (Gilbert, 1992), and the desire to achieve a higher and more spiritual understanding of self and relationships in general (Welwood, 1984).

The men's therapy group reflected similar findings. Demographically, these men closely paralleled the mythopoetic group, including exposure to counseling to address depression or relationship difficulties. Many times these men were drawn to this approach by curiosity about the all-male atmosphere and as an alternative method of coping with difficulties and increasing self-understanding. Overall, a consistent increase in the quality of communication and intimacy, spanning both genders, was reported by these participants.

An understanding of both groups of men might be summarized by saying that each reported similar motivation, experiences, and reactions but couched in the vernacular of the specific approach. The mythopoetic members interpreted change through their own terms and tended to lean toward an analytical and spiritual understanding, which provided a richer metaphorical description (and possibly deeper personal meaning) of the group processes. The men's therapy group responses were devoid of such terms as *shadow* or *archetype* but relayed in pragmatic terms the difficulties and restrictions experienced in being a man and what has helped them become more fully "human." Virtually all men had struggled with depression or difficulties with relationships, or both. Although these are not uncommon, most men report that the group (despite orientation) has had a positive effect in relieving these symptoms.

The words of these men boldly and honestly reflected the difficulty they experienced in searching for some method to alleviate their suffering. It seems that when all else failed or at least was unsatisfactory, they had turned to a group of men. The strongest therapeutic component for all of the men surveyed has been the support, sharing, and closeness they felt with other men, which has seemed to "reawaken" many positive aspects of the men's personalities (emotional expression, clearer communication, and honesty), which may be critical to the development and maintenance of fulfilling relationships. It may also have allowed them to overcome the fear and secretiveness of being relational and of the environments that accept and nurture this quality.

Of course, in both groups there were men who had not experienced a profound change or been transformed by these experiences. The myth and ritual of one group or the idea of a transformed view of masculinities in another seemed to carry very little meaning and left some confused, and these men seemed out of place. The benefit for these periphery of men seemed not on a grand scale or as a spiritual event, but on a more subtle or practical level. The wisdom they had gained seems reflected in the techniques, insights, and support they gleaned from the group. The magnitude of gains seemed varied but consistent.

The leaders of the groups also had many common characteristics. Age, race, and other demographics were similar. The leaders' education reflected at least bachelor's level, extending to graduate study and a variety of specialized training that enhance the notion of credibility and competency. Within the mythopoetic group, the leaders' theory, assumptions, processes, and mechanisms of change seemed to possess commonalities. The metaphorical nature of Jungian and shadow work was mentioned frequently, as well as the process and necessity of integrating body, mind, soul, and emotion through insight. It seemed as though the mythopoetic leaders take a largely active approach in the gatherings and employ a number of activities, exercises, and "re-creations" to increase awareness, prompt self-evaluation, and generate a vibrant atmosphere conducive to change.

The men's therapy group leader, by contrast, seems less active but uses his position to challenge and guide the men to practice new behaviors during situations that arose throughout the course of the group. The here-and-now philosophy may allow the men to try out new strategies within the safe environment of the group before applying them outside the meetings. It is interesting to note that in the age of short-term, focused treatment, both approaches have collaborately set goals with the participants and use this focus as a general framework for the process. Both also have additional or extended meetings to further the gains and allow more opportunity to integrate what is learned into "real life." The leaders felt the overall impact on men was characterized by the safety and acceptance that is fostered in the group allowing men to behave in less restrictive ways.

Psychological Impact

To a large extent, the group process itself seems to provide validation for the men's experiences and affirmation of their struggle (Rabinowitz & Cochran, 1987). The activities, exercises, and events that pull men away from a purely cognitive understanding of their difficulties may, for some, increase or intensify the therapeutic gain. To draw a parallel for the mental health practitioner for the purpose of technical clarification, between mythopoetic activities and a traditional system of psychotherapy there seem to be some similarities between the NWTA and Gestalt (therapy) techniques. The founder of the system, Fritz Perls, likened the unfolding of adult personality to the peeling of an onion, suggesting that psychological maturity is attained by stripping off five layers of neurosis (Corey, 1994). Similarly, the NWTA uses a script—the "infinite journey" following the "Golden Child" (raw psychic energy) through stages to the "Rational Man" (mature psychological development). Furthering this connection, Corey (1994) suggests that Gestalt therapy "may be most effective with overly socialized, restrained, constricted individuals who are often described as phobic, perfectionistic, ineffective and depressed" (p. 299). This would seem to describe many of the mythopoetic participants' difficulties. The experiential rather than verbal or interpretive approach of both may be a key element in bringing into awareness and reintegrating various unacknowledged parts of the personality, unlocking resources, and empowering the men. In addition, the ritual and spiritual component may create a new environment and set of beliefs and expectations that result in a removal from ordinary reality. This may prompt a transcendent understanding of the difficulties and jolt the men into a new way of perceiving (Goleman, Smith, & Dass, 1985).

Given the proposed benefits of the mythopoetic experience, the question might be why more men have not become involved. As one leader of a men's group stated at a national conference (in Wilson, 1993), "I don't believe that there issuch a thing as the 'Men's Movement.' At best what we have right now is the 'White-Men's-Upper-to-Upper-Middle-class-Educated-with-Discretionary-Income-and-Weekends-to-Go-Somewhere-Movement.' " This may indicate that the mythopoetic branch, or the men's movement in general, does not touch all men and is not available or critical for those who may not fit this narrow definition of the contemporary male. The question might also be asked: Why follow a movement at all? Although proponents of the mythopoetic claim to support spiritual needs (and the Promise Keepers seem to verify that men have a spiritual hunger) rather than gender politics and social construction of gender, this idea, in itself seems to be a political statement (Chapter 1, this volume). On a personal level the men may not feel part of anything larger than themselves. Whether in a political, religious, or therapeutic context, there may be a sense of support and solidarity that begins a process of transformation.

In some instances the mythopoetic may present an oversimplified view of feminism as it relates to the women's movement. There also seems to be a polarization of gender and essentialist assumptions (Kimmel & Kaufman, 1994), which may create a false dichotomy between the sexes, but Kimmel (1995) later attempts a reconciliation.

Throughout the literature (Moore & Gillette, 1990; Bly, 1990) examples are used, in Jungian fashion, to promote integration of "complementary opposites" and clarify the male predicament. It may also serve, however, to fracture a holistic view of "human" into male or female. This "dissection" of gender might ultimately be warranted, however, as Tannen and Bly (1993) suggest: "There is more danger in not knowing our differences than in knowing." This lends credence to the idea that in order to realize one's humanity fully, what it is to be a man or woman must first be examined.

CLINICAL IMPLICATIONS

Attitudes toward the concept of health may be changing. If the increasing number of holistic practices, seminars, and publications is indicative of this change, it might suggest both a broadening of awareness and alternatives and a dissatisfaction that contemporary culture may be expressing with the limitations of traditional methods. With this new appreciation for nontraditional complementary approaches comes great potential for the field of mental health. People may be more receptive to alternative approaches to self-understanding and well-being. If this perception of a shifting attitude toward a more holistic understanding of health is accurate, then the amalgam of psychotherapeutic, myth, ritual, and spirituality of the mythopoetic approach may be a viable alternative for many men who might otherwise shun treatment in its strictest sense.

If used as an adjunct to traditional counseling, the clinician needs to realize when and how to recommend this approach. Those suffering from chronic low-grade depression or anxiety may be good candidates, while severely compromised individuals diagnosed as schizoid, personality disordered, or with impaired reality testing may not be the best candidates (Williams & Myers, 1992). Introducing this approach to clients might be accomplished by presenting the idea of returning to a more "historical" way of being a man—a way that is more "natural" and less "complicated," reducing the initial resistance of attending a men's gathering. These gatherings may also function as a gateway service and tap issues worthy of deeper discussion in individual or group therapy.

Applying principles, techniques, and ideas of the mythopoetic might also be an option for mental health practitioners. As judged appropriate, the clinician might suggest readings, offer poetry, or incorporate the richness of myth and metaphor into therapy sessions (Chapter 8, this volume). Those working in a group context might employ themes of the mythopoetic or use a ritual process to simulate transitions and passages of clients. In some ways the therapist, regardless of age, symbolizes a mentor to the client. If the importance of this relationship is honored, it can be used as a positive force in aiding the client to new understandings and therapeutic experiences. It is also strongly suggested that the therapist experience his or her own ritual work enhancing personal growth, congruence, and experiences in this North American culture devoid of meaningful spiritual journeys, symbols, and rituals.

This exploration of the mythopoetic perspective within the framework of contemporary psychological theory and application has supported the approach as a viable psychoeducational experience for many men, while at the same time capturing only a fleeting glimpse of the richness and meaning for those who have grown, been transformed, and continue on their own hero's journey.

REFERENCES

Allen, J., & Gordon, S. (1990). Creating a framework for change. In R. L. Meth & R. S. Pasick (Eds.), *Men in therapy: The challenge of change*. New York: Guilford Press.

Berman, J. J., & Zimpfer, D. G. (1980). Growth groups: Do the outcomes really last? *Review of Educational Research, 50*(4), 505–524.

Bergman, S. (1995). Men's psychological development: A relational perspective. In R. Levant & W. Pollock (Eds.), *A new psychology of men*. New York: HarperCollins.

Bly, R. (1990). *Iron John: A book about men*. New York: Vintage Books.

Bolen, J. S. (1984). *Goddesses in every woman*. San Francisco: Harper & Row.

Boudewijnse, B. (1990). The ritual studies of Victor Turner: An anthropological approach and its psychological impact. In H. G. Heimbrock & B. Boudewijnse (Eds.), *Current studies on rituals: Perspectives for the psychology of religion*. Atlanta, GA: Rodolpi.

Brannon, D. (1985). A scale for measuring attitudes about masculinity. In A. Sargent (Ed.), *Beyond sex roles* (pp. 110–116) St. Paul, MN: West.

Bray, L. H. (1992). *A preliminary exploration of the men's movement: Demographics and motivating factors*. Unpublished thesis, University of Alberta, Edmonton.

Corey, G. (1994). *Theory and practice of group counseling*. Pacific Grove, CA: Brooks/ Cole.

Douglas, C. (1995). Analytical psychotherapy. In R. Corsini & D. Wedding (Eds.), *Current psychotherapies* (pp. 95–127) Itasca, IL: F. E. Peacock.

Dunn, P. H. (1998). *Gender-role conflict, sex role egalitarism, egalitarian behavior, and emotional behavior among men involved in groups seeking to redefine masculinity*. Unpublished Masters in Social Work Thesis, Smith College School of Social Work: Northampton, MA.

Epstein, S. (1994). Integration of the cognitive and the psychodynamic unconscious. *American Psychologist, 49*(8), 709–724.

Erikson, E. (1966). *Ontogeny of ritualization in man*. New York: Bantam.

Fine, R. (1988). *Troubled men*. San Francisco: Jossey-Bass.

Franklin-Panek, C. E. (1978). Effects of personal growth groups on the self-concept and decision-making ability of normal adults. *Psychology, 15*(3), 25–29.

Freudenberger, H. J. (1990). Therapists as men and men as therapists. *Psychotherapy, 27*(3), 340–343.

Gergen, K. J. (1985). The social constructionist movement in modern psychology. *American Psychologist, 40*(2), 266–275.

Gilbert, R. K. (1992). Revisiting the psychology of men: Robert Bly and the mythopoetic movement. *Journal of Humanistic Psychology, 32*(2), 41–67.

Gilligan, C. (1982). *In a different voice: Psychological theory of women's development.* Cambridge: Harvard University Press.

Goleman, D., Smith, H., & Dass, R. (1985). Truth and transformation in psychological and spiritual paths. *Journal of Transpersonal Psychology, 17*(2), 83–114.

Graham, S. R. (1992). What does a man want? *American Psychologist, 47*(7), 837–841.

Hartman, B. T. (1995). *Masculine gender role stress and the men's movement.* Unpublished doctoral dissertation, Indiana State University.

Hearn, J. (1993). The politics of essentialism and the analysis of the 'men's movement(s).' *Feminism and Psychology, 3*(3), 405–409.

Heimbrock, H. G., & Boudewijnse (Eds.), *Current studies on rituals: Perspectives for the psychology of religion.* Atlanta, GA: Rodolpi.

Herek, G. M. (1987). On heterosexual masculinity: Some psychical consequences of the social construction of gender and sexuality. In M. Kimmel (Ed.), *Changing men: New directions in research on men and masculinity.* Newbury Park, CA: Sage.

Hjelle, L. A., & Ziegler, D. J. (1992). *Personality theories: Basic assumptions research, and applications* (3rd ed.). New York: McGraw-Hill.

Jung, C. (Ed.) (1964). *Man and his symbols.* New York: Doubleday.

Kaufman, M. L. (1994). Men, feminism and men's contradictory experiences of power. In H. Brod & M. Kaufman (Eds.), *Theorizing masculinities* (pp. 142–163). Thousand Oaks, CA: Sage.

Kaufman, J., & Timmers, R. (1983). Searching for the hairy man. *Women and Therapy, 4*(4), 45–57.

Kimmell, M. S. (1995). Afterword to M. S. Kimmel (Ed.), *The politics of manhood: Profeminist men respond to the mythopoetic men's movement (and the mythopoetic leaders answer).* Philadelphia, PA: Temple University Press.

Kimmel, M. S., & Kaufman, M. (1994). Weekend warriors. In H. Brod & M. Kaufman (Eds.), *Theorizing masculinities* (pp. 259–288). Thousand Oaks, CA: Sage.

Kupers, T. (1993). *Revisioning men's lives: Gender, intimacy and power.* New York: Guilford Press.

Lesser, A. (1995). *Masculine psychological development and the mythopoetic men's movement: A relational perspective.* Unpublished manuscript, Smith College of Social Work, Northampton, MA.

Levant, R. (1990a). Introduction to special series on men's roles and psychotherapy. *Psychotherapy, 27*(3), 307–309.

Levant, R. (1990b). Psychological services designed for men: A psychoeducational approach. *Psychotherapy, 27*(3), 309–315.

Levant, R. (1995). Toward a reconstruction of masculinity. In R. Levant & W. Pollock (Eds.), *A New Psychology of Men* (pp. 180–194). New York: HarperCollins.

Levant, R., & Pollock, W. (Eds.). (1995). *A new psychology of men.* New York: HarperCollins.

Levin, J. (1997). *Psychological impact of a mythopoetic initiation on participants.* Unpublished doctoral dissertation, Adler School of Professional Psychology: Chicago IL.

Lewis, R. (1981). Men's liberation and the men's movement: Implications for counselors. *Personnel and Guidance Journal, 60*(4), 256–259.

Lips, H. M. (1993). *Sex and gender: An introduction.* Mountain View, CA: Mayfield.

Mankowski, E., Maton, K., Burke, C., & Hoover, S. (1997). *Participation and retention rates in a men's mutual support organization.* Unpublished manuscript, University of Illinois, Urbana/University of Maryland, Baltimore.

Mathews, B. (1996). Parts are parts—or are they? The men's movement. Available at: http://web.Indstate.edu.spsmm/.

Meth, R. L., & Pasick, R. S. (1990). *Men in therapy: The challenge of change.* New York: Guilford Press.

Moore, R., & Gillette, D. (1990). *King, warrior, magician, lover: Rediscovering the archetypes of the mature masculine.* San Francisco: HarperCollins.

Moyers, B., & Bly, R. (1990). *A gathering of men.* McCarthy, B. (Producer), & Ewing, W. (Director) (Videorecording). (Available from Mystic Fire Video, New York, NY 10012–0008)

Nahon, D., & Lander, N. (1992). A clinic for men: Challenging individual and social myths. *Journal of Mental Health Counseling, 14*(3), 405–416.

Osherson, S. (1992). *Wrestling with love: How men struggle with intimacy with women, children, parents, and each other.* New York: Ballantine.

Pasick, R. (1992). *Awakening from the deep sleep: A powerful guide for courageous men.* New York: HarperCollins.

Pasick, R., Gordon, S., & Meth, R. (1990). Helping men understand themselves. In R. L. Meth & R. S. Pasick (Eds.), *Men in therapy: The challenge of change.* New York: Guilford Press.

Pedersen, L. (1991). *Dark hearts: The unconscious forces that shape men's lives.* Boston: Shambala.

Pentz, M. (1997). *Ethnographic study of the new warrior training adventure: A vision of a mature masculinity or a repackaging of a dominant patriarchy.* Unpublished manuscript, Indiana University Purdue at Indianapolis: Indianapolis, IN. See Chapter 13, this Vol.

Pleck, J. H. (1981). *The myth of masculinity.* Cambridge, MA: MIT Press.

Pleck, J. H. (1987). The contemporary man. In M. S. Kimmel (Ed.), *Changing men: New directions in research on men and masculinity.* Newbury Park, CA: Sage.

Rabinowitz, F., & Cochran, S. (1987). Counseling men in groups. In M. Scher, M. Stevens, G. Good, & G. Eichenfield (Eds.), *Handbook of counseling and psychotherapy with men.* Newbury Park, CA: Sage.

Richter, T. (1994). *A descriptive study of a men's support group.* Unpublished manuscript, University of Wisconsin, Stout.

Scher, M. (1990). Effect of gender role incongruities on men's experience as clients in psychotherapy. *Psychotherapy, 27*(3), 322–326.

Scher, M., Stevens, M., Good, G., & Eichenfield, G. (Eds.). (1987). *Handbook of counseling and psychotherapy with men.* Newbury Park, CA: Sage.

Schulz, G. (1997). *The rise of the mythopoetic mens movement: A psychosocial analysis.* Unpublished Doctoral Dissertation, Illinois School of Professional Psychology: Chicago, IL.

Schwalbe, M. (1996). *Unlocking the iron cage: The men's movement, gender, politics, and American culture.* New York: Oxford University Press.

Tannen, D., & Bly, R. (1993). *Men and women: Talking together* [Videorecording]. New York: Mystic Fire Video.

Thompson, K. (1991). A man needs a lodge. In K. Thompson (Ed.), *To be a man in search of the deep masculine.* Los Angeles: Perigree Books.

Vanderlans, J., & Geerts, H. (1990). The impact of the liturgical setting: An empirical study from the perspective of environmental psychology. In H. G. Heimbrock & B. Boudewijnse (Eds.), *Current studies on rituals: Perspectives for the psychology of religion* (pp. 87–102). Atlanta, GA: Rodolpi.

Vandermeerch, P. (1990). Psychotherapeutic and religious rituals: The issue of secularization. In H. G. Heimbrock & B. Boudewijnse (Eds.), *Current studies on rituals: Perspectives for the psychology of religion* (pp. 151–164). Atlanta, GA: Rodolpi.

Warren, L. J. (1976). The therapeutic status of conscious-raising groups. *Professional Psychology, 7*(2), 132–140.

Welwood, J. (1984). Principles of inner work: Psychological and spiritual. *Journal of Transpersonal Psychology, 16*(1) 65–73.

Wicks, S. (1996). *Warriors and wildmen.* Westport, CT: Bergin & Garvey.

Williams, R. C., & Myers, R. A. (1992). The men's movement: An adjunct to traditional counseling approaches. *Journal of Mental Health Counseling, 14*(3), 393–404.

Wilson, S. (1993). *Beyond the drum: An exploratory study of the men's movement and its impact on men.* Unpublished master's thesis, University of California, Long Beach. See chapter 2 of this volume.

Wong, M. R. (1978). Males in transition and the self-help group. *Counseling Psychologist, 7*(4), 46–50.

Wikstrom, O. (1990) Ritual studies in the history of religions. In H. G. Heimbrock & B. Boudewijnse (Eds.), *Current studies on rituals: Perspectives for the psychology of religion* (pp. 57–67). Atlanta, GA: Rodolpi.

PART III _____
RESEARCH ON THE MANKIND PROJECT

Chapter 12

Collaborative Research with a Men's Organization: Psychological Impact, Group Functioning, and Organizational Growth

Eric S. Mankowski, Kenneth I. Maton,
Christopher K. Burke, Sharon A. Hoover, and
Clinton W. Anderson

Indicators of socialization and quality of life show men to be especially prone to alcohol and drug addiction, incarceration, early mortality, heart disease, suicide, perpetration of domestic violence, physical and sexual abuse of children, abandonment of parental responsibilities, and poor school performance (Kilmartin, 1994). In the past twenty-five years, a social movement of men has emerged that has focused on the dysfunctional aspects of masculine behavior and the male gender role as the cause of these health and behavioral risks (Clatterbaugh, 1997).

Along with the increased criticism of traditional masculinity and masculine roles has come the call for the development of new models of masculine socialization and new means to influence men's development and behavior positively (Levant & Kopecky, 1995). As Levant (1995b) has written, there is great opportunity and need to construct positive forms of masculinity, guided by both empathy toward men and an affirmation of feminist critiques of traditional masculinity. The ManKind Project (MKP) is one response to this call. Based on mobilization of peer rather than professional resources, the MKP is an international men's mutual support and self-development organization that describes itself as "an order of men called to reclaim the sacred masculine for our time through initiation, training and action in the world" (New Warrior Network, 1997). The organization is concerned with the support and transformation of men striving to develop more healthy and mature masculinity. Its mission and scope make it an important organization to study for psychologists and others who want to understand the impact of the mythopoetic branch of the contemporary men's movement on men's lives and society more generally.

A BRIEF DESCRIPTION AND HISTORY OF THE MANKIND PROJECT

The MKP is a rapidly expanding organization. Founded as the New Warrior Network in 1985 by Bill Kauth, Rich Tosi, and Ron Hering, the MKP has grown in size to twenty-three regional training centers located in the United States, Canada, and England. To date, over fifteen thousand men have completed an experiential, initiatory, adventure weekend (New Warrior Network, 1997; Virgin, 1998).

Participation in the MKP begins with the New Warrior Training Adventure (NWTA), an experiential, weekend-long gathering focused on deep, personal work with and among men. During the NWTA, men work on becoming aware of emotional wounds, overcoming barriers to intimacy and trust with other men, and developing a vital and constructive mission in life. The weekend encourages "deep self-exploration, emotional connection with other men and male initiation . . . [taking place] in the context of a mutually-supportive male social environment, but . . . also includes confrontational methods geared toward the individual issues presented by each participant" (Hartman, 1994, p. 13). There is also a theme of nature spirituality, strongly influenced by Native American traditions.

After the weekend adventure, men are assigned to a small, supportive, integration group (I-group), formed from the weekend participants. The groups are intended to help men integrate changes begun during the weekend into their daily lives. During an initial eight-week period, the I-groups are led by a facilitator trained by the organization in group process skills. The MKP provides a protocol for facilitators that has evolved over the years. Typically it includes exercises and drills for emotional awareness, communication skills, anger management, cognitive restructuring, and taking responsibility and ownership for one's behavior and thoughts. After eight weeks, the I-group is facilitated by its own members, similar to self-help and mutual-aid groups (Levine, 1988).

To further assist men's development, an array of experiential workshops and additional training programs are available: workshops to train the staff leaders of the NWTA weekend and I-groups and workshops focused on specific psychoeducational techniques and processes used in the weekend or I-groups. The MKP also sponsors a number of social events and civic volunteer activities in which men are encouraged to participate as part of their involvement in the organization and action in the world. Although many of the MKP activities are all male, the local community with which we have collaborated has a significant relationship with the sister organization, Woman Within, that shares structural similarities in that both include an initiation weekend experience and follow-up mutual support groups.

As with other mythopoetic branch organizations, the MKP's program of training and activity is based in part on archetypal theories regarding masculine personality development over the life span (Moore & Gillette, 1990). In this view, the modern masculine self is composed of four structures or energy forms that must be balanced and integrated for healthy and mature male personality functioning: the king, magician, lover, and warrior. Archetypal personality theory suggests that all four aspects of the male psyche have both positive and negative aspects. The MKP uses archetypal theory to help men more clearly understand their shadows—what they call "that part of ourselves which we hide, deny, or repress." By providing men a safe environment and a structured process for interaction and self-development, the MKP attempts to foster greater expression of the positive aspects of the archetypes and reduce the negative consequences of their shadow aspects. For example, the warrior archetype represents both "the capacity for aggression and the ability to serve a cause. The energy of the Warrior is that energy of focused discipline, boundaries, service and mission. . . . When immature, undeveloped, and uninitiated, this energy causes all kinds of trouble, from passivity to rampant violence, both of which we are facing globally." (Moore, 1997, p. 10).

ANALYTIC FRAMEWORK AND GOALS FOR COLLABORATIVE RESEARCH WITH MKP-GW

Theory and systematic research on therapeutic men's groups (Andronico, 1996) and mythopoetic men's organizations (Schwalbe, 1996) and groups (Chapter 2, this volume) have suggested a number of potentially positive outcomes for men who participate in a men's mutual support group, such as an I-group. For example, involvement appears to reduce men's gender role stress (Hartman, 1994). However, there are still large gaps in our understanding of how these groups and organizations work and what factors contribute to their creation, sustenance, and effectiveness in supporting and changing men. We know relatively little about who participates in these groups, who benefits from this kind of intervention, what, if any, changes men experience (e.g., in their psychological well-being, attitudes toward women, gender role conflict, and sense of purpose in life) as a result of participation in these groups, and how social-psychological processes in the groups contribute to these changes. Furthermore, we do not know how these organizations fit into the larger picture of community-based services addressing the needs of men and how they influence men's gender roles and contributions as partners, fathers, and coworkers. We have formed an ongoing, collaborative research relationship with an MKP training center in order to investigate some of these questions.

Following Maton (1993) and other community psychologists, we believe that mutual support organizations such as the MKP are most usefully described and analyzed at three distinct but related levels of analysis: the individual participants, the ongoing group work (i.e., small, peer mutual support groups), and the organizational structure and culture. At the individual level of analysis, for example, we ask: Are the participants making positive changes in their masculinities? Do they have more prosocial life goals, reduced gender role conflict, reduced anxiety and depression, and more respectful and less sexist attitudes toward women? Are they less isolated, and do they have better friendships with men and women? Are these potential changes sustained long after the initial period of involvement? To address these questions we are drawing on longitudinal survey data, intensive interviews, and family and peer reports about the members.

At the group level, we ask: How do small men's mutual support groups (in this case, integration groups) facilitate such changes? What kind of social interactions and processes occur in the group? What factors are related to groups lasting long enough to allow change to occur in individual members? This work is based on surveys of and interviews with I-group representatives about the rate and duration of individual participation in I-groups, reasons for members dropping out of the I-groups, the rate of I-group formation and disbandment, the duration of the I-groups, and group processes that may be related to these outcomes.

Finally, at the organizational level, we ask: How can a supportive organizational culture and structure assist individual men and groups in making these transformations in their masculinities? How does such a network develop and expand? What organizational processes and functions are related to the recruitment of members and the effectiveness and growth of groups? How do different group facilitation protocols relate to individual and group-level outcomes? Does the organization contribute to community well-being and to society's changing representations of masculinities? Although this level has not yet been formally incorporated into our research design, we are benefiting from informal conversations and meetings with local and international organization leaders.

Our research collaboration with the Washington, D.C., center of MKP (MKP-GW) began in 1996, after two of the authors completed the initiation adventure weekend (NWTA). The research team was purposefully composed of both members and nonmembers of the organization, as well as men and women. We think there are several advantages to our research that derive from having a relatively diverse team of collaborators. Because there are several members of MKP-GW on the research team (K.M., C.B., and C.A.), we are able to build on insiders' experiential knowledge. Their role as participant observers is helpful in gaining access to and establishing cooperative and trusting relationships with other members and leaders of the organization, as well as allowing us to communicate the implications of our research findings to leaders of the organization (Brydon-Miller, 1998). These relationships have also been crucial to the successful conduct of research on the potentially sensitive and personal experiences that occur in MKP. Our research team also contains the perspective of both a man and a woman (E.M. and S.H.) who are not members of MKP and may provide more balanced or objective viewpoints on the research questions, methodology, or data interpretations.

INDIVIDUAL AND PSYCHOLOGICAL IMPACT OF THE MANKIND PROJECT NWTA

Does the NWTA have a measurable psychological impact on participants? In particular, does it positively influence men's life goals, gender role conflict, self-development, and attitudes toward women? An abbreviated summary of the research methods and findings is provided here (for more detailed results, see Maton, Anderson, Burke, Hoover, & Mankowski, 1998 and Hoover, Burke, Maton, & Mankowski, 1998).

In summer 1997, we began surveying men before and after their participation in the NWTA.[1] Of the 119 men who received preweekend questionnaires to date, 70 (58.8 percent) completed them, with forty-two of the men (35.3 percent) completing postweekend questionnaires as well. The average age was 48.0, 51.2 percent were married, and 30.0 percent had children in the home. The majority of men were Caucasian (91.9 percent) and had postcollege graduate or professional degrees (58.5 percent).

Life Goals

The survey asked participants to assess the importance of fifteen life goals; having lots of money; being successful in work; having a high-quality relationship with a significant other; having a happy family life; having leisure time; working to correct social, racial, or economic inequalities; serving as a model for other men; helping other men develop and grow; having strong friendships with other men; developing a deep spiritual life; assuming leadership roles; developing leadership qualities; and having good physical health.

Following the NWTA, men reported significant increases in the importance of a number of life goals, including serving as a model for other men, helping other men develop and grow, having strong friendships with other men, working to correct social, racial, or economic inequalities, having a deep spiritual life, and having strong friendships. Changes in these particular life goals are consistent with the content and process of the weekend. The lack of change on life goals such as presence as a father and high-quality relationship with a partner likely reflect a ceiling effect, as men at baseline already had these as primary personal goals. The lack of change in goals related to work success and money earned likely reflect the reality that the MKP focus is on psychological, interpersonal, and societal goals, not traditional success-oriented pursuits.

Gender Role Conflict

Questionnaires also assessed gender role conflict (O'Neil et al., 1986). Following the NWTA, men reported significant reductions in gender role conflict, including restrictive affectionate behavior between men, success, power and competition orientation, and restrictive emotionally. The reduced levels of gender role conflict after the weekend are not surprising given the personal work and deep sharing with other men, and the psychoeducational focus on learning relationship and growth-oriented skills and overcoming barriers that inhibit affect, expression, and intimacy. MKP seeks to empower men to be affectionate, expressive, and intimate *as men* rather than as women would.

Psychological Well-Being and Self-Development

Questionnaires assessed several domains of psychological well-being, including depression and anxiety symptoms (SCL-90-R; Derogatis & Melisaratos, 1983; Boulet & Boss, 1991), self-esteem (Rosenberg, 1979), life satisfaction (Diener, Emmons, Larsen, & Griffin, 1985), and sense of mastery (Pearlin, Lieberman, Menaghan, & Mullan, 1981). In addition, a number of questions developed for this project tapped facets of self-development (beliefs, feelings, behaviors, and motivations) consistent with the NWTA. Members of MKP-GW, including but not limited to those on the research team, suggested these items— for example: "A man's personal growth requires tapping an inner, untamed part of himself"; "I am learning to accept total responsibility for all aspects of my life"; "I am learning to live in the world with an open heart"; "I carry around a lot of shame, especially involving sexuality and other aspects of my masculinity"; and "I am a man of power, a man among men."

Compared to before the weekend, men had significantly lower levels of depression and significantly higher levels of life satisfaction, self-esteem, and sense of mastery, although no change was found in anxiety symptoms. The reduction in depression symptoms and the enhanced levels of self-esteem, life satisfaction, and sense of mastery can be viewed as a direct result of the sharing, uncovering, catharsis, bonding, and positive formulation of goals and perspectives that form the core of the weekend experience.

Consistent with the view that the NWTA is linked to the changes reported, men also reported large and significant increases on most of the self-development process items developed for the research. Some of the increases were one standard deviation in magnitude. For example, men reported enhanced equality of power in relationship to other men ($M = 2.3$ versus 3.7), increased clarity of life "mission" ($M = 2.3$ versus 3.3), greater ability to live from the deepest core being or truth ($M = 3.4$ versus 4.3), greater acceptance of responsibility for their life ($M = 3.6$ versus 4.4), and increased openness to the world ($M = 3.6$ versus 4.4). Reductions were reported in internal shame and negative feelings toward other men. Enhanced sense of equality to other men, clarity of life mission, importance of tapping deep internal resources, focus on integrity and openness, and reductions in shame and negativity toward other men all represent focal points of the MKP. Furthermore, participants' increased sense after the weekend that involvement in ritual had contributed to their growth, health, and development suggests a direct link between the NWTA (ritual) and the other outcomes reported.

Attitudes Toward Women

Finally, we asked thirteen questions to assess participants' attitudes toward women,[2] including views of women's roles in society (e.g., "There should be more women leaders in important jobs in public life, such as politics"; "If a woman has a job outside the home, her husband should share the housework, such as washing dishes, cleaning, and cooking"), views of the women's movement (e.g., "The women's movement has made society a better place for women"), views of women's interactions with men (e.g., "I feel that many times women flirt with men just to tease them or hurt them"; "Generally, it is safer not to trust women"), and views of both physical and sexual aggression against women (e.g., "A man is never justified in hitting a woman"; "It is okay for men at times to be sexually aggressive, even when a woman does not seem interested"). One therapist who specialized in working with men before the therapist did the NWTA sees men as taking "sexually aggressive" to equate with "assertive" or "not passive" (Rose, D.S., personal communication, 2000).

Men's reported attitudes toward women did not change much, although that baseline levels were already quite high on most items. They did, however, demonstrate significant change on three items. Specifically, they reported more agreement with the suggestion that there "should be more women leaders in important jobs in public life," less agreement with the statement, "Sometimes women bother me just by being around", and a significant increase in their agreement with the statement, "It is okay for men at times to be sexually aggressive, even when a woman does not seem interested," which may have meant——to the men.

The last response above seems to be inconsistent with the other aspects of this research and other research reported in this volume. It is possible that the question did not really measure what it purported. Often the men indicated that they felt more assertive in their lives. That is assertive, not dominant or dominating. When the men were asked about sexual aggressiveness they may have really been thinking assertiveness rather then sexual aggressiveness.

These changes are of particular interest in the context of debates about the implications of the mythopoetic men's movement for women (Hagan, 1992). While some have argued that adopting a feminist philosophy is central to the mission of the men's movement (Tillitski, 1995), some feminist scholars have greeted the mythopoetic men's movement with critical skepticism and apprehension (Adair, 1992). Specifically, critics fear that the mythopoetic branch may worsen participants' attitudes and corresponding behavior toward women. Our preliminary findings do not provide a clear answer to these concerns; some items indicate a positive change in men's attitudes toward women, while another item suggests a possible negative change. In addition, the small number of items used to assess a broad attitude domain, as well as a lack of previous empirical validation for some of the scale items, caution against confident interpretations. Continued investigation may clarify the nature of these seemingly contradictory, initial changes in men's attitudes toward women.

Summary of the Impact of the NWTA on Participants

Participants initially report a striking, positive impact of participation in the NWTA on their life goals, gender role conflict, psychological well-being, and self-development, although the changes in their attitudes toward women are less clear. This evidence of immediate change in men was expected, as direct experience and observation of the weekend (both as initiates and staff) by three members of the research team indicate that it is indeed a powerful personal experience for many men, involving the deepest levels of personal work. Men who sign up for the NWTA are aware that it has the potential to be a life-changing experience, and some have seen friends and peers who have been significantly and positively affected by involvement in the weekend as well. Whether these changes are sustained after continued participation in the I-groups is an important question that our research is currently investigating.

Several features of these data should be kept in mind when thinking about the degree to which they are indicative of the MKP in general. Many men who were not affected by the NWTA or were negatively affected may not have returned questionnaires and thus are not represented in the sample. The relatively low return rate (35 percent), reliance on self-report measures, and the absence of a comparison sample of men who did not complete the NWTA somewhat limit our confidence in the validity of these initial findings. As our research continues, a larger sample size and longer-term follow-up will be available. Obtaining a similar comparison sample will remain a difficult problem, however, given the lack of control over assigning self-selected group men to participate in a different men's organization. But even with these limitations, the findings suggest that the NWTA has a substantive impact on at least some of the men who attended—an impact that can potentially result in healthier forms of masculinity and increased positive involvement of men in their families and society.

MKP I-GROUPS: MUTUAL SUPPORT FOR CONTINUING AND INTEGRATING INDIVIDUAL CHANGES

The second goal of our research project was to analyze whether MKP I-groups support the initial changes men make during the NWTA. I-groups can be understood as an instance of a larger, growing cultural phenomenon: the self-help or mutual-aid group (Kessler, Mickelson, & Zhoa, 1997). Both self-help and I-groups are designed to empower members in that they are peer led and draw on members' experiential knowledge with a shared condition or problem. Such small groups may be a natural setting for those who, having become dissatisfied with the traditional forms of community, are turning inward for answers to their questions but still yearn for a communal touch (Wuthnow, 1994). A cofounder of the MKP, Bill Kauth (1992), suggests that within I-groups, "a process has emerged by which a group of men who are reasonably compatible and who come together with a mutuality of intention will learn rapidly to trust, love, resolve conflict, and care for each other" (p xiii).

As in many other forms of effective group helpfulness (Yalom, 1985), the I-group meeting consists of exercises and drills designed to facilitate emotional awareness, communication skills, anger management, cognitive restructuring, and taking responsibility and ownership for one's behavior and thoughts. These I-group activities can create a "safe container" (Kauth, 1992), which enables members to take emotional risks that further the initial changes begun during the weekened adventure and enable them to integrate these individual changes into their everyday social lives and lived experiences.

Factors Affecting I-Group Duration, Member Retention, and Effectiveness

If MKP I-groups are to be effective in supporting the changes members initially make on the NWTA, they must be stable and retain active participants. Yet we know very little about the levels of participation and retention in men's peer mutual support groups in general or about I-groups in particular, or about how stable and effective groups are created and maintained (Jesser, 1996).

We reviewed the literature concerning mutual support groups in general (Maton, Leventhal, Madara, & Julien, 1989) and men's mutual support (MMS) groups in particular (Taylor, 1995) to identify factors affecting group duration and effectiveness. In addition, we consulted with experienced members of MKP-GW in order to build on their knowledge. Based on this effort, a number of possible factors affecting group outcomes were identified: group leadership (peer versus professional), group process, size of the group, diversity in age, background, and orientation of members, the availability of a stable meeting place, frequency of meeting, and several other factors related to the level of a member's commitment to the group, including the regularity of attendance. Most discussions of these issues suggested that stable and effective groups meet relatively frequently (two to four times a month), in an environment that is accessible and free of distraction, are not too small or too large (four to eight men), have members who attend regularly, and have a clear policy for missed attendance.[3] These factors might create group effectiveness and stability by fostering a group environment in which commitment, intimacy, and trust flourish.

In addition to knowing why and how groups are effective, it is also important to understand why members might drop out of their groups and why groups disband. An understanding of the most common reasons for leaving groups could inform guidelines for the process, content, and structure of MPMS groups (Kauth, 1992).

The initial phase of our research project therefore attempts to examine the levels of participation and retention within the I-groups and to increase understanding of the factors that contribute to stable and effective groups. Group representatives from every MKP-GW I-group formed between 1990 and 1996 ($N = 35$)[4] completed a historical survey[5] that asked, for example, about important dates in the group's formation and development; characteristics such as meeting location, frequency, and number of members; and reasons that members dropped out of the group. Understanding why some I-groups succeed whereas others do not is clearly a complex endeavor because of the diverse pathways to group durability, effectiveness, and disbanding. To contribute to such understanding, in a subsequent phase of the research, two of us (K.M. and C.B.) interviewed a subsample of I-group representatives about a variety of factors that may affect I-group effectiveness and duration.[6]

Organizational Growth and I-Group Duration

MKP-GW has grown substantially during the center's seven-year history. On average, there was a net increase of about four I-groups per year, although there was no growth in the most recent year. Interestingly, groups that were formed earlier in the history of the center tended to last longer. From 1990 to 1994, 95 percent (nineteen of twenty) of the groups continued two years or longer. Among groups developed more recently, during 1995 and 1996, we cannot yet determine the percentage of group disbandment two years after group formation, but since 40 percent (six of fifteen) have already disbanded, it is clear that the previous benchmark of 95 percent cannot be achieved. Groups formed earlier in the MKP-GW area may have been composed of men with especially strong initiative, motivation, or prior experience in and dedication to men's mutual support groups or other mythopoetic activities. Alternatively, the expanded size, structure, and functions of MKP-GW may have decreased recent members' identification with and commitment to the organization. Additional research is necessary to examine these and other possible explanations, especially to see whether these trends occur in other MKP centers and whether they represent a temporary or long-term change in the organization. Active groups had been meeting, on average, for twenty-nine months, whereas disbanded groups met, on average, for nineteen months. Groups formed with an average of eight members; currently active groups average seven members. Group duration was positively related to the number of men attending each meeting ($r = .34$). The overall portrait of MKP-GW I-groups painted by these data suggests that groups are fairly stable, typically lasting about two years, and, until recently, rapidly increasing in number (cf. Maton et al., 1989).

Groups met in a variety of locations: members' homes, churches, office buildings, and schools. On any given year, about 52 percent of the groups met in homes, 25 percent in churches, 10 percent in office buildings or schools, and 15 percent varied among these locations. Interestingly, a logistics regression analysis showed that groups that had a stable meeting location and met weekly (instead of only every other week) were significantly less likely to disband. Without the consistency of frequent meetings in stable location, groups appear to be less able to survive. The deep personal work occurring in MKP I-groups may require the safety and continuity provided by a stable, secure meeting location (see also Yalom, 1985).

I-Group Effectiveness

I-groups were rated as moderately effective ($M = 7.0$ on a 10-point scale, S.D. $= 1.63$). Overall, the eleven disbanded groups were viewed as significantly less effective than the twenty-four continuing groups, many of which are still active in 2000.. As would be expected, it seems that ineffective groups are more likely to disband. We explored other factors that might be related to group effectiveness and found that groups that met in a stable location during their first year were rated as significantly more effective.

Overall, our findings on I-group duration and effectiveness suggest that groups that are not rated as highly and eventually disband show signs of difficulty early in the group's history (Yalom, 1985). It is also noteworthy that perceived group effectiveness was higher for the later years of a group's history. There are several possible explanations for this outcome. Effectiveness ratings might be higher for groups in later years because only the most effective groups last this long. On the other hand, the growing strength of the group and its success in fostering the ability of the members to become more intimate and communicate more clearly may explain the higher ratings.

Our analysis of members' reasons for leaving an I-group identified additional factors that may contribute to group effectiveness. I-group representatives reported that most members left their group because they were too busy with work, family, or school commitment (26 percent); the group disbanded (20 percent); they moved away from the area (18 percent); or they disagreed with the group, individuals in the group, or MKP-GW (15 percent). What does it mean that the most common reason men leave an I-group is that they are too busy? While not discounting the importance of members' other commitments, the constant pressure to compete, achieve, and perform that is part of the traditional masculine gender role seems to prevent some members from continued participation in the potentially valuable activities of their I-group. Indeed, continued participation in MKP-W might assist these men in making changes at the personal and societal level that would alleviate pressure to be overly competitive and achievement oriented in the first place.

The second most common *proactive* reason for leaving a group was disagreement with the group, specific members in the group, or the MKP-GW organization. This finding seems important given that the ability of I-groups to stick to an agreed-on procedure for holding members accountable for their feelings and actions, and the presence of key members who can manage conflicts, may be important factors contributing to group effectiveness and stability. Additional training in conflict resolution might create more sustainable I-groups by aiding men to deal with conflict in productive ways rather than "running away," escaping, or striking back.

Consistent with observations of group psychotherapy, these data also suggest that groups rated as less effective and that eventually disband show signs of difficulty during the early stages of development. These signs of difficulty are men not attending, low accountability, inability to process emotions and conflicts between members (Yalom, 1985). MKP may want to take additional preventive steps to help groups that show these early signs of difficulty. One solution could be to invite the facilitators to return to the group for a period of time to address problems that the group identifies in their process.

Individual Member Participation and Retention

From the survey of I-group representatives, we found that as with I-group formation, the net number of new MKP-GW members increased every year ($M = 31$) except 1996, when there was no net growth. We also found that 16 percent of all active group members have been involved in their I-group for four to six years, 26 percent have been involved two to four years, and 58 percent less than two years. Members of active groups participate (or participated) about twice as long as those in disbanded groups ($M = 2$ years versus 1 year).

Group dropouts were most likely during the first year of participation in an I-group. Among men who dropped out, 3 percent were involved more than two years, 40 percent one to two years, and 57 percent less than one year. In addition, a significant portion of the men less than thirty years of age stopped their participation at an early stage of their involvement in MKP-GW (which we defined as less than eight weeks, before the completion of the organization's initial period of facilitating the groups). Overall, the level of member retention in MKP-GW I-groups, even considering disbanded groups, is considerably higher than has been reported for some other kinds of mutual support groups (Luke, Roberts, & Rappaport, 1993).

Corroborative Evidence from Interviews with Group Representatives

Preliminary analyses of the in-depth interviews with I-group representatives were carried out by two of the participant-observer researchers on our team (K.M. and C.B.). Based on the initial interviews and notes kept during the interviews, qualitative summaries were developed of I-group representatives' views regarding the main factors underlying their group's level of effectiveness and stability. The summaries of these factors were then discussed and evaluated by the entire research group. Special attention was given to comparisons between active and disbanded groups that formed after the same NWTA weekend in order to eliminate possible variance due to minor differences between the training weekends.

Our analysis of the interviews confirms and extends the main quantitative findings about I-group effectiveness and retention. Several salient factors at the individual, group, and organizational levels were identified and supported during our analysis of the transcripts that appear to corroborate findings from the surveys (see Table 12.1). This convergence of data obtained from different research methods on different occasions suggests that some confidence can be placed in the validity of the findings.

Table 12.1
Factors Related to Effective I-Group Functioning

Individual Level	Group Level	Organizational Level
1. A sense of "Fierce Caring"	1. Chemistry and balance	1. Quality of facilitation
2. A level of energy, intensity and personal engagement	2. Commonality in group members' experiences and goals for group work	2. Adding new members or facilitating group mergers
3. Accountability	3. Safety and trust	3. Organizational linkage
4. Willingness to do personal work	4. Accountability	4. Consultation from the ManKind Project
5. Commitment to the group process	5. Presence of 2 or 3 energetic, intense, and interpersonally engaging men	5. Meeting location planning
		6. Providing a paradigm of behavior

At the individual level, a number of characteristics were commonly noted in members who belonged to particularly stable or effective I-Groups:

1. A sense of fierce caring—or a persistent, intense, and caring challenging of men, at times in a confrontational but encouraging manner to perform personal work and relate to others at the deepest possible level. This quality may prevent members from "treading water" and hiding behind traditional defenses and modes of relating.

2. A level of energy, intensity, and personal engagement, which describes men who are invested in the process of men's work, bring ideas to the group, have good interpersonal skills, and lead in a cooperative spirit and without domination.

3. Accountability or responsibility—the willingness to show up for meetings on time, attend most meetings, and take responsibility for one's actions and feelings. This characteristic may encourage honesty and reduce passive-aggressive modes of dealing with frustration and hostility.

4. Willingness to do personal work—or the desire to understand one's true motives and feelings.

5. Commitment to the group process as indicated by loyalty and vested interest in the workings of the group.

At the group level, several qualities that an I-group embodies as a whole, values, or supports were noted among particularly effective and stable groups:

1. Chemistry and balance—or a good balance of gifts and capabilities and a positive spark resulting from the balance of personalities, characteristics, and styles.

2. Commonality in group members' experiences and goals for group work—or the lack of conflict about special issues that the group might undertake.

3. Safety and trust—an ingredient that was found necessary for the men to undertake the risks of exploring emotions and deep personal issues within the group setting.

4. Accountability. At the group level this describes the group's ethos of not letting the individual members become lax in relation to both commitments and personal work.

5. The presence of two or three energetic, intense, and interpersonally engaging men—
   describing a core of men in the group who model healthy masculinity and bring
   substantial interpersonal skills and new ideas to the group.

Finally, at the organizational level, a number of resources provided by the
MKP-GW organization were present in particularly effective and stable groups:

1. Quality of facilitation—or the skill with which the organization prepares the I-group
   facilitators to lead the men in performing group work.
2. Facilitating group mergers or the addition of new group member—when the organization helps groups that are getting smaller stay alive by connecting them with other
   smaller groups or with men who wish to continue group work.
3. Organizational linkage—which describes how supplemental events and workshops
   offered by the MKP-GW may infuse new energy, expertise, and techniques into a
   group that has members in attendance.
4. Consultation from the MKP-GW—which refers to the help the parent organization
   gives to groups that seek out help or facilitation if the I-group is having difficulty.
5. Location—or the organization's ability to choose members for groups in a way that
   makes good geographic sense.
6. Providing a new paradigm or way of understanding men that validates men for engaging in healthy yet atypical behaviors.

The interviews provided substantial information about possible processes by
which an I-group successfully challenges and supports men to continue the kinds
of changes begun during the NWTA. The factors described above, which appear
to contribute to group effectiveness and stability, were found to be common to
many of the groups. The analysis also revealed an interesting contrast. At each
level of analysis, certain qualities stood in juxtaposition, resulting in a tension
between opposing values that was successfully balanced by those I-groups that
survived and prospered. For instance, at the group level of analysis, two
concepts—challenging the group members and providing safety and comfort to
them—were found to affect the groups' functioning positively. However, any
group that overidentified with either of these factors to the neglect of the other
fared poorly. In almost every case of disbandment, the groups failed to provide
this balance. If a group became too challenging and provided no comfort, the
members found it alienating and were more likely to drop out. If a group focused
on comforting its members, it did not provide them with the difficult but adap-
tive awareness they needed to grow. These groups, to borrow a phrase, tended
to disband "not with a bang, but a whimper." A successful navigation between
these two qualities was the hallmark of an effective group.

In addition, successful groups used resources from all three levels analyzed
in our study. Groups that isolated themselves from the larger organization tended
not to fare as well as groups that used the additional trainings and resources

available through MKP-GW. Groups whose members were too invested in their own personal issues and were not concerned about the health of the group also tended not to do as well.

Summary and Limitations of the I-Group Research

This initial study of the MKP-GW I-groups revealed that the organization has successfully established member-led MPMS groups that can enable members to continue changes they began during the weekend training. Representative members view the groups as moderately effective. Retention rates and group duration are greater than reported for some kinds of mutual support groups (Luke et al., 1993) and open men's council groups. Finally, a number of qualities and processes were identified that help explain how the I-groups function effectively.

The findings about disbanded I-groups provide information that is potentially useful to the MKP and other men's organization that are working to create effective stable groups. The importance of a consistent meeting location during the first year suggests that men's organizations may want to assist new groups to find reliable meeting space. Given the importance of the early stages of group development for subsequent stability, organizations could arrange for group facilitators to consult with groups periodically about signs of loss of focus, accountability, or conflict management. Finally, although the optimal combination of individual characteristics, such as intense interpersonal engagement, age, common bonds, and chemistry among members, may be difficult to arrange, some attention to the matching of personal characteristics among members may be called for when feasible. Different types of I-groups and alternative models for I-group development may also be worth considering. For example, new members could join effective, existing groups with openings. I-groups could be formed that go beyond emotional work to focus on the development of life mission for members who have been in a group several years. Specialized groups for men with shared interests or experiences (e.g., young fathers, widowers) could be started.

Some limitations to this initial study suggest how future work could contribute to our understanding of MPMS groups. For example, instead of collecting data from only a single representative of the group, all members of a MPMS group could be surveyed to obtain a more representative sample of perceptions about I-group effectiveness and processes. Other members may have had different judgments about a group's effectiveness or about the reasons that certain members left the group. In addition, the survey of members' reasons for leaving an I-group do not allow us to discriminate between proactive (e.g., dissatisfied with the group) and involuntary (e.g., moving) reasons for leaving. Overall rates of member retention in I-groups would be higher if we had excluded members who dropped out for involuntary reasons, such as moving away from the area.

A second limitation is that data from groups at a single training center may not represent the membership of the MKP in general. With larger samples, more powerful and appropriate statistical models such as survival analysis could be used to predict factors that lead to group disbanding and member retention (see, e.g., Luke et al., 1993). Third, these data are retrospective and therefore subject to errors in recall. Our current research follows groups prospectively, beginning at the time of their formation. Finally, these results may not be applicable to other men's groups and organizations that are structured differently from MKP and have different purposes and organizational missions. For example, many men's groups have an open structure to their meetings in which men from the general public can attend any given meeting without making any commitment to return. We suspect that the relationships developed among men who attend such open groups are not as deep and that their ability to challenge each other and hold each other accountable for their feelings or actions is not as great. Our initial findings suggest that the tightly knit structure that the MKP provides does in fact create greater opportunities for group development than more open groups. Nevertheless, there is a qualitative difference in the nature of the groups, and the direct applicability of these findings may be limited.

GENERAL CONCLUSIONS: MKP IN THE CONTEXT OF CURRENT GENDER RELATIONS

The ManKind Project is one response to the problems associated with masculinity and male gender roles that we described at the beginning of this chapter. Based on our preliminary research, men appeared to be psychologically healthier after participation in the NWTA, although it was unclear whether this included a parallel improvement in their attitudes toward women. Our research also identified several factors, such as a stable group location and frequent meetings, that were related to the duration and effectiveness of I-groups. Groups with these qualities may be especially effective in supporting men's efforts to sustain initial improvements in their well-being.

Small, peer-led groups, such as an I-group, may be an especially effective form of intervention with men. Men are generally hesitant to seek traditional forms of counseling (Levant, 1990). This hesitancy to seek psychological health resources may be due to the format of the therapeutic relationship, which men often perceived as giving a power advantage to the therapist and encourages emotional vulnerability (Good, Dell, & Mintz, 1989). Given that power and emotional restriction are traditional male ego defenses (O'Neil et al., 1986), these may be significant barriers to the effectiveness of traditional therapy with men. Peer-led MMS groups may allow men to overcome these defenses by creating a setting in which emotional literacy and intimacy are positive and normative.

In thinking about the larger implications of these observations, several features of the sample should be kept in mind. Despite our collaborative relationship with the MKP-GW organization, which has been invaluable in facilitating our research and providing practical opportunities to disseminate the results back to the organization, collecting data from all active participants as well as men who have dropped out remains a challenging goal. The sample also does not include men who were initially interested in the organization but later declined to participate. Nor does it include men who belong to other kinds of men's groups and organizations (e.g., National Organization of Men Against Sexism, Promise Keepers) or the vast majority of men (including men of color and working-class men) who never join a men's group but nevertheless experience problems associated with masculinity. These observations raise the question of whether the particular men who self-selected into our study are unique in some way that is associated with the changes they report having made after the NWTA. The men in our sample might have changed regardless of their involvement in MKP-GW. Studies of MMS groups and organizations need to move to another level of rigor by incorporating comparison or control groups of men into the research design. For example, men participating in different kinds of men's mutual support groups, psychoeducational interventions, or men's therapy groups (Chapter 11, this volume, Levin, 1997) could be compared with respect to the same set of outcome variables. These designs will allow researchers to determine whether men's group participation is responsible for changes they report, or whether men who simply would have changed due to some other influence in their lives selected themselves into a group.

Finally, in this chapter we have generally skirted some important issues related to the topic of group effectiveness. By what standards should a group, or the changes that individual participants make in a group, be judged, and by whom? Reviewers of our research who ask about the ManKind Project's mission statement have raised a similar version of this question: "What exactly is meant by the 'sacred masculine' that men are intending to reclaim?" Another question is whether scarce psychological research resources should be directed to studies of primarily middle-class white men rather than more disenfranchised groups. These are excellent questions that go to the heart of evaluation research on MMS organizations. Thus far in our research, we have generally investigated individual-level variables representing men's psychological health such as gender role conflict, life goals and purpose in life, self-esteem, sense of mastery, and life satisfaction. Certainly many other criterion variables or outcomes could be used to define "effective change" in men's lives and masculinity, such as the quality of men's relationships with others and the effect their masculine-related behavior has on others. For example, our research investigates whether men's attitudes toward women are affected by participating in the NWTA. Another important question, given rates of violence associated with men and masculine ideology (Levant, 1995a), is whether men reclaiming "sacred masculinity" are more or less likely to behave violently toward women and other men. We believe these are important questions to ask about any organization dedicated to changing men's lives and masculinities and urge evaluation researchers to assess variables reflecting the range of issues and outcomes connected to diverse forms of masculinity.

ACKNOWLEDGMENTS

We thank the members of the MKP-GW who generously participated in the research reported in this chapter.

NOTES

1. Men who registered to complete the MKP-GW NWTA received a preweekend research packet from the MKP-GW center office. A postweekend questionnaire was included in the packet of materials distributed at the end of the NWTA weekend. Additional copies of the postweekend questionnaire were mailed at six months and eighteen months postweekend by the research team. In addition, men were interviewed at twelve months and nominated two peers to complete rating scales six months and eighteen months postweekend. For the current report of preliminary findings, only pre- and initial postweekend findings are reported.

2. Some of the items were selected from existing scales of attitudes toward women (e.g., Hostility Toward Women Scale Check, Malamuth, Elias, & Barton, 1985, and the Simplified Attitudes Toward Women, Nelson, 1988). However, because the wording of many of the items on existing scales seemed outdated, we generated additional items for the purposes of this study.

3. This discussion is based on closed men's groups—those that are generally private and open only periodically to add new members. Size and attendance factors may differ for open groups, in which men from the public are welcome to attend any meeting.

4. One representative from each active ($N = 24$) and disbanded ($N = 11$) I-group participated. Groups were counted as disbanded if members had stopped meeting or members had merged into another larger group. Two additional groups began to form but never met after the eight-week facilitation period. Because this study focused on factors determining group stability and effectiveness only after the eight-week facilitation period, these groups were removed from all analyses.

5. Drawing on organizational records, each representative was sent a survey and asked to complete it—if possible, in consultation with other members of their group. The survey asked when the I-group started and (if applicable) stopped meeting, the number of members in the group over its history, the age of each member, when each member joined and (if applicable) left the group, and the reason(s) that he left the group (a list of the following choices was presented: moved, work too busy, family life too busy, disagreement with the group, disagreement with an individual in the group, disagreement with MKP-GW, just stopped going, got what he wanted from the group, unknown, and other, with the option of describing the reason). In addition, for each year of the group's history, we asked how often the group met, where it met, the average number of members at meetings, and for a rating of the group's effectiveness. Unless otherwise reported, analyses were conducted using the group's score on a variable averaged over the years that it met.

6. For instance, representatives were asked to describe any changes in the group's functioning over the course of its history and the factors that contributed to these changes, the effectiveness of the initial eight-week facilitators, how closely the group followed MKP-GW rules and guidelines and whether this affected group functioning, and the specific techniques and processes used by the group and the effect these had on the group's functioning.

REFERENCES

Adair, M. (1992). "Will the real men's movement please stand up?" In K. L. Hagan (Ed.), *Women respond to the men's movement: A feminist collection* (pp. 55–66). San Francisco: Harper.

Andronico, M. P. (Ed.) (1996). *Men in groups: Insights, interventions, and psychoeducational work*. Washington, DC: American Psychological Assoc.

Boulet, J., & Boss, M. W. (1991). Reliability and validity of the Brief Symptom Inventory. *Psychological Assessment, 3*, 433–437.

Brydon-Miller, M. (1998). Participatory action research: Psychology and social change. *Journal of Social Issues, 53*, 657–666.

Burke, C. K., Maton, K. I., Hoover, S. A., & Mankowski, E. S. (1998, August). Qualitative analysis of mutual support groups in a men's transformative organization. In E. Mankowski & K. Maton (Chairs), *Psychological impact and group characteristics of a mythopoetic men's organization*. Symposium presented at the meeting of the American Psychological Association, San Francisco.

Check, J. V. P., Malamuth, N. M., Elias, B., & Barton, S. (1985, April). On hostile ground. *Psychology Today*, 56–61.

Clatterbaugh, K. (1997). *Contemporary perspectives on masculinity: Men, women, and politics in modern society*. 2nd ed. Boulder, CO: Westview Press.

Coyle, A., & Morgan-Sykes, C. (1998). Troubled men and threatening women: The construction of "crisis" in male mental health. *Feminism and Psychology, 8*, 263–284.

Derogatis, L. R., & Melisaratos, N. (1983). The Brief Symptom Inventory: An introductory report. *Psychological Medicine, 13*, 596–605.

Diener, E., Emmons, R., Larsen, R. J., & Griffin, S. (1985). The Satisfaction with Life Scale. *Journal of Personality Assessment, 49*, 71–75.

Good, G. E., Dell, D. M., & Mintz, L. B. (1989). Male role and gender role conflict: Relations to help seeking in men. *Journal of Counseling Psychology, 36*(3), 295–300.

Gossett, H. (1992). "Men's movement??? A page drama" In K. L. Hagan (Ed.), *Women respond to the men's movement: A feminist collection* (pp. 19–25). San Francisco: HarperCollins.

Hagan, K. L. (1992). *Women respond to the men's movement*. San Francisco: HarperCollins.

Harrison, J. (1978). Warning: The male sex role may be hazardous to your health. *Journal of Social Issues, 34*, 65–86.

Hartman, B. T. (1994). *Masculine gender role stress and the men's movement*. Unpublished doctoral dissertation, Indiana State University, Terre Haute.

Hoover, S. A., Burke, C. K., Maton, K. I., & Mankowski, E. S. (1998, August). *Men's movement or misogyny? Men's group members' attitudes toward women*. Poster presented at the meeting of the American Psychological Association, San Francisco.

Jesser, C. J. (1996). *Fierce and tender men: Sociological aspects of the men's movement*. Westport, CT: Praeger.

Jung, C. G. (1956). *Two essays on analytical psychology*. New York: Meridian.

Kauth, B. (1992). *A circle of men: The original manual for men's support groups*. New York: St. Martin's Press.

Kessler, R. C., Mickelson, K. D., & Zhoa, S. (1997). Patterns and correlates of self-help group membership in the United States. *Social Policy, 27*, 27–46.

Kilmartin, C. T. (1994). *The masculine self*. New York: Macmillan.

Kimmel, M. S. (1987). Rethinking "masculinity": New directions in research. In M. S. Kimmel (Ed.), *Changing men: New directions in research on men and masculinity*. Beverly Hills, CA: Sage.

Kimmel, M. S. (Ed.). (1995). *The politics of manhood: Profeminist men respond to the mythopoetic men's movement (and the mythopoetic leaders answer)*. Philadelphia: Temple University Press.

Kimmel, M. S. (1996). *Manhood in America: A cultural history*. New York: Free Press.

Levant, R. F. (1990). Psychological services designed for men: A psychoeducational approach. *Psychotherapy, 27*, 309–315.

Levant, R. F. (1995a). Male violence against female partners: Roots in male socialization and development. In C. D. Spielberger, I. G. Sarason, J. M. T. Brebner, E. Greenglass, P. Laungani, & A. M. O'Roark (Eds.), *Stress and emotion: Anxiety, anger, and curiosity* (Vol. 15, pp. 91–100). Washington, DC: Taylor & Francis.

Levant, R. F. (1995b). Toward the reconstruction of masculinity. In R. F. Levant & W. S. Pollack (Eds.), *A new psychology of men* (pp. 229–251). New York: Basic Books.

Levant, R. F., & Kopecky, G. (1995). *Masculinity reconstructed: Changing the rules of manhood: At work, in relationships and in family life*. New York: Penguin.

Levin, J. (1997). *Psychological impact of a mythopoetic initiation on participants*. Unpublished doctoral dissertation. Adler School of Professional Psychology, Chicago.

Levine, M. (1988). An analysis of mutual assistance. *American Journal of Community Psychology, 16*, 167–187.

Luke, D. A., Roberts, L., & Rappaport, J. (1993). Individual, group context, and individual-group fit predictors of self-help group attendance. *Journal of Applied Behavioral Science, 29*, 216–238.

Mankowski, E. S., Anderson, C. W., Burke, C. K., Hoover, S. A., & Maton, K. I. (1998, August). Participation and retention in a men's mutual support organization. In E. Mankowski & K. Maton (Chairs), *Psychological impact and group characteristics of a mythopoetic men's organization*. Symposium presented at the meeting of the American Psychological Association, San Francisco.

Maton, K. I. (1993). Moving beyond the individual level of analysis in mutual help group research: An ecological paradigm. *Journal of Applied Behavioral Science, 29*, 272–286.

Maton, K. I., Anderson, C. W., Burke, C. K., Hoover, S. A., & Mankowski, E. S. (1998, August). ManKind Project's impact on men's goals, gender-role conflict, well-being, and self-development. In E. Mankowski & K. Maton (Chairs), *Psychological impact and group characteristics of a mythopoetic men's organization*. Symposium presented at the meeting of the American Psychological Association, San Francisco.

Maton, K. I., Leventhal, G. S., Madara, E. L., & Julien, M. (1989). Factors affecting the birth and death of mutual-help groups: The role of national affiliation, professional involvement, and member focal problem. *American Journal of Community Psychology, 17*, 643–671.

Moore, R. (1997). Masculine initiation for the 21st century: The global challenge. In New Warrior Network (Ed.), *The New Warrior Handbook* (pp. 10–15). London: New Warrior Network.

Moore, R., & Gillette, D. (1990). *King, warrior, magician, lover: Rediscovering the archetypes of the mature masculine*. New York: HarperCollins.

Nelson, M. C. (1988). Reliability, validity, and cross-cultural comparisons for the Simplified Attitudes Toward Women Scale. *Sex Roles, 18*, 289–296.

New Warrior Network (1997). *The New Warrior handbook*. London: New Warrior Network.

O'Neil, J. M., Helms, B. J., Gable, R. K., David, L. and Wrightsman, L. S. (1986). Gender-role conflict scale: College men's fear of feminity. *Sex Roles,* 14, 335–350.

Pearlin, I. I., Lieberman, M. A., Menagan, E. G., & Mullan, J. T. (1981). The stress process. *Journal of Health and Social Behavior, 22,* 337–356.

Rosenberg, M. (1979). *Conceiving the self.* New York: Basic Books.

Schwalbe, M. (1996). *Unlocking the iron cage: The men's movement, gender politics, and American culture.* New York: Oxford University Press.

Shiffman, M. (1987). The men's movement: An exploratory empirical investigation. In M. S. Kimmel (Ed.), *Changing men: New directions in research on men and masculinity* (pp. 295–314). Newbury Park, CA: Sage.

Taylor, G. M. (1995). *Talking with our brothers: Creating and sustaining a dynamic men's group.* Fairfax, CA: Men's Community Publishing Project.

Tillitski, C. J. (1995). The men's movement: Substance and significance for mainstream men. *Humanistic Psychology, 23* (1), 83–96.

The trouble with men. (1996, September). *Economist*, pp. 19–20.

Virgin, P. (1998). Integration groups: A (rough) survey. *The Rattle*. London: ManKind Project.

Wuthnow, R. (1994). *Sharing the journey: Support groups and America's new quest for community.* New York: Free Press.

Yalom, I. D. (1985). *The theory and practice of group psychotherapy.* New York: Basic Books.

Chapter 13 _____

Heuristic and Ethnographic Study of the ManKind Project: Initiating Men into a "New Masculinity" or a Repackaging of Dominant Controlling Patriarchy?

Marty Pentz

At the opening staff meeting on Thursday of the New Warrior Training Adventure, each man was to share what he needed to learn for himself on this weekend. He was then to ask for a mentor to come forward to be his teacher. Some of the knowledge these thirty-six men asked for was on fathering, bringing this New Warrior energy home, leadership, and how to be connected with their children. Some wanted mentoring or were learning how to release and experience joy, openly dealing with grief, and learning to be of more service to the world. At the point where each man came forward with a need, another man would come forward with his willingness to teach what he has of this knowledge.

One man came forward asking for a mentor to teach him about living and grieving. With his arms out and palms upward, as if to accept something, this man tearfully said, "I need to learn how to truly live within my grief." The man who came forward (who had lung cancer and died a month and a half after this weekend) stated, "I would be honored to teach you what I know about living in joy while you grieve."

Many of the men expressed fear in being vulnerable in this way, and many were tearful. In a world where men are often taught that it is not manly to show tears or ask for help and where they are disconnected from themselves and others and the consequences of their actions (Gilbert, 1992; Gutmann, 1987), it was a unique occurrence for me to watch myself and thirty-five other staff men being this vulnerable with each other. Among other things, the detailed experience illustrates men making emotional connections with other men.

This chapter presents two qualitative examinations of The ManKind Project

(MKP) (formerly the New Warrior Network): an ethnographic study of the New Warrior Training Adventure (NWTA) weekend and a heuristic examination of the New Warrior Integration Training (NWIT) or I-groups.

LITERATURE REVIEW

Why should a social worker study the contemporary men's movement (CMM)? Reamer (1995) stated that the "profession of social work historically has been committed to enhancing the welfare of people who encounter problems related to poverty, mental health, health care, employment, shelter and housing, abuse, aging, childhood, hunger, and so on" (p. 893). If this is what the social work profession is based on, why study a movement that is considered to be populated primarily by middle-class white males (Adair, 1992)? According to the two studies (Pentz, 1996, 1997) some of the issues were that the men in MKP deal with violence, trust with men and trust with women, being victims of and perpetrating all forms of child abuse, how to be a father, homophobia, depression, and addictions, to name a few. These are certainly issues that many social workers deal with on a daily basis.

The Men's Movement and Its Context

Many assert that the contemporary men's movement consists of men responding to the women's movement (Ruether, 1992). Others state that it is "angry" white men wanting their power back (Brown, 1992). These reasons may be true for some men, but for the staff and the initiates on the NWTA weekend and the I-group studied, it appeared to be none of the above. One man came "afraid and angry" and wanted to find his "truth." Another man was looking at life through a young boy's filter and wanted to grow up. One staff member originally came to this work because he could not control his rage, now he can face it, honor it, release it without hurting anyone, and use it in a healthy manner. Other men came because of relationship problems, sexuality issues, abuse issues, and many other reasons. Many came just to be with other men. In the heuristic study, a group of new men were asked what brought them to the NWTA. These are the issues they presented: trust issues, fathering, spirituality/God, feelings of fear, masculinity, and loneliness, among others.

Some feminist writers (Ruether, 1992; Starhawk, 1992) have voiced a need for a "men's movement" but are frightened of its possible ramifications. Starhawk (1992) sums up the fear and the hope of many feminist writers: "Feminists long for men to heal. . . . Our fear is that the men's movement will do what men have always done, at least since the advent of patriarchy: blame women for their problems and defend their own privileges" (pp. 27–28). This quote is similar to the description in the New Warrior brochure (1996) describing the New Warrior; "The New Warrior is a man who has confronted this destructive 'shadow' form and has achieved hard-won ownership of the highly focused, aggressive energy that empowers and shapes the inner masculine self. Sustained by this new energy, the New Warrior is at once tough and loving, wild and gentle, fierce and tolerant. He lives passionately and compassionately, because he has learned to face his own shadow and to live his mission with integrity, and without apology" (p. 2).

Few writers on the CMM and masculinity have focused on the NWTA, but a number have written about what is called the mythopoetic branch of the CMM (Bliss, 1992; Keen, 1992). The MKP would be considered a part of this branch. A number of writers have critiqued the mythopoetic branch of the CMM from the outside. However, Brod (1992), a member of the profeminist branch, stated that he finds much of value in the mythopoetic movement. When talking about Bly, he states, "He is answering real needs for men to reach out across generations, for men to honor their fathers . . . to have a positive, assertive sense of self, to heal men's grief" (p. 232). However, Brod (1992) takes exception to the way Bly recalls the history of masculinity: "The history of masculinities, the history of men in families, at work, with each other, must be told as the history of patriarchy, or it is not truly being told at all. Without that perspective, we are in the presence of myths as falsehood, rather than myth as deep truth. I find an awareness of patriarchy utterly lacking in the story of our past which the mythopoetic movement tells us" (pp. 233–234).

Feminist writers have critiqued the men's movement as well. Ruether (1992) equates the mythopoetic branch with three of its leaders (Bly, 1990; Keen, 1991; Moore & Gillette, 1990) and lumps the thousands of men who have participated in various events into this mold. She sees this version, the mythopoetic branch of the CMM, as simply a reiteration of the old patriarchal scripts. Starhawk (1992) states:

The problem with men is not, as Robert Bly suggests, that the male initiatory process has broken down. The problem is that it's working all too well to shape young boys and girls into the type of men and women required by a society dominated by war. . . . War requires soldiers. Not mythical warriors, independent, self-sacrificing masters of strategy, not "a warrior in service to a True King—that is to a transcendent cause" (Bly, 1990, 151)—not inner warriors or archetypal warriors or spiritual warriors, but soldiers: weapon like, obedient to their handlers, and unthinkingly, unfeelingly brutal to their victims. (p. 32)

Starhawk (1992) also calls the term *warrior* into question. She agrees that the old warrior needs to be retired and something else needs to take its place: "But let's call ourselves something else, healers, maybe, even simply fighters, lest we idealize what we are struggling against" (p. 33). She acknowledges that we have plenty of battles to fight. This kind of concern is one of the reasons for the recent organizational name change to the MKP.

One writer (Kingsolver, 1992) sees the mythopoetic branch as a direct response to feminism and that the women's movement is fighting for women's lives and the mythopoetic branch is men looking for peace of mind. This seems rather simplistic and would probably only end dialogue between men and women rather than encourage it. Every man that I interviewed in the heuristic and ethnographic studies stated that he was fighting for his life and for the lives of those in his family constellation. Eisler (1992) views the mythopoetic branch as an important social movement. She agrees with the mythopoetic stance that we need different definitions of success for men. Eisler sees as confusing the mythopoetic stance that "urges men to identify with dominator archetypes such as the warrior and king, while at the same time often talking about equal partnership between women and men and a more generally just and equitable society" (p. 47). Eisler advocates for a partnership movement, with which many of the men in the MKP would agree.

Adair (1992) admittedly takes her impressions of the mythopoetic branch solely from a reading of Bly's *Iron John*. She believes that the mythopoetic branch sustains the status quo. Another view that she expressed was that the mythopoetic branch is not about social change and that connecting with nature through the "inner wild man" and warrior continues the pattern of male domination. The skepticism by feminist and other profeminist writers is understandable. None of their critique of the NWTA experience or the mythopoetic branch is based on empirical evidence. This does not invalidate their points. There are other ways of seeing that do not include empirical evidence.

Social Movement Theory

Is MKP itself a social movement, or is it a part of a larger social movement of men? Thiele (1993) stated that "social movements are political organizations that attempt to restructure attitudes, values, and behavior; they are composed of and oriented to a relatively nonexclusive population; and they function primarily through communicative rather than coercive means" (pp. 281–282). Popenoe (1995) describes different types of social movements. The expressive movement, for example, attempts "to provide their members with some type of personal transformation, which may include emotional satisfaction, a new identity, or a different ideology. Expressive movements can be either religious or secular in nature" (p. 490).

With these definitions it would appear that MKP is a social movement by itself and may also be part of a larger social movement. Jesser (1996) states the following about the mythopoetic branch, which is what brings many men to the NWTA weekend:

I see some resemblance to the general stages of germinating social movements in the stirrings of men in the last decade. First, there is some, usually murky, sense of dissatisfaction in one's life—rumblings that something is "out of kilter"; there is a period of discussion, at first faltering, but finally some clearer raising of consciousness among the distressed that identifies the struggle, the anomalies, the deficits, or the *ennui*. In present men's work, the notion of "wound," arising from such sources as isolation, father ab-

sence, unspoken shame, lack of initiation, and mentoring, and the unjustified scapegoat-
ing of men, serve as examples. (p. x)

I will show that the NWTA and the NWIT attempt to "restructure attitudes,
values, and behaviors." I will also demonstrate that MKP is an expressive social
movement in that it attempts to change the people in it.

THE WEEKEND NWTA

The NWTA processes are designed to lead a man to the "hero's journey."
On this journey he can do his "work," find a "mission," be "accountable" for
himself, and confront his destructive "shadow" side. "Work" is the effort needed
to go on the hero's journey and come out with the "gold" (new awareness and
behaviors). The bulk of the individual work on a NWTA is in the process called
the "hero's journey." This journey can be analyzed as follows:

To the degree that any one of us reaches toward autonomy, we must begin a process of
sorting through the trash and treasures we have been given, keeping some and rejecting
others. We gain the full dignity and power of our persons only when we create a narrative
account of our lives, dramatize our existence, and forge a coherent personal myth that
combines elements of our cultural myth and family myth with unique stories that come
from our experience. (Keen & Valley-Fox, 1989, p. xiv)

One staff member described the hero's journey as being critical and crucial
for men to become initiated: "It gives men a chance to get past figuring and
into feelings. It is a centering process that gets at the real core shadow pieces,
this is a real deep journey into who Fred is" (Wolfred, personal communication,
1996). Another staff member said the hero's journey was shadow work into
what gets in the way of life. He described it as a "descent into hell to find one's
own personal dragons, fight them, and come out with a victory" (T. Lankford,
personal communication, 1996). To another man, the hero's journey was a cathartic experience that allowed him to purge years of anger, terror, and frustration and then fill the space up with "good stuff." Healing and letting go are the
ultimate objective, with the end result being the "evolution of personhood" (D.
Gray, personal communication, 1996). This is the hero's journey on which the
staff took these initiates.

After the hero's journey, the new men were led through the woods to a
ceremony honoring each new warrior brothers in turn. In addition to the thirty-
six staff members, there were twelve men who came for this ceremony to honor
the new brothers. The ceremony involved drumming, dancing, playing of a flute,
and the giving of a gift to the new brothers signifying their initiation as new
warriors.

The knowledge detailed during this process was the belief that every man needs a reason and purpose to be on this planet. A mission is what helps a man to be fulfilled. One of the staff made this statement to begin the mission work: "We are greater then we appear to be. All matter is one, I am in union with God, Tao, Spirit, Nature, and Self. Ultimately I am alone as a man, but I have to live in relationship with others." Later in the process another of the staff stated that the mission and vision is of service. He also stated that "how I am in relationship to others is my decision, but it does not involve domination or destruction and must involve love and service."

A major aspect of NWTA work is for a man to determine what this mission is and then live it. One of the staff members stated during the process on missions that a man's mission in the MKP is generally one of service to men, women, children, or an ideal. The missions were to be grandiose and a means for changing the world, one person at a time. Examples of mission statements from the new brothers are: "To make the world a place that honors men's pain by honoring my own," "To make the world a place that is safe for all children by helping men to heal their pain," and "To make the air safe to breath by working to decrease or end air pollution." The belief is that a man's mission will evolve as he grows and develops in his life after the NWTA and during and after NWIT.

The human shadow consists of those elements of ourselves that we do not want others to know and often we do not know ourselves. A "shadow always manifests where there is an immature, fragmentary psyche, because splitting is always a symptom of unintegrated development" (Moore & Gillette, 1992). The shadow is also said to have a mission. Shadow mission is whatever is inside a person that block him from performing his true mission. This is often thought to be the opposite of affirmation—a statement about what or who a man is. Examples of affirmations are, "As a man among men I speak my truth" or "As a man among men I am connected." Not speaking one's truth is thought to be a barrier to living out one's mission. Not feeling connected is a barrier to living one's true mission.

Accountability was heavily stressed during a number of the processes. One process was entirely devoted to being accountable for oneself. A number of the new men were confronted on what their behavior, as opposed to their words, is saying to other people. One of the men was confronted on what his being late and making the other men wait is saying to those men who waited. The learning is that one's behavior always has meaning and consequences. The attitude of the MKP is that one is accountable for knowing and owning one's behavior, its meaning, and its consequences.

Throughout the NWTA there were a number of visualizations, similar to the hypnotic process of guided imagery used by many therapists and counselors (O'Hanlon & Martin, 1992). They are designed to help the men gain access to their feelings and promote the expressive aspects of themselves. The visualizations dealt with the "wild man" as depicted by Bly (1990):

The Wild Man, then, through his disciplines, prepares an emotional body that can receive grief, ecstasy, and spirit. . . . The Wild Man's energy is that energy which is conscious of a wound . . . and leads the return we eventually have to make as adults back to the place of childhood abuse and abandonment. . . . The Wild Man's qualities, among them love of spontaneity, association with wilderness, honoring of grief, and respect for riskiness, frightens many people. Some men, as soon as they receive the first impulses to riskiness and recognize its link with what we've called the Wild Man, become frightened, stop all wildness, and recommend timidity and collective behavior to others. . . . The aim is not to *be* the Wild Man, but to be *in touch with* the Wild Man (Bly, 1990, pp. 225–227).

It is the wild man energy that is believed to give a man the courage and power to confront his demons on his hero's journey.

In this center on the Thursday following the NWTA, there was a graduation for the new men. The new men were encouraged to invite their families and anybody else with whom they wanted to share this honoring ceremony. The ceremony began with a staff member talking about MKP. He stated that we are here to hold men accountable for their actions. The trappings and rituals are used to get away from the material world. All faiths as well as those of no particular faith are invited. This man also stated that "deep, inner work is what this is all about."

During the honoring of the new men, they were invited to speak of their experience. When asked what he had gained from the training adventure weekend, one man said: "I came afraid and angry. I wanted to find my truth, and the strength I have gotten is beyond words. This is a strange, but safe place, and the gift will not stop with me." Another man said he was looking at life from a young boy's filter and now feels equality and a newly found lightness. This was a "spiritual experience." The next man spoke of facing issues with his father and finally felt love for himself for the first time. He continued, "I came an anxious boy and left a strong man." One man found that he could now "measure up." Another felt a deep connection to his life that he did not have before. Another man shared about making friends on the weekend. He found a group of men who were "totally honest without snickering." Honesty to him was the core of the weekend. The last man to speak said he found out that as a strong man he did not have to be violent. He could be peaceful and calm.

What have their families seen as a result of the weekend? One man's spouse said she does not understand men. She added that her husband's new-found calm assurance of knowing who he is she has not seen in years. Another woman always knew that he was a good and important person with good women friends. She and another woman were grateful that their husbands now had good male friends.

The initial part of the New Warrior Integration Training (NWIT) is a ten week I-group process with eight to fifteen men who have been through the most recent NWTA in their area. This group is facilitated by two or three staff members. After the initial ten-week group, the men are invited to continue in their I-group as an ongoing closed men's peer mutual support group, designed to integrate into the man what was learned on the NWTA and continue to grow as a mature man. The I-groups continue the hero's journey, working on accountability and the other aspects and issues detailed in these two studies.

DESCRIPTION OF THE STUDIES

Ethnographic Study

The main purpose of this study was to examine the assumption that men are disconnected from themselves, their own feelings and the feelings of others, the consequences of their behavior, society, and the impact of the NWTA experience on these dynamics. I also wanted to gain an understanding of the NWTA experience and its relevance and purpose to the men, their families of whatever configuration, social work, and society. One further goal was to examine the attitudes and knowledge that were being influenced and disseminated on a NWTA. The method for the ethnographic phase of the study was a qualitative design with quantitative aspects.

The NWTA is a relatively new phenomenon that claims to connect men to themselves and others in meaningful ways. It does this through rituals and experiences with male mentors and elders who are also doing their own inner work. An ethnographic study is appropriate for study of a new phenomenon and gaining an understanding of the experience from those involved (Marshall & Rossman, 1995). Creswell (1994) cites the utility of using a combined qualitative and quantitative design for some studies. Combining methods is a way to triangulate in a study and therefore neutralize bias in data sources, investigator, and method (Creswell, 1994).

My being a member of the MKP is the only reason I was able to gain the trust of the men to do this study. I was an initiated man in MKP prior to becoming a doctoral student. The role of the researcher was that of a participant observer–ethnographer. I was a full member of the staff of the NWTA, in addition to being a researcher. During the initial staff meeting (two months prior to the NWTA studied) for the weekend under study, it was necessary to be identified as a full staff member to gain the trust of the men on staff. The duties that I performed as a staff member were conducive to this dual role.

Data were collected by ethnographic observations, literature review, in-depth interviews with staff and initiates, field notes, artwork, poetry, a survey questionnaire, and the NWTA brochure. The observations began with a meeting of the MKP Center at which the board approve this study. Observations continued with staff and rookie meetings (a rookie is an initiated man staffing his first or second NWTA), proceeded throughout an NWTA weekend, and concluded with the NWTA graduation ceremony following the weekend.

The in-depth interviews of staff and members (tape-recorded with permission) took place during the NWTA and afterward. The interviews were conducted using an interview guide, and observations were conducted with an observation guide, both constructed prior to the initiation weekend. Field notes were taken throughout the entire course of the study. A survey was administered to twelve of the thirteen new men on the first night of the weekend and again to eleven of the thirteen men at a three-month follow-up. One man declined to participate in this study, and one of the men could not be reached for the follow-up. This group of new men was chosen for this study because the men were on the weekend chosen and approved for study.

I expected to find men seeking what they had not found before. I was looking for connections and disconnections from themselves and others and the consequences of the violent behavior of some men on society. I wanted possible answers to the questions: What is "mature masculinity"? What short- or long-term impact, if any, does the NWTA weekend have on these men as individuals, their relationships, and their families of whatever configuration? Is this part of a social movement? Another aspect under study was what attitudes were being addressed in a given process and what knowledge was being disseminated. I expected to find a story about men seeking their "truth." I expected to learn about the processes used to initiate men into MKP. I intended to explore the essence of the NWTA and NWIT experiences.

Heuristic Study

The New Warrior brochure states that the New Warrior is "at once tough and loving, wild and gentle, fierce and tolerant. He lives passionately and compassionately, because he has learned to face his own shadow and to live his mission with integrity, and without apology" (1996). I wanted to find out *what* impact this work has on the men and those around them. I wanted to get at the meaning of the NWTA experience.

The MKP organization is open to all men who are willing to go through the weekend NWTA experience. Only those who have been through the NWTA know what happens during the training weekends, but all else is open to the world. The initiatory experience is kept secret so the new man can experience it fully and completely. It would take a full participant to study this type of group in depth, always keeping bias in mind and up front. The primary researcher is a member of MKP. The heuristic approach calls for the researcher to be part of the lived experience under study. Subjectivity was monitored by having transcripts coded with my classmates and instructors in a seminar setting. Themes that were extracted from the transcripts were also taken back to the coresearchers for verification.

Initial Research Process

The method of study was the heuristic approach: "The qualitatively oriented heuristic scientist seeks to discover the nature and meaning of the phenomenon under study from direct first-person accounts of individuals who have directly encountered the phenomenon" (Moustakas, 1990, p. 38). The focus of heuristic inquiry is on recreating the lived experience. The overall question posed in this study fits the qualitative framework.

The leadership of this MKP center gave permission to proceed with the study. From a cohort group of thirteen New Warrior brothers who had been through the weekend experience in the past three months, six men, including myself, were part of the study:

- All were Caucasian.

- Ages ranged from 27 to 65, with a mean of 38.5.

- Length of involvement in the MKP was three months at the time of first contact (with the exception of the three years I have been involved).

- Four were single, one was getting a divorce, and one was married.

- Two of the six men have children of their own.

- All six of the men were heterosexual (however, this is not representative of the center under study).

Part of the MKP experience is an opportunity to attend, with the men with whom one went through the NWTA, an ongoing group. It is in this I-group that the weekend experience is integrated into the lives of the men. I attended an NWIT meeting of these men and outlined what I proposed to do for the research. It was from this meeting that the men were chosen for the study. Thirteen men, including myself, filled out the survey. All thirteen on the most recent NWTA filled out the quantitative questionnaire, but only six (including myself) were in the I-group under study. The nature of the heuristic process required that I use my experience as a New Warrior fully. I was and am immersed in what this experience means to me.

FINDINGS

Heuristic Study

All of the interviews were tape-recorded and then transcribed, which allowed for thorough and in-depth analysis. All of the interviews began with a certain amount of rapport building, followed by the men telling their story of the lived experience of being a New Warrior through the use of the interview guide. Sometimes the questions followed from what the man said, and other times they were from the general interview guide. After the four data reductions and a group interview to see if there was agreement on the core themes of the experience, five core themes evolved:

1. Fathering. The themes of feeling cared for by a man, who he is is ok, receiving love from men, pain and emotion, and pride.

2. Relationships. The themes of boundaries, trust with men and women, honesty, understanding, and love.

3. Rites of passage/masculinity. The themes of shadow, feelings and their expression (fear, anger, joy, exhilaration, sadness, grief), power, accountability, service, access to emotions, men as teachers, mission, being a man, loneliness, men's work, energy, and macho. .

4. Spirituality/God. The themes of soul/inner work, service, and surrender.

5. The experience of being a New Warrior and feelings. The essence of all the above themes plus integrity.

These men all had a very individualized experience, but the experience centered around an essential core. One of the issues that brought all of these men to the MKP was relationships. Four of the men had recently ended what they termed "dysfunctional" relationships. All six stated a need for relationships with men. What follows are samples of the responses to the question: What was going on in your life that brought you to the NWTA?

Relationships

"It was a relationship. Mainly a relationship. It was an addictive, painful relationship for me." Another man responded, "touched on the fact that my father was married to his practice, and that left little time for raising his five boys. I found out that I had lost out on a lot and my restlessness and my inability to commit in a relationship. I had been through several failed relationships in my life. I was trying to get at the root cause of that, and I discovered that a lot of it had been from a lack of nurturing as a child. I needed to find a group of men."

These men were to the point of being willing to go on an NWTA because of problems in interpersonal relationships with women. As a result of the New Warrior experience, one man touchingly responded, "What I ended up getting out of the weekend was I felt cared for by other men in a way I had never felt cared for by other men before. They cared about me as a man. Basically that I was okay, that I was a man." Another man said, "I went to the weekend and I just came back not needing a woman. I went from needing a woman to just wanting the companionship of a woman, which is a very different perspective."

There appears to have been a big change in how these men viewed and operated in relationships with men and women. This went from the struggle to express themselves emotionally to the willingness and courage, in spite of the fear, to share who they are with other people. The survey had questions about increases in the ability to share feelings with their family—anger, fear, joy, and sadness. A Likert scale used was 5 for "greatly increased," 4 for "increased," 3 for "stayed the same," 2 for "decreased," and 1 for "greatly decreased." All four feeling variables surveyed (anger, fear, joy, sadness) had a mean of 4, indicating an increased ability to share feelings.

It is apparent that a large part of the essence of the NWTA and the NWIT experience is in the area of relationships.

Fathering

Fathering can be thought of in at least four contexts: fathering one's own children, the fathering one did or did not receive as a child, fathering received from one's own father as an adult, and replacement fathering one might receive as an adult from other men. Five of the six men in the I-group study talked about having issues around fathering they did not receive as a child. The two following examples are from the individual and group interviews:

The weekend to me means stepping through a lot of my childish fears or at least putting them out in front of me and then getting the love I wanted from a man, my father, through the men in group.

In my life I had discovered through counseling the void that lack of fathering had left in my life. I touched on the fact that my father was married to his practice, and that left little time for raising his five boys.

I was very lonely. I didn't have close relationships at all with my father or brothers. I never gave myself permission to have friends, male friends. Ten years ago to twelve years ago, I had a male friend. We didn't talk about things close, but that was the closest thing to a male friend I could come to.

I did not have an emotional relationship with my father. He worked all the time or was drunk. My relationship with my brothers was either competition or fighting.

All but one of these men had father issues that dated to early childhood. The increasing number of men who are seeking connections in men's peer mutual support groups is testimony to this need for fathering of men. A number of authors (Gerzon, 1992; Meth & Pasick, 1990) are writing about and researching the need we have as a society for healthy fathering—fathering that teaches about nurturing, loving, sharing, and embracing of all who one is, not about control and conquest. Dollahite, Hawkins, and Brotherson (1997) postulate the need for a conceptual ethic of generative fathering—"fathering that meets the needs of children by working to create and maintain a developing ethical relationship with them" (p. 18). This sounds like an appropriate mission statement for an MKP father.

Spirituality

Spirituality was of importance to five of the six men, as the following statements show:

This was a part of the weekend too, where the mission statement comes up, and each person has to come up with a mission for their life. My mission statement is to spread God's truth around the world on a daily basis in my daily life. It also helped bring together a lot of past work in my life on spirituality. I was raised in a fundamentalist Protestant church, and had religion given to me in a nice, neat, orderly way. But it didn't feel right to me as a young man. After I finished my course of medical school and residency, I began my own search for a religion and a philosophy that would carry me through the rest of my life. I felt in touch with the Higher Being, the Higher Spirit, and I felt, too, it was okay, not a sense of again I had to have all the answers. That God did live close to me and within me, and going back in a sense in a search with the New Warrior's to our ancestors and how they lived their lives and how they believed, and the common spirit that would bind us all together is a spirit of God and Nature and how there are guiding principles in life that I can embrace, and that I can make part of my life. It made me feel more at home with many things I had discovered on my own beforehand.

The NWTA and the NWIT experiences appear to have deepened the spirituality of these men and grounded it more within who they are as a human being.

Rites of Passage and Masculinity

The men talked about NWTA as a rite of passage and how they view mature masculinity.

The group encompasses people from all walks of life, all colors and creeds and what have you, and it's just an enriching experience. Not only is it your own rite of passage, but working with the other people's. It's a passage into manhood and into self. You learn to be accountable for your actions. I think that's the main thing. Learn to say our feelings, whatever they are and whatever that causes. Good, bad or indifferent, then you have to accept the consequences of your actions.

I think it's a rite of passage into living in the mature male masculinity, from a destructive immature male masculinity. What it means to me to be a man is . . . it's hard for me to explain that. I have felt, you know, before that I was a man, but I couldn't really put it into words. It means knowing, really knowing who I am—what I feel or think or value, and being able to speak that and live that. That pretty much is what I think a man is. He knows who he is, what he values, what he esteems, feels. A man treats other people with love. He treats them with honesty and with love, which means that he does not do anything to maliciously harm another human being, but he will not allow a person to maliciously harm him or those that he cares about.

The NWTA brochure talks about being initiated into what some people call a new masculinity. I think that men, with our egos, our competition with other men and things like that, we have distorted what masculinity is all about. This brings that more into focus—that being male, being masculine isn't about hurting other men. It's about having power. It's about having anger. It's about having joy, and having all this stuff. In the past it has been used in such negative ways, and it's caused a lot of damage.

These men all spoke of a need they have had since childhood to be taught what it is to be a man. They all could describe rites of passage that they had experienced, but none that taught them what it is to be a mature man. The mature masculine was described as being in integrity with himself and others, being honest, treating people with kindness and courtesy, but with the ability to be fierce when needed. They explained that the mature man honors his responsibilities to other people and the environment, serves others and has a mission in life that they were living toward. All the men stated they did not yet consider themselve truly mature men.

The Experience of Being a New Warrior and Feelings

The last theme deals with men's overall experience of the I-Group and the New Warrior Training Adventure Weekend.

The essence of it has been to put me in touch more with myself and with my feelings and understand my feelings and understand that they are all right no matter what they are, and that I need to talk about them to others. Another part I like about it is it's an ongoing program. Our integration group has been meeting every Saturday morning. Those that need to do work, do work like the work we did on the weekend.

I'm trying to get a grip on it here, but, I don't know if that is even a correct statement or not. But, coming out of the NWTA, out of the weekend and everything, I felt closer to men than I'd ever felt before. Now I have a tendency to focus in when I'm talking to other men about what it is to be a man. And what it is to have our shadows out in front of us. Before I might be talking about not drinking or doing an inventory. Now I'm bringing in more what I got out of the weekend.

In response to a comment that the warrior is the wild man rather than the savage, one man answered:

And the wildman is incredible. The wonder of being a man with the fear of being a man. I love that. Carlos Castenada says the "real accomplishment in life is the art of being a warrior which is the only way to balance the terror of being a man with the wonder of being a man." That's basically what it's about."

During the group interview one man shared how he saw the essence of the experience, and the others agreed that his statement covered much of what the experience is all about.

The meaning and essence is to unite our spirits as one. To do that is to allow our barriers to come down and to acknowledge who we are and to reach out to one another as fellow human beings in our search for truth and in our search for a better world.

The experience these men described of being a New Warrior is settling deeper into their own experience. This experience appears to be different for every man, yet it is much the same. They all spoke of the five core themes and the need for other men in their lives, which until now was unfulfilled.

Follow-up Findings

Eleven of the thirteen men in the ethnographic study who were the initiates on the investigated weekend were contacted for follow-up interviews and survey and asked the same set of questions as the original survey. They were also asked what, if any, changes in their life they would attribute to their experience with the NWTA. The dominant themes were changes in relationships and friendships, confidence level, openness with feelings, integrity, and connections with other people. All eleven said they were glad they had participated in the weekend experience. One man called it the best experience he has had in years. Nine of the eleven noted improved or new connections with other men and the significant people in their lives (partners and children) as the primary change they have noticed in their lives. One of the men stated that he now has two male friends whom he does things with, whereas he had had no male friends prior to the weekend.

Having more integrity in their lives was a change detailed by nine of the eleven men in the follow-up. Integrity in MKP experiences can be defined as firm adherence to values of honesty, accountability, responsibility, equality, and sharing of one's thoughts and feelings. One man said that he now knows what it is to be a man with "commitment and integrity." Positive changes in relationships and friendships, confidence levels, and being open with feelings was mentioned by six of the eleven men.

The survey was administered to the initiates on Friday of the first day of the weekend (time 1) and at a three-month follow-up (time 2). A significance level of $p < .10$ was used due to the small sample size and this being an exploratory study. At $p < .10$, two variables were statistically significant. The variable "a strong man inhibits his emotional expression" goes with the following question: "I live by the creed that a strong man inhibits his emotional expression," "I do not often share my feelings" is the other question that is significant at the .10 level. One of the attitudes that the MKP attempts to change is the male prohibition against the sharing of feelings. Although it is not possible to know what produced this reported change, the assumption is that the NWTA had some influence on the sharing of feelings. The two variables were written to measure the same construct. This psychological construct deals with men sharing feelings and this lack of sharing affecting other areas of their lives. The participant responses were consistent ($r = .75$) between these two items the first time the survey was administered. At the three-month follow-up, the positive correlation between these two items changed to .09. With this correlation not holding up over time, it is probable that these two items are not measuring the same construct. A larger sample size and further analysis are needed to determine if and how these items relate to each other.

A quantitative analysis of this research is problematic. There are problems with reliability due to a small N. There is possibly a type II error due to the small sample size. A quantitative analysis with this small an N has little power to find changes that did occur due to the NWTA. Another problem is confirmation bias, which I attempted to control by having a noninterested third party audit the process throughout.

The questions dealing with violence and threats of violence went in the direction of less violence from the pre- to posttest phase, although they were not statistically significant. With the absence of fathers being reported as detrimental to the raising of children (Kimmel, 1987), it is important to note that all ten of the eleven men who had children reported that they were close to their children. An area for further research is the impact of the NWTA and the NWIT on the lives and relationships of the significant people in these men's lives.

SYNTHESIS AND IMPLICATIONS

Ethnographic Study

During the discussion of coding themes, one of my classmates brought up ethics and morality theory (Smurl, 1996), which dictate that there are ethical and value principles that "appear regularly in the oral and written traditions of the world's major cultures and religions" (Smurl, 1996, p. 3):

A. Self-cultivation consists of developing one's self.

B. Truth telling consists of communicating one's opinions accurately. This is not an unrestricted obligation; it applies only to free (versus coerced) communications between fully responsible (versus incompetent or mad) persons; involves telling the truth to self and others.

C. Promise-keeping is a form of doing what you agreed to. Included under such agreements are not only explicit promises, but also implicit ones, as in the understood assurance of competent, proper, and due care of oneself and others; keeping promises to self and others.

D. Beneficence (love) involves doing what is in another's best interest, or at least not harming another (nonmaleficence or "no harm"); showing love for self and others.

E. Justice consists of acting fairly in our exchanges with self and others. (Smurl, 1996, p. 3)

The essence of the NWTA and the NWIT experience is encompassed in this theory and is well defined in the five core themes of the experience of being a New Warrior and feelings, relationships, fathering, rite of passage and masculinity, and spirituality. The self-cultivation of the ethics and morality theory (Smurl, 1996) is in all of the core themes. According to the men in this study, the NWTA and the NWIT experiences are about developing one's self. Truth telling and promise keeping are represented in the core themes of masculinity, the essence of being a New Warrior in feelings, fathering, and relationships. Beneficence and justice are represented by the core themes of the experience of being a New Warrior of feelings, relationships, fathering, rite of passage and masculinity, and spirituality.

The theories that guided these studies were social learning (Bandura, 1977) and symbolic interaction (Charon, 1995). Social learning theory states that learning is largely from modeling and reinforcement. It appears that the NWTA and the NWIT experiences changed the reward system of these men so that nonviolent and more helpful behavior is the norm. Other studies will be needed to determine if these men are practicing what they claim to have been taught.

Blumer (1986) stated the three basic principles of symbolic interaction: (1) we act toward things according to the meaning we give them, (2) the meaning we give to things is the result of social interaction and (3) in any situation, we go through an internal process of interpretation in order to give the situation a meaning and decide how to act. If the men of the MKP are beginning to follow the five core themes of this study and ethics and morality theory (Smurl, 1996), they are changing their interactions. This study and its themes were not put through the lens of social learning theory or the principles of symbolic interactionism, although they were used to guide the development of the study. Ethics and morality theory (Smurl, 1996) was added later because it spoke to the themes that emerged from the data.

Social Policy and Practice Implications

The men depicted in these studies displayed a need for other men and a mature masculinity that was and is being met by the MKP experiences. This is a need that the literature review appeared to show that many men have (Campbell & Moyers, 1988) and that social workers see on a daily basis—men who have no connection to an ethic or morality other than "what I want is right" and an ethic that says "I can get what I want any way I want it."

The social policy implications of these studies are that we need to study the possibility of programs to initiate young men into a mature masculinity that is nurturing and loving and encompasses the five aspects of Smurl's (1996) ethics and morality theory: self-cultivation, truth telling, promise keeping, beneficence (love), and justice. Social workers can advocate and write grants for programs such as this. In the absence of programs, social workers can investigate the MKP experiences and consider referring their male clients there. Male social workers can also become initiated by going through the NWTA (female social workers can investigate, or become involved with, the Woman Within experiences, a sister program to the MKP). There is potentially a great deal that social work can learn about holding men and others accountable for their behavior, regardless of their circumstances.

The New Warrior brochure (1996) states that "New Warrior men and centers are involved in mentoring disaffected youth, working with gangs and incarcerated young men, building shelters for the homeless, creating programs for Vietnam-era veterans, and other causes that cry out for healthy masculine presence" (p. 4). With this outreach mission, these men are working with some of the same problems and issues that social workers handle and struggle with.

Qualitative data obtained from both studies suggested that the NWTA was addressing attitudes and knowledge about mature masculinity, the value of rituals and initiations, owning one's own shadow, and making connections. Other attitudes and knowledge areas addressed were about accountability; honesty; integrity; the need to heal father wounds, mother wounds, and sibling wounds from childhood, all behavior having meaning in the man's life; and the value of having a mission in life. Two major aspects of the NWTA for these men were accessing the "wild man" energy and the inner work of the "hero's journey."

The MKP seems to be saying that a mature man is one who has integrated the mature aspects of the four archetypes of the king, warrior, magician, and lover and continues to confront the destructive shadow and golden shadow (that in us that is good and we do not recognize) in each of us (Moore & Gillette, 1990). These men also appear to be saying that it takes time away from society with initiated men for some men to access these attributes in themselves. The initiation weekend used rituals, Jungian psychology, visualizations, times of open sharing, Native American traditions, adventures, and aspects of Gestalt therapy to attempt to help initiates grow into this vision of a mission of service and a mature masculinity.

The qualitative data from the men in the ethnographic study suggest that some of these missions were accomplished. Nine of the eleven new men who participated in all aspects of the study said the weekend helped them to live with more integrity and to make better connections with the people in their lives. Six of the eleven stated that the weekend helped them with relationships and friendships, confidence in themselves, and being more open with their feelings. From this it appears that the NWTA affected, at least qualitatively, the lives of these men in positive ways. Although only two variables in the survey showed statistically significant changes, both dealing with the sharing of feelings, all but one of the other variables moved in the direction of a mature masculinity, as defined by Bly (1990) and Moore and Gillette (1990) and as used by the MKP.

Study Limitations

The MKP center that the men in these studies are part of is predominantly Caucasian and with the active involvement of a number of gay men. There have been efforts, with some success, to broaden the appeal of the training adventure weekend to a more diverse population. It is not known if what these men experienced would be beneficial for men of other races, classes or cultures. There is still much work to be done in the area of serving a much more diverse group of men. Interpretive bias was guarded against by an ongoing audit performed by my faculty advisers. Even so, bias cannot be ruled out. The following research questions should be studied by researchers outside the MKP in the effort to eliminate possible interpreter bias:

- What in the weekend experience changes these men, and are the changes long term?
- What is the impact of the MKP experiences on the family structure, relationships, and others around these men?

CONCLUSION

The NWTA and the NWIT do not appear to be a repackaging of a dominant controlling patriarchy. It appears from the research that the overall mission of MKP is to lead men to lives of service. That is not a dominant controlling patriarchy. What about the name *warrior* in the work of the MKP? Starhawk (1992) makes the point that the word *warrior* carries a lot of negative and violent images with it and suggests that *healers* or *fighters* may be a more appropriate name for men who claim to be discarding the old vision of the warrior conqueror. She makes a valid point. If we are to make positive changes, we need to do it in a way that treats all people with integrity, dignity, and respect. The NWTA and the NWIT appear to be doing this.

Social workers need many avenues to help alleviate the suffering of the various groups of people they serve. If these studies are any indication, the MKP may be helping to alleviate the suffering of many men. It is our job as social workers to learn what we can from this organization and training, and participate if we are male and choose to participate, so as to use what we can to help those who suffer. Where do we go from here? Moore and Gillette (1992) stated, "We believe both men and women have encoded deep inside an understanding of how to use their power for blessing and liberation. With the Navajo, we have faith that human beings can once again find the *Blessingway*" (p. 9).

NOTE

The papers on the two studies are (1) "Heuristic Study of the New Warriors Experience: A Rite of Passage into a New Masculinity," and (2) "Ethnographic Study of the New Warrior Training Adventure. A Vision of a Mature Masculinity or a Re-packaging of Dominant Patriarchy." Anyone wanting a copy of the complete research studies may contact the author or order them through inter-library loan from the "Changing Men Collections." Michigan State University Libraries, East Lansing, Michigan.

REFERENCES

Adair, M. (1992). Will the real men's movement please stand up? In K. L. Hagan (Ed.), *Women respond to the men's movement* (pp. 55–68). New York: HarperCollins.

Balcom, D. (1991). Shame and violence: Considerations in couples' treatment. *Journal of Independent Social Work, 5,* 165–181.

Bandura, A. (1977). *Social learning theory.* Englewood Cliffs, NJ: Prentice Hall.

Berne, E. (1964). *Games people play.* New York: Grove Press.

Bliss, S. (1992). What happens at a mythopoetic men's weekend? In C. Harding (Ed.), *Wingspan: Inside the men's movement* (pp. 95–99). New York: St. Martin's Press.

Blumenkrantz, D., & Gavazzi, S. (1993). Guiding transitional events for children and adolescents through a modern day rite of passage. *Journal of Primary Prevention, 13*(3), 199–213.

Blumer, H. (1986). *Symbolic interactionism: Perspective and method* (3rd ed.) Berkeley: University of California Press.

Bly, R. (1990). *Iron John: A book about men.* Reading, MA: Addison-Wesley.

Brod, H. (1992). The mythopoetic men's movement: A political critique. In C. Harding (Ed.), (pp. 232–236). New York: St. Martin's Press.

Brown, L. S. (1992). Essential lies: A dystopian vision of the mythopoetic men's movement. In K. L. Hagan (Ed.), *Women respond to the men's movement* (pp. 93–100). New York: HarperCollins.

Campbell, J., & Moyers, B. (1988). *The power of myth.* New York: Doubleday.

Chalk, F., & Jonassohn, K. (1990). *The history and sociology of genocide: Analysis and case studies.* New Haven: Yale University Press.

Charon, J. (1995). *Symbolic interactionism. An introduction, an interpretation, an integration* (5th ed.). Englewood Cliffs, NJ: Prentice Hall, 1995.

Creswell, J. W. (1994). *Research design: Qualitative and quantitative approaches.* Thousand Oaks, CA: Sage.

Daly, K. J. (1995). Reshaping fatherhood: Finding the models. In W. Marsiglio (Ed.), *Fatherhood: Contemporary theory, research, and social policy.* Thousand Oaks, CA: Sage.

Dollahite, D. C., Hawkins, A. J., & Brotherson, S. E. (1997). Fatherwork: A conceptual ethic of fathering as generative work. In A. J. Hawkins & D. C. Dollahite (Eds.), *Generative fathering: Beyond deficit perspectives.* Thousand Oaks, CA: Sage.

Eisler, R. (1992). What do men really want? The men's movement, partnership, and domination. In K. L. Hagan (Ed.), *Women respond to the men's movement* (pp. 43–54). New York: HarperCollins.

Faludi, S. (1991). *Backlash: The undeclared war against American women.* New York: Crown Publishers.

Fasick, F. (1988). Patterns of formal education in high school: As rites of passage. *Adolescence, 23*(90), 457–468.

Gerzon, M. (1992). *A choice of heroes: The changing faces of American manhood.* Boston: Houghton Mifflin.

Gilbert, R. (1992). Revisiting the psychology of men: Robert Bly and the mythopoetic movement. *Journal of Humanistic Psychology, 32,* 41–67.

Gutman, D. (1987). *Reclaimed powers: Toward a new psychology of men and women in later life.* New York: Basic Books.

Hough, J., & Hardy, M. (1991). *Against the wall: Men's reality in a codependent culture.* Center City, MN: Hazeldon.

Hyden, M., & McCarthy, I. (1994). Woman battering and father-daughter incest disclosure: Discourses of denial and acknowledgment. *Discourse and Society, 5*(4), 543–565.

Jesser, C. J. (1996). *Fierce and tender men: Sociological aspects of the men's movement.* Westport, CT: Praeger.

Johnson, N. (1984). Sex, color, and rites of passage in ethnographic research. *Human Organization 43,* 108–120.

Jung, C. G. (1993). Psychological types. In V. S. De Laszlo (Ed.), *The Basic Writings of C. G. Jung.* New York: Modern Library.

Kauth, B. (1992). *A circle of men: The original manual for men's support groups.* New York: St. Martin's Press.

Keen, S. (1991). *Fire in the belly: On being a man.* New York: Bantam Books.

Keen, S. (1992). Rapacious normality: The war between the sexes. In C. Harding (Ed.), Wingspan: Inside the men's movement (pp. 237–241). New York: St. Martin's Press.

Keen, S., & Valley-Fox, A. (1989). *Your mythic journey: Finding meaning in your life through writing and storytelling.* Los Angeles: Jeremy T. Tarcher.

Kimmel, M. S. (1987). Rethinking "masculinity": New directions in research. In M. S. Kimmel (Ed.), *Changing men: New directions in research on men and masculinity* (pp. 9–24). Newbury Park, CA: Sage.

Kingsolver, B. (1992). Cabbages and kings. In K. L. Hagan (Ed.), *Women respond to the men's movement* (pp. 39–42). New York: HarperCollins.

Kovaks, M. G. (Trans.). (1989). *The epic of Gilgamesh.* Stanford: Stanford University Press.

MacNab, T. (1990). What do men want? Male rituals of initiation in group psychotherapy. *International Journal of Group Psychotherapy, 40*(2), 139–153.

Marshall, C., & Rossman, G. B. (1995). *Designing qualitative research* (2nd ed.). Thousand Oaks, CA: Sage.

McBride, A., & Darragh, J. (1995). Interpreting the data on father involvement: Implications for parenting programs for men. *Families in Society: The Journal of Contemporary Human Services,* 76, pp. 490–497.

Meth, R. L., & Pasick, R. S. (1990). *Men in therapy: The challenge of change.* New York: Guilford Press.

Miedzian, M. (1988). *Boys will be boys: Breaking the link between masculinity and violence.* New York: Doubleday.

Moore, R., & Gillette, D. (1990). *King, warrior, magician, lover: Rediscovering the archetypes of the mature masculine.* San Francisco: HarperCollins.

Moore, R., & Gillette, D. (1992). *The king within: Accessing the king in the male psyche.* New York: Avon Books.

Mosher, D., & Tomkins, S. (1988). Scripting the macho man: Hypermasculine socialization and enculturation. *Journal of Sex Research, 25*(1), 60–84.

Moustakas, C. (1990). *Heuristic research: Design, methodology, and applications.* Newbury Park, CA: Sage.

Musgrove, F., & Middleton, R. (1981). Rites of passage and the meaning of age in three contrasted social groups: Professional footballers, teachers, and Methodist ministers. *British Journal of Sociology, 32*(1), 39–55.

New Warrior Network. (1996). *The new warrior training adventure* (Brochure). Wendell, MA: Author.

O'Hanlon, W. H., & Martin, M. (1992). *Solution-oriented hypnosis: An Ericksonian approach,* New York: Norton.

Pentz, M. (1997a). *Heuristic study of the "New Warriors" experience: A rite of passage into a new masculinity*. Unpublished manuscript, Indiana School of Social Work, Indianapolis, IN.

Pentz, M. (1997b). *Ethnographic study of the New Warrior Training Adventure: A vision of a mature masculinity or a re-packaging of a dominant patriarchy*. Unpublished manuscript, Indiana School of Social Work, Indianapolis, IN.

Popenoe, D. (1995). *Sociology* (10th ed.). Englewood Cliffs, NJ: Prentice Hall.

Reamer, F. G. (1995). Ethics and values. In R. L. Edwards (Ed.), *Encyclopedia of social work* (19th ed., Vol. 1, pp. 893–902). Washington, DC: NASW Press.

Ruether, R. R. (1992). Patriarchy and the men's movement: Part of the problem or part of the solution? In K. L. Hagan (Ed.), *Women respond to the men's movement* (pp. 13–18). New York: HarperCollins.

Smurl, J. F. (1996). *A primer in ethics*. Unpublished manuscript, Indiana University, Department of Religious Studies.

Starhawk. (1992). A men's movement I can trust. In K. L. Hagan (Ed.), *Women respond to the men's movement* (pp. 27–38). New York: HarperCollins.

Thiele, L. P. (1993). Making democracy safe for the world: Social movements and global politics. *Alternatives, 18*(3), 273–305.

Vachss, A. (1993). *Sex crimes: Ten years on the front lines prosecuting rapists and confronting their collaborators*. New York: Henry Holt & Co.

Williams, J. (1982, Winter). The ritual of initiation. Implications for the liberal arts. *Educational Record*, pp. 29–31.

PART IV
FEMINIST ROUNDTABLE

INTRODUCTION TO FEMINIST ROUNDTABLE

Part IV consists of chapters by authors from the United States, United Kingdom, and Canada.

The first in the Roundtable is Jorgen Lorentzen (1998) of the University of Oslo, Norway, and his review of Kimmel's *The politics of manhood: Profeminist men respond to the mythopoetic men's movement (and the mythopoetic leaders answer).* After discussing the question of what is a movement and essentialism, Lorentzen tackles the topic of "women and feminism."

It is pretty daring to say that someone with a foggy understanding of feminism is an antifeminist. I agree that the mythopoets have been unclear and weak on this issue.

On the other hand,

I find it puzzling to read some of the articles' harsh words against Bly and the movement, when Bly has worked with the feminist movement before some of the writers in this book could walk. The same goes for Shepherd Bliss and others. Is it not strange that the only ones who call themselves feminists are the mythopoets, Marvin Allen and Shepherd Bliss, while their critics call themselves profeminist? In my thinking, either you are feminist or not, either you are working to end oppression of women and the patriarchy, or you are not, feminism is a theory and a practice, not a gender. Men are feminists as are women. If American profeminists started to think this way, they would not be so afraid of being politically correct. Perhaps the profeminists need a retreat into the woods to work on how to be less politically correct, which means how to be honest and unafraid of your own inner meanings. And which could also mean, in another language, how to be wild and carry your inner warrior. It takes a lot of warrior energy to fight patriarchy, and sometimes we even have to fight against biased and incorrect thinking of feminist women, without being antifeminist because of that (pp. 113 and 114).

You are invited to read the rest of Jorgen's short essay for his additional comments about it being appropriate for straight, white, middle-class men to be healing themselves spiritually. They are the "model." They need to change. They need to change by healing. Then join in reading the rest of the international roundtable that follows.

REFERENCE

Lorentzen, J. (1998). Book review of *The politics of manhood*, edited by Michael Kimmel. *Men and Masculinities*, 1, 112, 115.

Chapter 14
A Feminist Looks at the Men's Movement: Search for Common Ground
Holly Sweet

The day I was preparing a talk on which this chapter is based, I met some friends for dinner to discuss how we could help a man we knew who had been incarcerated for many years and was struggling to get parole. Twenty years ago, he had been an adolescent with an absent father and a brother-in-law (a career criminal) who became his surrogate father. For Eddie at age sixteen, manhood meant being tough and emulating macho men with guns.

When I arrived home after dinner, the telephone rang. It was Jim, a male friend who lived in another part of the country. He said he had just had a bad ulcer attack. "Do you know what my main problem was?" he asked. "I couldn't think of anyone I was close enough to be able to ask for a ride to the hospital. I didn't want anyone to know I was in such pain."

Jim and Eddie represent just two of the ways in which men are damaged in our culture by their attempts to live up to the standards of "real men" who have to be tough, self reliant, and aggressive, no matter how destructive the consequences are for themselves or others. What is particularly poignant is that so many men, whatever their race, ethnic background, social class, and sexual orientation, are either unaware of this damage (because our culture still holds on to the myth that men "have it all"), do not know how to talk about it, or are afraid to talk about it for fear of being ridiculed or blamed. The mythopoetic branch of the emerging men's movement is a step in the right direction; it gives men a framework with which to gain awareness of gender-related problems and begin to find practical ways of dealing effectively with those problems.

I know the power of having a framework about the social construction of gender and how that construction can constrict and demean women. Robin Morgan first gave it to me when she edited *Sisterhood Is Powerful* in 1970. Additional feminist authors over the next twenty-five years and my own women's support groups have helped me use that framework both personally and professionally for the past thirty years. I believe that when men's eyes are opened about how male sex role norms can hurt themselves and others (and they are able to explore those roles in supportive environments such as men's support groups), they will have the desire to make constructive changes in their own lives and in the institutions in which they live and work that will benefit men and women alike.

This chapter examines the similarities and differences between only two branches of the men's movement: profeminist and mythopoetic. I chose these approaches because I believe they represent what the men's movement should be about and are well allied with feminist principles in general.

MANHOOD IN TRANSITION

Increasing attention has been paid to studying the male sex role in American culture as a social construction that carries painful aspects for men as well as power and privilege. Although a handful of books in the mid-1970s began to talk about problems with the male sex role (Goldberg, 1976; David & Brannon, 1976), it was not until the early 1980s that the concept of male sex role strain (introduced by Pleck in 1981 in his book *The Myth of Masculinity*) made its way into mainstream academic literature. Since that time, a growing number of scholarly books have been devoted to men's studies (Doyle, 1995; Levant & Pollack, 1995; Kimmel & Messner, 1995); courses on men's studies have risen from seventeen before 1975 to fifty-seven in 1992 (Femiano, 1992); and as of July 1995, the American Psychological Association formed a new division (Division 51) to study men and masculinities.

It is clear from men's studies scholarship that there are significant problems associated with the male sex role: an unhealthy emphasis on aggression, independence, oversexualization of relationships, success, domination, and restriction of vulnerable feelings and a general attitude of antifemininity that contributes to both homophobia and the demeaning of women. Awareness of the destructiveness of male sex role norms on both personal and societal levels (particularly the norms of aggression, dominance, and emotional restriction) has resulted in men (and women) coming together in informal groups, retreats, and conferences to take a critical look at hegemonic "hypermasculinity." This critique has been accompanied by an emphasis on how we can go about changing expectations of what it means to be a man in mainstream U.S. culture. The men's movement thus consists of personal and political efforts by men and women to examine and change the roles that men have been expected to play in our culture.

SIMILARITIES AND DIFFERENCES

Based on information in a collection of writings about the mythopoetic and profeminist branches of the men's movement (Kimmel, 1995) and a series of interviews with men involved in the mythopoetic men's gatherings (Schwalbe, 1996), it is probable that both groups would agree on the following points:

- Men need to be able to bond with other men in intimate, meaningful ways that do not demean women, gay men, or other marginalized men.
- Men should be allowed to show a full range of feelings without being labeled as unmanly or weak, especially more vulnerable feelings such as sadness, fear, and the need for intimate, caring contact with both males and females.
- Men need to find ways to take a more active role in mentoring younger men in healthy, nurturing ways.
- Men need to be better connected to their families (of whatever configuration those families might be) in a more responsible, egalitarian, and intimate fashion.
- Relationships with partners would work better if there was less dominance and violence on the part of men, more respect for the feminine aspects of life, and a better balance of sexuality and emotional intimacy by both genders.
- Economic and political power in our society should be shared more equally between men and women.

Despite many basic points in common, mythopoetic and profeminist men differ in emphasizing the importance of these points and how one might best reach these goals.

- Profeminist men see gender differences as an artifact of a sexist culture (a more sociological perspective); mythopoetic men see gender differences as having a more fundamental base in biology and psychology (a more psychological perspective).
- Mythopoetic men focus more on personal growth; profeminist men focus their efforts more on social and political action.
- Profeminist men openly encourage women to work with them in fighting patriarchy; mythopoetic men find it important to spend time alone with other men in order to express safely feelings of anger, shame, guilt, and sadness in order to heal their own emotional wounds.
- Mythopoetic men focus more on the damage done to men by patriarchal norms; profeminist men focus more on the damage done to women.
- Profeminist men are more likely to acknowledge the negative aspects of masculinity on a social level; mythopoetic men are more likely to acknowledge the positive aspects of masculinities on a social level while working to understand their own "shadow side."

Of these differences, only the first is actually a true opposite. It is also not clear how many mythopoetic men actually believe that any biological differences that exist between women and men account for the problems that exist with male sex role norms. The remaining differences are simply a shift in focus on the same problem: that traditional male norms hurt us all. As Bliss (1995) mentions in Kimmel's book *The Politics of Manhood*, "There is much work to be done. I choose to do mine in certain ways. Others choose different ways. . . . Let us honor diversity" (p. 292).

MENDING FENCES

These two branches of the men's movement (and their feminist supporters) need to confront several problems that have caused some acrimony and misunderstanding among those who are involved with changing men's roles. First is a distinct tendency (certainly not limited to the men's movement or feminism) to view differences in a dualistic, either-or sense. This approach has been called the zero-sum approach: if one side gains something, the other side must lose an equal amount. This kind of thinking leads to the following false assumptions:

• If you're doing personal growth work, then you aren't doing political work.
• If you're spending time working with men, then you aren't helping women.
• If you express negative ideas about how men act, then you have nothing positive to say about men.
• If you talk about how men are in pain, then you ignore women's pain.

Bly (1995) argues that this kind of linear, oppositional thinking is misleading and gets in the way of genuine growth and insight. I would argue that the opposite of the zero-sum paradigm tends to be true: women benefit as more attention is paid to men's problems (and men benefit as more attention is paid to women's problems). For example, as men work on their own problems more, they tend to become more egalitarian and compassionate toward women, not less. People who do personal growth work (whether through traditional individual and group therapy, weekend retreats and workshops, or ongoing support groups) are usually better able to engage productively in political and social action, having taken steps to work on their own issues that might cloud their ability to see clearly what is happening around them.

One way to overcome the tendency to think dualistically is always to acknowledge the value of another's viewpoint and see how it can enlarge and transform one's own worldview. Dash (1995) stresses this point and says that "the two movements need each other. We need to combine activism with inner work" (p. 355). Robert Bly and Michael Kimmel demonstrated this synergy well in their 1996 public debate sponsored by the Men and Masculinity Conference in Portland, Oregon. The debate was humorous, respectful, passionate, and conciliatory, with a call by both Kimmel and Bly to end the infighting and focus instead on their common goals. Kimmel acknowledged that profeminist men could use some of the positive spirit, emotional release, and intimate relations with men found among mythopoetic men. Bly acknowledged that mythopoetic men could learn more from profeminist men about the importance of fighting institutionalized sexism and homophobia.

Both factions must demonstrate a greater respect for and understanding of their differences. In the process of setting up straw men to knock down (a common debate technique), viewpoints are distorted. In *The Politics of Manhood* (1995), some authors make pejorative and provocative comments about other points of view. For example, Connell (1995) states:

Bly's muddled fantasy of masculinity might be laughable if all it led to was middle class men sitting under pine trees and pretending to be bears. But I think it is more dangerous than that. Racist, myth-mongering warrior cults of masculinity have existed before: in Germany in the 1920s for instance. (p. 85)

Not surprisingly, statements like this are met with defensiveness on the part of some Bly supporters. Kipnis (1995), for example, accuses some profeminist men (and feminists) of making "blatantly misleading" and "maliciously careless" statements about mythopoetic theory that he believes results in continued male bashing. This kind of polemic interaction is unfortunate, since it assumes the worst motives of one's critics and encourages combative debate rather than a collaborative dialogue. It is discouraging when well-intentioned men who are dedicated to reforming male norms, including the norms of aggression and competition, fall prey to their power instead. One wonders if the decline of the once active National Organization for Men Against Sexism may be related.

Kimmel begins and ends his book with a call to both sides to engage in what he calls "compassionate challenge, nourishing debate, and loving engagement." In order to do this, however, it is important that both sides are well informed about other points of view, open to changing their own points of view, and willing to see that other people's ideas do in fact change. We need to see people where they are now and where they are headed, not where they were. For example, people often refer to Bly's ideas as expressed in *Iron John* (1990) rather than where he stands today (with a far more balanced and aware view of gender and sexual orientation, as evidenced in his remarks in the 1996 Men and Masculinity debate).

The kind of work men do in mythopoetic men's gatherings has been called "whining" by some critics. Perhaps some of the discomfort with the kind of emotionally cathartic work that occurs in these gatherings is linked to the fact that it violates one of the core norms for men: to be in emotional control at all times. It is crucial to keep in mind that some men need time to heal their own wounds before they can get involved in political action. Many men in the mythopoetic movement are doing just that. Bullock (1995) points out that "buried feelings, especially the feeling of pain, [can] become the appropriate starting point for men's awareness and transformation" (p. 236). Stopping men from expressing their vulnerable feelings by shaming them with negative labels may be just another example of adherence to a harmful norm that men are fighting to overcome.

Finally, it is important that men involved with mythopoetic men's gatherings take their work into a more political arena. Their new wisdom must be brought into public places like government and industry that are in need of transformation to accommodate a healthier vision of manhood for everyone concerned. This is what profeminist men like Kimmel are asking of people involved in the mythopoetic movement: to bring back the insights they have gained in private retreats into the public arena so that key issues like shared child care, promotion of gay rights, and support of affirmative actions programs can be tackled.

REACHING OUT TO A WIDER AUDIENCE

There appear to be two main reasons that the general public is not becoming involved with the men's movement. The first is that the movement is largely invisible. If you were to ask an average man what he thinks the men's movement is about, he will either stare blankly or say something along the lines of "drumming" or "sweat lodges." Last summer I conducted a small, nonscientific survey of the men in a local sports club and found some interesting results. None of the men knew what the men's movement was. This in itself was not at all surprising. However, all the men expressed an interest in finding out more about the men's movement. They spoke to me quite openly about some of the problems they had had in adhering to male norms, such as emotional restrictiveness and success at all costs. These men need to be reached; people in the men's movement need to learn how best to reach them.

The men's movement (like the women's movement) began in academia, a relatively small and sometimes isolated section of American society. Those in academia must consider ways to reach men outside academia who have never heard of Robert Bly or do not understand what the term *sex role strain* means. New formats that attract mainstream men (like the Million Man March or the Promise Keepers) should be analyzed to see why their message appeals to men and incorporate those aspects (such as compassion) that can be incorporated into the men's movement without violating its integrity.

The interest that many men have shown in John Gray's book *Men Are from Mars, Women Are from Venus* (1992) is testament to the fact that some men care very much about how to get along better with women. In my experience as a trainer in gender relations, I have found repeatedly that men will show up for workshops on "improving relationships between men and women" much more often than they will for workshops on men's issues. If this is so, then one way to reach men would be to include breakout sessions for men on men's issues within the context of gender relations workshops.

Better marketing is needed about what the men's movement stands for and who is involved in it. Names like *profeminist* and *mythopoetic* are esoteric and unintelligible to many men and women. Bly has suggested the term *expressive* as a replacement for *mythopoetic*. The term *profeminist* could also be replaced by a new term (perhaps something to do with social activism) that would more clearly define its philosophy to the general public.

As O'Neil (1995) suggests, more empirical research on gender role strain in men is needed, especially on groups of men who are not white, middle-class American heterosexual men—that is, men with different sexual orientations and different class, racial, and ethnic backgrounds. More research needs to be conducted on why men are attracted to movements like the Promise Keepers and what changes men undergo as a result of participating in such programs. Feedback from women who work and live with men who have been involved in men's work should be solicited. Surveys, interviews, and questionnaires would help find out whether women consider their male colleagues and partners to be more compassionate, emotionally open, egalitarian, less homophobic, and more respectful of women after attending rallies and workshops organized by any of the groups involved with challenging traditional male norms.

The second reason that the men's movement is not reaching as many men as possible is that it too often carries a negative message: that men's ways of being in the world are inherently bad. Schwalbe (1996) suggests that even men who are familiar with and sympathetic to the men's movement can be turned off by what they see as a negative, blaming, or self-righteous attitude. For example, Brod (1995) writes:

We serve no one . . . if the only message we bring is that . . . men are simply wrong about their experience of power, or that they're not being honest, or that they suffer false consciousness. None of the standard, arrogant, elitist responses put forth by those who think they're more enlightened works to persuade those they think are less enlightened. (pp. 92–93)

In order to reach people, they must be approached with a positive message that they are drawn to rather than a negative message that they are shamed into. Promoting a positive image of masculinity is exactly what the Promise Keepers have been doing, and they are packing men by the thousands into football stadiums around the country. Although I may not agree with all the promises they want men to keep, I do agree with one of their basic tenets: that you reach men (especially wounded men) better through compassion than blame. As Bly (1995) says: "Many young men, rather than being ashamed of being patriarchal, are ashamed of being men. We must be more clear. To be ashamed of your gender is not healthful for anyone" (p. 274).

HOW WOMEN WILL BENEFIT FROM THE MEN'S MOVEMENT

Many of the authors in *Women Respond to the Men's Movement* (1992) are guarded about how useful the mythopoetic branch will be to women. They fear that in some way, the mythopoetic branch is nothing more than an attempt to return to dominating and misogynist ways under a new name. In her preface, Hagen (1992) says:

I've heard women respond in many ways—from cautious hope that men are coming to terms with the realities of true partnership and shared power, to utter disgust at the chorus of whining white men, to a deep-rooted fear that the men's movement has only legitimized a fashionable new form of woman-hating. (p. xi)

On the other hand, most of the authors in this book express some optimism about a movement that is truly centered on helping men become more integrated and whole. Starhawk (1992) speaks for the feminists she knows:

Feminists long for men to heal. . . . We dream of a world full of men who could be passionate lovers . . . capable of profound loves and sorrows, strong allies of women, sensitive nurturers . . . sweet without being spineless, proud without being insufferably egotistical, [and] fierce without being violent. (p. 27)

As men become less aggressive, less hypersexual, more emotionally open, and less driven by norms of power, success, and control, all women will benefit. Women will find themselves with male colleagues, friends, and partners who are better able to respect their ways of being and doing without resorting to defensiveness or detachment and who are better able to connect with women in mutually satisfying ways. Women will enjoy the company of men who are not afraid of the feminine in themselves and will not feel compelled to denigrate the feminine in others.

HOW WOMEN CAN HELP PROMOTE THE MEN'S MOVEMENT

First, judging harshly the motives of men who are truly struggling to change old patterns is not helpful and too often leads to continued patterns of anger and defensiveness. If their efforts to change are respected, they are more likely to continue to want to change. Although it may be difficult for some women to continue to engage with men who lapse into old patterns of chauvinism, it is important to acknowledge the positive direction in which men are headed rather than focus on the negative direction from which they have come (and occasionally return to).

Second, men need the freedom to work with other men—alone. Pathologizing men's support groups as just another version of old boys' clubs is misleading and unhelpful. Feminists have been involved with women's groups for many years. These groups have served women well and allowed them to work together on both personal and political issues. Men must be allowed the same opportunity.

Third, as men change and become more emotionally intimate with each other, they may not need women to do as much caretaking and nurturing as women did in the past. Although this is what women say they want, in practice women may feel as though they are no longer needed as much by men. Women may have some trouble in letting go of the roles they have played for so long. In addition, women may still respond negatively, on a *gut level*, to men who cry easily or cannot change a flat tire. Many women were born and raised in times that taught them that men should be tough, in control, and competent at all times. Openly and honestly acknowledging the difficulty that change poses for everyone, even changes that are seen as positive, would be helpful for both men and women.

Finally, both men and women need to move beyond the zero-sum approach to gender relations. For example, Kingsolver (1992) compares men's problems to hangnails and women's problems to cancer and says that women are fighting for their lives, while men are looking for some peace of mind. Although it is undoubtedly true that women are more harmed economically and physically by patriarchy than men are, comparisons of suffering that minimize difficulties that men experience are not useful in alleviating men's pain. We must acknowledge that both men and women have been hurt by a system of rigid roles that has limited each gender (although in different ways). The important point is not to compare who suffers more but to change a system under which everyone suffers.

CONCLUSION

It is of paramount importance that men and women who are concerned about the damage done by rigid and restrictive male norms learn to work together to challenge traditional structures rather than argue about who has the better approach or who is more politically correct. Feminist women, profeminist men, and mythopoetic men are all involved in what should be a shared struggle to change definitions of manhood to include norms for men that are more balanced, humane, and affirming of the feminine than existing models of hypermasculinity allow in contemporary society. All groups seek to find personal and institutional ways of helping men become less aggressive and more receptive, less competitive and more collaborative, less self-reliant and more connected, less emotionally available to themselves and others. This is the common ground that profeminist men, feminist women, and mythopoetic men share. It is essential that they support and respect one another as they pursue different but complementary ways of finding that ground.

REFERENCES

Bliss, S. (1995). Mythopoetic men's movements. In M. Kimmel (Ed.), *The politics of Manhood*. Philadelphia: Temple University Press.
Bly, R. (1990). *Iron John*. New York: Vintage Book.

Bly, R. (1995). Thoughts on reading this book. In M. Kimmel (Ed.), *The politics of manhood*. Philadelphia: Temple University Press.

Brod, H. (1995). The politics of the mythopoetic men's movement. In M. Kimmel (Ed.), *The politics of manhood*. Philadelphia: Temple University Press.

Bullock, C. (1995). Psyche, society, and the men's movement. In M. Kimmel (Ed.), *The politics of manhood*. Philadelphia: Temple University Press.

Connell, R. W. (1995). Men at bay: The "men's movement" and its newest best-sellers. In M. Kimmel (Ed.), *The politics of manhood*. Philadelphia: Temple University Press.

Dash, M. (1995). Betwixt and between in the men's movement. In M. Kimmel (Ed.), *The politics of manhood*. Philadelphia: Temple University Press.

David, D. & Brannon, R. (Eds.). (1976). *The forty-nine percent majority: The male sex role*. Reading, MA: Addison-Wesley.

Doyle, J. (1995). *The male experience*. Madison: William C. Brown and Benchmark.

Femiano, S. (1992). *Directory of men's studies courses taught in the United States and Canada*. Northampton, MA: American Men's Studies Assoc.

Friedan, B. (1962). *The feminine mystique*. New York: Norton.

Goldberg, H. (1976). *The hazards of being male*. New York: Signet.

Gray, J. (1992). *Men are from Mars, women are from Venus*. New York: HarperCollins.

Hagen, K. (Ed.). (1992). *Women respond to the men's movement*. San Francisco: HarperCollins.

Kimmel, M. (1995). *The politics of manhood*. Philadelphia: Temple University Press.

Kimmel, M., & Messner, M. (Eds)., (1995). *Men's lives*. (3rd ed.). Reading, MA: Allyn and Bacon.

Kingsolver, B. (1992). Cabbages and kinds. In K. Hagen, (Ed.), *Women respond to the men's movement*. San Francisco: HarperCollins.

Kipnis, A. (1995). The postfeminist men's movement. In M. Kimmel (Ed.), *The politics of manhood*. Philadelphia: Temple University Press.

Levant, R., & Pollack, W. (Eds.). (1995). *A new psychology of men*. New York: Basic Books.

Morgan, R. (Ed.). (1970). *Sisterhood is powerful*. New York: Vintage Books.

O'Neil, J. (1995). Fifteen years of theory and research in men's gender role conflict: New paradigms for empirical research. In R. Levant & W. Pollack (Eds.), *A new psychology of men*. New York: Basic Books.

Pleck, J. (1981). *The myth of masculinity*. Cambridge, MA: MIT Press.

Schwalbe, M. (1996). *Unlocking the iron cage*. New York: Oxford University Press.

Starhawk. (1992). A men's movement I can trust. In K. Hagen (Ed.), *Women respond to the men's movement*. San Francisco: HarperCollins.

Chapter 15
Men and the Search for Common Ground
John Rowan

I have been in the profeminist men's movement since 1972. I have been involved in five consciousness-raising groups, have organized groups at conferences, and have led workshops in six different countries. In 1978 the antisexist magazine *Achilles Heel* came into being, and I have been writing and coediting it from its early days.

Holly Sweet (Chapter 14, this volume) names the mythopoetic approach but restricts this to the work of Robert Bly and his followers and imitators. My own work (1987, 1997) attempts to show that there is a profeminist version of the mythopoetic approach associated with the work of Starhawk (1989) and others in the neopagan tradition. This tradition is older and larger than anything connected with Bly, and I think has more to offer for both men and women.

Far too many of those who want to urge a new masculinity seem to think that it can be reached by a short-cut. All we men have to do, they seem to say, is to welcome and embrace our maleness in all its pristine depth and purity. But I agree with David Tacey (1997) when he says, "Before we remake masculinity we must unmake it, and understand why it had to fall apart" (p. 14).

Holly Sweet says "Mythopoetic men focus more on personal growth: profeminist men focus their efforts more on social and political action." In my experience this is much too neat. Profeminist men, in my experience in the United Kingdom, find personal growth an essential part of their work. I remember a cartoon from about 1980 produced by one such group, which had a Fred Flintstone figure saying, "I just ain't going to be much help in smashing the system because the system is doing a pretty good job of smashing me." Personal de-

velopment and political action seem to me to be like two legs on which we have
to walk. Neither is sufficient on its own.

One of the reasons for the importance of personal work is that we have to
deal with the whole question of the patripsych: the whole body of assumptions
and identifications coming from a hierarchical and patriarchal society that we
have introjected at an unconscious level. Because the patripsych is unconscious,
it is not available to take part in the changes that we are trying to adopt consciously in political action. Consequently it can hit us in what seem to be in-
explicable ways when we try to practice equality and mutuality. We have to
deal with it in therapy. If we can find the right kind of therapy, as I have argued
at length (1997), we can be initiated into a new kind of masculinity because we
have dealt with the patripsych.

Sweet (chapter 14) also says, "Mythopoetic men focus more on the damage
done to men by patriarchal norms: profeminist men focus more on the damage
done to women." (p. 231). Although there is a great deal of truth in this, I find
it too neat. Profeminist men increasingly do justice to the problems involved
through the damage done to men by patriarchal norms. Life is more difficult for
them just because of this: some feminists may be antimale, and withdraw from
all contact with men, but men do not have that luxury.[1]

And Sweet herself lays out four false assumptions held by critics of the men's
movement about how men act or should act. These are very important, so I
comment on each one.

1. *If you're doing personal growth work, then you are not doing political
work.* This is important because it is often denied by political activists. In fact,
I have known people who were thrown out of political organizations because
they were "too interested in therapy." Andrew Samuels (1993) makes a good
point when he says, "I do not agree that therapy inevitably siphons off rage that
might more constructively be deployed in relation to social injustices. In fact, I
think that it is the reverse that often happens: Experiences in therapy act to fine
down generalized rage into a more specific format, hence rendering emotion
more accessible for social action" (p. 51).

2. *If you're spending time working with men, then you are not helping
women.* The point here is that men relate to women as husbands, lovers, sons,
fathers, brothers, and so forth. They can relate to them either as equals, in
mutuality and respect, or they can oppress or attempt to oppress them. Such
oppression may be conscious or unconscious. A man who is in touch with his
own center (whether conceptualized as self, soul, or *hara*) does not compulsively
need to control or exploit others. The case for working with violent men hardly
needs to be argued, but other men, too, are subject to the same unthinking
norms—the whole package that Bob Connell (1995) calls "hegemonic masculinity." This is what men need to question and ultimately leave behind.

3. *If you express negative ideas about how men act, then you have nothing
positive to say about men.* I know from my own experience how easy it is to
appear to be antimale when critiquing false forms of masculinity. Many men

find it hard to avoid the black-and-white thinking of being either "for or against men." Yet it is this very black-and-white thinking that needs to be questioned and ultimately abandoned. Men and women are not playing a zero-sum game, as Sweet so rightly points out. We can go for win-win solutions rather than win-lose.

4. *If you talk about how men are in pain, then you ignore women's pain.* This can be done, but there is no logical connection. You might just as well say that if you talk about how bears are hunted to extinction, then you ignore the rhinoceros. Yet in reality someone who cares about the bear is far more likely than not to care about the rhinoceros too. Again it is possible to concentrate on one to the exclusion of the other, but so far as men and women are concerned I have found that most profeminist men are proman as well as prowoman.

Questioning all four of these false assumptions may lead us to make common cause with critical psychology. Consider this quotation from Prilleltensky Nelson (1997), "By contrast, critical psychology generally views the individual and society as so fundamentally intertwined that they cannot be separated from one another in any way that makes sense. Individuals and the social world they inhabit are one and the same thing, two ways of looking at the same phenomenon. The problem then becomes explaining this reality, not in terms of a *relationship* between two separate phenomena, but in terms of some sort of totality or whole" (Nightingale & Neilands, 1997, p. 73). The personal is political. What we are interested in is social justice. The main problem is oppression. Why we are particularly interested in the oppression of women is that they have become so articulate about the problem and are closer to us than any other oppressed group. They have made it easier for us as men to see and deal with our own tendencies to oppress. The reason that we have to be interested in men too is not that they have equal problems, but that their—our—attitudes get in the way of dealing with oppression. We are part of the problem, and we can also be part of the solution.

John Gray's book (1992) has sold so well because it tells the sad and terrible truth about the way men and women mostly relate in our culture. But it tells only the most superficial and titillating part of the truth and makes it seem as if that is the way things have to be. It offers no prescription for change, because it sees no need for change. It just tells us how to oil the wheels. If we want to do more than that and make a difference in the way women and men relate in our culture, we have to dig a lot deeper and be prepared to make some ugly discoveries. We have to own up to the way in which power and control are important to men in relationships. We have to dare to find out how curiosity and the will to learn work better in relationships than the intent to protect ourselves. We have to learn that teasing put-downs are not humorous; they are killers. We have to open up our awareness of how all our attitudes have been powerfully distorted by society and how we are perpetuating a culture of hostile humor directed at women in particular.

Sweet raises the question of how we make these insights popular. I do not think we can make them sweet. We are just not going to be "packing men by the thousands into football stadiums around the country." We are too critical. Social justice is not a popular cause. Opposing the establishment is not for the many.

We cannot even make these ideas popular among feminists. One of the crushing discoveries for men who discover the profeminist men's movement is that feminists do not trust them more or like them any better. We as men discover that there is not just one kind of feminism. If we seek approval from one lot, that puts us in bad with another lot. If we look for accountability by trying to relate to feminists, we are faced with an infinite regress, because there is no ultimate group of feminists to whom all feminists are accountable. All we succeed in doing is to divide feminists into those who are pro-profeminist men and those who are anti-profeminist men. It is all very confusing and difficult. Men love to get things right, and to discover that there is no way of getting it finally and ultimately right is bad news, and sad news.

Even the language in which we discuss these things is suspect. Adrian Coyle and Caroline Morgan-Sykes discuss the way in which much of the talk about men's problems actually reinforces the notion of hegemonic masculinity while purporting to critique it. And they also come to the view that only deep and far-reaching personal therapy can do the job of changing this state of affairs in any radical way: "Such radical, social constructionist therapy can then become a discursive context in which men who are experiencing problems grounded in a struggle with enactments of masculinity can be helped to reposition themselves in relation to changes which they may view as having been foisted upon them by a changing social context" (Coyle & Morgan-Sykes 1998, p. 281).

All kinds of interesting things are happening now. In Norway has emerged an organization called IASOM (International Association for Studies of Men), which is trying to draw together the threads of men's groups and publications worldwide. Its web site is http://www.ifi.uio.no/~eivindr/iasom. In France there emerges a web site that also produces CDs dedicated to information about gender politics and social change (http://www.menprofeminist.org). Achilles Heel now has a web site with links to these and others (http://www.stejonda. demon.co.uk/achilles/index.html). The Internet is now one of the main channels through which ideas are being exchanged and worked over. And perhaps the multitudinous nature of the Internet makes it easier to see that all these issues have to be pursued at many levels. Isaac Prilleltensky and Geoffrey Nelson make the point like this: "Continuing with this illustration, the interdependence of micro, meso and macro contexts draws attention to how sexism is manifested at multiple levels of analysis. Women experience sexism in their families and close relationships (the micro level) and in their work, school and religious setting (the meso level). Both levels are affected by the larger macro context: social norms that objectify women, socioeconomic inequality, and social policies that harm women and children. A social justice focus requires changes at all three levels of analysis" (Prilleltensky & Nelson, 1997, pp. 178–179). Seeing things in this way brings us up against the sheer size of the problem. Anything that raises awareness is going to be of some use, no matter how ultimately limited it may be. So I agree with Holly Sweet when she urges us not to knock Bly and his supporters too much: his work may be limited, but it at least problematizes men and does not take them for granted. It questions what it is to be a man, and this is valuable. It is only when it offers answers rather than questions that its limitations become cruelly apparent.

We come back again and again to the difficulty with the profeminist men's movement—the sheer size of the problem that it has identified so accurately. I have had some interesting experiences in labeling men's groups at conferences. If a workshop is labeled "Men Examining the Problems of Sexism," about three men may attend. If it is labeled "Men Examining the Problems of Relationships," about ten men may come. If it is labeled "Men Finding Their Strength and Joy as Men," anything up to fifty men may roll up. This leads me to the rather simple conclusion that people prefer pleasure to pain. Therapy involves pain, which is why so many people—men and women alike—avoid therapy if they can. And if they do go to therapy, they more often choose a form of therapy that is not too challenging and offers quick results. Similarly, people prefer political action that is not too challenging or demanding. At the other extreme is the overly dedicated follower, who obeys the definition of the fanatic that I saw once: "A fanatic is someone who, when faced with the failure of some action, redoubles his efforts at it." The compulsive activist, the compulsive militant, is dangerous to himself and others. The workshop junkie is just as unfortunate, but may not do as much harm to others. But most people are not at these extremes; they prefer a quiet life.

If we are asking men to shake up their ideas, to look at themselves and their actions with a critical eye, to delve into the causes of their problems, we are making huge demands. I do not know whether we shall ever have a Million Men March or fill a stadium. All I know is that the workshops I have been to that have made the most difference to me have often been the least well attended. And the ones with hundreds of enthusiastic men chanting and drumming have been much more problematic in terms of their content. It is possible to run a high-energy workshop with deep content, and I have done it myself, but it is hard to achieve.

I ran a weekend workshop to go deeply into each man's experience of relating to women, using ritual. Each man constructed his own ritual, and we played them through. Three men turned up, and it was one of the most meaningful and excellent workshops I had ever been to. Out of this weekend came the consolidated and integrated version of what I called "A Ritual of Wounding and Healing" (Rowan 1987, pp. 120–125, 1997, pp. 209–212). I presented this at a conference of the British Association for Counselling (a large organization with some thousands of members), and about twelve men participated; it went quite well. I presented it again at a men's international conference in Austin, Texas, with about twenty men, and there it went extremely well, ending up with a drumming procession through the hotel where the conference was located.

Another ritual that my partner and I devised for an international conference on the island of Lanzarote went extremely well (Rowan 1997) with twenty men and thirty women. This was more elaborate, and we never found the occasion to repeat it, but it was a wonderful experience, and I think went quite deep.

On the other hand, I was not so pleased with a ritual some of us devised for an international men's conference in Koszeg, Hungary. One of the men was leaving one day to get married. Before he went, he wanted to feel that he had attained manhood. Some of the men devised a spontaneous ritual that involved the elders gathering round him, lifting him up high, speaking some words about manhood, and giving him a blessing. It seemed to do something important for him. This impressed the group so much that other men wanted to do the same thing. Eventually something like twenty men went through it. Yet in spite of the fact that this was referred to as initiation, it was relatively superficial, and I wonder how much it really meant in terms of different consciousness or action after the conference.

I believe that long-term therapy rather than a brief workshop is needed for a true initiation. We do not have a quick fix to offer, so I am perhaps less sanguine than Holly Sweet about the possibility of large-scale success. That does not mean that such a desirable outcome is not worth talking about or working for— just that I want to be realistic about what can be achieved. Reality is better than illusion, even if it is not so comforting in the short run.

NOTE

1. It is true that John Stoltenberg (1990) wrote a striking book called *Refusing to Be a Man*, but this is a rare exception, which went too far for most men.

EDITOR'S NOTE

Regarding the reference to the "initiation" of men at the first European Men's Gathering, I was the one who developed the ritual with the help of other men.

My contribution was initially called 'a gift to Peter'. . . . Peter was leaving early to go home to get married. [I offered to give him a gift.] It was an initiation by the elders. What could be more appropriate than to initiate one who was leaving later that day to get married?

After that initiation, there were several concerns expressed to me because I had offered to repeat the process on the last morning for the other men who wanted to be initiated. One man suggested that I had not followed Joseph Campbell's three stages of initiation sufficiently. Another indicated that there was not enough participation by those who were not elders.

Accordingly, by Saturday morning, in consultation with the other elders, modifications evolved and many more men wanted to be initiated than I had expected. It was the traditional lifting by the elders after being drummed into the room, with the outer circle chanting in concentric circles. It was an interesting touch to have the effect of 'monks' chanting in the outer circle as each man was initiated. That maintained the energy and provided a European Gregorian touch to the ceremony." (Barton, E. [1998]. "One man's small step, one giant step for mankind: Reflections on the 1st European men's gathering." *Transitions*, 18, 8, 20.)

Today, I probably would call the ritual an elder blessing, rather than an initiation. First of all the men felt a need and asked to participate in the ritual that was developed rather spontaneously. I feel the men felt an emptiness that this ritual blessing helped fill.

I agree with John that this was rather superficial, especially compared to the intense weekend initiatory experience of the New Warrior Training Adventure and still the blessing by older men fulfilled a need, want, and hunger that the men felt.

Neither John nor I know what the long term impact of that elder blessing has or will be. Yes, intense therapy often is necessary to make permanent, transformative change. These men's work events can and do move men toward therapy and can enhance the therapeutic process for those already in therapy.

REFERENCES

Connell, R. W. (1995) *Masculinities*. Berkeley: University of California Press.

Coyle, A., & Morgan-Sykes, C. (1998). Troubled men and threatening women: The Construction of "crisis" in male mental health. *Feminism and Psychology, 8*, 263–284.

Gray, J. (1992) *Men are from Mars, women are from Venus*. New York: HarperCollins.

Nightingale, D., & Neilands, T. (1997). Understanding and practising critical psychology. In D. Fox & I. Prilleltensky (Eds.), *Critical psychology: An introduction*. London: Sage.

Prilleltensky, I., & Nelson, G. (1997). Community psychology: Reclaiming social justice. In D. Fox & I. Prilleltensky, (Eds.), *Critical psychology: An introduction*. London: Sage.

Rowan, J. (1987). *The horned god: Feminism and men as wounding and healing*. London: Routledge.

Rowan, J. (1997). *Healing the male psyche: Therapy as initiation*. London: Routledge.

Samuels, A. (1993). *The political psyche*. London: Routledge.

Starhawk (1989). *The spiral dance: A rebirth of the ancient religion of the great goddess* (2nd ed.) San Francisco: Harper & Row.

Stoltenberg, J. (1990). *Refusing to be a man*. London: Fontana.

Tacey, D. J. (1997). *Remaking men: Jung, spirituality and social change*. London: Routledge.

Chapter 16
Justice, Joy, and an End to the Gender Wars
Amanda Goldrick-Jones

I want to live in a world without patriarchy. And like many other feminist women, I want to share that world joyfully with men. I have experienced many intellectually and emotionally fulfilling relationships with men, not least among them my father, who nurtured my mind and curiosity; my articulate and artistic brother; and my husband—my equal partner in life who will not call himself a feminist yet cannot imagine not being married to one.

But deeply satisfying personal and professional relationships between women who are feminists and men seldom make headlines. Instead, especially in North America, a rhetoric of "the gender war" is fed by accounts of men's sexism and violence and women's suspicion, pain, and hostility to men. No race or economic class is untouched; both the Hill-Thomas hearings and the Clinton-Lewinski affair underscore how deeply entrenched are Western mythologies about gender and power. In these real-life tales, all men are oppressors and all women are victims.

Sometimes, tragically, these mythologies are borne out. In Canada, the December 1989 massacre of fourteen young women at the University of Montreal's Ecole Polytechnique shook the faith of many feminists who envisioned better relations between women and men. In his suicide note, the man who shot those fourteen women wrote that "feminists have always enraged me. They want to keep the advantages of women . . . while seizing for themselves those of men" (Malette & Chalouh, 1991, pp. 180–181). In this climate of heightened awareness of male violence, I and many other women felt old fears reawakening. For some women, distrust of "all men" reached new levels; according to one Canadian commentator on the massacre, an Alberta professor is "reported to have

said in a public lecture that men have been masquerading as human beings"
(Crowley 1994, p. 2).

This perspective was not shared by "all feminists." Nor were "all men" prepared to be labeled as subhuman. Many men were as sickened and horrified as
women by this massacre and began to speak out publicly with women about
men's violence. Men still stand with women each year at December 6 memo-
rials, and every feminist I know welcomes men's presence at these vigils (in
Winnipeg, when it is often well below zero fahrenheit on December 6, one group
of men stands on the sidelines with hot tea and soup). At least two men's groups,
the Halifax-based Men for Change and the Toronto-based White Ribbon Campaign, were formed because of the massacre. Neither group was motivated by
guilt or by women pointing fingers, but by a desire to achieve gender justice
and help men examine in their own lives the links between violence and problematic concepts of masculinity.

What does the December 6 massacre, this true myth, have to do with mythopoetic men's search for deeper connections with other men and their own feelings? I mention it partly because the massacre could have been the catalyst for
a very long gender war in which women, distrusting men, lash out in rage or
retreat into "womanspaces" (Clatterbaugh 1990, p. 53), and men withdraw from
women in confusion and anger. Indeed, many feminists argued passionately, and
in highly respected publications, that the massacre was not an aberration but
proof of "an ongoing pattern of sexist, misogynist violence" (Menzies, 1991, p.
26). Faced with women's rage, men may want to rage back; according to Michael Kimmel (1995), at mythopoetic gatherings the emotions rising to the surface can be frightening: "Undiluted rage against mothers . . . venomous anger at
wives . . . and seeming incomprehensible fury at feminist women" (p. 7).

But the anger and grief unleashed by the Montreal massacre also motivated
some groups of women and men to communicate more with each other and try
to work together to address gender oppression and violence. Notably, very little,
if any, of this antiviolence work has been about "guilting men out" or labeling
"all men" as oppressors, nor should it be. Like many other feminists, I have
never believed that feminism is about male bashing, and I deplore the fact that
somehow along the way, "feminism" has often become equated with hating men.

Yet even feminists who want to work with men are often not immediately
prepared to trust men's methods or motives. A major reason is that masculinity
has been linked with the power to control ideas and resources. (Lips, 1991,
summarizes this notion succinctly.) However, many theorists reject notions of
power as a "commodity" someone can own and control, but rather conceptualize
it as a network of forces working independently of individual will, intention, or
agency (Lips, 1991) and shaping the production of societal "truths" (Foucault,
1978; 1984; Smart, 1985). Feminists have drawn attention to the ways these
power structures have oppressed women, marginalized entire peoples, and re-
inforced the privileges of elite men. But Foucault's conception of power has
also been used to explain an apparent paradox: while men as a group appear to

have "power," many actually feel quite powerless in their daily lives (Pratt & Tuddenham, 1997).

Perhaps it is unfair to jump down the throats of men who want to change themselves for the better. Indeed, as Holly Sweet points out in Chapter 14 of this volume, "Awareness of the destructiveness of male sex role norms on both personal and societal levels . . . has resulted in men (and women) coming together in informal groups, retreats, and conferences to take a critical look at hegemonic hypermasculinity."

But ambivalent attitudes about "male power" help explain why many feminists (and profeminists) view with deep suspicion men who uncritically celebrate and invoke what appear to be mythologies of male power in order to empower themselves. Mythopoetic men's groups were especially criticized soon after they came into prominence, notably in Kay Leigh Hagan's 1992 collection, *Women Respond to the Men's Movement*. The book's title does not reflect the fact that several of the contributors, including bell hooks and Elizabeth Dodson Grey, are aware of other branches of "the men's movement" and differentiate profeminist men's groups from Robert Bly's mythopoetic groups. Time and again the writers issue urgent calls for men to change themselves and work with women to redress inequalities. They are not convinced that Bly's "deep masculine" or "wild man," which they deem essentialist, will engender the kinds of public, political engagement necessary for social change.

Similarly, a highly critical attitude toward the mythopoetic branch characterizes the politically aware, activist profeminism exemplified by the U.S.-based National Organization of Men Against Sexism (and to some extent by the White Ribbon Campaign). Despite some attempts at dialogue, notably in Michael Kimmell's 1995 collection, *The Politics of Manhood*, relations between mythopoetics and profeminists in North America are still a long way from cordial. One reason is that in North America and Australia, and to some extent in Britain, profeminism has been largely influenced by the radical feminist adage, "The personal is the political." Many profeminist men have interpreted this as a call to protest gender-based injustices or inequalities like restrictions on abortion or violence to women, or publicly taking a feminist stance on an issue like pornography or violent toys. Kimmel (1995), Michael Kaufman (1993), and Harry Brod (1998), among other high-profile profeminists, are concerned that focusing on mythical images of masculinity and articulating feelings associated with those images encourage men to avoid taking responsibility for larger social and political changes.

Yet not all profeminists see such a schism between antisexist work and mythopoetic work. During a recent visit to London, I talked with several of the men who publish *Achilles Heel*. This "radical men's magazine" has a long profeminist pedigree (also see Chapter 15, this volume). Yet when I asked, "What do you think of the mythopoetic men's movement?" most indicated that men engaged in men's work in Britain see considerable overlap between profeminist and mythopoetic goals.

This statement needs some qualification: at least two contributors to *Achilles Heel* have expressed concern about the implications of uncritically adopting "Iron John"–inspired archetypes. Mick Cooper sees archetypes as "vital" for psychological health, but in his view, concepts like Bly's "Wild Man" romanticize tribal society and implicitly celebrate the "sexual division of labour that paved the way for patriarchy in the first place" (1991, pp. 30–31). Similarly, Paul Wolf-Light criticizes Bly's "romanticising of the warrior" and apparent blindness to issues of race and homosexuality (1994, pp. 16–17). But Wolf-Light is reluctant to dismiss Bly on the basis of these failures, for he sees much "value and beauty" in Iron John, as well as a "genuine wish to address the conflict between men and women honestly" (1994, p. 17).

My impression is that British profeminist men are more likely than their North American counterparts to see improving relationships among men and changing individual behaviors as "political" acts, and that there is a place for mythopoetic work on the agenda. As I have described elsewhere (Goldrick-Jones 1998), British profeminists seem more prepared to see the value of addressing individual behaviors and psychological influences around issues like violence and to question the effectiveness of purely educational initiatives, like the Duluth model described in *Education Groups for Men Who Batter* (Pence et al., 1993).

At the same time, North American profeminists and other writers on masculinities have long since stopped totalizing "the men's movement" or equating it solely with mythopoetic groups. Since Kenneth Clatterbaugh's first edition of *Contemporary Masculinities*, various other schemas have emerged whose purpose is to distinguish among aspects of men's movements. Clatterbaugh (1997) continues to define "the mythopoetic men's movement" as distinct from other kinds of men's movement, as have Kimmel (1995) and Messner (1997). But Clatterbaugh carefully differentiates Bly's uses of archetypes from John Rowan's "more feminist" grounding in Wiccan tradition (1997, p. 96). Clatterbaugh also describes Bly and Rowan as practitioners of "the spiritual perspective" of men's movement. This term seems to me more respectful of this branch of men's work than Messner's "essentialist retreats" (1997), a chapter title covering both mythopoetic groups and the Promise Keepers.

Indeed, as Rowan contends (Chapter 15, this volume; see Clatterbaugh, 1997, chap. 5, on Rowan), personal or spiritual work informed by feminist principles is an important part of political work. Ideally, the personal and the political energize and inform each other, though ironically, the schism between mythopoetic and profeminist work in North America illustrates the extent to which the personal and the political can drift apart. Yet not all men's groups emphasize the one to the point of almost obliterating the other. Perhaps instead of buying into the false dichotomy that "if you're doing personal growth work, then you aren't doing political work" (Rowan, Chapter 15, this volume) or vice versa, women and men who are envisioning a world free of violence, inequality, and repressive gender stereotyping should be asking, What kinds of personal work will help men conceptualize masculinities in positive ways and also motivate men to work with women for gender justice?

Some men's groups have managed to combine a political agenda with a variety of personal, male-positive, or therapeutic activities—for example:

- The Everyman Centre in Devon, England, relies on feminist perspectives of male violence, treating men and supporting their female partners through therapy and cocounseling (Bell, 1998; Wolf-Light, 1998), publishing articles and educational materials, and participating in political events like International Women's Week (Everyman, 1997).

- Men for Change, based in Halifax, Canada, seeks to combine "political accountability" with "consciousness raising amongst members about the dynamics of traditional 'male culture.' " Members share their feelings and reflect on their experiences as men in small, supportive groups; they also occasionally go on retreats (though Men for Change does not practice Bly's mythopoetics [Men, 1991]). At the same time, members hold public meetings, speak at schools and community centers, and have created a "Healthy Relationships Violence-Prevention Curriculum" package, now being piloted in some Canadian high schools.

- The Men's Resources Center of Massachusetts celebrated its Seventeenth anniversary in 2000. Founded in 1983, it wanted to raise men's awareness of male violence and related issues through consciousness-raising and political events. Although it is not as overtly political as Men for Change, the MRC continues to work against violence with a combination of men's work, support groups, and community event, including a youth education program designed to raise awareness of gender stereotyping and encourage mutual respect (Valley, 1998).

My impression is that the men in these groups combine a strong sense of justice with enjoyment, mutual support, and empowerment. At times, they even have fun. After several years of exploring the histories and activities of profeminist groups in Canada, the United States, Britain, and Australia, I have come to appreciate how difficult it can be for men to maintain a strong sense of gender justice and a strongly positive image of who they are as men. While many men may need other men's support during the process of examining their own feelings and experiences of masculinity, men may also need women's support to use this knowledge and strength for transforming oppressive gender relations.

I have been fortunate in my relationships, but there have been far too many casualties in the gender wars. More dialogue and coalition work between feminist women and profeminist men is an important first step in transforming gender relations. It seems equally important for profeminist and mythopoetic groups to understand their own differences, develop a stronger dialogue, and explore possible alliances. The future of gender relations may well rest not only on women's activism, but on men's ability to rejoin the political with the personal and justice with joy.

REFERENCES

Bell, C. (1998, January). Personal interview.

Brod, H. (1998). To be a man, or not to be a man—that is the feminist question. In T. Digby (Ed.), *Men doing feminism* (pp. 197–212). New York: Routledge.

Clatterbaugh, K. C. (1990). *Contemporary perspectives on masculinity: Men, women, and politics in modern society.* Boulder, CO: Westview.

Clatterbaugh, K. C. (1997). *Contemporary perspectives on masculinity: Men, women, and politics in modern society* (2nd ed.). Boulder, CO: Westview.

Cooper, M. (1991, Autumn). A wander on the wild side. *Achilles Heel, 12,* 28–31.

Crowley, B. L. (1994). *The road to equity: gender, ethnicity, and language.* Toronto: Stoddart.

Everyman Centre. (1997, August). *Everyman Centre Newsletter,* p. 1.

Foucault, M. (1978). *The history of sexuality* (Vol. 1), (R. Hurley, Trans.). New York: Vintage Books.

Foucault, M. (1984). Truth and power. In P. Rabinow (Ed.), *The Foucault reader* (pp. 51–75). New York: Pantheon Books.

Goldrick-Jones, A. (1998, Summer). Politics and profeminisms across the pond. *Achilles Heel, 23,* 32–34.

Hagan, K. L. (Ed.). (1992). *Women respond to the men's movement.* San Francisco: Pandora.

Hemsworth, W. (1992, December 4). 89 massacre spurs action across Canada. *Calgary Herald,* p. B6.

Lips, H. (1991). *Women, men, and power.* Mountain View, CA: Mayfield.

Kaufman, M. (1993). *Cracking the armour: Power, pain and the lives of men.* Toronto: Viking.

Kimmel, M. S. (Ed.). (1995). *The politics of manhood: Profeminist men respond to the mythopoetic men's movement (and the mythopoetic leaders answer).* Philadelphia: Temple University Press.

Malette, L., & Chalouh, M. (Eds.). (1991). *The Montreal massacre.* (M. Wildeman, Trans.). Charlottetown: Gynergy Books.

Men meeting because we're men. Halifax, N.S.: Men for Change.

Menzies, H. (1991, December). *Canadian Forum, 70,* 26–27.

Messner, M. A. (1997). *Politics of masculinities: Men in movements.* Thousand Oaks, CA: Sage.

Pence, E., et al. (1993). *Education groups for men who batter.* New York: Springer.

Pratt, S., & Tuddenham, R. (1997, Summer–Autumn). Masculinity and power. *Achilles Heel, 22,* 23–25.

Rowan, J. (2000). Men and the search for common ground. In E. Barton (Ed.), *The mythopoetic perspective of men's healing work: An anthology for therapists and others.* Westport, CT: Greenwood.

Smart, B. (1985). *Michel Foucault.* London: Tavistock.

Sweet, H. (2000). Men and the search for common ground. In E. Barton (Ed.), *The mythopoetic perspective of men's healing work: An anthology for therapists and others.* Westport, CT: Greenwood.

Valley men: the magazine of the Men's Resource Centre of Western Massachusetts (1998, Spring/Summer). Men's Resources Centre.

Wolf-Light, P. (1994, Autumn). The shadow of Iron John. *Achilles Heel, 17,* 14–17.

Wolf-Light, P. (1998, January). Personal interview.

Conclusion

Four main themes run through this book: the parallels between feminists, feminism, and mythopoetic men's work; the emotional healing aspect of mythopoetic men's work, which is beneficial to the men who participate as well as those with whom they interact; men reinterpreting old stories and myths for themselves as part of their personal healing process; and the mythopoetic perspective as a useful approach for people in the healing professions for assisting men, women, and children in the healing process.

On a more personal note, I have struggled with whether to write this conclusion from my head or from my heart. Will I be liked for what I say or will I be criticized/ridiculed/shamed if I write from my heart? If I do the latter, will it prevent me from getting an academic position and/or will it block future promotions? As I write this, I am reminded of Carlos Castenada's reporting of Don Juan's comment that "the real accomplishment in life is the art of being a warrior, which is the only way to balance the terror of being a man with the wonder of being a man." There is a similar terror and wonder as I write this conclusion. I am walking through my fears/my terror and writing this by being vulnerable, open, and sharing my thoughts, feelings, and fears from a mythopoetic perspective.

In 1998 there were three main men's work events in which I participated that had an influence on me, each of which corresponds to one of the main themes of this book. The first event was Men & Masculinity (M&M) SUNY-Stonybrook. The key event for me at M&M was the speech by Gloria Steinem. It was not so much what she said but the fact that I bought her book *Revolution from Within* and read it during the rest of the year.

In the first chapter of this book parallels are drawn between mythopoetic men's work and selected feminist theories. This theme of some similarities is again addressed in Part IV of this book What struck me so about *Revolution from Within* were the repeated similarities between what Steinem went through as she discovered her lack of self-esteem and her recovery largely through writing that book. The table of contents and phrases in the book are very similar to words and my experiences in mythopoetic men's work; authentic self, circle of true selves, self esteem and needing no master, "hitting the wall," hitting bottom, radical empathy for self, ordinary men, paradigm shift, "my own authentic body" and fearfulness passes, age and blessing, shadow, religion versus spirituality, inner awareness, stories as medicine, and a meditation guide (p. 363).

Another parallel in *Revolution from Within* is in the Afterword to the 1993 edition. Steinem shares much of the negative responses from the press, critics, and even women writers. This criticism did not come from the hundreds of women who wrote to her and talked to her about how much the book had helped them. The criticism came from the "experts," the critics, the media. This is very similar to the criticism of the mythopoetic branch that Joel Morton wrote about in Chapter 6.

In the dedication I spoke about my family of choice. Steinem (1993) suggests four principles for an effective psychic family. "That someone who has experienced something is more expert in it than the experts; that shared experience and desire for change can bind us to each other, that mutual confidentiality and commitment are to be honored; that everyone participates but no one dominates (p. 178). This is very similar to the guidelines and my experiences in men's peer mutual support groups, many of the aspects of mythopoetic men's events, and the data from research of the NWTA that was reported in earlier chapters.

Admittedly, Steinem has a different lived experience as a woman and active feminist. However, in her book about self-esteem, there was a surprisingly large number of similarities to mythopoetic men's work. By seeing the similarities and commonalties, it would seem that there could be more of a basis for co-operation among various branches of the contemporary men's movement, particularly, in this instance, the profeminists and the mythopoets.

The second event mirroring the second theme was over Labor Day weekend when John Lee, Pat Love, and Martin Prechtel facilitated a weekend for men and women near Kalamazoo, Michigan. In all the mythopoetic events that I have attended, this was only the second one in which I have participated in which there were women and men. That in itself was a challenge for me.

One of the emotional high points for me was Pat Love's presentation about attachment theory. It took me back to remembering a family story. We lived on a farm. My parents were busy with field work and house work, and my younger sister came along when I was three. I clearly remember going to the farm dump and picking up old bottles with which to play. I am told that I would be tethered to the corn crib and I would sit there by the hour and amuse myself by playing with those old bottles.

As Pat Love relayed it, that would not be considered "secure attachment." I also remember my friend Paul being so angry that as a young child I would be tethered like I was and apparently did not resist. I had a lot of tears that afternoon about my memories about being tethered. As I search for meaning and understanding of this family story, I look to see how I might reinterpret it for my healing.

The third event was the last weekend in September when I was staffing my eighteenth NWTA at the Windsor/Detroit Center. At one point in the weekend, one of the leaders instructed us to put our little boy somewhere where he would be safe for the rest of the afternoon. I tried to put my little boy somewhere on the site that was safe, but that did not work. The place that was safe was tethered to the corn crib at home, and that is where I put him for the rest of that afternoon so I could focus on the job of initiating men.

I must admit that I am still pondering what all this means to me and the psychic ramification. I am not clear why Pat Love's talk brought up such emotional feelings of sadness, and yet later that month the corn crib was the safe place to put my little boy so he would be safe and could play with his bottles.

I must also admit that I continue to look, search, feel, and think as I continue on my mythopoetic path of healing and helping other men heal. A man's mission as defined by the ManKind Project is something that will never be accomplished in a lifetime, but steps toward it will make this world a better place. My mission is to create world peace through healing and emotionally empowering men. I see my men's work, my midlife presentations, and even editing this book as part of my mission. Providing this information about mythopoetic men's healing work will help men heal by giving therapists and others in the healing professions information about the benefits of mythopoetic men's healing that will save men's lives and improve the lives of their children, partners, families of whatever configuration, community, and the world.

This book has just scratched the surface of theory building on the mythopoetic perspective of men's healing work and transformation. There are few theoretical models (Cornish, 1999, is a recent example of a model for personal change and social transformation).

There are a number of other theories and literatures that seem to have relevance to the study of mythopoetic perspective on men's healing work and personal transformation. Directions for future research would be the impact of mythopoetic activities on fathering and parenting plus literature on adults as learners, experiential education, family paradigms, phenomenology, Lerner's (1989) developmental contextualism and goodness of fit, symbolic interactionism, communications theory, linguistics theory, exchange theory, conflict theory, change theory, ecological theory of human development (Bronfenbrenner, 1979), social supports, storytelling and poetry as healing, narrative therapy, marriage and family therapy, gender identity, identity theory, and social movements, to name some of them. There are also the instrumental-expressive and structural-functional concepts, along with the concept of emancipatory research. There are the major frameworks of gender: essentialist, socialization, social constructionist, and structural theories (Fish, 1999), which provide lenses for further research. There are probably many more. Accordingly, there is much more research that can be done and is being done to augment and extend the knowledge of the value of the mythopoetic perspective of men's healing work.

In today's world of managed care and brief therapy, it would seem that any therapist and others in the healing professions would seem to be ethically bound to recommend additional resources for their male friends and clients. These resources could be from an array of mythopoetic support groups, weekend events, initiatory events, and other mythopoetic perspective events. The research reported in this book strongly indicates that mythopoetic perspective activities are helpful in the healing process and can be a successful adjunct to therapy in the healing of men's (and women's and children's) lives.

REFERENCES

Bronfenbrenner, U. (1979). *The ecology of human development*. Cambridge, MA: Harvard University Press.

Cornish, P. A. (1999). Men engaging feminism: A model of personal change and social transformation. *Journal of Men's Studies, 7,* 173–199.

Fish, R. (1999). *The mythopoetic men's movement and the shaping of masculine identification*. Paper presented at the 7th American Men's Studies Association Conference, Vanderbilt University Divinity School, Nashville, TN.

Lerner, R. M. (1989). Developmental contextualism and the life-span view of person-context interaction. In M. Bornstein & J. Brunner (Eds.), *Interactions in human development*. Hillsdale, NJ: Erlbaum.

Lorentzen, J. (1998). Book review of *The politics of manhood*, edited by Michael Kimmel. *Men and Masculinities, 1,* 112–115.

Lynd, S. (1999). Feminism for men. *Journal of Men's Studies, 7,* 165–172.

Steinem, G. (1993). *Revolution from within: A book of self-esteem*. Boston: Little, Brown.

Glossary

Accountability: The willingness to take responsibility for one's actions and their effects, regardless of their intent, on others in a relationship, group, or community. In Integrity Therapy, accountability is linked to the second leg of the Integrity stool of honesty, responsibility, and emotional closure. From the Integrity Therapy perspective, accountability points to the fact that individuals must take full responsibility for their actions and must fully own their 50 percent of the responsibility in any conflict situation.

Agency: Personal agency is the power of an individual to take an active part in an act such as actions to change one's life.

Archetypal Personality Theory: Drawn from Jung's theory of archetypes. Mythopoetic groups draw upon the archetypes that are commonly found in stories and myths and reinterpret them to make them meaningful to men today as a guide in discovering healthier ways of expressing their emotions and their individual masculinity.

Archetypes: Defined by Jung as universal patterns or predispositions in the collective unconscious that influence how human beings adapt to and understand their world.

Attachment: An affectional bond that one individual forms for another and that endures across time and space. An attachment is expressed in behaviors that promote proximity and contact. One's first attachment is usually with the primary care giver.

Authentic Masculinity: A postulated way of being a male that arises from the deepest essence of men. It emanates from "hard wiring" rather than from socialization or socially constructed masculinity. Understanding of authentic masculinity is based on archetypal patterns of the male human psyche as theorized by Jung, and more recently by Robert Moore.

Block: An emotional block is something which prevents or obstructs a person from getting to the issues. A block prevents that person from reaching and working on the resolution of the emotional issues in that person's life.

Check In: The process at the beginning of a meeting of making all group members aware of where each person is emotionally, spiritually, and/or psychologically. The beginning of a men's group during which time men take turns briefly telling each other about their current or recent feelings and experiences and in I-Groups the man may also check in with the shadow he brings to the meeting. Compare this to the outer check in and inner check in in Chapter 2.

Closed Men's Peer Mutual Support Group: A group where the membership is fixed. A closed group allows for the development of more intimate sharing among members because of the higher level of trust that can be developed among members. The closed group may open membership briefly and then close the membership when the desired number of members is reached.

Cognition: The most basic level of thought. In a wider sense it is a series of thoughts which form a particular concept. Cognition is "thinking" activities as opposed to "feeling" activities. The ability to keep cognitions ordered and avoid major distortions in the cognition process is the key to emotional health.

Collective Unconscious: Jung's notion of collective unconscious is said to be inherent in humanity as a race of beings. Among the features of this collective unconscious are archetypal patterns of being. These can be said to be "hard wired," a product of biology rather than learned through socialization as they are said to be stored memory of all images and ideas the human race has accumulated.

Community: A group of people banded together by shared goals and ideas. With urbanization and mass movement of people in this mobile society, there is a loss of traditional community. The fact of not really knowing your neighbors is an example compared to the more rural setting where everyone knew their neighbors and their neighbor's children. Men's healing work is often an attempt to build and restore that sense of community and caring among the men involved.

In Integrity Therapy, community was the original third leg developed by Mowrer. Community means that the ultimate intent of any interaction, particularly when trying to resolve conflict, should be to bring about a sense of increased closeness or rapprochement with the other.

Conscious: The quality or state of being aware especially of something within oneself; the state or fact of being conscious of external object, state, or fact; concern awareness; the state of being characterized by sensation, emotion, volition, and thought: mind; totality of conscious states of an individual; normal state of conscious life; the upper level of mental life of which the person is aware as compared with unconscious processes.

Consciousness Raising Groups: Groups exploring personal development without a pathological or dysfunctional orientation. These groups form for the purpose of raising one's awareness about certain ideas or issues. At times these groups are confrontive in nature and at other times may be more informative in nature. CR Groups may be a form of social support and/or a self help group. The groups may be formed informally by persons interested in a topic or issue; or they may be formed formally by a person or agency in response to a particular need.

Consilience: William Whewell, in his 1840 synthesis *The Philosophy of the Inductive Sciences*, was the first to speak of consilience. He spoke of it as meaning " 'a jumping together' of knowledge by the linking together of facts and fact-based theories across disciplines to create a common groundwork of explanation" (Wilson, 1998, p. 8). Whewell added the following, "The Consilience of Inductions takes place when an induction, from one class of facts coincides with an induction from another different class. This Consilience is a test of the truth of the theory in which it occurs" (Wilson, 1998, p. 8).

At this point in history, Wilson (1998) observes that the possibility of consilience beyond science and across the great branches of learning is not yet science, but rather, a metaphysical worldview. Its surest test, Wilson suggests, will be its effectiveness in the social sciences and humanities.

Contemporary Men's Movement (CMM): The CMM emerged in the 1960's and 1970's in response to the women's movement. There are different branches such as the pro-feminist, mythopoetic, and the men's rights/father's rights branches which emerged regarding the felt need of the members of each branch as to how it's members were being impacted by feminism and the women's movement.

Container: A metaphor of the alchemist's crucible, a vessel capable of containing the energetic processes of transformation. The container must be adequate to contain the energy of the process. It must be emotionally safe yet be psychologically evocative ritual space. In the work of initiation, or other men's healing work, it is physically, emotionally, and spiritually energetic, which requires a substantial container. In the case of men's healing work, the container is the group of men assembled and the dynamics of that group. The container is created by the common intent and focus of the assembled group.

Contextualization: Represents a method for analyzing phenomenon; a way of viewing. The contextual approach to the rise of psychological ideas utilizes the assumption that intellectual phenomenon may be best understood in relation to surrounding circumstances, i.e., context, as opposed to merely viewing the internal contents of the phenomenon itself. The reason for this is the idea that the phenomenon itself may be best understood as a composition of elements drawn from and influenced by past and surrounding circumstances, i.e., contexts.

Denial: An ego defense mechanism whereby the individual essentially refuses to acknowledge what is true about himself. Denial functions to protect the individual from facing uncomfortable realities, such as when one first learns of the death of a loved one.

Discourse: Linguistic expression either written or spoken.

Dissociation: A psychological process whereby an individual separates one part of their consciousness from another part. Amnesia is one example of dissociation. The separation may be partial or complete. Most people practice partial dissociation and it may be required for some occupations (a surgeon cutting open a human being, a soldier in combat). In complete dissociation, an individual may be totally unaware in one dissociative state of what was done in another such in multiple personalities.

Elder: An older man or woman, usually over 50 years old, who accepts the challenge of providing mature leadership for the younger generation of women and men. The elder, in many traditional societies, would initiate the young man or women into the mysteries of life, work, responsibility, marriage, and masculinity or femininity. The elders provide a workable blueprint for boys and girls to achieve adult maturity.

Emotional Closure: In Integrity Therapy, emotional closure is the third leg of the three-legged stool of integrity theorized by Lander and Nahon which means that the ultimate intent of any interaction, particularly when trying to resolve a conflict, should be to bring about a sense of increased closeness or rapprochement with the other(s).

Essentialists: The idea that men's actions are caused by innate or universal characteristics of men as a male sex. Essentialist theory explains sex-linked variation in behavior to biological, genetic, hard-wired, or other fixed causes as opposed to social influences that are relatively variable meanings which are socially constructed, varying over time, by context, and setting.

Existential Framework: A framework which integrates a philosophical and psychological perspective of the nature of being human. It focuses on the need for individuals to reflect on their lives and values and to find a personal and unique sense of meaning for their existence.

Father Absence: A phenomenon brought about by the physical and/or emotional absence of the father. Father absence often causes a father hunger in men and women.

Gender Role Conflict Strain: A set of values, attitudes or behaviors learned during socialization that causes negative psychological effects on a person. The four components include success, power and competition; restrictive emotionality; restrictive affectionate behavior between men; and conflict between work and family relationships, of whatever configuration. Exercising these components causes Gender Role Strain.

GRCS: Gender Role Conformity Scale is a psychometric instrument to assess adherence to stereotypical gender roles.

Gestalt: A psychological approach focusing on the wholeness of the human experience, including both mind and body and the life setting of the individual.

Gold: From the Integrity Therapy perspective of the story of Iron John, the gold in the wound is the realization that the self has inherent positive values and attributes, and that one always has the choice of choosing good over evil.

Golden Shadow: Something which is a part of an individual which is to be valued and affirmed (i.e., golden), but of which the person may not be aware, or may choose to deny, hide, or repress.

Group Process: Activities and practices that typify the interactions of men in a mythopoetic men's group or at a mythopoetic event.

Health Side: A concept of Integrity Therapy framework. It refers to that part of human motivation which is in tune with one's underlying values and which leads to a positive and creative use of one's own personal power.

Hegemonic Masculinity: A term introduced by Bob Connell to name a kind of masculinity which is so all-pervasive that it does not have to be enforced. It is socially constructed in relation to various subordinated or marginalized masculinities as well as in relation to women.

Hermeneutics: In its general sense this refers to theories of interpretation, that is, the question, "what does a text mean?" Hermeneutics, as understood by Paul Ricoeur, refers not to an absolute interpretation of a text, but an understanding of a text that always includes an element of self-understanding. The text is always and only understood in a context of a historical moment and a real life. Hermeneutics thus becomes the meaning of human life and human action. No one singular interpretation of a text becomes definitive with this approach.

Hero's Journey: The hero's journey is an internal quest to fight one's own demons. The premise is that a man cannot fight the dragons of the world until a man has fought and conquered his own internal demons. A New

Warrior's demons are represented by his shadow. The myths of Gilgamesh, Homer, and Perceval are often seen as symbolic carriers of the journey of every man. In order to integrate the four archetypes of the King, Warrior, Magician, and Lover one has to take the internal quest of the hero's journey.

Homophobia: An often irrational fear or hatred of gay people or of intimacy with other men, especially expressions of physical intimacy which is often internalized. Homophobia may be rooted in fear of being viewed as or being treated or perceived as a woman by other men.

Honesty: A key concept in Integrity Therapy. Honesty is the first leg of the three-legged stool of integrity. It is essential to be honest with one's self and others, but honesty alone is not enough; it must be used responsibly and with the intent to close the space with others.

Hypermasculinity: The exaggerated expression of traditional gender role norms, sometimes called hegemonic masculinity.

Identity: The pervasive and continuing sense a person has of who he or she is and those characteristics make him or her unique.

I-group: A small, supportive group of men who regularly meet after completing the ManKind Project's New Warrior Training Adventure and have completed their Integration Training. The I-Group continues as a closed men's peer mutual support group.

Imago: Idealized and personified images of the self that play the role of characters in a person's life story. Imagoes take the form of role models, mentors or heroes. Two imagoes commonly described in Mythopoetic texts are the warrior (used as part of the New Warrior name) and mentor.

Initiation: For men, a process used to transmit and model a healthy understanding of what it is to be a man. It includes rituals, activities, and ceremonies designed to create a meaningful sense of inclusion and identity as a man. As opposed to the term "rites of passage" which connotes a focus on the societal and cultural functions of rituals and ceremonies, initiation focuses on the personal and psychological impact of the process.

Integration Training: Men who have completed the NWTA are encouraged to participate in an eight to ten week, meeting weekly, facilitated support group format where the container for a closed men's peer support group is developed through a different set of processes each week, centered around a weekly theme which continues the man's work on the issues he faced on his initiatory weekend. This is sometimes called the New Warrior Integration Training (NWIT).

Integrity Therapy: An existential therapeutic framework, based on the work of psychologists O. Hobart Mower, Nedra R. Lander, and Danielle Nahon, which views the human being as a valued animal. Difficulties with living, living stress and mental illness are seen as arising from a lack of integrity to one's personal value system, and from a lack of personal integrity which is defined as the three-legged stool of honesty, responsibility, and increased community and/or increased emotional closure.

Interview Protocol: A set of questions or probes asked of participants in a research study. The questions are often asked in a particular style and in a particular order. In quantitative research, the interview protocol may be an instrument or scale.

Introjection: The process of taking in beliefs, without judgment. As an example, it is normal for children to adopt wholesale their parents' belief systems during their early years of development.

Interpellation: Louis Althuser illustrates the process of interpellation through the analogy of the police officer hailing an individual: "Hey, you there!" When hailed and the individual responds, that person has been interpellated. That means that the person has become the subject of the officer's ideological discourse and takes on, becomes subtext to, and of, the officer's identification of that person. Roughly speaking, this is the same process by which narrators of realist texts interpellate or "hail" their readers, subjecting them to seemingly common sense or natural point of view of the narrator, a point of view which is in fact ideologically specific to the narrator's position within social, racial, and gendered power relations.

Jungian Psychology: The body of theory developed by Carl Jung and his followers, especially as it relates to the unconscious parts of the human psyche.

Liminal: Relates to a sensory threshold or to something that is barely perceptible, hence the notion of extra-ordinary experience on the edges of day-to-day experience. A common example of a liminal experience is the experience of entering one of the great cathedrals of Europe, with its stained glass windows and vaulting arches of immense grandeur, and feeling or sensing a greater power or presence.

ManKind Project (MKP): An order of men called to reclaim the sacred masculine through initiation, training and action in the world formerly known as the New Warrior Network, with the New Warrior Training Adventure as the entry way for membership.

Mature Masculinity: The mature male is one who has integrated the four archetypes of the king, warrior, magician, lover, and continues to confront the destructive shadow side of each.

Masculine Identity: A man's pervasive and continuing sense of being a man and the experience of seeing himself as masculine and the context and quality of that masculinity.

Masculinities: There is no single definition of masculinity, but many different masculinities socially constructed which vary by social class and which change over time. They can also be constructed by men, particularly in mythopoetic activities, as they consciously redefine what their own masculinity means to them.

Men & Masculinity: The annual meeting of the National Organization for Men Against Sexism (NOMAS).

Men's Peer Mutual Support Group (MPMSG): A generic term referring to any support or non-professionally led self-help group focused on men's issues and masculinities, and that provide emotional support (being a form of social support) for its members. MPMSG is peer lead in that men participate in sharing the facilitation and providing mutual support to each other.

Men's Work: The process by which men turn inward into their hearts, souls, and minds, both by themselves and in the company of other men, in order to better understand and access their feelings, who they are as men, and how they relate to others in their lives. It is the activities of mythopoetic men as they work on emotionally healing themselves, their families, of whatever configuration, their relationships, their community, and their planet, but primarily each one is working on emotionally healing himself, his spirit, and his spirituality.

Metaphor: A figure of speech in which one object is likened to another. [As an example, the use of the word castle in a fable is a metaphor for home.]

Mentor: A person who serves as a teacher or guide, or one who models a different way of being. It may also be a person who is involved in some form of initiation into a more mature identity.

MKP-GW: The Greater Washington, D.C. Center of the ManKind Project.

Mission Work: Developing a life's mission which guides a person's work and action in the world, which he or she will not complete in his or her lifetime.

Myth: A story dealing with the cosmological, supernatural, or archtypical traditions of a people such as their gods, culture, heroes, or religious beliefs.

Mythological: The realm of human experience that reveals itself in and through images and stories.

Mythopoetic: Reinterpreting and reworking old stories and myths in ways that are relevant to the emotional healing of contemporary men; a revisioning of masculinity for our time.

Mythopoetic Branch of the Contemporary Men's Movement: The branch consisting of men interested in spiritual growth.

Mythopoetic Men's Peer Mutual Support Groups: A group operating from a mythopoetic perspective of men's emotional healing work.

Mythopoetic Men's Work (MPMW): Uses stories, myths, and poetry as vehicles for accessing inner emotions, inner realities, and feelings. The accessing of these feelings is part of the remythologizing of the man and his masculinity for this time.

Narcissistic Injury: It is any injury to the exaggerated sense of self or exaggerated valuation of self. As a concept of Integrity Therapy, it refers to the

sense of wounded pride that arises from the realization of one's own im-
perfection and/or from a sense of frustration or thwarting of one's desires
for immediate gratification.

National Organization for Men Against Sexism (NOMAS): NOMAS is an
activist organization of the pro-feminist branch of the contemporary men's
movement. It supports positive changes for men. It advocates a perspective
that is pro-feminist, gay-affirmative, anti-racial, and committed to justice on
a broad range of social issues. It affirms that working to make the nation's
ideal of equality real and substantive is the finest expression of what it
means to be a man.

New Warrior Network (NWN): The organizational name for the organization
consisting of centers which offer the New Warrior Training Adventure
(NWTA) which is the gateway for membership, now named the ManKind
Project.

New Warrior Training Adventure (NWTA): The introductory, experiential
weekend-long men's gathering and initiation of the ManKind Project, focused on deep, personal work. The NWTA is a men's initiatory experience.
It is modeled largely after Joseph Campbell's cross cultural research and
uses Campbell's stages of initiation; separation, dissent, ordeal, and welcoming back into the community of initiated men.

Object Relations Theory: A theory of personality development based on social
interaction rather than sexual drives. The term "object" refers to both external objects, which are actual people, and internal objects, which are internal representations. It is the integration of the multitude of internal
objects that result in a consolidated self of the individual.

Open Men's Peer Mutual Support Group: An open group, sometimes called
a drop-in group, that meets at a fixed location, may be advertised or pro-
moted, and that any man may attend and participate in the meeting that
night. Sometimes open groups may have a topic or book as the focus of
the group's discussion for that meeting. Compare this with the facilitated
open men's support group in chapter 2.

Ordeal: A severe trial or experience in the context of masculine initiation.

Paradigm: A general way of thinking about a problem or topic that is widely
shared and accepted by a community of individuals. An example is the
concept of gender role, which is a paradigmatic or theoretical way of explaining consistencies across men's behavior.

Patripsych: Consists of internal versions of the external relations of patriarchy,
and is based on assumptions about authority figures that have been internalized and may be unconscious. This makes transformative changes difficult, and group work or group therapy work is usually necessary.

Personality Theory: A model representing an individual's style of relating, both
intrapsychically and socially.

Personal Unconscious: That part of the unconscious that is unique to each individual. It includes material that has been forgotten as well as material that has been repressed or introjected.

Phenomenological: A personally unique way of perceiving and interpreting the world.

Post-Enlightenment: Commonly associated with the onset of the nineteenth century and the philosophy of Immanual Kant (1724–1804). Kant began to differentiate a variety of ways to look at human reason. He suggested that human reason is not a singular concept, nor a singular event, but involves many movements and elements of human living. Thus pure reason, as constructed by the Enlightenment, was deconstructed to include other elements and facets of human life. Reason lost its authority and began to include, for example, elements of the aesthetic. Post-Enlightenment thus refers to a breakdown of strict rationalism as the only way to monitor and discern human action.

Post-Heideggerian: An ontology of agency or action that began to be developed by Martin Heidegger (1889–1976) but was made more precise through the textual hermeneutics of Paul Ricoeur. Ricoeur has explicated and included a more intimate link between human action and ontology through a new analysis of the writings of Aristotle. Furthermore, a post-Heideggerian approach seeks to correlate ontology with epistemology. Therefore, ontology, human action, and epistemology are all linked in a post-Heideggerian approach to textual interpretation.

Presenting Problem: The initial focus of treatment in the client's "own words," i.e., what the patient identifies as the issue when the person comes for treatment. It is often a symptom of some deeper issue. A person may present an issue of being unable to sleep and the actual issue may be dissatisfaction with work or problems in a relationship. The presenting problem is the starting place for any therapy.

Projection: One of several ego defense mechanisms. Feelings, urges, and other unconscious matter are said to be projected onto another person. A projecting person cannot see the quality as being in themselves, but instead sees it in another person who mirrors the quality for the person doing the projecting. A strong emotional reaction usually accompanies the projection because the person is highly invested in suppressing the quality.

Proxemics: The study of body space in relation to each other.

Psychodrama: An extemporized dramatization designed to afford catharsis and social relearning for one of the participants, or initiates, from whose life history the plot is abstracted.

Quasi-myth: A story which uses the characteristics of a myth but is not a part of the formal, historical mythological literature.

Realistic Narrative: The dominant theory of 19th century English literature, realist narrative remains the dominant popular mode of expression in literature, film, and television, as well as popular magazine writing. It retains the "naturalist fallacy" now debunked by more recent theories of literature. This fallacy is the belief that literature (including its contemporary popular modes) may be understood as a "true" reflection of reality or personal experience, and that the realist author—and, by extension, the reader of realist texts—is somehow free from or outside of ideology.

Repressed: Material which is repressed is material which has been forced into the unconscious of an individual. This is usually done as a way to avoid pain or discomfort associated with that material. It is repressed when the ability to readily access the material is compromised. If the material cannot be accessed on desire, it is suppressed. Forgotten material is different in that it cannot be recalled no matter how one approached the material. Repression is a defensive process and repressed materials may present a serious danger to the person. However, despite the repression, repressed materials still are available on an unconscious level and may affect behaviors and attitudes of an individual. Note that repressed material, as with all memory, is reconstructed and may or may not be actual representations of an event which occurred.

Rescript: In transactional analysis this concept holds that an individual writes a life script early in life which that person then proceeds to live out. In order to change a maladaptive script, one rewrites the script through some process and in so doing, can live out the new script.

Responsibility: Taking and being [responsible] for ones own actions, not blaming someone else, not projecting onto someone else. In Integrity Therapy, responsibility is the second leg of the three-legged stool of integrity. It means that one must own 100 per cent of one's 50 percent in any conflictual interaction, make amends for it, and that one must resist the temptation to blame others for their contributions to the conflict.

Ritual: A set pattern, internal or external, for performing some action. There is usually a goal associated with the pattern. A ritual may help focus one's attention on a specific situation or help one disconnect from things that are interfering with the current situation. Rituals can be as common as the batter hitting his bat against his foot before batting or a person taking a deep breath as she or he starts a speech, or as unique as the very formal rituals used to start group processes in the ManKind Project or the beginning of a worship service.

Ritual Space: An area or space removed from ordinary reality which has been given some symbolic or sacred intent. In men's healing work, it is an area, often in a natural setting, out doors, where men can meet free from the influences of civilization within a container that feels safe and blessed, often through spontaneous ritual, often a circle, created for the men to do their emotional healing work.

Sacred Space: A place where group interaction can take place. The difference between ordinary space and sacred space is that for a period of time the ritual space is dedicated to a particular function. This dedication is often done through a ritual process. In sacred space there are different rules for interacting among those in the sacred space.

Safe Container: A metaphorical term relating to a place in which emotional work can be done. It is a group context in which a person can take risks in examining personal issues. This is a metaphorical description of a critical property of men's groups, describing the group's capacity to provide safe boundaries and support in the group context that reduces men's fears thereby enabling the men to share more deeply, work on sensitive personal issues, and honestly confront themselves and others.

Safety: In support groups, safety means that a container has been built wherein the man feels safe in sharing feelings that might shame him or be considered unmanly or unmasculine in his contemporary culture.

Schema: A term from developmental psychology which refers to an organized way of approaching a subject so that it can be identified, have meaning applied to it, and appropriate actions decided upon without a formal thought process. Another way of understanding this is that a schema is a stored pattern that allows for rapid decision-making.

Sense of Mastery: A personality construct describing positive beliefs in one's abilities, skills, and control as sufficient to the demands of life situations.

Shadow: Jung defined the shadow as "the thing a person has no wish to be." Jung considered the shadow to be an archetype, and thus a powerful, yet usually unexplored, part of a person which often is not examined, thereby hampering the process of individuation.

For New Warriors, the shadow consists of those elements of ourselves that we do not want others to know and often we do not know ourselves. The shadow is those parts of ourselves that we hide, repress, or deny.

Shame: An amalgam of guilt, embarrassment, unworthiness, and/or disgrace. It may be biological and/or learned. It may be internalized. Guilt is about doing something wrong and shame is about the individual's perception of being flawed or worthless.

Smudging: A custom, taken from Native American traditions, is ceremonially performed in some men's groups by brushing the wafts of sage smoke on a man to purify and momentarily cleanse him.

Social Construction: A theory that explains sex-linked activities to cultural and social influences that vary, over time, within cultures and sub-cultures as well.

Social Support: Support from a group of persons, be it family or support group. Informal social support is often found in self-help groups and mutual support groups, while formal social support is found from existing groups such as family and extended family. Mythopoetic support groups offer mainly emotional social support, while father's rights groups offer mainly informational social support.

Splitting: The psychological action of separating experience into two categories, usually "good" and "bad." When splitting occurs, everything is identified as one category or the other. This is considered a process of human psychological development.

Standpoint Theory: In feminist standpoint as developed by Hartsock, its components are oppression of women and the perspective that women have due to their unique lived experiences because of their oppressed position.

Subconscious: The mental activity just below the threshold of consciousness.

Sweat Lodge: A space which comes from a variety of traditions around the world but which in the United States is most often associated with Native American rituals. It is a closed space where the temperature can be elevated, usually by the introduction of heated rocks. The participants will sweat in the high temperature and humidity. It is thought that the sweating process will help in purifying the body. During this time prayers of various types are offered and there is a corresponding purifying of the body and the spirit.

Symbolic Approach: The use of symbols such as in metaphors for men's healing.

Talking Stick: An object, often a staff, passed around in a group to empower only the person holding it to speak in a particular, focused way. The person is to speak briefly and honestly, describing his or her own experience only, and "in the moment".

Templates: A model or pattern that can be used to reproduce itself. A template could be a narrative that is used as the basis for authoring a similar life story, but which is based on different events and different characters who share the similar life story.

Unconscious: The part of the psychic apparatus that does not ordinarily enter into the individuals awareness. It is below the level of consciousness manifested in overt behavior, such as slips of the tongue or dreams.

Visualizations: Images that people are guided to see. "To visualize" can be defined as "to see or form a mental image."

Vulnerability: The risk of injury. That injury that could occur may be psychological, spiritual, or physical. A person is at risk of injury either directly, as a result of some action of another, or indirectly, because someone may take information which is provided or shared, and use it in a way which harms the individual or exposes the individual to ridicule.

Warrior: Jesser defines warrior as focused energy (in the service of a noble mission), accountability, integrity, and the embracement of one's own feminine. The positive energy of the warrior is that energy of focused discipline, protecting boundaries, service, and mission.

Warriorhood: True warriorhood is adopting the authentic warrior archetype of the defender of the boundaries of the realm, as opposed to a mercenary soldier. Thus the selection of the name NEW Warrior by the founders of the New Warrior Training Adventure.

White Ribbon Campaign Against Men's Violence: This campaign was started as a reaction to the massacre of 14 female engineering students at the University of Montreal's École Polytechnique on Dec. 18, 1989. The young man, a semi-recluse, shouted "You're all a bunch of feminists, and I hate feminists" before he raised his semiautomatic and started shooting. The campaign was initiated by Michael Kaufman and others in Toronto after the massacre as a grass roots campaign to draw attention to and discourage men's violence against women. During White Ribbon Week in late November to early December, men are encouraged to wear a white ribbon to demonstrate their opposition to men's violence. The campaign has also undertaken educational campaigns in schools and companies, and has inspired men in Australia, New Zealand, Norway, and the United States to start similar efforts.

Wild Man: The Wild Man prepares an emotional body that can receive grief, ecstasy, and spirit. The Wild Man's energy is that energy which is conscious of a wound. The Wild Man's qualities, among them love of spontaneity, association with wilderness, honoring of grief, and respect for riskiness, frighten many people. Some men, as soon as they receive the first impulses to riskiness and recognize its link with what we've called the Wild Man, become frightened, stop all wildness, and recommend timidity and collective behavior to others. The aim is not to *be* the Wild Man, but to be *in touch with* the Wild Man. It is the Wild Man energy that is believed to give a man the courage and power to confront his demons in the hero's journey.

Work: Work on a New Warrior Training Adventure weekend is the effort expended to go on the hero's journey and come out with the "gold." Gold in this sense is new awareness and behaviors. The work of a New Warrior is similar to what one would do in therapy, but the NWTA is a psychosocial experiential educational event, not therapy. Work is also seen as identifying, developing, and implementing steps toward one's personal mission.

Wound: A deep emotional injury to the psyche.

Wounding: A term used in mythopoetic discourse, referring to an emotional or psychological hurt of deep and lasting consequence in a man's life.

Index

About the Editor and Contributors

CLINTON W. ANDERSON is the Lesbian, Gay and Bisexual Concerns Officer of the American Psychological Association Public Affairs Directorate in Washington, DC. He received his M.A. in Psychology from Harvard. Clinton is currently a Doctoral student at UMBC in the Community-Social Psychology Program.

EDWARD READ BARTON is a graduate candidate in Family Science in the Department of Family and Child Ecology at Michigan State University where he teaches courses in Men & Masculinity, Boys: Trauma & Violence, and Family Law & Relationships. He is an Associate Editor of the Journal of Men's Studies. His dissertation is a qualitative study of an open Mythopoetic men's support group, a NEW Warrior Integration Group, and a father's rights group. He received a M.P.A. and a J.D. from Cornell University in 1964 and a M.A. from Michigan State in 1993 in Family Studies with a minor in Family Intervention. He is chairman of the board of Mankind Project–Windsor/Detroit Centre.

THOMAS M. BRUNNER completed his Master's Degree in the Social Sciences at the University of Chicago in 1996. At Chicago, he studied the history of psychology, participated in men's work stimulated by Mythopoetic men's movement figure Robert L. Moore, Ph.D. Currently, he is pursuing a Ph.D. in Clinical Psychology at the University of South Florida.

CHRIS BULLOCK is a full professor in the Department of English at the University of Alberta, Edmonton, Canada. He is a joint compiler of A *Guide to*

Marxist Literary Criticism (Indiana Univ. Press, 1980), joint author of *Essay Writing for Canadian Students* (4th Ed., Prentis-Hall, 1998), and author of numerous articles on modern American and British authors, environmental writing, and men's issues in modern literature. Most recently he has jointly edited "Examining and Experiencing Masculinities" a special issue of *Mattoid* (Deakin University, Australia). He is interested in exploring the links between ritual, psychological process, and literature. He is a member of MKP–Canada–West.

CHRISTOPHER K. BURKE is a graduate student in psychology at the University of Maryland, Baltimore County. He takes a personal interest in men's work being a member of the ManKind Project, and works clinically with domestically violent men and veterans. He has an avid interest in his research and is excited to discover and describe new and alternative ways of working with men.

AMANDA GOLDRICK-JONES was born and raised in Vancouver, British Columbia, and spent time in Toronto as a freelance newspaper reporter before receiving her B.A. and M.A. from the University of British Columbia. She taught composition, rhetoric, and communications at several institutions before completing her Ph.D. in communications and rhetoric at Rensselaer Polytechnic Institute in Troy, NY. She combined her studies in rhetoric and her long-time interest in men's relations with feminism in a dissertation exploring how Canada's all-male White Ribbon Campaign against violence to women created alliances with feminist groups. Since arriving at the University of Winnipeg in 1994, she has researched a variety of men's profeminist groups and is writing a book on attitudes towards, and crisis-points in, profeminist activism.

WESLEY R. GOODENOUGH is a psychotherapist working in the field of addictions treatment, including chemical dependency, sexual, and gambling addictions. He has also worked in treatment of male domestic violence perpetrators. Wes has life experience beginning in Bolivia, S.A., as a missionary and in business as a computer systems designer and information systems manager. He is currently active in Mythopoetic men's work in association with the ManKind Project and is producing and facilitating workshops on fathering. He is the father of two daughters and two grandsons.

SHARON A. HOOVER is a doctoral student in the Clinical Psychology Program at the University of Maryland Baltimore County (UMBC). She graduated from Miami University of Ohio after completing an honors thesis investigating the contextual factors involved in dating violence among college men, and has continued researching domestic violence in her graduate studies. In addition Sharon has worked with colleagues at UMBC to investigate the change process among individuals involved in men's support organizations, and has examined how participation in such groups impacts attitudes toward women. She has served as a clinician in the Men's New Behaviors program, a treatment program for perpetrators of domestic abuse, at the Domestic Violence Center of Howard Co. in Maryland.

NEDRA R. LANDER, Ph.D., C. Psych. is Senior Psychologist, Civic Site, Ottawa Hospital and Associate Professor of Psychiatry, Faculty of Medicine, University of Ottawa. Her work with Dr. O. Hobart Mower at the University of Illinois introduced her to the concept of Integrity Therapy, an existential psychotherapy approach which she rekindled in the professional and academic communities through her writing and her work with men. In collaboration with Dr. Danielle Nahon, Nedra founded the Men's Clinic at the Ottawa Hospital in 1986—the first tertiary care clinic for men in North America (if not the world)—and co-hosted the First International Multi-Disciplinary Congress on Men held at Carleton University in Ottawa, Canada, in 1995. Her career is dedicated to the development of the fields of Integrity Therapy, psychotherapy with men, health promotion for men, and men's health.

ROSS THOMAS LUCAS obtained his M.Ed. in Counseling and Guidance from Southwestern Oklahoma State University, Weatherford, OK, his M.Div. from Southern Baptist Theological Seminary in Louisville, KY, and his Ph.D. in Educational Psychology from Indiana University, Bloomington, IN. Ross is a licensed Psychologist, Fellow in the American Association of Pastoral Counselors, and is certified in Clinical Hypnosis by the American Society of Clinical Hypnosis. He has previously served as a Pastor of the American Baptist Churches/USA and as Executive Director and Clinical Director of Samaritan Counseling Center of Central Michigan, Inc. Ross is currently affiliated with Lansing Psychological Associates, P.C. and serves as Centre Director of the ManKind Project Windsor/Detroit.

ERIC S. MANKOWSKI received his Ph.D. in Psychology in 1997 from the Personality and Social Ecology Program at the University of Illinois, Urbana-Champaign. He is assistant Professor of Psychology at Portland State University, where he teaches courses on Men and Masculinity, Community and Social Psychology, and Qualitative Research Methods. His research focused on self-help groups, community and identity narratives, and social support processes. In addition to his current research with the ManKind Project, he is studying processes of change in male batter's intervention treatment programs.

KENNETH I. MATON is Professor of Psychology at the University of Maryland, Baltimore County, Director of the Community-Social Ph.D. Program in Human Services Psychology, Immediate Past-President of the Society for Community Research and Action, Division 27 of the American Psychological Association. He has co-authored or co-edited four books, and has published widely in areas of minority youth development and education, community psychology, self-help groups, and religion. He is a member of MKP–Greater Washington.

JOEL MORTON is Senior Instructor of Humanities and Western Civilization at the University of Kansas, where, as a Ph.D. candidate in American Studies, he is completing his dissertation, "Disciplining Men: Cultural Studies of the Men's Movement." Centering on participant-observation research in anti-sexist men's groups in Kansas City and Birmingham, U.K., the project combines historical, cultural, and ethnographic analysis of men's movement activity. His research includes a year as a visitor to the Cultural Studies and Sociology Department at the University of Birmingham.

DANIELLE NAHON, Ph.D., C. Psych., has a practice in Clinical, Counseling and Consulting Psychology, and is Assistant Professor of Psychiatry, Faculty of Medicine, University of Ottawa, Ottawa, Canada. In collaboration with Dr. Nedra Lander, Danielle founded the Men's Clinic in 1986 at the Ottawa Hospital and co-hosted the First International Multi-Disciplinary Congress on Men. Her dissertation topic was "The Effectiveness of "Masculinist" Group Psychotherapy with Recently Separated Men" at the University of Montreal. She has extensively published scholarly and popular articles including "A Clinic for Men: Challenging Individual and Social Myths" co-authored with N.R. Lander published in the Journal of Mental Health Counseling in 1992.

MARTY PENTZ is a clinical social worker teaching at Indiana University East. He teaches primarily research and practice. His research interests are masculinity and hope in older adults with cancer, Marty is an active member of the ManKind Project. He is committed to leading men to lives of service.

DAVID B. PERRIN grew up in a family of seven children on a small farm in Petawawa, not far from Ottawa, ON. He obtained a B.S. in Chemistry from the University of Western Ontario in 1978. After a two-year teaching sojourn in Haiti, and then some philosophy studies at the University of Ottawa, his career path led him to further studies at Gregorian University in Rome, Italy. He specialized in the area of spirituality. He returned to Ottawa, Canada, to complete a Ph.D. at St. Paul University and is currently the Dean of the Faculty of Theology at that University. He has published three scholarly books, the latest is "The Sacrament of Reconciliation: An Existential Approach" (Edwin Mellen Press, 1998). He has also published popular and scholarly articles on mysticism, asceticism, spirituality, men's studies, and other related subjects.

DANIEL J. RICHARD is a licensed therapist practicing in the South Shore Boston area. His interests include the psychology of men, forensic evaluation, adult and group treatment, and spirituality. He has over 19 years experience teaching and training in the martial arts and Eastern healing practices. He is an avid "risk-taker," philosopher, and artist.

JOHN ROWAN is the author of a number of books, including *The Horned God: Feminism and Men as Wounding and Healing* (Routledge, 1987) and *Healing the Male Psyche: Therapy as Initiation* (Routledge, 1997). He is on the Editorial Board of *Self & Society, Journal of Humanistic Psychology, The Transpersonal Psychology Review*, and *Masculinities*. He is a past member of the Governing Board of the UK Council for Psychotherapy, representing the Humanistic and Integrative Section. He is a Fellow of the British Psychological Society (member of the Psychotherapy Section and the Counseling Psychology Division), a qualified individual and group psychotherapist (AHPP), chartered counseling psychologist (BPS) and an accredited counselor (UKRC). He practices Primal Integration, which is a holistic approach to therapy, teaches, supervises, and leads groups at the Minster Centre. He also helps to produce the magazine *Achilles Heel*.

HOLLY SWEET, Ph.D., is the Co-Director of the Cambridge Center for Gender Relations (a consulting company specializing in improving relations between men and women) and is an administrator and lecturer at Massachusetts Institute of Technology. She holds a doctorate in Counseling Psychology from Boston College and has a psychotherapy practice in the greater Boston area.

STEVE R. WILSON received his Masters in Social Work from California State University, Long Beach, in 1993 and went into direct practice working with the terminally ill elderly persons. He is Adjunct faculty in Human Development and Social Work at California State University, Long Beach, and is pursuing his doctorate in social work at the University of Southern California. His current research interests involve cross cultural grief and bereavement.